Leaning Into Politics

A volume in
Research on International Civic Engagement
Walter F. Heinecke and Carah Ong Whaley, *Series Editors*

Research on International Civic Engagement

Walter F. Heinecke and Carah Ong Whaley, *Series Editors*

The State of Citizen Participation in America (2012)
    Hindy Lauer Schachter and Kaifeng Yang

Civic Engagement in a Network Society (2008)
    Erik Bergrud and Kaifeng Yang

Leaning Into Politics

Higher Education and the Democracy We Need

edited by

Abraham Goldberg
James Madison University

Carah Ong Whaley
University of Virginia

INFORMATION AGE PUBLISHING, INC.
Charlotte, NC • www.infoagepub.com

Library of Congress Cataloging-in-Publication Data

A CIP record for this book is available from the Library of Congress
http://www.loc.gov

ISBN: 979-8-88730-700-8 (Paperback)
       979-8-88730-701-5 (Hardcover)
       979-8-88730-702-2 (E-Book)

Copyright © 2024 Information Age Publishing Inc.

All rights reserved. No part of this publication may be reproduced, stored in a retrieval system, or transmitted, in any form or by any means, electronic, mechanical, photocopying, microfilming, recording or otherwise, without written permission from the publisher.

Printed in the United States of America

CONTENTS

Acknowledgments ix

1 Building the Democracy We Need: How Can Higher
  Education Meet the Moment? 1
  Abraham Goldberg and Carah Ong Whaley

SECTION I

NAMING AND FRAMING: CHALLENGES AND PATHWAYS FOR HIGHER EDUCATION'S NECESSARY ROLE IN STRENGTHENING DEMOCRACY

2 Authoritarianism and the University: Global Perspectives
  From the Last Century 19
  Lauren L. Shepherd

3 Caught in the Middle: (In)Civility, Compliance, and "Norms
  of Appropriateness" 35
  Angela Kraemer-Holland

4 Leaning Into Institutional Politics: Paradoxes of Success
  in Higher Education Civic Learning and Democratic
  Engagement Initiatives 49
  Caroline W. Lee

5 Focusing on How Not Why: Examining the Role of Nonprofit Partner Organizations in Campus-Based Civic Engagement Programming 65
Allison D. Rank

6 Bridging the Complexities of Higher Education and Philanthropy 83
Teresa Taylor

SECTION II

BUILDING INSTITUTIONAL AND ADMINISTRATIVE CAPACITY FOR POLITICAL LEARNING AND DEMOCRATIC ENGAGEMENT

7 Fostering Campus Cultures That are ALL IN for Nonpartisan Democratic Engagement 101
Stephanie King and Jennifer Domagal-Goldman

8 How America's Community Colleges Support Democracy 121
Belinda S. Miles, George Keteku, Tiago Machado, Glenetta Phillips, and Rinardo Reddick

9 Embracing the Politics of the Possible: Voter Engagement at an R1 Institution 141
Karen M. Kedrowski

10 Who's in the Room When It Happens? Use of Data Driven Analysis and Power Mapping to Build an Inclusive Political Engagement Coalition 157
Leah A. Murray

11 Opening the "Pod" Doors: The Public Intellectual in an Age of Democratic Decline 171
Saladin Ambar

SECTION III

STRENGTHENING STUDENT VOICE AND ENHANCING CIVIC SKILLS AND DISPOSITIONS

12 Developing Empowered Citizens: How Universities Help Build Efficacy 183
Laurie L. Rice and Kenneth Moffett

13 Political Socialization in Campus Life: Can Student
    Organizations Replicate Civic Learning in Tocqueville's
    Voluntary Associations? 199
    J. Cherie Strachan, Michael R. Wolf, and Elizabeth A. Bennion

14 Fostering Civic Resilience: A Framework for Campus
    Misinformation Reduction 227
    Ryan W. Flynn and Elora A. Agsten

15 Indoctrination, Education, and Deliberative Democracy:
    A DEI Case Study 243
    David Moshman

16 The Proximate Power of Student-Led Nonpartisan Political
    Engagement Efforts 259
    Alexander S. Kappus

17 Space, Place, and Community: Engaging With College
    Students Where They Are 277
    Brian F. Harrison and Robert Healy

SECTION IV

CHARTING COURSES: CREATING CLASSROOMS THAT PREPARE STUDENTS FOR DEMOCRACY

18 Teaching and Modeling Democracy in the Classroom
    During Political Polarization: The Amalgamation
    Pedagogy Project 293
    Mark K. McBeth and Donna L. Lybecker

19 Moving Fast Without Breaking Democracy: Computer Science
    Education for a Just Future 309
    Julie M. Smith

20 Forced Migration, Civic Engagement, and Educational
    Exchange in the Time of COVID-19 321
    Prakash Adhikari

21 Poetry at the End of Democracy: Envisioning Democracy
    Through Poetry 339
    Angelo Letizia

22 Reading Banned Books: Preparing Elementary Teachers
    to Navigate the Politics of Teaching and Learning 357
    Aaron R. Gierhart

ACKNOWLEDGMENTS

This volume is motivated by our deep concern about the state of democracy in the United States and around the world, our commitment to building a more just and inclusive society and the value we place on education. Young people are coming of age during a time of high levels of socioeconomic inequality, persistent inequities in access, voice and participation in political and decision making processes, a fragmented and unstable information ecosystem, pernicious partisan polarization and an increasing distrust in political institutions. Meanwhile, public issues persist and questions are being raised about whether democracy is up to the task of identifying and implementing solutions.

As we have worked together over the years, we have shared a belief that higher education has a critical role in strengthening democracy. We have questioned whether and to what extent colleges and universities are preparing people with the knowledge, skills and dispositions to be active and informed participants in civic and political life and to build a better democracy. We have also sought to examine whether institutions of higher education are structured to support (and protect, when necessary) the students, faculty and staff doing the work, especially in light of external pressures from public officials and the donor class. As the chapters ahead show, the results are mixed, but the work by contributors to this volume give us hope.

We are grateful for our students who motivate and inspire us to improve our pedagogy and praxis in order to build the democracy and society we need. We also express our sincere gratitude to AASC&U's American Democracy Project, the American Political Science Association's (APSA) Civic

Leaning Into Politics, pages ix–x
Copyright © 2024 by Information Age Publishing
www.infoagepub.com
All rights of reproduction in any form reserved.

Engagement Section and to the Lumina Foundation for providing space for connections and conversations around these pressing issues.

This work is impossible without partnering organizations and the communities in which our institutions are situated. Many of the projects described in this volume require mutually beneficial and reciprocal relationships with, and the goodwill and support of, state and local legislators, public institutions and local nonprofits.

Any book, and particularly edited volumes, depends on the labor of many individuals. To that end, we thank George Johnson at Information Age Publishing for his partnership and support; the many reviewers for their outstanding substantive and constructive comments; and all of the chapter authors for their collaboration, vision, brilliance and commitment. This book is not just words on a paper; more importantly it represents a community of individuals dedicated to positive social change and strengthening democracy.

Finally, each of us extends our gratitude to our family, friends and personal networks for supporting us as we added editing this volume to our existing heavy workloads.

Abe: My participation in a project like this would not have happened without the mentorship I received at Ohio University, West Virginia University, the University of South Carolina Upstate and James Madison University, as well as from the many leaders in the "strengthening democracy" space that I have had the privilege of collaborating with and learning from. I thank the Mahatma Gandhi Center for Global Nonviolence as a funding partner and especially as an organization with a beautiful and impressive record of supporting faculty, students and community organizations in shared efforts to create a more equitable and just society. Carah, you are the best colleague, co-conspirator and dear friend a person could ask for. Thank you for continually reminding me that I have not lost my mind, as that has certainly been needed over the years. Finally, I thank my parents for instilling in me the importance of education and Roni, Leo and Hazel for being my favorite people on the planet.

Carah: I am incredibly grateful to Larry Sabato and my colleagues at the Center for Politics at the University of Virginia and at Issue One for giving me the opportunity and support to focus on political learning, engagement and scholarship for a more just and inclusive democracy. I am also incredibly lucky to have Sonjia Smith as an advocate—thank you for caring deeply about democracy and justice. Abe, "what a long strange trip it's been" filled with laughter, tears and everything in between. I couldn't have asked for a better collaborator and confidante. To Ben, Ever, Cade and Phantom (our dog), thank you for your unconditional love, unwavering support and daily walks that get me to laugh and breathe.

CHAPTER 1

BUILDING THE DEMOCRACY WE NEED

How Can Higher Education Meet the Moment?

Abraham Goldberg
James Madison University

Carah Ong Whaley
University of Virginia

It was an exciting professional opportunity. We were charged with building out a campus-wide political learning and democratic engagement initiative at an institution that seemed ready to prioritize this work. Civic engagement appeared prominently in a newly developed vision statement and strategic plan, which led to the creation of an academic center fully dedicated to preparing students—all students—to be active and informed participants in our democracy. Distinct from service-learning and student volunteer programs, we were laser focused on finding ways for students in and out of the classroom to grapple with pressing public issues and the structural and political frameworks they inhabit. We sought to promote voter education and engagement as part of the year-round learning process, and not as a procedural and episodic activity that is divorced from the academic enterprise. We rejected claims about young people being uninterested and ambivalent about public issues and instead would ask them what they cared about and challenged them to think about what they could do about it. Rather than being off-limits due to inherent divisiveness, we aimed to lean into politics as a way to prepare students to address issues through the democratic process.

Of course, none of this work was to occur in a vacuum. National higher education organizations such as the American Association of Colleges and Universities (AAC&U) and the American Association of State Colleges and Universities (AASC&U) have established track-records for supporting campuses in efforts to promote political learning and engagement. Other groups, such as Campus Compact, the Institute for Democracy and Higher Education (IDHE) and Project Pericles have provided extensive resources and shared learning opportunities for faculty, staff and civic engagement professionals. And, more recently, organizations such as the ALL IN Campus Democracy Challenge and the Campus Vote Project, along with many others affiliated with the Students Learn Students Vote Coalition, have emerged to specifically bolster nonpartisan college student voter education and engagement.

Leveraging this network, one of our first major projects was to develop a campus climate study for political learning and engagement. We were one of a dozen campuses across the country to work directly with AASC&U's American Democracy Project and IDHE to engage in this endeavor and the timing was perfect. Both being new to our institution, we did not have prior relationships to depend on or a record of accomplishments from which to build trust with our new colleagues and students. We also did not yet have a good sense of our campus. The climate project provided a substantive outlet for a small advisory board we created to get involved in our work and brought us in close partnership with our institution's proud assessment office. Our team conducted focus groups—11 in total—with faculty, students, staff and administrators as part of the project to learn about how conducive our campus was for political learning and engagement. It proved to be quite a learning opportunity.

Several findings emerged from the climate study that framed our experiences as leaders of a campus-wide civic engagement initiative in the years ahead. First, we learned about how challenging in-class discussions about political issues can be for both students and faculty. Students spoke about their hesitation to engage in such conversations out of fear that discussions would get out of hand and that they could even be attacked for expressing their views. They also spoke about wanting to avoid offending other students while trying to form a community of friends, as well as concerns that their opinions may differ from those of their professors. Faculty spoke about not having the skills needed to successfully facilitate discussions on political issues in their classes and about fears of being reprimanded by students and the university, especially in light of course evaluations and prospects for promotion. For both populations, avoiding discourse on public issues seemed to be the safe approach.

Second, we learned that people had mixed views on the state of free speech and activism at our institution. Some faculty and students saw the entire campus as a venue for political discourse and activity, whereas others spoke about designated free speech zones and that student protests needed pre-approval and were highly monitored. Physical space was also mentioned in light of discussions about free speech in our focus groups. The campus was widely seen for its beauty, cleanliness and well-manicured landscaping; however, some people shared the perception that this served to mute activism by citing examples of sidewalk chalk being immediately removed and a lack of public posting locations. Despite these observations, some discussed how the institution does not restrict speech from outside groups on campus, even when such speech is considered offensive or hateful.

Third, we learned in great detail about ways in which cultural aspects of the institution affected political learning and democratic engagement. Focus group participants spoke about the "culture of niceness" where people are generally respectful, kind and hospitable. These, of course, are seemingly positive attributes of any institution, however, students and faculty alike spoke about how that could inhibit discourse on public issues and that it could even be relied upon so much that deeper exploration into what it really means to be inclusive would be avoided. Further, people noted a general risk aversion from the campus administration as a public institution with an important stake in maintaining positive relationships with elected officials, alumni and donors. Finally, people spoke about concerns they had about concentrated, opaque decision-making processes likened to a "country club" or "old boys club" culture, though others noted that decision-making, at least within academic affairs, is decentralized to the college and unit level.

It became clear that the lived experiences and perceptions of many faculty, staff and students were misaligned from the rhetoric about the institution's commitment to civic engagement found in public-facing documents. Our work was at the center of that disconnect and it was something that demanded considerable attention as we built out our initiative. In the years that followed, we eagerly collaborated with faculty to integrate political learning opportunities into courses and academic programs, while recognizing and appreciating the types of legitimate concerns many had expressed in the climate study. Our co-curricular programs were high profile and well-received by students from across the political spectrum, especially those that demystified and normalized open discussions about public issues. However, those same programs created a great deal of friction with key administrators as the climate study suggested they could. We worked through the political implications of the global pandemic as well as the so-called nationwide "racial reckoning" that followed the murders of Ahmaud Arbery, Sean Reed, Breonna Taylor, Tony McDade, George Floyd, Daunte Wright and others. This included an intense and public battle that culminated in the removal of the names of three Confederate leaders from academic buildings on our campus. We also worked through the 2020 election and violent insurrection that followed. Our programs were specifically designed to lean into politics and provide outlets for students and the public to learn about and grapple with not only the issues they care about most, but also the issues others raised. Doing so often left us in the crosshairs of skeptical public officials and donors, as well as administrators tasked with maintaining relationships with them.

We were a very small (three full-time employees, including us) unit that quickly built a positive reputation among faculty and students across the institution, national higher education associations, nonprofit organizations, other campuses across the country and the national media. The work was highly regarded for providing academic outlets for people to better understand public issues and their consequences and to promote democratic engagement, such as voting in elections. Despite this, we ultimately succumbed to the local pressures we faced and the climate we inherited, but were unsuccessful in changing. The work had become untenable and we ended our relationship with the center for civic engagement after five grueling years. We remain firmly committed to the idea that colleges and universities have a duty and perhaps a unique position to strengthen democracy, though our experiences, if reflective of the broader landscape, left us wondering how this can even happen during such a hyperpartisan and perniciously polarized era, and at a time when higher education itself is being attacked.

BROADER CONTEXT

Work like ours, at the university level, comes at a time when both higher education and democracy are facing significant challenges. Democratic decline, both in the United States and globally, lack of confidence in political institutions and an increasingly violent and divisive political climate raise many questions about the state of political learning and civic engagement in higher education. About ten years ago, a task force commissioned by the United States Department of Education called on colleges and universities to affirm their missions to educate for democracy (Association of American Colleges and Universities, 2012). Relatively few have made the investment, though dozens of higher education associations and organizations have publicly committed their support to prepare students to address the persistent public issues they are inheriting (College Civic Learning, 2021; Daniels, 2021).

While there has been a recent upward spike in rote civic knowledge and historically high youth voting rates in recent elections, the United States has seen a decline in political rights and civil liberties over the last decade and has been listed as a backsliding democracy (Annenberg, 2021; CIRCLE, 2019; International IDEA, 2021; Repucci, 2021). Since 2010, state legislatures have passed laws making it harder to vote, with access to the ballot increasingly dependent on the partisanship of state legislatures (Brennan Center, 2023). There has also been a rise in the politicization of election administration (Pew Research Center, 2022) and extreme partisan and racial gerrymandering (Ong Whaley and Kondik, 2023). Meanwhile, substantial dysfunction and hyperpartisanship in Congress, concerns over the impartiality of the judiciary and limited accountability and oversight of the executive branch have contributed to the loss of institutional capacity to address pressing public problems and amounted to declining public confidence in political institutions (Williamson, 2023).

This coincides with deeply problematic rhetoric and growing scrutiny from public officials on how colleges and universities educate students on public issues, particularly those centered on race, ethnicity and social justice. The budgets for some universities have been slashed for promoting such programming while several states have passed legislation targeting related instruction (Bauer-Wolf, 2021; Reilly, 2022). The issues of free speech and expression were further nationalized following a high-profile hearing of the House Committee on Education and the Workforce that questioned the presidents of Harvard, Massachusetts Institute of Technology and University of Pennsylvania about antisemitism on their campuses. Two presidents (as of this writing) lost their jobs as a result of their inability to satisfy the Congressional committee and the scrutiny and public outrage that followed. Since then, we have witnessed violent responses to peaceful protests emerging on campuses across the country regarding the United States' role in the Israel-Gaza war. All of these episode served as a loud warning shot to colleges and universities across the country. Academic freedom and freedom of speech—core tenets of a liberal education—are at risk.

Countering political overreach into higher education, PEN America assembled over 100 *former* college and university presidents to "defend higher education against a barrage of state legislation and policies that seek to restrict campus free expression and college and university autonomy" (PEN America, 2023, para. 1). The effort is built to "advocate individually and collectively against efforts by public officials to censor and chill campus free expression and the right of students to learn, and against attempts to delegitimize and defund public colleges and universities" (PEN America,

2023, Statement of Purpose section, para. 1). Indeed the initiative recognizes that *current* university leaders are poorly positioned to defend academic freedom from educational gag orders given their dependence on funding, though this is surely an unsettling vulnerability. We have yet to see whether efforts such as this can provide a formidable defense of campus free expression and academic freedom, however, we anticipate politically-charged oversight from both the federal and state governments to persist.

Fortunately, and perhaps surprisingly given its troubled state, people still generally prefer democracy to other forms of government. In a recent Open Society Foundation poll of over 30,000 respondents across 30 countries, 86% want to live in a democracy and 62% report that it is preferable to any other form of government. However, the numbers are not as strong for young people globally or among adults in the United States (Open Society Foundations, 2023). Within the United States, well over half of adults say that laws and policies are not reflective of what most people think across a range of issues including immigration, government spending, reproductive rights and gun policy according to a recent AP-NORC poll. Further, 49% report that democracy is not working well, whereas only 10% say its' working extremely well and 40% only somewhat well (Riccardi & Sanders, 2023). A national poll from YouGov found that a whopping 31% of 18—29 year-olds agree that democracy is no longer a viable system and that America should explore alternative forms of government to ensure stability and progress (Frankovic & Montgomery, 2023).

Public sentiments about the state of American democracy have been worsening. Examining the American National Election Survey, we found a notable shift toward greater dissatisfaction with how democracy is working from 2012 onwards and 2020 stands out with heightened levels of both "Not Very Satisfied" and "Not at All Satisfied" across race, ethnicity and partisan self-identification (Figure 1.1). Young people in particular have heightened levels of dissatisfaction. Nearly half of 18—29 year-olds reported being either "Not Very Satisfied" and "Not at All Satisfied" in 2020 compared to one-third of those 60 and older. Just 12 years earlier, only 22% of the youngest age group reported being "Not Very Satisfied" and "Not at All Satisfied" (ANES, 2023).

Coupled with growing dissatisfaction in American democracy, particularly among young people, is a significant dip in the rates that college students believe their First Amendment rights are secure across a five year period. The Knight Foundation's College Student Views on Free Expression and Campus Speech report found that 74% of students believed that freedom of speech was secure in 2016, compared to just 47% in 2021. Similarly, 81% believed freedom of the press was secure in 2016 while 55% believed the same in 2021. Despite these trends, 84% of college students believe that free speech rights are extremely or very important in a democracy. There is a sizable racial gap when it comes to who feels protected by the First

Building the Democracy We Need • 7

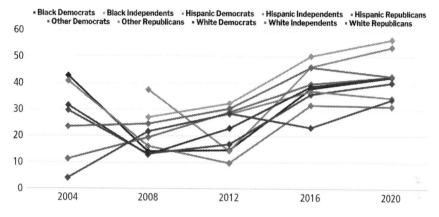

Figure 1.1 Dissatisfaction with how democracy is working by race/ethnicity and partisan identification.

Amendment. A mere 5% of Black students believed the First Amendment protected people like them in 2021, which was down from 25% in 2019. Numbers for White students on the same question were 43% in 2021 and 53% in 2019 (Knight Foundation, 2022).

The same poll provides important revelations about the state of free expression on college and university campuses. Close to two-thirds of American college students strongly or somewhat agreed that the climate of their campus prevents people from saying things they believe because others might find it offensive. Slightly less than half reported feeling comfortable voicing disagreement with ideas expressed by their instructors or other students in their classes. About two-thirds of students supported restrictions on use of racial slurs, whereas less than half supported other forms of limitations such as wearing clothing with the Confederate flag or passing out pamphlets with Christian messages (Knight Foundation, 2022).

SO WHERE DOES THIS LEAVE US?

We envision a multi-cultural, multi-racial democracy that embraces the strengths and experiences that everyone brings to the table. A responsive political system that accounts for both scientific discovery and popular sentiments while being grounded in the core values of freedom, equality and justice. We dream of a thriving and fully accessible public square across all levels of government where people come together to talk through the pressing issues of the day and learn from each other. And, we recognize that education is a bedrock for democracy and must provide equitable opportunities for people to acquire the knowledge, skills and disposition necessary to participate and ask challenging questions.

Colleges and universities find themselves in a place where both liberal education and core components of a healthy democracy are being attacked. Despite prominent calls by higher education associations for campuses to serve their civic mission and affirm their commitment to democracy, university leaders have a short-term disincentive to defend academic freedom leaving countless faculty and staff in precarious positions. Young people are, understandably, increasingly dissatisfied with American democracy and we have seen massive declines among college students believing that their First Amendment rights are secure.

Perhaps the experiences we had as leaders of a campus-wide civic engagement initiative were subject to these macro-level dynamics; however, we are left with more questions than answers. Through our great fortune and privilege, we have collaborated with teacher-scholars from across the country, leaders of national nonprofit organizations supporting higher education's civic mission, university administrators and foundation program officers to dive deeper into higher education's role in building the democracy we need, which we continue to believe requires leaning into politics. The stakes of course are high and democracy is not guaranteed.

VOLUME STRUCTURE AND CONTENTS

The volume is divided into four sections. The first section explores ways in which colleges and universities interact with and are influenced by external political and economic pressures. The following section addresses institutional challenges and capacity and is written by authors from a diverse set of institutions, including community colleges, regional comprehensive institutions and large land grant universities. These authors share their insights and approaches to campus-wide political learning and democratic engagement within the context provided in the first section. The third section focuses on building civic skills, efficacy and dispositions through curricular and co-curricular programming. Finally, noting that colleges and universities have a duty to prepare all students for democracy, not just those majoring in political science, the final section includes chapters that outline innovative approaches to building political learning into fields ranging from poetry to computer science. Although the volume is divided into four sections, readers will notice that many of the contributions offer insights that transcend the focus of a particular section. While each chapter stands alone, they also speak to each other and, taken together, provide a better understanding of how higher education as a field and its various specific interlocutors—students, faculty, staff—can leverage resources and capacity at a moment when our societies and democracy needs them most.

Section I provides a multifaceted view of the complex relationship between higher education, democracy and societal change. It underscores the need for colleges and universities to navigate and respond to various external pressures while maintaining their core democratic and educational values. The diverse perspectives offered in these chapters highlight both the challenges and opportunities for higher education in contributing to a democratic society, with an emphasis on the tension between external pressures (political, economic, etc.) and the intrinsic values of academic freedom and open inquiry. Each chapter deals with the challenges of institutionalizing civic engagement in a way that genuinely contributes to democracy. In "Authoritarianism and the University: Global Perspectives from the Last Century," Lauren Lassabe Shepherd focuses on the historical relationship between authoritarian regimes and higher education. She explores how authoritarian governments have targeted universities and liberal education and highlights the impact on academic freedom, as well as how intellectuals' have responded to political assaults with lessons for modern contexts, including in the United States. The next chapter is "Caught in the Middle: (In)Civility Compliance and 'Norms of Appropriateness' by Angela Kraemer-Holland which analyzes how neoliberal and conservative policies affect academic freedom and open inquiry and explores the tensions between civility, compliance and academic freedom within U.S. colleges and universities. Both Lassabe Shepherd and Kraemer-Holland prompt us to consider the political, economic and ideological challenges to academic freedom and open inquiry in higher education and how these challenges impact the ability of colleges and universities to contribute to democratic societies.

The subsequent chapter, "Leaning into Institutional Politics: Paradoxes of Success in Higher Education Civic Learning and Democratic Engagement Initiatives" by Caroline W. Lee focuses on the challenges and paradoxes of institutionalizing civic learning and democratic engagement in U.S. higher education. Lee illustrates the unintended consequences of top-down efforts for institutional change (with a particular focus on the Carnegie Community Engagement Classification), including how they focus the attention of colleges and universities on self-auditing and compliance rather than addressing broader societal issues. The shift toward proceduralization and professionalization in civic engagement and the inward-looking nature of these initiatives has led to failures to significantly impact political and economic inequalities and reinforced existing institutional hierarchies. Thus, higher education needs a more outward-directed focus in civic engagement initiatives.

Similarly, Allison Rank provides a critical analysis of the influence of organizations like ALL IN Campus Democracy Challenge, Students Learn

Students Vote and Campus Vote Project, and the ways in which these organizations direct college and universities' approaches to civic learning and political engagement. In her chapter entitled, "Focusing on How Not Why: Examining the Role of Nonprofit Partner Organizations in Campus-Based Civic Engagement Programming," Rank highlights the importance of these organizations in providing resources and frameworks for campuses to encourage student voting and political participation, but also finds that their focus on action planning centered around the Strengthening American Democracy Guide constitutes an auditing process that can shape priorities and behaviors of campus actors. Through an analysis, Rank finds that while these organizations frame their work as promoting civic learning and democratic engagement, what is explicitly and implicitly encouraged is the process of casting a ballot with little discussion of where that process fits within the larger political landscape.

The final chapter in the first section by Teresa Taylor of the Lumina Foundation, entitled "Bridging the Complexities of Higher Education and Philanthropy," explores the dynamic relationship between higher education and philanthropy and discusses how both sectors can collaborate to address the challenges of authoritarianism and democratic reform. Taylor emphasizes the need for higher education, in collaboration with philanthropy, to develop new solutions and engage with diverse constituencies in order to respond to societal and political challenges.

The chapters in Section II underscore the crucial role of higher education institutions, whether community colleges, research intensive (R1) universities, or others, in cultivating a democratic ethos among students. The first chapter by Stephanie King and Jennifer Domagal-Goldman targets all higher education institutions with a focus on voter registration and turnout. The second chapter by Belinda Miles et al. specifically focuses on the unique role and contribution of community colleges in expanding democratic principles and citizenship in a broader sense. Karen Kedrowski's chapter is tailored to the context and capabilities of research-intensive (R1) universities. Leah Murray's chapter focuses on a teaching-centered institution and she introduces specific concepts like power mapping and inclusive coalition building. The section concludes with a chapter by Saladin Ambar, which takes a more theoretical and intellectual approach, focusing on the societal role and impact that public intellectuals can have in a period of democratic decline.

Whereas Section I provides framing and critical analyses, all of the chapters in Section II present a diverse array of strategies and perspectives on fostering nonpartisan democratic engagement, civic learning, and political engagement to enhance student's capacity to create positive social change. And all of the chapters in this section emphasize the need for inclusivity and diversity in shoring up democratic institutions, norms and processes.

The chapter by Miles et al. provides a framework for practical, hands-on education experiences and the successes they've achieved at a community college that can serve as an example for reaching and developing the civic agency of a broader array of individuals in order to strengthen democratic principles and citizenship. Several chapters (particularly those by King and Domagal-Goldman and Murray) focus on using data-driven approaches and empirical evidence to inform strategies that promote political engagement. While these chapters are unified in their commitment to enhancing democratic engagement within higher education, they differ significantly in their focus on specific types of institutions, methodological approaches, target audiences, engagement tactics and the scope of their impact. This diversity reflects the multifaceted nature of the challenge of fostering democratic engagement in the complex landscape of higher education. While King and Domagal-Goldman, Kedrowski and Murray are relatively more focused on immediate student engagement in political processes, Miles et al. and Ambar discuss the broader, long-term impact on how students understand and interact with democracy.

Building on Section II, the chapters in Section III focus on enhancing civic engagement and building political efficacy among students. Chapters in Section III explore the potential for long-term impact of engagement experiences on students' future aspirations and commitment to civic participation. They also highlight the importance of context (e.g., cultural, spatial) and inclusivity in effective civic engagement efforts. Each chapter offers a unique perspective on how higher education can foster civic skills, dispositions, and democratic participation among students and each approach contributes uniquely to the broader goal of nurturing meaningful contributions to building democratic societies.

In "Developing Empowered Citizens: How Universities Help Build Efficacy," Laurie L. Rice and Kenneth W. Moffett examine how a college education, specifically classes on government and politics, influences students' political efficacy. The authors use data from surveys conducted at Southern Illinois University Edwardsville in 2016. Rice and Moffett find that students who took classes in government and politics felt more informed about politics. Furthermore, being encouraged to vote in the 2016 presidential election was associated with a decreased perception that one's vote does not matter. Moffett and Rice find that educational content and encouragement to participate in democratic processes enhance students' beliefs in their ability to understand and impact politics (internal efficacy) and in the effectiveness of their political actions (external efficacy).

In "Political Socialization in Campus Life: Can Student Organizations Replicate Civic Learning in Tocqueville's Voluntary Associations?," J. Cherie Strachan, Michael Wolfe and Elizabeth Bennion present a detailed exploration of how student organizations can foster civic learning and political engagement, akin to what Alexis de Tocqueville described in his observations of American voluntary associations. Their study addresses the decline in civic and political participation among young people, emphasizing the need for effective political socialization to prepare college students for public-spirited participation in democracy. While Strachan et al. find significant political socialization occurring within student organizations, they also identify gaps in fully leveraging the potential of campus life for civic learning. Their findings highlight the need for more effective strategies to engage diverse student populations, including women and minoritized students, in political activities, also addressed in the chapter by Murray in Section II. They recommend instilling a broader sense of civic duty and public-spirited participation in student organizations.

Next, Ryan W. Flynn and Elora A. Agsten acknowledge the persistent problem of misinformation, particularly online, and its impact on democratic processes and civic engagement in their chapter entitled, "Fostering Civic Resilience: A Framework for Campus Misinformation Reduction." Flynn and Agsten present an innovative framework for higher education institutions to combat and reduce misinformation and foster civic resilience by focusing on the importance of students feeling connected and valued within their campus community, which is crucial for effective misinformation education. Their framework emphasizes the unique position of colleges and universities as both living and learning communities, which can counter misinformation through education and community engagement. They argue that campuses can be "third places," which are neutral, comfortable spaces for students to engage in open dialogue and develop personal agency.

While Flynn and Agsten provide a new community-based approach, David Moshman centers individuals in what he defines as "education for rationality," which emphasizes respect for reasons, persons, truth, and intellectual freedom. Education for rationality respects students as rational agents and promotes their rationality by providing reasons for teachings and encouraging critical thinking. Moshman highlights the importance of respecting reason in both education and governance, encouraging rational deliberation and respect for evidence. This involves treating individuals as rational agents with legitimate reasons for their beliefs and emphasizes that freedom to express and explore diverse viewpoints is crucial in both education and deliberative democracy.

In the subsequent chapter, Alexander S. Kappus focuses on the challenges faced by students in their efforts, including the politicization of voter education, hostile interactions, and institutional barriers. The varying levels of support (or lack thereof) from educational institutions in facilitating student-led political engagement efforts can greatly impact efforts. Kappus also highlights the unique experiences of students of color in political engagement activities, underscoring the need for inclusive approaches in civic education (see also Miles et al., Murray and Strachan et al. in this volume). The final chapter of this section is written by faculty and student co-authors Brian F. Harrison and Robert Healy. The authors discuss tactics and strategies for engaging students in their own spaces and communities, acknowledging the importance of context in civic engagement.

The final section of the book features contributions from faculty at a range of colleges and universities and emphasizes flexible and innovative teaching methods that foster civic engagement and participation in democratic processes to respond to contemporary challenges, including pernicious polarization and global crises. Each chapter contributes to the overarching theme of preparing students for democracy, but they differ in their specific focus areas—from technology and arts to literature and virtual exchange programs, highlighting the multifaceted nature of democratic education. The authors in this section also focus on developing critical thinking skills, encouraging students to question, analyze, and form their own opinions, while acknowledging diverse perspectives and experiences as vital to understanding and participating in democracy. Whether through technology, literature, or arts, there's a continuous thread through the chapters on teaching the ethical implications and responsibilities inherent in a democratic society.

The first chapter in the section by Mark K. McBeth and Donna L. Lybecker addresses challenges to teaching democracy during political polarization. Their innovative Amalgamation Pedagogy Project (APP) combines civil discourse and exploring opposing views to enhance student understanding of democracy. Their unique approach helps provide a better understanding of how pedagogy itself impacts a student's view of the world. They also recommend that faculty focus on balancing optimism and pessimism, helping students recognize today's problems, and believe in the possibility of solutions.

Taking up the contemporary challenge of Big Tech, Julie M. Smith argues that problems of democracy-breaking algorithms extend to virtually every corner of modern technology from facial recognition software used to suppress political dissent to Google searches that sexualize young women from minoritized groups. She argues that as an ever-increasing number of students learn computer science concepts, it is important to explore what they are—and are not—learning about responsible computing. Smith considers the status quo of undergraduate computer science education in relation to democratic norms and explores alternative approaches to teaching future computer scientists about their professional responsibilities. She concludes with a framework of best practices for the development of responsible computing.

The subsequent chapter by Prakash Adhikari explores how the institutional infrastructures of campuses can be leveraged to support civic engagement and the ways in which students can remain engaged even during disruptive natural calamities. During the COVID-19 pandemic, Adhikari developed two innovative humanitarian programs through his courses to provide college level education to people experiencing forced migration around the world, while also engaging students within the affected population. Adhikari highlights some of the strategies adopted in engaging students in conversation with individuals living in a refugee camp in Malawi to foster better understanding of some of the most challenging issues of our time, including migration. Based on program evaluations of 250 participants to date, his findings suggest that higher education institutions can leverage their resources and capacity to implement innovative programs that foster civic engagement while also expanding access to university education to displaced persons, even in the middle of disasters such as a pandemic.

The final two chapters of this section focus on the role of literature in fostering democratic values and both of the authors provide a framework for how others might replicate assignments. Grounding his analysis in John Dewey's notion of creative democracy, Angelo Letizia shows how professors and students can use poetry to strengthen their current democracies and imagine new political and social arrangements when those democracies end. The chapter also uniquely includes actual professor and student-created poetry which illustrates how democracy and more generally, a robust social life, can be reimagined. Aaron Gierhart examines how legislation banning or censoring books and art not only greatly impacts teaching candidates' future work by restricting discourse and knowledge about a range of issues, but it is also antithetical to the democratic ideals upon which the United States was founded. His chapter presents a case study in a multicultural children's literature course for pre-service elementary teaching candidates that considered how state laws might impact teaching and learning in public schools and he offers a theoretical framework and an assignment that can be adapted by other educators to help future teachers find creative ways to strive towards democratic ideals as they navigate the politics and legislation that impact their work.

CONCLUSION

Nearly a century ago, education reformer John Dewey described democracy not as a utilitarian means to a political end, but as an ethical way of life that "had to be enacted anew in every generation, in every year and day, in the living relations of person to person in all social forms and institutions" (1937, pp. 473–474). If, as Dewey urged, democracy has to be made real and relevant to each new generation, higher education has an important role to play in building the knowledge, skills, values and agency of the communities it serves and works alongside. With all of the pressing public problems facing societies around the world and with democratic backsliding happening both in the United States and globally, revitalizing higher education's role in building the democracy we need is crucial. Can higher education step up and meet the moment?

REFERENCES

Annenberg Center. (2021, September 14). *Americans' civics knowledge increases during a stress-filled year.* Annenbergpublicpolicycenter.org. Annenberg Public Policy Center. https://www.annenbergpublicpolicycenter.org/2021-annenberg-constitution-day-civics-survey/

ANES. (2023). *ANES guide to public opinion and electoral behavior.* Electionstudies.org. ANES. https://electionstudies.org/data-tools/anes-guide/anes-guide.html?chart=how_satisfied_with_way_democracy_works

Association of American Colleges and Universities. (2012). *A crucible moment college learning and democracy's future. A national call to action.*

Bauer-Wolf, J. (2021). Idaho lawmakers cut $2.5M in funding for social justice education at 3 public universities. In highereddive.com. Higher Education Dive. https://www.highereddive.com/news/idaho-lawmakers-cut-25m-in-funding-for-social-justice-education-at-3-publ/599613/

Brennan Center. (2023, October 19). *Voting laws roundup: October 2023.* Brennancenter.org. Brennan Center for Justice. https://www.brennancenter.org/our-work/research-reports/voting-laws-roundup-october-2023

CIRCLE. (2019, April 29). *Half of youth voted in 2020, an 11-point increase from 2016* [Review of *Half of youth voted in 2020, an 11-point increase from 2016*]. Circle.tufts.edu; CIRCLE. https://circle.tufts.edu/latest-research/half-youth-voted-2020-11-point-increase-2016

College Civic Learning. (2021, September). *Shared commitment statement.* Retrieved December 29, 2023, from https://www.collegeciviclearning.org/shared-commitment

Daniels, R. J. (2021, October 3). *Universities are shunning their responsibility to democracy.* The Atlantic. https://www.theatlantic.com/ideas/archive/2021/10/universities-cant-dodge-civics/620261/

Dewey, J. (1937). Education and social change. *Bulletin of the American Association of University Professors, 23*(6), 472–474.

Frankovic, K., & Montgomery, D. (n.d.). *Most Americans support democracy and oppose dictatorship.* Today.yougov.com; YouGov. Retrieved December 29, 2023, from https://today.yougov.com/politics/articles/48238-most-americans-support-democracy-and-oppose-dictatorship

IDEA. (2021). www.idea.int THE GLOBAL STATE OF DEMOCRACY 2021: Building Resilience in a Pandemic Era. In *idea.int.* International Institute for

Democracy and Electoral Assistance. https://www.idea.int/gsod-2021/sites/default/files/2021-11/global-state-of-democracy-2021.pdf

Knight Foundation. (2022, January). *College student views on free expression and campus speech.* Knightfoundation.org; Knight Foundation. https://knightfoundation.org/wp-content/uploads/2022/01/KFX_College_2022.pdf

Ong Whaley, C., & Kondik, K. (2023, June 28). *Why partisan and racial gerrymandering should be abolished ft. Mitchell Brown.* University of Virginia Center for Politics.

Open Society Foundations. (2023, September). *Open Society barometer: Can democracy deliver?* Opensocietyfoundations.org; Open Society Foundations. https://www.opensocietyfoundations.org/uploads/e6cd5a09-cd19-4587-aa06-368d3fc78917/open-society-barometer-can-democracy-deliver-20230911.pdf

PEN America. (2023, April 14). *118 former higher education presidents launch initiative to combat educational censorship.* Pen.org; PEN America. https://pen.org/press-release/118-former-higher-education-presidents-launch-initiative-to-combat-educational-censorship/

PEN America. (2023). *Champions of Higher Education statement of purpose.* Pen.org; PEN America. https://pen.org/champions-statement/

Pew Research Center. (2022). Two years after election turmoil, GOP voters remain skeptical on elections, vote counts. In *pewresearch.org.* Pew Research Center. https://www.pewresearch.org/politics/2022/10/31/views-of-election-administration-and-confidence-in-vote-counts/

Reilly, K. (2022, April 22). *Florida's governor just signed the "Stop Woke Act." Here's what it means for schools.* Time. https://time.com/6168753/florida-stop-woke-law/

Repucci, S. (2021). *From crisis to reform: A call to strengthen America's battered democracy.* Freedom House. https://freedomhouse.org/report/special-report/2021/crisis-reform-call-strengthen-americas-battered-democracy

Riccardi, N., & Sanders, L. (2023, July 14). Americans are widely pessimistic about democracy in the United States, an AP-NORC poll finds. *AP.* https://apnews.com/article/poll-democracy-partisanship-trump-biden-trust-221f2b4f6cf9805f766c9a8395b9539d

Williamson, V. (2023, October 17). *Understanding democratic decline in the United States.* Brookings. https://www.brookings.edu/articles/understanding-democratic-decline-in-the-united-states/

SECTION I

NAMING AND FRAMING:
CHALLENGES AND PATHWAYS
FOR HIGHER EDUCATION'S NECESSARY ROLE
IN STRENGTHENING DEMOCRACY

CHAPTER 2

AUTHORITARIANISM AND THE UNIVERSITY

Global Perspectives From the Last Century

Lauren L. Shepherd
University of New Orleans

ABSTRACT

Authoritarianism is on the rise globally, and education remains at the center of the political crosshairs of illiberal regimes—as it has been for a century and more. Gaining an understanding of why and how antidemocratic movements have sought out institutions of higher education as political targets can help scholars anticipate forthcoming assaults on the university at home and abroad. This essay takes a global and historical perspective to examine how autocratic governments have targeted universities and liberal education more broadly from the 20th century to the present. It further explores how intellectuals have grappled with the fallout of these interventions. This narrative analysis spans authoritarian regimes across South America, Europe, South Asia, and the Pacific from the 1920s to the present, connecting historical themes from across the globe to the contemporary United States.

If scholars are committed to protecting universities for their vital role in fulfilling a nation's liberal democratic missions, we would be remiss to ignore that the current assaults on our academic institutions are neither unprecedented nor unique to the United States. Authoritarianism is on the rise globally, and education remains at the center of the political crosshairs of illiberal regimes—as it has been for a century and more. Gaining an understanding of why and how antidemocratic movements have sought out institutions of higher education as political targets can help scholars anticipate forthcoming assaults on the university and, more broadly, on our collective freedoms.

This chapter takes a global and historical perspective to examine how illiberal governments have targeted the academy (and education generally) from the 20th century to the present. A narrative analysis offers readers case studies of authoritarian impositions, spanning nationalist regimes across South America, Europe, Asia, and the Pacific, from the 1920s to the present. It further explores how intellectuals have grappled with the consequences of these interventions. Under these illiberal regimes, academics, students, journalists, and other intellectuals have been fired, jailed, and even killed for their actual or perceived political biases, which were deemed a threat to the given regime's legitimacy. These examples offer themes from the past which I connect to the contemporary state of the academy and its adversaries in the United States.

In the following analysis, I use the terms "authoritarian," "illiberal," and "antidemocratic" to qualify the different regimes presented within. Each of these terms describes a form of neo-nationalism, which John Aubrey Douglass defines as "extreme right-wing movements...often characterized by anti-immigrant and xenophobic rhetoric; economic protectionism; constraints on civil liberties; attacks on critics...and the emergence and empowerment of demagogues and autocrats" (Douglass, 2021, p. vii). The examples that follow demonstrate how autocrats and their political agents have forcefully promoted their own historically privileged cultures over minority groups within the same political jurisdiction. Such efforts have been most apparent through legislation that privileges dominant ethnicities and/or religions in political and cultural institutions. These laws have helped demagogues appeal to their followers by fostering and reinforcing a sense of belonging in the dominant culture of which they are already members or to which they aspire to belong. Attacking critics has been central in autocrats' rise and their ability to maintain control once in power (Albright, 2018; Ben-Ghiat, 2021; Finchelstein, 2022; Kuklick, 2022; Rosenfeld & Ward, 2023; Ross, 2017; Stanley, 2018).

In the examples that follow, autocrats were propelled into authority when their nation's majority culture imagined threats to their social, political, and economic status, frequently in the aftermath of a war. The demagogues in these cases commonly rose to power in democratic societies. In many cases, they rose up when supposed threats to the dominant culture's status were mere fantasy, but the autocrat convinced his constituents that demographic changes were an impending or existing danger to their privileges. The populations authoritarians have captivated came to believe their respective demagogue's propaganda through repeated exposure, fearfully accepting claims regarding the imminence of their own social and financial demise. Once in power, universities, libraries, and schools have tended to be among their first targets (Albright, 2018; Ben-Ghiat, 2021; Rosenfeld & Ward, 2023; Stanley, 2017).

For the autocrat to retain power in a pluralist society, a steady stream of disinformation and propaganda is necessary. Universities are thus ripe targets for the ways they foster and promote free inquiry. Faculty encourage students to explore libraries and archives, conduct scientific experiments, engage in debate, and—in the broadest sense—expose themselves to ideas that may challenge their traditional worldviews. Uncomfortable though such challenges may be, the purpose of these explorations is to further human knowledge by discovering innovative solutions to problems of science and society. Often, the quest for knowledge and progress gives rise to ideas that contest the traditional understandings on which authoritarians rely. Nationalist demagogues thus characterize the type of free inquiry that universities promote as seditious, harmful to the national order, and deserving of punishment and elimination. Faculty and scientific researchers are characterized as biased and elitist, projected onto the masses by way of propaganda as hostile actors waging war on tradition.

A global history of authoritarian attacks against the university helps expose the inaccuracy and disingenuousness of such portrayals. The deceit becomes apparent when analyzing the political advantages that authoritarians gain from these assaults, and by examining how their power relies on public opposition to dissent. Demagogues know that information bans serve their interests, even when the faculty and students who seek banned knowledge do so for reasons unrelated to politics. But autocrats do not frame their attacks against unencumbered inquiry as the outright rejection of learning that it is. Instead, in need of an enemy to assail, they position free inquiry as treasonous to the dominant culture. Authoritarians demand conformity and obedience to maintain national homogeneity, which they claim only their rule can protect. Condemning places of learning and critical reasoning is paramount in their propaganda campaigns.

AUTHORITARIAN REGIMES AND HIGHER EDUCATION, 1922–1989

Ironically, higher education cannot entirely disassociate from its own authoritarian past. The very first European institutions in Bologna, Paris, and

Oxford in the 11th and 12th centuries were all created by authoritarian edicts of crown, church, or both. Even the earliest research universities of Germany in the 19th century emerged from the zeitgeist of nation building (Douglass, 2021). But by the 20th century, the same institutions that helped unite the German and Italian states were under attack by authoritarians promoting National Socialism and National Fascism.

Once in power, loyalty tests have tended to be the autocrat's primary method to ensure that blind allegiance replaces truth, principle, and inquiry. Throughout the 1920s in Italy, Benito Mussolini expelled hundreds of Jewish faculty and thousands of students from Italian colleges for their supposed unfaithfulness to fascism. By 1931, the regime demanded that those left on campus make loyalty oaths and attest to their "Aryan" status (Adler, 2022, p. 528). The following year, faculty were required to become bona fide members of the fascist party to retain employment, and were expected to be seen publicly donning the paramilitary's black shirt (Ben-Ghiat, 2020). To enforce his vision, Mussolini appointed fascist partisans to the Ministry of Education, regardless of their lack of professional experience in the field. Minister of Education Giuseppe Bottai confessed that schools "had to be defended and protected," as they were "central to the transmission of Fascist values and Italian identity" (Adler, 2022, p. 525). Throughout the 1920s and into the 1930s, party loyalists developed state textbooks that glorified fascist worldviews, including national supremacy and, especially, the racial inferiority of Jews and other groups (McLean, 2023).

Around the same time, National Socialists in Germany followed the Italian model by instituting their own loyalty oath requirements to determine which faculty to purge or replace. The Nazis' particular brand of anti-intellectualism went well beyond simply replacing a faculty expert with an ideological ally in the classroom—they also destroyed records of knowledge. In 1933, Joseph Goebbels infamously spoke at Humboldt University in Berlin before the flames of a fire that engulfed 20,000 books by Jewish, gay, and other "un-German" authors. The same year, the Nazi regime fired an additional 250 Jewish professors and ordered the deportation of an unknown number of foreign students under the Law for the Restoration of the Professional Civil Service (Douglass, 2021, p. 8). In 1939, Nazi troops swept Czechoslovakian universities and, in response to student protests, stormed residence halls and city living quarters. The incursion killed nine students and directed more than 1,200 others to concentration camps (European Network of Remembrance and Solidarity [ENRS], 2023). By 1945, the Russian occupation of East Germany ended the Nazis' control over the University of Berlin. The Soviets took over and implemented yet another faculty and student purge (prompting some faculty and students to flee to West Germany) and installed Soviet academic stand-ins (Douglass, 2021, pp. 10–11).

Not long after, in 1949, the Chinese Revolution under nationalist Chiang Kai-Shek led to a similarly swift denigration of the academy. Following the example of the Soviet system of higher education, colleges were overhauled to serve the regime's specific economic needs. Instead of conducting research, faculty trained students for work as the state demanded. By the time of the Cultural Revolution in 1967, populists under Mao Zedong had sent thousands of faculty to be reeducated in camps, or to fields where they performed forced labor. The number of college students across China fell drastically, from an estimated 700,000 to less than 50,000 (Douglass, 2021, p. 15). The Chinese government's policy of punishing dissent continued well into the 20th century and continues today. The most infamous example of China's state-enforced conformity took place in 1989, when student protests for civil liberties in Tiananmen Square were violently crushed by the state military.

In postwar Latin America, attacks against the academy followed a similar pattern. Throughout this era, the United States sponsored coups d'états across the global South to solidify its political alliances against the Soviet Union. American leaders coordinated the overthrow of socialist governments and replaced them with right-wing strongmen and juntas who shared typical autocratic views about unsupervised and unguided learning. In 1973, in Chile, the US-backed military dictator Augusto Pinochet (quietly known as an academic himself) led his own faculty purges and installed loyalists in key administrative roles. To signal the beginning of his tenure as rector of the University of Chile, Air Force General César Ruiz Danyau made a striking entrance by parachuting onto the campus, foreshadowing the authoritarian rule that would follow. From 1973 to 1975, Danyau expelled 24,000 faculty and students and closed the departments of philosophy and sociology completely. Under Pinochet's junta, Chilean universities became sites of show trials in which faculty witnesses turned against one another. As a result of the trials, convicted "extremists" were imprisoned or tortured. Other faculty were sentenced to internment camps on islands off the Pacific coast (Ben-Ghiat, 2020).

In each of these cases of autocratic rule in Europe, Asia, and Latin America, totalitarian leaders employed similar tactics when seizing control of universities. They first submitted students and faculty to tests of loyalty, purging those who failed. Undesirable faculty and administrators were then replaced with regime supporters. Knowledge was forbidden through book bans, or quite literally destroyed through book burnings. Curricula were transformed to prioritize the regime's ideology over historical and scientific accuracy. In the extreme cases of Germany, China, and Chile, disloyal faculty were punished in forced labor and death camps.

There were successful instances of faculty and student resistance in other cases, though these types of occurrences were exceptional. Throughout the

1970s and early 1980s, Polish faculty were unique in finding ways to reject nationalist annexations of their classrooms. During the Russian Empire's crackdown on higher education, Polish faculty designed the "flying university," a clandestine network of scholars and their students who met secretly in private residences to continue teaching and learning in the tradition they had formerly known (Daniels, 2021, p. 4). With few exceptions, faculty and student dissidents were usually subjected to forced exile, imprisonment, or execution.

AUTHORITARIANS AND THE UNIVERSITIES IN THE 21ST CENTURY

Previously, economic dislocation and status anxieties were major factors that fueled authoritarian movements across Europe, Asia, and South America. Today's iteration of right-wing populism has three additional factors: globalization, demographic change, and advanced technology that allows for surveilling and targeting political opponents (Douglass, 2021, p. vii). The target demographic has also been expanded from ethnic and religious minorities to include the LGBTQ community, though persecution of gay citizens is known to have occurred in Nazi Germany and elsewhere.

In addition to their attacks on the academy, today's authoritarians have also spearheaded efforts to transform primary and secondary (K–12) education to serve their political interests. Schools are often easier targets than universities, where politicians have less direct control over daily operations and curricula. In other instances, rather than repurpose universities and schools to fit their ideological liking, dictators have simply shut them down. This has been the case in Russia, where Vladimir Putin has closed universities on grounds ranging from formatting errors in course syllabi to the supposed architectural shortcomings of campus buildings (Daniels, 2021, p. 5).

In the 21st century, autocrats continue to fire, replace, and imprison their academic challengers. Modern regimes now strip colleges of funding, fire faculty and order hiring freezes (rather than institute loyalist replacements), and generally starve institutions so that they atrophy from within. This was the case in 2019, when Brazil's Jair Bolsonaro froze new faculty hires, slashed public research funds, and rerouted millions in funding for universities to vocational education and other sectors (Douglass, 2021, p. 27). While in power, he elevated right-wing narratives about slavery in the former Portuguese colony, insisting that, more than White Europeans, African merchants were chiefly responsible for the transatlantic slave trade (Machado & Zeeman, 2023). In promoting these false claims, Bolsonaro called back to 20th-century fascist rulers who purposefully distorted the past to appeal to a nationalist political base.

Twenty first-century autocrats have expanded their list of political scapegoats to include the LGBTQ community. From his campaign in 2018 and throughout his time in office, Bolsonaro attacked the statewide high school exit test, the National Secondary Education Exam (ENEM), for its questions related to gender. After forcing several questions to be removed from the ENEM, 37 education ministers resigned, and Bolsonaro bragged that the exam would finally begin "to resemble this administration" (Radio France Internationale [RFI], 2021). Similarly, Brazil's conservative political movement, the *Programa Escola Sem Partido*, purports to protect children from educational indoctrination, especially regarding Brazil's colonial past and the histories of Black and Indigenous people. Advocates urge students to film teachers, and for parents to report perceived teacher bias to a hotline (Machado & Zeeman, 2023). In the United States, we have seen similar tip lines in Virginia and Arizona.

Nations such as Hungary and Poland have banned gender studies as a field of research, categorizing the discipline as an ideology rather than an academic field of study—an attitude quickly gaining a foothold in both higher education and K–12 schools in the United States. The K–12 education system in Hungary prohibits the teaching of gender and sexuality, labeling these subjects as types of child abuse and "sexual propaganda," while equating homosexuality with pedophilia. The instruction in sex education that does exist in Hungary and Poland promotes a view of family life rooted in Christian teachings of marriage; same-sex marriage is illegal in both nations. Public schools in Hungary and Poland are now subject to their respective states' national curricula, which prescribe textbooks that glorify Christian nationalism and minimize historical wrongdoings, such as each country's participation in the Holocaust. The Polish education minister has proudly stated that he has eliminated an "education of shame" from schools and replaced it with an "education of pride," echoing Bolsonaro's boasts about the revised ENEM exit exam (American Historical Association, 2023).

Following Putin's example of forced university closures, Hungary's Viktor Orbán ordered Central European University to close its doors in Budapest. It has been reinstated today in its new location in Vienna, Austria, outside of the Orbán regime's control. The initial closure was a result of the university's mission to promote open societies in the former Soviet bloc, as well as its ties to philanthropist founder and *bête noire* of the far-right, George Soros. Orbán has further used the power of the Hungarian government to take over both the Academy of Sciences and the University of Theatre and Film Arts in Budapest, replacing their board members, administrators, and faculty with his own partisans (Gall, 2020). As of January 2023, 21 Hungarian universities are under the control of Orbán-approved asset management companies—a red flag for the European Commission, which has threatened to withdraw those institutions from the European Union's study abroad program (Woods, 2023).

In perhaps the most retrograde and disturbing present-day example, the Chinese government under Xi Jinping has jailed Uighur academics, placing them in hard labor camps reminiscent of the Soviet Union's Gulag. China's National Security Law in 2020 has allowed for state crackdowns on faculty and student dissidents in Hong Kong and elsewhere. To identify rebels, China uses a modern software equivalent of the historic loyalty oath—a digital program called the Social Credit System that allows the communist government to monitor and rank its citizens for trustworthiness. Consequences for citizens' infractions range from restricted internet access to travel bans (Donnelly, 2023).

Likewise, India's current right-wing prime minister, Narendra Modi, has followed in the footsteps of 20th-century demagogues by intensifying radical Hindu nationalism, or Hindutva, and fueling ethnic and religious divisions across the subcontinent. Since 2019, the Modi government has censored history textbooks that describe inter-caste social conflicts. In 2021, the state issued a revised undergraduate history curriculum for Indian public universities that deemphasizes Muslim and Mughal contributions and elevates Hindu religious history (Machado & Zeeman, 2023).

Similar curriculum wars are currently being waged in the Philippines, where President Ferdinand "Bongbong" Marcos Jr., son of former dictator Ferdinand Marcos Sr., has lambasted history textbooks for their portrayal of the Marcos family's ill-gotten wealth and human rights violations; Marcos Jr. frequently characterizes such claims as "political propaganda" (Jalea, 2020). After appointing loyalists to the education ministry, the Commission on Filipino Languages banned five books highlighting the abuses of the former Marcos regime. Though the ban has since been rescinded, the commission continues to characterize the authors as "communist," and the books on its list of censored texts as "subversive" (Machado & Zeeman, 2023).

In addition to loyalty oaths, book bans, and washing the historical record in nationalist propaganda, faculty purges have also endured in the 21st century. Since 2016, Turkey's President Recep Erdoğan has fired 8,500 faculty and 1,350 university staff, closed institutions, and restructured those allowed to remain open. The Erdoğan regime ordered over 550 faculty and students be apprehended as terrorists and coup plotters and charged with sedition. Of the thousands of faculty, students, and staff who were dismissed, each was banned from future employment with the state, and all have been required to reapply for their passports (Kaya, 2018).

DISCUSSION

An examination of both past and present examples shows that the strategies and priorities of authoritarian control over universities differ among various regions of the world. In the 21st-century United States and the United Kingdom, for example, there have been strong anti-immigrant currents, best exemplified by Donald Trump's immigration bans and Brexit restrictions on research visas. Conversely, in Hungary, Poland, and Turkey, many native faculty members have fled the repressive regimes of their home countries (Douglass, 2001, p. ix).

Despite these variations, a distinct pattern has emerged among the authoritarian regimes of the 21st century that involves the consolidation of power through information restriction and manipulation. Under the modern nationalist model, autocrats appoint their allies as college presidents and other principal administrators, dictate faculty dismissals and hirings, punish student dissent, and refuse funding for areas of research that challenge their ideological frameworks. In both higher education and K–12 schools, autocratic regimes prioritize patriotism at the expense of academic freedom and access to education, as they undoubtedly see the ability of citizens to question the state as a threat to their authority. In K–12 textbooks and curricula, authoritarian governments attempt to eliminate the representation of minority groups whose cultural achievements contradict nationalist ahistorical narratives and political mythologies (Machado & Zeeman, 2023).

HIGHER EDUCATION IN THE CONTEMPORARY UNITED STATES

This essay has highlighted egregious assaults against the academy in cases from Brazil, Chile, China, Germany, Hungary, India, Italy, the Philippines, Poland, Russia, and Turkey. However, the antagonism between authoritarians and universities has also been well documented recently in Egypt, Indonesia, Myanmar, Turkmenistan, Venezuela, and elsewhere. These international cases may lead readers to the unwarranted conclusion that the present situation in the United States is less dire under the current Biden-Harris administration. We have yet to impose loyalty oaths or incarcerate government critics in labor camps, and we have also been spared the most extreme forms of genocidal violence inflicted upon academic dissidents in countries like Chile, China, Italy, Germany, and Russia.

Even during the previous presidential administration of Donald Trump, who was notably more hostile to journalists than academics, universities seemed to operate largely without political constraint. Perhaps the most contentious event regarding universities under the Trump administration came in 2017, when the former president tweeted his consideration to revoke federal funds from institutions that would not allow reactionary speakers on campus, such as extremist provocateur Milo Yiannopoulos, who had been banned from speaking at the University of California at Berkeley. In March 2019, Trump translated his online musings into law under Executive Order 13864, which mandates that institutions that receive federal funding "avoid creating environments that stifle competing perspectives." The order also includes the protection of hate speech from the type of far-right extremists known to endorse his politics (Exec. Order No. 13864, 2019). In effect, the order legitimizes hate speech by codifying it as an additional perspective to be protected.

Although the former president has been replaced in office and faces just under one hundred criminal indictments, as of the publishing of this manuscript, he is the frontrunner for the Republican Party's nomination to be president in 2024. During his current campaign, the former president has accelerated his attacks on the "woke" academy and promises to use his power to enforce further crackdowns if reinstated (Knott, 2023). Republican Party office holders with their own presidential aspirations have followed Trump's lead within their current jurisdictions. This is most apparent at the state level, where there has been an onslaught of legislative bans on "divisive concepts" since 2020.

According to the nonprofit PEN America, an organization dedicated to defending free expression, legislation targeting what the political Right frames as "divisive" can better be understood as a series of educational gag orders. These gag orders are partly a result of the pushback against Nikole Hannah-Jones' antiracist *1619 Project*, which was sponsored by *The New York Times* during the Trump era. While he was still in office, Trump's Executive Order 13950 on Race and Sex Stereotyping was the first to ban a range of allegedly divisive concepts associated with antiracist education, including diversity, equity, and inclusion (DEI) requirements in federal workplace trainings (Exec. Order No. 13950, 2020). However, the order was signed at the end of Trump's term and, along with his alternative *1776 Commission on Patriotic Education*, was dissolved on the first day of the Biden administration (American Historical Association, 2023).

When it became clear to Republican lawmakers that Trump's federal DEI ban would not be realized, there began a cascade of similarly spirited state legislation, now totaling over 300 proposed bills at the time of writing. Much like the Trump executive order, the state bills began by targeting trainings in state agencies but have since broadened their scope to encompass K–12 schools and universities, with higher education becoming an "increasing focus" (39% of the bills proposed in 2022 were targeted at colleges and universities, and the number of these bills is on track to exceed that level in the 2023–24 academic year). Nineteen states have approved this type of legislation through executive orders or state policy, bypassing the representative voting process (American Historical Association, 2023).

Even when the proposals fail to become law, the political assertions made by these gag order bills can still have a chilling effect on curricula.

The best examples of the gag orders affecting higher education include laws from the states of Texas and Florida. Texas law SB17 bans diversity, equity, and inclusion (DEI) offices, as well as DEI training. It prohibits affirmative action, race-conscious, and gender-conscious hiring. The law is enforced through regular compliance inspections by state auditors. In addition to external audits, the law provides a path for students and employees to sue their university to enforce compliance as a form of inspection from within (T.S.B. 17, 2023). Similarly, Florida law FL S0266 bans faculty from exposing students to any critical theory (including feminist theory, critical race theory, and queer theory), dismantles DEI programs, defunds and prohibits campus activities deemed discriminatory (defined at Republican politicians' discretion), and allows for post-tenure reviews by trustees appointed by the Republican governor (FL S0266, 2023). Under the law's original proposal, the partisan board would be granted statewide curricular control, which would allow it to rewrite mission statements and eliminate majors entirely (FL S0266, 2023).

Ron DeSantis, the Republican governor of Florida, demonstrated how this type of legislation could be enacted by appointing a numerical majority of party loyalists to the Board of Trustees at New College in Sarasota. Among the most threatening appointees is Christopher Rufo, the architect of anti-critical race theory hysteria among the political Right. Rufo has proudly declared that the "hostile takeover" of New College "would serve as a model for conservatives to copy all over the country," further elaborating that "If we can take this high-risk, high-reward gambit and turn it into a victory, we're going to see conservative state legislators starting to reconquer public institutions all over the United States" (Goldberg, 2023). What Rufo likely realizes but refuses to acknowledge is that this new "model for conservatives to copy" has long been part of the script of the autocratic and fascist regimes highlighted here.

Other legislation in Florida more specifically targets the elementary and secondary school spheres. Laws that forbid K–12 teachers from talking to their students about gender identity are characterized as a form of protection for children and families. This includes the Stop Wrongs to Our Kids and Employees Act (known as the Stop WOKE Act) and the Parental Rights in Education Act (known as the Don't Say Gay law). A direct nod towards the fascist method of taking control over institutions by feigning to protect parents and children, these laws mimic the Hungarian and Polish examples that ban classroom discussions of sexuality outside of Christian teachings. The purpose of the gag orders, as in any authoritarian sphere, is to promote a mythical past by conflating "faith with science, memory with history, and dogmatism with truth" (McLean, 2023). These laws blur the lines between church and state in the K–12 space, and as Rufo has promised, foreshadow the Right's plans for the university in the immediate future.

IMPLICATIONS FOR THE ACADEMY

Historians (McLean, 2023; Rosenfeld & Ward, 2023) have argued that focusing our energies on denouncing modern Republican efforts as "fascist" risks ignoring very real problems that existed long before GOP presidential hopefuls began pointing their political weapons at education. Underfunded schools, curricular oversimplifications of historical events, teacher shortages, and a preference for training students for jobs at the expense of educating future citizens who can think critically have resulted in the conditions that allow disinformation to thrive (McLean, 2023).

In the name of political compromise and neoliberal economic efficiency, law and policymakers outside of the Republican Party are also complicit in creating conditions for authoritarianism to take hold. In the higher education sphere, this applies to self-styled liberals as well as those on the Right. For decades, decision makers in higher education have pursued a strategy of administration and adjunctification. This model provides for investments in administrative employees whose jobs protect the university from legal liability. It offsets subsequent administrative salary and benefit costs by deprioritizing faculty budget lines. Under this design, college regents and administrators who do not consider themselves to be political conservatives have nonetheless compromised away necessary investments in faculty and researchers who would have the protection of tenure, especially those working in the humanities, social sciences, and libraries.

As a result of right-wing attacks and neoliberal concessions that reduce the importance of the faculty, decision makers across the political spectrum have failed to make higher education more accessible and affordable—another advantage for demagogues who rely on an undereducated populace to manipulate. Educators ourselves have also failed to correct the widely shared public misunderstanding that colleges are job training facilities or mere factories for credentialing technology workers. Regardless of our political intentions, illiberal political actors benefit from the fact that the humanities—their chief target—do not fit well into the college-as-workforce training conceptualization. The existence of multibillion-dollar endowments at public institutions is proof that the money required to alter our current trajectory is already available. The political will to do so is minimal, and actively under attack by our own authoritarians.

In the last year, thousands of faculty and graduate students have worked to combat this by unionizing the campus (Quinn, 2023). While their collective efforts are a powerful force and a hopeful sign of resistance, the burden of protecting our shared capacity to research, teach, and learn freely too often falls on those directly under attack. It is the responsibility of everyone, from faculty members with tenure protections (including those in the hard sciences who tend to bare the least of the attacks) to administrators, K–12 teachers, students, librarians, and the public to exhaustively advocate for the importance of the humanities and the fundamental right to free inquiry. We must defend books currently under fire by legislators who would ban them for political gain. The fates of higher education, K–12 education, and public libraries are interconnected, and the right to learn needs to be fiercely defended in each. What is at stake for one is at stake for all, as the history of authoritarianism around the globe has offered precedent.

Scholars have become increasingly more forceful in their warnings about what may lie ahead for the United States. Attacks against universities tend to serve as a bellwether for attacks against political freedoms writ large (Ben-Ghiat, 2020; Daniels, 2021). We should collectively emphasize, as Levinson & Erickson (2022) have argued, "that teaching and learning are not simply about mastery of technical content but also play an essential role in the transmission of human values, in shaping us as persons, and in preserving what matters in civilization" (p. xvii). Because education is a public good, faculty and students must engage with the public beyond the ivory tower and communicate our research and findings to the wider world. We should address the public as collaborators and equal partners in the fight to protect our right to learn and other freedoms next at stake. In doing so, we ensure the public is less receptive to the propaganda and disinformation of authoritarians.

Those who argue that the United States is not currently in a political situation reminiscent of 20th-century fascism obscure the real potential that such an outcome could materialize in the context of the Right's current illiberal aspirations. While the Republican Party's repressive educational measures do not yet match the historical precedents set by authoritarian regimes of the last century, they are a clear indication of the party's support for its most extreme right-wing members who favor an antidemocratic future for the country. This threat goes beyond the censorship of individual professors or teachers, but spans one or more generations of students and the public. Lest our colleagues in the sciences dismiss these assaults as aimed only at the humanities, it is important to remember the recent attacks against expertise itself, which include COVID-19 denialism and vaccine skepticism, to say nothing of climate change denial. Authoritarian discourse is consumed by "factual relativism," that fuels the degradation of both the humanities and the sciences, as well as our collective search for solutions to modern problems (Douglass, 2021, p. xiv). By putting global authoritarian violence against liberal education and free inquiry in a longer historical perspective, we can reach a better understanding of how to protect our most fundamental democratic institution—public education.

REFERENCES

Adler, F. H. (2022). Italian fascism: Decentering standard assumptions about antisemitism and totalitarianism. In B. M. Levinson & R. P. Erickson (Eds.), *The betrayal of the humanities: The university during the Third Reich* (pp. 522–544). Indiana University Press.

Albright, M. (2018). *Fascism: A warning*. Harper.

American Historical Association. (2023, February 6). Don't say gay, Stop WOKE, banned books, and anti-trans laws: Teaching through the backlash [Video]. *American Historical Association*. https://www.youtube.com/watch?v=UEGSYJaCNG0

Ben-Ghiat, R. (2020, October 15). The right's war on universities. *The New York Review of Books*.

Ben-Ghiat, R. (2021). *Strongmen: Mussolini to the present*. W. W. Norton.

Daniels, R. J. (2021). *What universities owe democracy*. Johns Hopkins University Press.

Donnelly, D. (2023, January 3). China social credit system explained—What is it & how does it work? *Horizons*. https://nhglobalpartners.com/china-social-credit-system-explained/

Douglass, J. A. (2021). *Neo-nationalism and universities: Populists, autocrats, and the future of higher education*. Johns Hopkins University Press.

European Network of Remembrance and Solidarity. (2023). German Nazi storming of Czech universities. ENRS. https://enrs.eu/news/german-nazi-storming-of-czech-universities

Exec. Order No. 13,950, 3 C.F.R. (2020). https://www.federalregister.gov/documents/2020/09/28/2020-21534/combating-race-and-sex-stereotyping

Exec. Order No. 13,864, 3 C.F.R. (2019). https://www.federalregister.gov/documents/2019/03/26/2019-05934/improving-free-inquiry-transparency-and-accountability-at-colleges-and-universities

F.H.B 999, 2023. (Fla. 2023). https://www.flsenate.gov/Session/Bill/2023/999/?Tab=BillText

F.S.B. 266, 2023. (Fla. 2023). https://legiscan.com/FL/text/S0266/2023.

Finchelstein, F. (2022). *Fascist mythologies: The history and politics of unreason in Borges, Freud, and Schmitt*. Columbia University Press.

Gall, L. (2020, September 3). Hungary continues attacks on academic freedom. *Human Rights Watch*. https://www.hrw.org/news/2020/09/03/hungary-continues-attacks-academic-freedom

Goldberg, M. (2023, January 9). DeSantis allies plot the hostile takeover of a liberal college. *New York Times*. https://www.nytimes.com/2023/01/09/opinion/chris-rufo-florida-ron-desantis.html

Jalea, G. (2020, January 10). Marcos pushes for revision of history textbooks: "You're teaching the children lies." *CNN Philippines*. http://www.cnnphilippines.com/news/2020/1/10/Marcos-wants-to-revise-history-textbooks.html

Kaya, M. (2018). Turkey's purge of critical academia. *Middle East Research and Information Project*. https://merip.org/2018/12/turkeys-purge-of-critical-academia/

Knott, K. (2023. May 4). Trump's 'secret weapon'? College accreditation. *Inside Higher Ed.* https://www.insidehighered.com/news/government/2023/05/04/trumps-secret-weapon-college-accreditation

Kuklick, B. (2022). *Fascism comes to America: A century of obsession in politics and culture.* University of Chicago Press.

Levinson, B. M., & Erickson, R. P. (Eds.). (2022). *The betrayal of the humanities: The university during the Third Reich.* Indiana University Press.

Machado, J. B., & Zeeman, R. (2023, April 4). Censoring history education goes hand in hand with democratic backsliding. *History News Network.* https://historynewsnetwork.org/article/185267

McLean, E. (2023, April 7). Fascism's history offers lessons about today's attacks on education. *Scientific American.* https://www.scientificamerican.com/article/fascisms-history-offers-lessons-about-todays-attacks-on-education/

Network of Concerned Historians. (2023.) *Compilation of annual reports, 1995–2022.* https://concernedhistorians.org/content_files/file/ar/compilation.pdf

Quinn, R. (2023, September 6). Grad worker unionization is booming, even down south. *Inside Higher Ed.* https://www.insidehighered.com/news/faculty-issues/labor-unionization/2023/09/06/grad-worker-unionization-booming-even-down-south

Radio France Internationale. (2021, November 16). Bolsonaro govt accused of censoring Brazil school exam. *RFI.* https://www.rfi.fr/en/bolsonaro-govt-accused-of-censoring-brazil-school-exam

Rosenfeld, G. D., & Ward, J. (Eds.). (2023). *Fascism in America: Past and present.* Cambridge University Press.

Ross, A. R. (2017). *Against the fascist creep.* AK Press.

Stanley, J. (2020). *How fascism works: The politics of us and them.* Random House.

T.S.B. 17, 2023. (Tex. 2023). https://legiscan.com/TX/text/SB17/2023

Woods, J. (2023, January 10). After the EU ban: What will happen with the Erasmus program in Hungary? *Daily News Hungary.* https://dailynewshungary.com/after-the-eu-ban-what-will-happen-with-the-erasmus-program-in-hungary/

CHAPTER 3

CAUGHT IN THE MIDDLE

(In)Civility, Compliance, and "Norms of Appropriateness"

Angela Kraemer-Holland
Kansas State University

ABSTRACT

This chapter explores the current social and political contentions affecting United States colleges and universities. These contentions mirror national debates around civility and divisiveness, autonomy and external pressure, and democracy and dogma. I draw on Van Dijk's (2008) critical discourse method to show how colleges and universities employ anti-democratic tactics in the name of civility, and in practice, operate counter to their missions of academic freedom and open inquiry. This is a result of the rise of neoliberalism and conservatism in academia, which is explored in this chapter to place the present situation in political context. Specifically, neoliberal and conservative policies and initiatives that necessitate alleged civility jeopardize the institutional missions and roles of colleges and universities as democratic spheres of academic freedom, while weaponizing the very notion of civility for these policies mandate. Consequently, this chapter highlights how neoliberal and conservative discourses of hegemonic civility have infiltrated colleges and universities, exacerbated by a deeply polarized United States and further challenging the position of colleges and universities as civic-oriented institutions of open inquiry.

> *If the university does not take seriously and rigorously its role as a guardian of wider civic freedoms... then some other regime or ménage of regimes will do it for us, in spite of us, and without us.*
> —Morrison, 2001, p. 7

Once revered enclaves of critical thought and ideological boundary-pushing (Giroux, 2014), current political and public assault through discourse and policy threatens the missions, structures and positions of colleges and universities as spaces to engage with more significant social issues through scholarly and civic dissent. As politics continue to intrude on "the life of the mind" (Gross, 2013, p. 17), the discursive and legislative attacks and the erosion of democratic principles underscoring higher education simultaneously grow (Young & Friedman, 2022). Educational institutions maintain increasingly socially organized and sanctioned norms, behaviors and knowledge that re-socialize their educational stakeholders while negotiating their fragile roles fostering invention and contention (Ball, 2003; Goodin, 2012). Moreover, far from possessing immunity from policies and discourses shaping public institutions and public life, colleges and universities are now increasingly situated within the crosshairs of civility, criticality and outside neoliberal and conservative influence that consequently intrude on institutional structure, practice and governance. As a result, institutional autonomy and academic freedom resemble capitalistic parodies of the democratic principles that are the hallmark of higher education (Giroux, 2014). Instead, practices of "civility" reflect a more profound, insidious effort to shape the behavior of faculty, students and the institutional structure of colleges and universities to align with external Right-leaning political and economic interests.

In this context, this chapter explores higher education's complicated position as it seeks to achieve its broader public missions while satisfying competing (and sometimes nefarious and Right-leaning) political and financial interests. It will illuminate how policy and discourse complicate universities' efforts to adhere to their missions and sustain policies and practices that value and maintain its reputation as a critical and democratic space. Drawing from the framework of critical discourse studies (Van Dijk, 2008), this chapter critiques discourses that appear to champion civility through institutionally sanctioned "norms of appropriateness" (Van Dijk, 2008, p. 8). Instead, calls for civility mask neoliberal and conservative goals to reorganize college and university governance and faculty subjectivities toward *hegemonic* civility (emphasis added). Finally, this chapter calls attention to how neoliberal and conservative discourses weaponize civility and consequently jeopardize criticality and democratic principles in higher education.

THE HISTORICALLY COMPLICATED POLITICAL POSITION OF HIGHER EDUCATION

As sites of knowledge production and debate, colleges and universities are required to accommodate competing, nuanced ideas and perspectives to create a more democratic and inclusive society (Castro, 2019; Gross, 2013; Seis, 2019), endeavoring to serve the common good rather than individual or institutional interests (Dutt-Ballerstadt & Bhattacharya, 2021). In this way, higher education occupies dominant and subordinate social positions through its implication in broader political and economic landscapes. Therefore, it is essential to situate historical and contemporary assaults on higher education within social, economic and political power struggles.

Historically, criticisms of higher education have lacked cohesiveness across states and institution types (Giroux, 2014). However, while the social movements of the 1960s and 1970s distinguished academia socially and politically from the general public (Gross, 2013), such movements similarly cultivated latent and pervasive distrust in higher education. Consequently, the 1980s ushered in attacks on colleges and universities that coincided with simultaneous assaults on public institutions and democratic principles under the dominant capitalist orientation (Giroux, 2014). As a result—although not always the case—college degrees tend to serve as political and cultural dividers between the university-connected and those removed from higher education (Fischer, 2022; Giroux, 2014), and consequently might mirror partisanship embedded in political and public discourse.

In addition to their initial positions as sites of knowledge production and debate, colleges and universities also socialize their inhabitants (Binder & Wood, 2013). Colleges and universities cultivate human and social capital through institutionally sanctioned norms of appropriateness that align with institutional missions, but also mirror outside debates and policies aimed at redefining institutional structure and individual subjectivities (Van Dijk, 2008). Modern assaults on the public university and its democratic missions underscore how colleges and universities are susceptible to outside economic and political influences that seek to restructure academia. Challenges to the university as a space for critical thought and academic freedom coincide with more widespread attacks on our nation's democratic principles writ large. In this climate, colleges and universities paradoxically negotiate competing initiatives: adhering to their institutional missions and supporting students' civic participation while also enacting cost-cutting strategies to offset defunding and navigating restrictive educational policies that inhibit teaching and learning of specific topics and ideas (see PEN America's (2022) continuous compilation report of U.S.-educational gag orders). Furthermore, deepening partisan divides amplify academia's susceptibility to anti-democratic pressures and trends (Kaltefleiter, 2019), hardening the challenge to preserve institutional principles and practices grounded on open inquiry and civility.

(In)Civility, Compliance, and "Norms of Appropriateness"

It is essential to examine the complicated position of higher education within the larger discursive and policy efforts to constrict its enactment of academic freedom and democratic principles. Situating higher education within prevailing neoliberal and conservative discourses highlight how neoliberal and conservative language can shape institutional policies and governance (Van Dijk, 2008). Discourse represents socially sanctioned language that encompasses the speaker's beliefs, values and attitudes, all of which then shape the language context (Gee, 1996). Discourses consequently inform institutional policies, procedures, and values. These institutional norms are increasingly informed by broader beliefs of what is true and common sense—often established by more powerful entities—which consequently influence individuals' work and their identities (Ball, 2012; Foucault, 1977). In this way, discourse, policy and power are inextricably linked, whereby notions of truth are implicated in these larger discursive and political power structures, fostering institutional and social reorganization toward complicity and censorship over civility.

To that end, calls for civility surged following Donald Trump's election as president in 2016 (Boatright, 2019; Cloud, 2021), often from socially dominant groups (Cloud, 2021). As a result, colleges and universities revisited their own conduct codes, which establish norms of appropriateness around what is permissible for campus constituents, and which is anchored in the nebulous notion of civility. As a discourse, civility encompasses socially and contextually established norms and behaviors of expected politeness (Jamieson et al., 2015; Laden, 2019), increasingly aligned with White ways of knowing/being/doing (Dutta, 2021). However, civility also includes nonviolent dissent, despite its persistent conflation with compromise, neutrality, and majoritarianism (Zurn, 2013). Political theory grounds civility within deliberation principles that preserve civility's underpinning of respect and the individual's democratic position (Jamieson et al., 2015), while recognizing its implication in the power structures that define it (Abraham, 2021; Williams, 2021).

As this relates to higher education, campus civility codes govern controversies to avoid confrontation and to sustain both respect and a welcoming environment (Cloud, 2021; Dutta, 2021; Shahvisi, 2021), a normative concept embedded in *hegemonic* civility deployed to narrow and de-politicize open inquiry and social critiques to preserve institutional reputation. Coalesced around White ideals embedded in U.S.-aligned modes of communication (Dutta, 2021), *hegemonic civility* preserves the status quo through deliberate and organized efforts to silence opposition, consequently labeling dissenters as "uncivil" while simultaneously championing freedom of expression (Patton, 2004). This is done to satisfy the institution's reputation and maintain its positive relationship with donors, funding agencies, legislators, and status-quo oriented alumni. From there, those who define civility are positioned as models of the civility-focused norms of appropriateness they create.

Hegemonic civility can be easily co-opted as means of oppression as it can be disguised behind masks of allyship and progressive messaging (Dutta, 2021; Sheth & Croom, 2021). Additionally, discourses of hegemonic civility normalize conforming practices and policies of ideological and intellectual consensus as natural and objective (Williams, 2021). When calls for civility are deployed to silence dissent, we become aware of how hegemonic civility can be used towards anti-democratic and anti-egalitarian ends (Zurn, 2013). Through surveillance and prohibition practices such as curtailing academic freedom, hegemonic civility can become *in*civility by encompassing silencing functions wielded by those seeking widespread change or increased power. In academia, incivility hides behind the mask of discursive hegemonic civility to disempower dissent against the unjust (Dutta, 2021), jeopardizing alignment with institutional missions. As a result, colleges and universities exist in a double bind—they are tasked with responding to social issues while upholding their position as a democratic sphere founded on civil, open inquiry (Duncan, 2019; Giroux, 2014). It is squarely between this divisiveness and civility in which colleges and universities find themselves discursively, politically and structurally. Consequently, it becomes imperative to examine the structures defining and wielding (in)civility against higher education's position "as a democratic public sphere" and how these are implicated in larger neoliberal and conservative orientations (Giroux, 2014, p. 16).

PROFIT, POLICY, AND DISCURSIVE TURNS: INSTRUMENTS OF "THE UNCIVIL UNIVERSITY"

Neoliberalism's Pursuit of Profit and the Civil "Academic-Entrepreneur"

The increased neoliberalization of colleges and universities jeopardize their missions (Ball, 2012). Neoliberalism emerges as not only an economic structure and political orientation but, more fundamentally, as a way of being (Kirsten, 2019). Neoliberalism reflects an aggressive restructuring of capitalism that blurs the lines between the economic, social and political, eroding collective welfare and values in favor of individualized self-interest (Duncan, 2019; Seis, 2019). Macro-level neoliberalism manifests in state defunding of collective welfare programs and public institutions for financial market projects (Gross, 2013; Seis, 2019), and, in education, through political-corporate relationships that entrench school-as-business paradigms characterized as work force development (Juergensmeyer et al., 2019). Neoliberalism's insidiousness rests in its capacity to infiltrate policy, common sense and public discourse, shaping our relations with our environment, others and ourselves (Ball, 2012). As a result, neoliberalism as a regime of truth establishes its own appropriateness norms aligned to consumerism, competition and individual self-interest that stifles challenges to these ideals (Dutta, 2021; Juergensmeyer & Benz, 2019).

Alongside macro-level restructuring, neoliberalism reinvents individuals toward solitary, competitive and self-monitoring units of value under the guise of civility (Ball, 2012; Giroux, 2014; Patton, 2004). Through

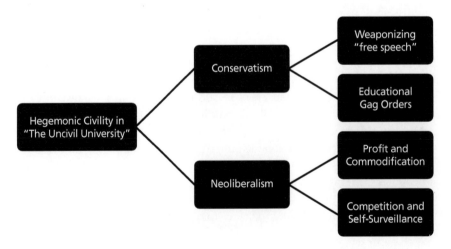

Figure. 3.1 Instruments of "The Uncivil University."

entrenched practices of ideological consensus and privileging narrow measures of scholarly productivity (Ball, 2003; 2016), neoliberal institutional policies and discourses subjugate and stifle faculty at the expense of faculty collectivity and academic freedom. Such neoliberal approaches prioritize consensus-building and scholarly and ideological control, which can often lead to faculty engaging in practices of self-surveillance over their teaching and scholarship. Furthermore, the neoliberal college or university normalizes situating education and knowledge as commodities, made evident through competitive grants and narrow impact factors as indicators of worthy, rigorous scholarship. These seemingly objective approaches to faculty scholarship and knowledge production demonstrate institutional efforts to normalize neoliberal principles as necessary parts of the status quo (Cloud, 2021; Dutta, 2021).

From there, neoliberalism and corporate power wield hegemonic civility through macro and micro-level efforts that illustrate commodification and academic repression. As defunding of higher education continues (Gross, 2013; Seis, 2019), colleges and universities often implement top-down institutional oversight to sustain revenue, competition, and institutional reputation (Ball, 2012; Giroux, 2014; Kirsten, 2019). While tenure and academic freedom held long-standing roles in academia, many institutions have curtailed or eliminated tenure and tenure lines that illuminate university preference for low-wage, temporary labor (Castro, 2019; Giroux, 2014; Kirsten, 2019); which consequently encompass an overwhelming majority of current college and university faculty. Packaged as a cost-cutting strategy, this practice positions contingent faculty as both disposable and exploitable. Hoping to remain employed, they are pressured to unite around the goal of sustaining the university as a business (Sheth & Croom, 2021). Employment uncertainty redefines faculties' understanding of their work and the boundaries of what constitutes academic freedom toward increased alignment with institutional hegemonic civility (Patton, 2004).

Augmenting employment precariousness, the neoliberal university establishes norms that quantify teaching, scholarship and education (Ball, 2012), in which tangibility of knowledge and faculty performativity eclipse criticality and academic freedom. Although donors cannot limit academic freedom, institutions can enact donors' wishes that could institutionally entrench neoliberal practices of hegemonic civility. Faculty become "academic entrepreneurs" who assess their work and worth alongside narrow metrics to maintain the university as a business (Giroux, 2014, p. 17). Academic entrepreneurs align their subjectivities toward hegemonic norms of competition and self-interest and engage in self-surveillance and censorship in fear of admonishment for challenging these neoliberal values (Dutta, 2021). In this way, hegemonic civility becomes a powerful tool for faculty control, as faculty must comply with oppression while detaching from and quantifying their intellectual work (Sheth & Croom, 2021; Williams, 2021). Other micro-level changes centrally position student learning outcomes and graduation pathways as keys to a skilled workforce, fostering pay-for-grade paradigms to entice student retention (Duncan, 2019), masquerading as critical scholarly inquiry and instruction that position students as consumers and faculty as entrepreneur-entertainers. When institutions prioritize consensus-building around such consumer-driven discourses and policies of entertainment, competition and self-surveillance, open inquiry becomes a performative gesture that serves donor interests and institutional missions become superficial (Dutta, 2021), thereby maintaining the status quo and entrenching practices of neoliberal hegemonic civility.

The Conservative Civility-Weapons: "Free Speech" and Gag Orders

Fueled by historic anti-intellectualism (Binder & Wood, 2013; Giroux, 2014; Moses, 2023), conservative defunding and political assaults on colleges and universities have swelled over time as Right-wing voices coalesced their messages and financial support around an entity that they could all oppose (Gross, 2013; Seis, 2019). When paired with anti-establishment messaging, rejection of the elite and the academic has united broad swaths of conservative voices into a movement of alleged protectors of traditional American values from progressive policies and democratic principles. These perspectives represent a collective identity emergent in current conservative educational policies curtailing diversity and inclusion practices, academic freedom and scholarly dissent. As a result, efforts to preserve academic freedom, independent institutional governance and fundamental civility amid the conservative onslaught prove significantly more difficult.

Since the initial waves of defunding and demonizing of higher education (Gross, 2013; Seis, 2019), conservatives have unified and sharpened discursive assaults to underscore their policy platform against academia, mirroring the broader culture wars that aim to fetter colleges and universities (Kirsten, 2019). Current conservative discourse alleges radically progressive professors' supposed discrimination of conservative perspectives (PEN America, 2022; Vivian, 2023), illustrating the ideological foundation for the current discursive repression of academia. Such discursive turns are especially evident in the Right's convolution of "free speech" and "academic freedom," amounting to the illegitimate use of both concepts. While the former positions hate speech and unfounded opinions as legitimate discourse, quality and informed speech is the nature of the latter (Shahvisi, 2021). In sum, the conservative policy platform admonishes colleges and universities allegedly threatening academic freedom and free speech, consequently entrenching existing public distrust of higher education and building on existing partisan divides (Taylor, 2022).

While academic freedom enshrines pedagogical and intellectual commitments endeavoring to mitigate ongoing fears of scholarly retribution—even when these challenge institutional policies (Sheth & Croom, 2021)—in an authoritarian fashion, conservative policies increasingly blur the lines between fact and fiction (Moses, 2023), and weaponize (in)civility to silence academics and curtail academic freedom (Shahvisi, 2021). Multiple bills introduced across the United States seek to curtail and control the teaching of particular concepts or topics, threats to academic freedom; restriction or elimination of diversity, equity and inclusion initiatives, and prohibition of instruction about racial justice and White supremacy (Dutt-Ballerstadt & Bhattacharya, 2021; Young & Friedman, 2022). The AAUP has joined PEN America in characterizing these bills as educational "gag orders," which aim to control genuine—and manufactured—pedagogies and behaviors under the guise of protecting free speech from alleged progressive indoctrination (AAUP, 2022; PEN America, 2022). Although often equated with a handful of states (see Kraemer-Holland, 2023), such gag orders span the country to illustrate a more widespread, chilling challenge to higher education's initial allegiance to open inquiry.

In this way, conservative gag orders create "norms of appropriateness" (Van Dijk, 2008, p. 8) over what constitutes the educational process in colleges and universities. Championing "equal presentation" and "balanced teaching" of contending viewpoints might seem both common sense and constitutionally aligned (PEN America, 2022, p. 9); however, such gag orders illustrate modes of surveillance and compliance toward hegemonic civility that deprofessionalize faculty and the broader existence of the higher education institution. Claims of "balanced" teaching superficially suggest a call to respectability, a weaponized "entry poin[t] to silence those [who] interrogate it" (Dutta, 2021, p. 46). Despite the largely tepid responses from university administrators against such gag orders (Golden, 2023), conservative policymakers have determined the boundaries around what constitutes instruction and academic "freedom" (Dutta, 2021). Hegemonic civility serves the status quo, albeit often on compulsory grounds. Rather than couching academic freedom behind veils of diversity and inclusion, conservatives and their policies equate civility with compliance and obedience, disingenuously redefining civility to further their political goal to oversee what it means to educate and be educated. PEN America's (2022) ongoing compilation of such policies exemplify the conservative nationwide effort to disingenuously redefine civility to constrain educational spaces, explicitly prohibiting the teaching of particular topics or withholding funding from colleges and universities accused of violating any portion of these decrees. Hidden behind allegations of institutional eroding of "free speech" and admonishing of conservative perspectives in academia, hegemonic civility emerges as a weapon wielded against academic freedom and the democratic university (Sheth & Croom, 2021). And, in the case of institutions in states like Florida and Texas for example (Fischer, 2022; Golden, 2023), politicians' weaponizing of hegemonic civility illuminates higher education's susceptibility to the whims of politicians and political movements.

THE UN/CIVIL UNIVERSITY? HIGHER EDUCATION'S UNCERTAIN FUTURE

Institutional and social debates regarding civility and divisiveness, autonomy and influence, sustainability and financial precarity, and democracy and dogmatism complicate higher education's political position, highlighting its uncertain future (Gross, 2013). This chapter outlines such difficulties facing academia, made so through economic and political intricacies embedded in wider neoliberal and conservative efforts to reshape academia's structures, procedures and constituents. As neoliberal influences continue to jeopardize colleges' abilities to attain their public-serving missions, economic and political pressures coalesce into institutional norms of hegemonic civility built upon repression, surveillance and the protection of institutional reputation and financial interests (Dutta, 2021; Patton, 2004). Wielding hegemonic (in)civility in these ways subsequently jeopardizes academic freedom, reorganizes faculty relationships and subjectivities (Ball, 2012), and disarms challenges to injustices (Cloud, 2021; Dutta, 2021). Higher education's uneven position further complicates adherence to respective institutional missions or cowering to outside economic and political pressures that deepen the question of how institutions enact civility *and* critical inquiry in an increasingly polarized society.

Because political extremism threatens truth and democratic principles, colleges and universities must recommit to their institutional missions to enshrine civic participation and productive scholarly dissent (Moses, 2023). Colleges and universities should scrutinize the nebulousness and weaponizing of "free speech" when campuses unilaterally decide that all parties—even those with views premised on violence and oppression—deserve spots at the discursive table. This kind of moral equivalence rightly calls into question how and the extent to which institutions can adhere to missions premised on and amid increased calls for civility. Collective resistance aligned with transformation, counter-discourse and civil disobedience in justice-oriented curricula and campus initiatives illustrate productive methods to offset hegemonic civility (Cloud, 2021). Although we should feel empowered to engage in these alternatives, it is crucial to recognize the credibility deficit levied upon womxn and scholars of color that often precludes their academic privilege (Sheth & Croom, 2021). In this case, academics of dominant groups have a responsibility to sideline civility and call out the unjust practices that constrict academic freedom of students and faculty, particularly for contingent faculty who are afforded little presence in institutional governance. To that end, prioritizing sustaining strong institutional and faculty governance signals strong support for long-term privileging of academic freedom over short-term financial fixes and external political desires. As agents of morality, criticality, and conduits between scholarship and the public, colleges and universities are responsible for exposing structures of political, social, and economic power that are often obscured to the American public (Giroux, 2014; Shahvisi, 2021), and as opportunities to lean into democratic notions of scholarly dissent and civility embedded in our academic and civic responsibility.

REFERENCES

Abraham, M. (2021). Civility and the bounds of the permissible: Scholars of color embodying the very social-political dynamics at the heart of their critique. In R. Dutt-Ballerstadt & K. Bhattacharya (Eds.), *Civility, free speech, and academic freedom in higher education: Faculty on the margins* (pp. 111–131). Routledge.

American Association of University Professors. (2022). *Political interference in higher ed.* AAUP data. https://www.aaup.org/issues/political-interference-higher-ed

Ball, S. J. (2003). The teacher's soul and the terrors of performativity. *Journal of Education Policy, 18*(2), 215–228. http://dx.doi:10.1080/0268093022000043065

Ball, S. J. (2012). Performativity, commodification and commitment: An I-spy guide to the neoliberal university. *British Journal of Educational Studies, 60*(1), 17–28. http://dx.doi.org/10.1080/00071005.2011.650940

Ball, S. J. (2016). Neoliberal education? Confronting the slouching beast. *Policy Futures in Education, 14*(8), 1046–1059. https://doi.org/10.1177/1478210316664259

Binder, A. J., & Wood, K. (2013). *Becoming right: How campuses shape young conservatives.* Princeton University Press.

Boatright, R. G. (2019). Introduction: A crisis of civility? In R. G. Boatright, T. J. Shaffer, S. Sobieraj, & D. G. Young (Eds.), *A crisis of civility? Political discourse and its discontents* (pp. 1–6). Routledge.

Castro, A. P. (2019). Foreword: The erosion of academic freedom. In E. Juergensmeyer, A. J. Nocella II, & M. Seis (Eds.), *Neoliberalism and academic repression: The fall of academic freedom in the era of Trump* (pp. xii–xiv). Brill.

Cloud, D. L. (2021). The rhetoric of civility as soft repression. In R. Dutt-Ballerstadt & K. Bhattacharya (Eds.), *Civility, free speech, and academic freedom in higher education: Faculty on the margins* (pp. 72–88). Routledge.

Duncan, T. (2019). Fun home, self-censorship, and emancipation beyond trigger warnings. In E. Juergensmeyer, A. J. Nocella II, & M. Seis (Eds.), *Neoliberalism and academic repression: The fall of academic freedom in the era of Trump* (pp. 123–137). Brill.

Dutt-Ballerstadt, R., & Bhattacharya, K. (2021). Introduction. In R. Dutt-Ballerstadt & K. Bhattacharya (Eds.), *Civility, free speech, and academic freedom in higher education: Faculty on the margins* (pp. 1–10). Routledge.

Dutta, M. J. (2021). Universities, civility, and repression in the age of new media: Surveillance capital and resistance. In R. Dutt-Ballerstadt & K. Bhattacharya (Eds.), *Civility, free speech, and academic freedom in higher education: Faculty on the margins* (pp. 41–58). Routledge.

Fischer, K. (2022, October 18). *A playbook for knocking down higher education.* The Chronicle of Higher Education. https://www-chronicle-com.er.lib.k-state.edu/article/a-playbook-for-knocking-down-higher-ed

Foucault, M. (1977). *Discipline and punish: The birth of the prison.* Random House.

Gee, J. P. (1996). *Social linguistics and literacies: Ideology in discourses* (2nd ed.). Falmer Press.

Giroux, H. (2014). *Neoliberalism's war on higher education.* Haymarket Books.

Golden, D. (2023, January 3). "It's making us more ignorant." Governor Ron DeSantis's anti-critical-race-theory legislation is already changing how professors in Florida teach. *The Atlantic.* https://www.theatlantic.com/ideas/archive/2023/01/ron-desantis-florida-critical-race-theory-professors/672507/

Goodin, R. E. (2012). Institutions and their design. In R. E. Goodin (Ed.), *The theory of institutional design* (pp. 1–53). Cambridge University Press.

Gross, N. (2013). *Why are professors liberal and why do conservatives care?* Harvard University Press.

Jamieson, K. H., Volinsky, A., Weitz, I., & Kenski, K. (2017). The political uses and abuses of civility and incivility. In K. H. Jamieson & K. Kenski (Eds.), *The Oxford handbook of political communication* (pp. 1–15). Oxford University Press.

Juergensmeyer, E., & Benz, B. (2019). Neoliberalism, discursive formations, and the educational intelligence complex. In E. Juergensmeyer, A. J. Nocella II, & M. Seis (Eds.), *Neoliberalism and academic repression: The fall of academic freedom in the era of Trump* (pp. 58–74). Brill.

Juergensmeyer, E., Nocella II, A. J., & Seis, M. (2019). Introduction: The academic industrial complex: The dangers of corporate education and factory schooling. In E. Juergensmeyer, A. J. Nocella II, & M. Seis (Eds.), *Neoliberalism and academic repression: The fall of academic freedom in the era of Trump* (pp. 1–12). Brill.

Kaltefleiter, C. K. (2019). Learning into labor: (Anarcha) feminism, the myth of meritocracy, incivility, and resistance for women in the neoliberal academy. In E. Juergensmeyer, A. J. Nocella II, & M. Seis (Eds.), *Neoliberalism and academic repression: The fall of academic freedom in the era of Trump* (pp. 175–193). Brill.

Kalven Committee. (1967, November 11). Report on the university's role in political and social action. *The University of Chicago Record, I*(1), 1–3.

Kirsten, P. J. (2019). Marx, neoliberalism, and academic freedom: Toward a dialectic of resistance and liberation. In E. Juergensmeyer, A. J. Nocella II, & M. Seis (Eds.), *Neoliberalism and academic repression: The fall of academic freedom in the era of Trump* (pp. 13–30). Brill.

Kraemer-Holland, A. (2023). Who holds [educational] authority? Framing the authoritarian turn in the conservative "gag orders" in the United States. *Teachers and Teaching: Theory and Practice.* https://doi.org/10.1080/13540602.2023.2273399

Laden, A. S. (2019). Two concepts of civility. In R. G. Boatright, T. J. Shaffer, S. Sobieraj, & D. G. Young (Eds.), *A crisis of civility? Political discourse and its discontents* (pp. 9–30). Routledge.

Morrison, T. (2001). How can values be taught in the university? *Michigan Quarterly Review, 40*(2), 273–278.

Moses, M. S. (Presenter). (2023, March 5). *Democracy, extremism, and the crisis of truth in education*. Address presented at Philosophy of Education Society Conference, Chicago, IL, United States.

Patton, T. O. (2004). In the guise of civility: The complicitous maintenance of inferential forms of sexism and racism in higher education. *Women's Studies in Communication, 27*(1), 60–87. https://doi.org/10.1080/07491409.2004.10162466

PEN America. (2022, January 18). *Educational gag orders: Legislative restrictions on the freedom to read, learn, and teach* (PEN America, Comp.). https://pen.org/report/educational-gag-orders/

Seis, M. (2019). Pondering the neoliberal public university with the ghost of Foucault. In E. Juergensmeyer, A. J. Nocella II, & M. Seis (Eds.), *Neoliberalism and academic repression: The fall of academic freedom in the era of Trump* (pp. 43–58). Brill.

Shahvisi, A. (2021). On the social epistemology of academic freedom. In R. Dutt-Ballerstadt & K. Bhattacharya (Eds.), *Civility, free speech, and academic freedom in higher education: Faculty on the margins* (pp. 59–71). Routledge.

Sheth, M. J., & Croom, N. N. (2021). Chronicles exploring hegemonic civility and the evisceration of academic freedom for critical womyn of color. In R. Dutt-Ballerstadt & K. Bhattacharya (Eds.), *Civility, free speech, and academic freedom in higher education: Faculty on the margins* (pp. 145–162). Routledge.

Taylor, B. J. (2022). Wisconsin. In B. J. Taylor (Author), *Wrecked: Deinstitutionalization and partial defenses in state higher education policy* (pp. 70–93). Rutgers University Press.

Van Dijk, T. A. (2008). *Discourse and power*. Palgrave Macmillan.

Vivian, B. (2023). *Campus misinformation: The real threat to free speech in American higher education*. Oxford University Press.

Williams, J. E. (2021). Afterword: The civility-incivility paradox. In R. Dutt-Ballerstadt & K. Bhattacharya (Eds.), *Civility, free speech, and academic freedom in higher education: Faculty on the margins* (pp. 179–184). Routledge.

Young, J. C., & Friedman, J. (2022, August 17). *America's censored classrooms*. PEN America. https://pen.org/report/Americas-censored-classrooms/

Zurn, C. F. (2013). Political civility: Another illusionistic ideal. *Public Affairs Quarterly, 27*(4), 341–368. https://doi.org/10.16997/jdd.30749=

CHAPTER 4

LEANING INTO INSTITUTIONAL POLITICS

Paradoxes of Success in Higher Education Civic Learning and Democratic Engagement Initiatives

Caroline W. Lee
Lafayette College

ABSTRACT

Since 2010, top-down, national-level civic learning and democratic engagement (CLDE) efforts have focused colleges and universities on the goal of institutionalizing responsible civic engagement more deeply in their programs and practices. Drawing on a multi-method ethnographic study of democratic engagement as an institutional practice in higher education, this chapter highlights how these efforts have been accomplished by reorienting institutional incentives and redefining campus professionals' work. The day-to-day efforts of staff are increasingly focused on self-auditing compliance with a set of formally prescribed procedures, acquiring credentials on best practices for compliance, and communicating and sharing these accomplishments

Leaning Into Politics, pages 49–64
Copyright © 2024 by Information Age Publishing
www.infoagepub.com
All rights of reproduction in any form reserved.

with other actors within the institution and the institutional field. The field has achieved widespread success in producing and documenting high-quality democratic engagement experiences, but I argue that the institutional politics of civic learning and democratic engagement in U.S. higher education are fundamentally inward-looking and fail to address political economic crises and inequalities in the larger society.

Top-down, national-level civic learning and democratic engagement efforts involving the federal government, industry and professional associations, and foundations have been broadly successful at focusing U.S. colleges and universities on the goal of responsible civic engagement in the past decade. The methods for achieving these changes, however, have created a number of tensions between the institutional politics of the higher education sector and the political economic needs of particular constituencies, campuses, and communities. Drawing on a multi-method ethnographic study of democratic engagement as an institutional practice in higher education, this chapter highlights key tensions that remain unresolved despite widespread success in producing and documenting high-quality democratic engagement experiences for students.

THE INSTITUTIONAL POLITICS OF HIGHER EDUCATION CIVIC ENGAGEMENT

The bulk of scholarship on higher education democracy efforts focuses on civic learning in terms of individual student outcomes and "best practices" as performed in particular projects (Chittum et al., 2022). But individual projects take shape as part of a portfolio of projects supervised by a community engagement center within an institution linked to others in the region and to national-level associations, funders, and regulators. By looking at the national scale of the larger field, at all of the institutional and field-wide efforts to promote and reward and count those activities, we can gain a very different understanding of the political economic forces driving the widespread enthusiasm for community engagement across all sectors of higher education and across the spectrum of national and statewide partisan politics.

What then are institutional politics, and who are the key actors in the case of higher education institutional politics? By institutional politics, I mean the ways that people act to achieve their goals within and through organizations. If we shift our focus to the larger agenda-setting and coordination going on within the field, we gain a very different perspective on the politics and relationship networks that matter for higher education community engagement. At the national scale in higher ed, there are industry organizations that issue reports, fund activities, and give awards and certifications, academic journals where research on civic engagement is reviewed and shared, and workshops, professional conferences, webinars, and trainings where people working within organizations meet to learn from each other. These organizations are deeply invested in institutional politics, that is, the power dynamics and status and resource hierarchies of organizational bureaucracies, associational networks, and competitive markets for student tuition dollars, foundation grants, and government spending.

Scholarship on institutional politics studies the patterned ways organizations interact within their fields, and can help us understand the organization of social change, where new understandings and practices become "institutionalized." Fligstein and McAdam (2019) define "strategic action fields" as "arenas where actors take one another into account in their interactions. These fields have complex internal dynamics that contribute to stability and change. They are, however, also embedded in a broader environment" (Fligstein & McAdam, 2019, pp. 1–2). For the purposes of this chapter, two major insights from institutional researchers are relevant. First, many scholars have highlighted the increasing attention to CLDE in higher education as part of a larger movement to change higher education (London 2010; Woolard 2017), and institutional politics can help us to understand innovation and disruption within and across organizations. Second, institutional theory can also help us understand stability and settlement, or why organizational change nevertheless has a tendency to favor sameness and reproduce existing hierarchies. DiMaggio and Powell's research on institutional isomorphism (1983) identifies an "iron cage" of collective rationality within institutions as a key result of the diffusion of organizational innovations across fields, whether through coercive, normative, or mimetic responses to crises and uncertainty. Fligstein and McAdam note that the dynamics of contestation within strategic action fields where insurgents encounter established actors who can mobilize resources and relationships to other fields "help us understand why most of the time incumbents are able to reproduce their positions even as fields continually evolve" (2019, p. 2).

Applying this kind of field-level perspective to higher education is not at all new, of course (see Stevens & Gebre-Medhin, 2016, and also Stevens et al., 2008). Scholars have done similar work in all kinds of programs and projects embraced in the field of U.S. higher education, from how a compliance bureaucracy was created for research on human subjects (Babb, 2020), to how elite reformers and foundations reshaped the higher education sector in the 20th century (Ris, 2022), how rankings affected the law school field (Espeland & Sauder, 2016), and how sustainability emerged as a field in U.S. higher education (Augustine & King, 2015). Adjacent to higher education, scholars have studied the emergence of fields related to civic learning and democratic engagement like social entrepreneurship (Spicer et al., 2019) and public engagement (Lee, 2015). Particularly relevant to this chapter's focus on community-based democratic learning, studies of related fields have even explored the extent to which advancing community development at the local scale is a political choice made within larger strategic action fields (Immerwahr, 2015).

By adopting a field-level view of institutional politics in this case, I focus primarily on the civic learning and democratic engagement subfield and the larger field of U.S. higher education, on national-level elites and foundations, federal actors like the U.S. Department of Education, and their dynamic interactions with each other, in addition to national and regional associations of higher ed organizations and professionals. Seeing the politics of the CLDE field in these contexts has the virtue of allowing us to understand patterns of stability and settlement and the tensions they produce not as social movement failures, but as expected outcomes of institutionalizing change.

Following a description of the methods used in this study, I begin the analysis by describing how higher education civic learning and democratic engagement efforts have been organized since the early 2000s, sketching a subfield of higher education characterized by top-down coordination of institutional change management efforts initiated by the federal government, national industry and professional associations, and foundations. Next, I sketch how efforts to change higher education through civic learning and democratic engagement have settled into characteristic institutional patterns, whereby organizational bureaucracies and existing hierarchies are reinforced rather than challenged.

METHODS

The research project on which this chapter draws focuses on contemporary civic learning and democratic engagement initiatives in U.S. higher education, and more specifically on publicly available professional discourse in the national strategic action field of organizations and entities pursuing civic learning and democratic engagement in higher education, drawing on a database of 1,000+ text sources and images collected between 2012 and 2023 from news coverage, press releases, publications, brochures, social media posts, web sources, and academic publications by field insiders. To supplement the archival research, I conducted participant observation between 2014 and 2023 at higher-education-focused sessions at dialogue and deliberation conferences, and at webinars, in-person conferences, and workshops for higher education professionals focused on civic learning and democratic engagement. Combined, these data are a useful guideline to "frontstage" understandings within a settled field on shared norms, best practices, and evaluation and certification standards (Augustine & King, 2019).

MEETING A CRUCIBLE MOMENT: TOP-DOWN COORDINATION OF FIELDWIDE INSTITUTIONAL CHANGE

In 2012, halfway through the Obama presidency, came *A Crucible Moment: College Learning and Democracy's Future*, a report commissioned by the U.S. Department of Education in 2010 and produced by the National Task Force on Civic Learning and Democratic Engagement, a group constituting many of the leading organizational actors in the higher education field. Over the preceding two years, a model deliberative democratic process had been convened by a consulting firm and the American Association of Colleges and Universities (AAC&U), in which "134 people representing 61 community colleges, four-year colleges, and universities; 26 civic organizations; 9 private and government funding agencies; 15 higher education associations; and 12 disciplinary societies" had debated their perspectives on the current state and potential future of civic learning in higher education in five National Roundtables (The National Task Force on Civic Learning and Democratic Engagement 2012, p. viii).

Synthesizing their insights, *Crucible Moment* argued that, just as the Truman Commission had met a difficult moment in 1947 with ambitious goals for a democratic future, higher education institutions and their allies should embrace their democratic missions by "investing on a massive scale" (2012, p. 2) in civic-capital-building efforts for their students. The United States and the world faced a number of striking ecological and financial challenges made worse by partisanship, polarization, and passivity. (In 2012, the authors saw a civic malaise but not democratic backsliding or rising autocracies, instead noting the rising number of democracies.) The way forward was reinvestment in the civic skills of students, and national organizations and the federal government would lead the way by hosting conferences and workshops to share best practices and demonstrate the importance of "expanding students' capacities to be civic problem-solvers using all their powers of intellect and inventiveness" (2012, p. 19). *Crucible Moment* noted the efforts already undertaken in this vein over the preceding decades, but urged higher education leaders to take things further by moving civic engagement from the periphery to the center of the collegiate mission. To do that, *Crucible Moment* spelled out precise, detailed recommendations for making civic problem-solving pervasive on campuses, including toolkits and templates for professional student affairs staffers and administrators to follow to measure and improve civic learning on their campuses.

In addition, several coalitions with overlapping memberships formed around the terminology of "civic learning and democratic engagement" and continue to advance the principles set forth in *Crucible Moment*. The Civic Learning and Democratic Engagement Action Network gathered together a number of national organizations from across the U.S. higher ed sector to advance civic learning: AAC&U, American Association of State Colleges and Universities (AASCU), American Democracy Project, Anchor Institutions Task Force, The Bonner Foundation, Bringing Theory to Practice, Campus Compact, Center for Information and Research on Civic Learning and Engagement (CIRCLE), Imagining America, Institute for Democracy and Higher Education (IDHE), Interfaith America, Kettering Foundation, and NASPA: Student Affairs Administrators in Higher Education. Today, the CLDE Coalition is led by AAC&U, College Promise, Campus Compact, Complete College America (CCA) and State Higher Education Executive Officers (SHEEO). Annually, NASPA and American Democracy Project host a "CLDE" conference for university and college leaders, staffers, students, faculty, and community partners to gather to celebrate best practices and "to advance institutions' commitment to advancing democracy."

As DiMaggio and Powell describe, activities of this sort are designed to effect institutional change as "formal and informal pressures exerted on organizations by other organizations upon which they are dependent and by cultural expectations in the society within which organizations function," while actors within organizations may also model their own efforts on those of others mimetically (1983, p. 151). By bringing actors from different institutions together to share new frameworks, listen to field leaders' presentations and webinars, and compete for fellowships, grants, and awards according to shared criteria for quality projects, for example, these coalitions create national expectations and standards for civic learning and democratic engagement, and diffuse common approaches.

It would be hard to overstate how intently focused the expressed goal of national-level actors in the field is on *institutional* change throughout the period under study, both within *Crucible* itself and throughout publications in the field. In 2012, the *Handbook of Engaged Scholarship: Contemporary Landscapes, Future Directions* (Fitzgerald et al., 2012) was published with Volume 1 exclusively dedicated to the topic of "Institutional Change." Also in 2012, field leaders Ira Harkavy and Matthew Hartley wrote a piece for the *Journal of Higher Education Outreach and Engagement* entitled "Integrating a Commitment to the Public Good into the Institutional Fabric." A panel for the 2023 NASPA conference was titled, "From Episodic to Institutionalized Involvement: Going ALL IN with Communities of Practice." If, as Colyvas and Powell argue, the "roads to institutionalization" in higher education entail "the self-reinforcing feedback dynamics of heightened legitimacy and a deeper taken-for-grantedness" (2006, p. 305), then the very idea of institutionalizing civic learning and democratic engagement in higher ed has itself been institutionalized as the sine qua non of civic engagement at the post-secondary level.

One of the most impactful ways in which institutional change has been diffused throughout the civic learning and democratic engagement field is through the Carnegie Community Engagement Classification, launched in 2006 and currently administered by the American Council on Education

(ACE) for The Carnegie Foundation for the Advancement of Teaching. While many are familiar with the Carnegie Basic Classification of U.S. higher education institutions, institutions must apply for recognition with the Elective Classification for Community Engagement on the basis of "extraordinary commitments" to community engagement efforts throughout the institution. In the words of the Elective Classification website:

> Elective Classifications are not awards. They are evidence-based documentation of institutional policy and practices focusing on areas such as institutional culture and mission, curricular and co-curricular programming, continuous improvement activities, and the recruitment and reward of faculty, staff, and students.
>
> To become a Classified institution requires the investment of substantial effort by participating institutions to provide evidence of the commitment to a special purpose, demonstrated with precision across the breadth of the institution.

From an initial round of 76 institutions selected in 2006, the CE Classification has recognized a total of 440 campuses, with 357 institutions currently classified (see Figure 4.1 for a map from the CE Classification website).

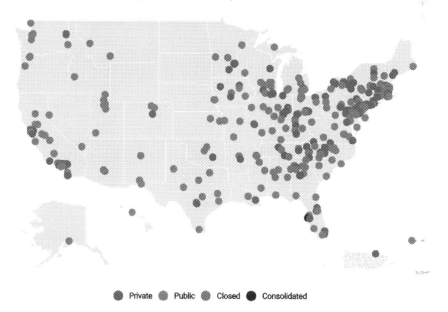

Figure 4.1 Screenshot of Current Classified Campuses from the ACE CE Classification website: (https://carnegieclassifications.acenet.edu/elective-classifications/community-engagement/, accessed September 21, 2023)

Each of these institutions has conducted an intensive, elaborate self-study intended to "engage [the] institution in the process of inquiry, reflection, and self-assessment." Typically, the timeline for this study is two years from the time an application is initiated to the time classified campuses are announced. As intended, participants in the self-study hail from across institutions, as a study of successful 2010 applicants found; see Figure 4.2 from Noel and Earwicker, 2015. While the average amount of time spent on applications in that study was 6.6 months, "respondents indicated they needed more time, Classification training courses, and support to complete their application" (2015, p. 52).

Part of why collecting such data is so labor intensive has to do with the intentional self-reflection built into the questions; the "process" itself is envisioned as its own outcome as it brings together stakeholders to deliberate on the pervasiveness of civic learning and democratic engagement in their institution and "aligns" these actors toward the common goal of "infusing" civic learning and democratic engagement in the institutional bureaucracy. For example, one of the 70 questions on the application asks first-time applicants to provide a table with data on the numbers of courses with community engagement designations, number of departments and faculty members offering such courses by status, etc. and then asks, "Describe how the data in the table above were derived. How was it gathered, by whom, with what frequency, and for what purpose? Reflect on how the data indicates the levels of pervasiveness and depth community engagement is infused in the curriculum" (Carnegie Foundation 2023). Espeland and Sauder (2016) have studied the extent to which ranking systems like U.S. News have transformed institutions by reorganizing work and creating new professional roles and market opportunities. In the case of the CE classification, the work of engagement professionals within their institutions

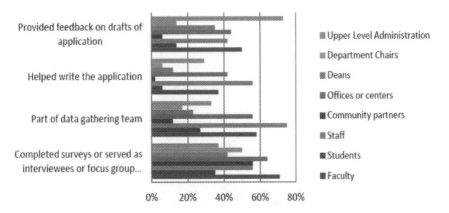

Figure 4.2 "Roles of Stakeholders," from Noel & Earwicker, 2015, p. 44.

has been reoriented toward the collection and analysis of data for ongoing, exhaustive self-study of the institution as a whole.

Not surprisingly, such professionals have sought out additional capacity and capital for their new administrative responsibilities, and new market opportunities have arisen to make the reflexivity required by the Carnegie CE Classification less labor-intensive and more visible to external audiences. ACE trains consultants in advising on Carnegie applications, provides its own webinars run by the consultancy Collaboratory, and has integrated the Carnegie Application itself into the GivePulse software that many campuses use to collect data campuswide for their applications.

Another national-level innovation, Campus Compact's Community Engagement Professional Credentialing Program, was initiated in 2015, piloted in March 2019, and implemented in 2020. Higher education engagement practitioners have the opportunity to earn 15 "micro-credentials" (digital badges) in "core competency areas that are key to success in higher education civic and community engagement," including "Institutionalizing Engagement," "Equity & Inclusion," and "Assessment & Evaluation" (Campus Compact 2023b). To prepare for the credential, practitioners are encouraged to engage in approved online graduate courses and communities of practice with like-minded others. Like a campus-wide self-study process, the community engagement credential entails a diagnostic self-assessment and the production of extensive[1] application materials documenting not only community engagement projects on which a practitioner has worked, but also "critical self-reflection" and "personal growth and on-going professional development" (Campus Compact 2023b).

It is important to note that the CE Classification and the Credentialing Program are just two manifestations of larger processes of institutionalization of community engagement throughout the higher education sector: other mechanisms, such as the promotion of certificate and degree programs in community engagement, community engagement in required general education curricula and orientation programs, and the integration of community engagement in accrediting bodies' standards are not focused on in this chapter, but are important components of institutionalization in this case (Paton et al., 2014; see also Rank's chapter in this volume).

Over the last two decades, the labor of civic learning and democratic engagement has been shifted from producing experiences with community stakeholders to properly documenting and assessing those experiences for external audiences of higher education professionals. This proceduralization (formalization of prescribed processes) and professionalization has resulted in an isomorphic field shaped by both coercive adoption of best practices through centralized external assessment and mimetic adoption through norm-sharing and networking throughout the field. The result has been an established record of success in integrating civic learning and democratic engagement assessment throughout bureaucratic infrastructures and as part of administrative roles on hundreds of campuses in the United States, but this achievement does not represent an endpoint for the civic learning and democratic engagement movement. The principle of continuous improvement, core to accountability cultures of higher education bureaucracies, means there are always more process improvements to be made, and more opportunities to further democratize assessment through institutional self-reflection (Lee, 2020; Strathern, 2000).

THE COSTS OF LEANING INTO INSTITUTIONAL POLITICS

Despite having infused civic learning and democratic engagement throughout higher education institutions, many higher education civic leaders find the contributions of colleges and universities to democracy or civic purpose sorely wanting (Daniels, 2022; Flores & Rogers, 2019; Hodges & Dubb, 2012; Tierney, 2021; Stoecker, 2016). As we might expect from the institutional politics research, the civic engagement movement has been successful at getting experiential civic work in the community, supervised by professionals, and catalogued and documented appropriately for external audiences, deemed a best practice pursued throughout U.S. higher education, but it has not disrupted existing inequalities and hierarchies in the higher education field or in the political system.

Indeed, at a 2022 Year in Review webinar for the Carnegie Elective Classification, organizers expressed dismay when they dug into the 2020 data on attainment rates by institution type. Organizers were "satisfied" with the overall "achievement rate" of 61%, "which means it's difficult but doable" (Campus Compact 2023a). However, only 4 HBCUs applied in the 2020 round, and only one was successful. Rates for community colleges were similar (21%, N=14) and Hispanic Serving Institutions were better (48%, N=29), but still below the average attainment rate. The presenter described the internal reaction to the data: "So for us, this really indicated both the areas that we needed to improve and do outreach, thinking about the ways that we could change our policies and practices to be more reflective of these kinds of institutions" (Campus Compact 2023a).

In both national level organizations and within higher education institutions, the reinforcement of existing institutional hierarchies is not because administrators don't care deeply about civic learning and democratic engagement, but because routine institutional politics focus, quite naturally, on the institution itself, even when the object of investigation is the institution's engagement with the community. One study of community engagement in nonprofits found that, despite "deep and passionate concern for the communities in which they work and for the people in those communities," community engagement for organization leaders was "defined in terms of the needs and interests of their organizations, and not those of the community":

> Despite their impulses and aspirations to undertake and sustain engagement, these organizations and leaders find themselves enveloped in a profound and airtight gestalt of inwardness, planning, and professionalism. (Harwood Institute, 2009)

Organizations face "intense internal and external pressure to deliver results" and demonstrate impact, such that even when organizations pursue engagement, they follow a project development model and typically seek out "participation from key community leaders and service providers who themselves hold an organizational stake in the program or initiative" (Harwood Institute, 2009, pp. 7, 10). Rigorous accountability measures such as those demanded by the CE Classification require well-resourced community partners who are able to use engagement software and participate in feedback routines, meaning the neediest cases and causes are riskier to tackle. These kinds of dynamics are typical for institutional actors feeling pressure to produce "good projects" (Krause, 2014).

Even within civic learning and democratic engagement trainings and workshops, organizers make reference to the "myth and ceremony" of civic learning and democratic engagement logics such as reciprocity. A description of an ACE webinar entitled "Community Assets, Reciprocity and Other Ideas We Don't Really Believe," acknowledges the omnipresence of idealistic claims in higher education community engagement that are very difficult to achieve in practice:

> Language about reciprocity and community assets is present in nearly every university grant proposal, statement of purpose and presentation related to university-community engagement. It is central to the Carnegie Elective Classification for Community Engagement. And yet, in the implementation of our engagement efforts, the community typically possesses far less authority than the university, and its assets are often overlooked or considered far less essential than the university's to achieve desired outcomes. (Email communication, January 27, 2023)

New projects may arrive in the context of longstanding institutional reputations for hostile and self-serving behavior; a study of successful community/university development partnerships found that "Each of the university projects featured in this study had to overcome significant skepticism among local residents and elected officials regarding their institution's motivation, commitment, and capacity to function as a respectful and dependable economic development partner" (Reardon, 2006, p. 106).

Universal prioritization of civic learning and democratic engagement as ideal outcomes of university-community relationships fails to address the very different types of secondary institutions, community contexts, and demographics of students across the enormously diverse U.S. higher education landscape, where, for example, adult learners, HBCU students, undocumented students, or commuters may have very different political orientations and knowledge bases regarding communities "outside" campuses (Klemenčič and Park, 2018; Reyes, 2018). Not surprisingly, making civic learning and democratic engagement central to institutional routines, and the fact that well-resourced institutions are the best-positioned to succeed at doing so, does not disrupt long-term dynamics of hierarchical resource and power relationships within higher education, or at the institution-level, university/community power relationships affecting local housing access, wage suppression, gentrification, and policing (Baldwin, 2021).[2]

Many civic leaders have highlighted these failures to move beyond the insular world of institutional change, despite 20-plus years of institutionalizing civic learning and democratic engagement. Eric Mlyn, a political scientist and the inaugural director of the Duke Center for Civic Engagement/DukeEngage, wrote an op-ed for Inside Higher Ed in August 2022 provocatively titled "Our House is Burning." In his call to action, Mlyn argues that "the civic engagement movement in higher education promoted its democratic mission primarily through student voluntarism in local and global communities," well-meant efforts that "fail fundamentally to meet the nature of the threat we're facing." (Mlyn 2022) As Mlyn notes, experiential civic action in communities is a universalized best practice in higher ed at this point, but it is not the only way to educate young people for democratic citizenship, and may not be an apt response to the systemic and structural challenges students and campuses will face in the present or future from state legislatures and their lobbyists or from disinformation campaigns. Such critiques, even when calling for fundamental change in institutional practices, still center the institution.

CONCLUSION

Higher education leaders in the United States in the 2010s and 2020s have confronted two inter-related and deepening crises, one of higher education's legitimacy, and the other, of democratic legitimacy writ broadly. While the solution to both seems to be the cultivation of a new era of democratic citizenship, this is not without its own dilemmas—a better understanding of which might contribute to imagining richer, more diverse alternatives to the civil society and citizenship cultivation practices we currently have. As this chapter has described, alliances of powerful associations and organizations in the field have spearheaded sweeping initiatives for civic learning and democratic engagement. Democratic engagement has been produced by reorienting institutional incentives and campus professionals' work. The day-to-day efforts of staff are increasingly focused on certification, credentialing, assessment, and communication of these accomplishments to elite (non-public) audiences. Overall, this proceduralization and professionalization of civic learning and democratic engagement work has had a number of paradoxical results. Chief among these is a turning away from civic spheres for labor-intensive self-study of campus change management processes in the name of continuous improvement. Given these results, I conclude with two seemingly simple, but actually quite difficult, common-sense recommendations for citizens and college and university administrators and leaders, both of which are predicated on making the institutional politics of higher education, and the way it intersects with community politics, visible.

The first recommendation is for colleges and universities to stop looking inward, at least when directed at continuous improvement of current institutional processes. An outward-directed focus on engaging unique community contexts and local, regional, and national politics is needed—one which sees that "institutions can be powerful enablers of... citizen leadership or they can seriously impede it" (White, 2011). Creativity, resistance, and ferment do not fit well into procedural and professional remedies, although they can be productive elements of citizenship education, as the example of HBCUs shows (Favors, 2020).

The second recommendation is to make accountability suspect, by accounting for the costs to communities and communal resources of foregrounding proceduralization and professionalization within colleges and universities. While "accountability requirements don't always improve performance or result in greater confidence in the institutions involved," they can also directly undermine civic learning, investments in local capacity-building, and innovation (Mathews, 2011). These outcomes are entirely consistent with institutions gaining in status and reputation from performing accountability well at the scale of field-level institutional politics. Those "positive" publicity outcomes for institutional leaders need to be interpreted alongside community awareness of the ways accountability favors those with disproportionate resources and professional expertise.

Finally, following these two recommendations will lead to a number of uncomfortable questions yet to be asked regarding the inequalities proceduralized engagement obscures: What are the consequences of focusing on college-educated youth engagement and citizenship to the exclusion of non-college-going young adults and non-citizens? What kinds of civic action do for-profit educational institutions subsidize and encourage in their students, and how do they differ from those encouraged by non-profits? How do students envision the continuum of their different engagement activities and their efficacy, and how do their perceptions of these vary by type of institution and other factors? Can the resistance of activists help us conceive of a more expansive democratic engagement that does not center institutions, and could thereby escape the vicious cycle of proceduralization and professionalization?

NOTES

1. For early career professionals, this includes a "narrated, 15–20 minute video presentation on the fundamentals of community engagement."
2. In fact, funding "non-partisan" civic education centers at state universities has become an increasingly popular strategy with Republican activists attempting entirely different institutional changes within higher education (Pettit, 2023), a sign of how flexible the value commitments that can be promoted through institutional politics are.

REFERENCES

Augustine, G., & King, B. (2019). Worthy of debate: Discursive coherence and agreement in the formation of the field of sustainability in higher education. *Socio-Economic Review, 17*(1), 1–31.

Babb, S. (2020). *Regulating human research: IRBs from peer review to compliance bureaucracy.* Stanford University Press.

Baldwin, D. (2021). *In the shadow of the ivory tower: How universities are plundering our cities.* Bold Type Books.

Boyte, H.C., ed. (2015). *Democracy's education: Public work, citizenship, and the future of colleges and universities.* Nashville, TN: Vanderbilt University Press.

Campus Compact. (2023a). *Carnegie elective classifications 2022 year in review.* Posted January 20. Available at: https://www.youtube.com/watch?v=4MFSHxB2cjw

Campus Compact. (2023b). *CEP credential program handbook.* Available at: https://compact.org/current-programs/community-engagement-professional-credential/cep-credential-program-handbook

Carnegie Foundation for the Advancement of Teaching. (2023). *Elective classification for community engagement: 2024 re-classification documentation framework.* Available at: https://carnegieelectiveclassifications.org/wp-content/uploads/2022/05/2024-Community-Engagement-First-Time-Classification-Guide-5.10.2022.pdf

Chittum, J.R., Enke, K.A.E., & Finley, A.P. (2022). *The effects of community-based and civic engagement in higher education.* Washington, DC: Association of American Colleges & Universities.

Colyvas, J., & Powell, W.W.. (2006). Roads to institutionalization: The remaking of boundaries between public and private science. *Research in Organizational Behavior 27*: 305–333.

Daniels, R.J. (2022). *What universities owe democracy.* Johns Hopkins University Press.

DiMaggio, P. J., & Powell, W. W. (1983). "The iron cage revisited: Institutional isomorphism and collective rationality in organizational fields." *American Sociological Review, 48*(2), 147–160.

Espeland, W., & Sauder, M. (2016). *Engines of anxiety: Academic rankings, reputation, and accountability.* Russell Sage Foundation.

Favors, J.M. (2020). *Shelter in a time of storm: How Black colleges fostered generations of leadership and activism.* The University of North Carolina Press.

Fitzgerald, H.E., Burack, C., & Seifer, S.D.. (2012). *Handbook of engaged scholarship: Contemporary landscapes, future directions: Volume 1: Institutional change.* Michigan State University Press.

Fligstein, N., & McAdam, D. (2019). States, social movements and markets. *Socio-Economic Review 17,* 1–6.

Flores, W.V., & Rogers, K.S., eds. (2019). *Democracy, civic engagement, and citizenship in higher education: Reclaiming our civic purpose.* Lexington Books.

Harkavy, I., & Hartley, M. (2012). Integrating a commitment to the public good into the institutional fabric. *Journal of Higher Education Outreach and Engagement 16,* 17–36.

The Harwood Institute. (2009). "The organization-first approach." Report produced for The Kettering Foundation. https://www.kettering.org/catalog/product/organization-first-approach-how-programs-crowd-out-community

Hodges, R. A., & Dubb, S. (2012). *The road half traveled: University engagement at a crossroads.* Michigan State University Press.

Klemenčič, M., & Park, B. Y. (2018). Student politics: Between representation and activism. In B. Cantwell, H. Coates, & R. King (Eds.), *The handbook on the politics of higher education,* (pp. 468–486). Edward Elgar Publishing.

Krause, M. (2014). *The good project: Humanitarian relief NGOs and the fragmentation of reason.* University of Chicago Press.

Immerwahr, D. (2015). *Thinking small: The United States and the lure of community development.* Harvard University Press.

Lee, C.W. (2015). *Do-it-yourself democracy: The rise of the public engagement industry.* Oxford University Press.

Lee, C.W. (2020). Who is community engagement for? The endless loop of democratic transparency. *American Behavioral Scientist, 64*(11), 1565–1587.

London, S. (2010). *Doing democracy: How a network of grassroots organizations is strengthening community, building capacity, and shaping a new kind of civic education.* Kettering Foundation.

Mathews, D. (2011). Democracy and accountability. In J. Johnson, J. Rochkind, & S. DuPont (Eds.), *Don't count us out: How an overreliance on accountability could undermine the public's confidence in schools, business, government, and more,* (pp. 3–5). A report from the Kettering Foundation and Public Agenda. https://www.kettering.org/catalog/product/don't-count-us-out-how-over reliance-accountability-could-undermine-public's

Mlyn, E. (2022). Our house is burning. *Inside Higher Ed.* August 22. https://www.insidehighered.com/views/2022/08/22/higher-ed-must-confront-threats-democracy-opinion

The National Task Force on Civic Learning and Democratic Engagement. (2012). *A crucible moment: College learning and democracy's future.* Association of American Colleges and Universities.

Noel, J., & Earwicker, D.P. (2015). Documenting community engagement practices and outcomes: Insights from recipients of the 2010 Carnegie Community Engagement Classification. *Journal of Higher Education Outreach and Engagement 19*, 33–61.

Pardo-Guerra, J.P. (2022). *The quantified scholar: How research evaluations transformed the British social sciences.* Columbia University Press.

Paton, V. O., Fitzgerald, H. E., Green, B. L., Raymond, M., & Borchardt, M. P. (2014). U.S. higher education regional accreditation commission standards and the centrality of engagement. *Journal of Higher Education Outreach and Engagement, 18*(3), 41–69.

Pettit, E. (2023). How a center for civic education became a political provocation. *The Chronicle of Higher Education,* February 22. https://www.chronicle.com/article/how-a-center-for-civic-education-became-a-political-provocation

Reardon, K. (2022). Promoting reciprocity within community/university development partnerships: Lessons from the field. *Planning, Practice & Research, 21*(1), 95–107.

Reyes, D.V. (2018). *Learning to be Latino: How colleges shape identity politics.* Rutgers University Press.

Ris, E. W. (2022). *Other people's colleges: The origins of American higher education reform.* University of Chicago Press.

Spicer, J., T. Kay, & M. Ganz. (2019). Social entrepreneurship as field encroachment: how a neoliberal social movement constructed a new field. *Socio-Economic Review 17*, 195–227.

Stevens, M.L., & Gebre-Medhin, B. (2016). Association, service, market: Higher education in American political development." *Annual Review of Sociology 41*, 121–142.

Stoecker, R. (2016). *Liberating service learning and the rest of higher education civic engagement.* Temple University Press.

Strathern, M. (Ed). (2000). *Audit cultures: Anthropological studies in accountability, ethics, and the academy.* Routledge.

Tierney, W.G. (2021). *Higher education for democracy: The role of the university in civil society.* SUNY Press.

White, B.P. (2009). Navigating power dynamics between institutions and their communities. Kettering Foundation. https://www.kettering.org/catalog/product/navigating-power-dynamics-between-institutions-and-their-communities

Woolard, C. (2017). *Engaging civic engagement: Framing the civic education movement in higher education.* Lexington.

CHAPTER 5

FOCUSING ON HOW NOT WHY

Examining the Role of Nonprofit Partner Organizations in Campus-Based Civic Engagement Programming

Allison D. Rank
State University of New York at Oswego

ABSTRACT

Any assessment of the challenges and opportunities for higher education to strengthen democracy requires focusing our attention not only on college campuses but on the substantial ecosystem of partner organizations dedicated to civic engagement and, particularly, to the most measurable form of civic engagement—voting. To that end, this chapter offers two overarching claims. First, as partner organizations provide a wide range of needed resources—including but not limited to funding, credibility, training and materials—we need to carefully consider how these organizations direct our attention. More specifically, I argue that the voter engagement action planning process centered around the partner-produced *Strengthening American*

Democracy Guide constitutes an auditing process that can shape priorities and behaviors of campus actors. Second, through an analysis of the *Strengthening American Democracy Guide* and campus action plans produced using the guide, this chapter finds that while partner organizations frame their work as promoting civic learning and democratic engagement, what is explicitly and implicitly encouraged is the process of casting a ballot with little discussion of where that process fits within the larger political landscape.

In the wake of the 2018 midterm election, I received an invitation to travel to Washington, D.C. to participate in a Post-Election Gathering funded by the Students Learn Students Vote Coalition, then hosted at an organization called Young Invincibles. At the Post-Election Gathering, or PEG in youth vote parlance, I was introduced to world of "partner organizations": non-profits, largely but not entirely national in their scope, that work with colleges and universities—variously targeting faculty, staff, students and even administrators—in a quest to support civic engagement and particularly voter turnout on college campuses. Given the scope of these nonprofits, any assessment of the challenges and opportunities for higher education to strengthen democracy requires focusing our attention not only on college campuses but on the substantial ecosystem of partner organizations dedicated to civic engagement and, particularly, to the most measurable form of civic engagement—voting. To that end, this chapter offers two overarching claims. First, as partner organizations provide a wide range of needed resources—including but not limited to funding, credibility, training, and materials—we need to carefully consider how these organizations direct our attention. More specifically, I argue that the action planning process centered around the partner-created *Strengthening American Democracy Guide* constitutes an auditing process that can shape priorities and behaviors of campus actors. Second, an analysis of action plans produced using the guide leads me to conclude that while these organizations frame their work as promoting civic learning and democratic engagement, what is explicitly and implicitly encouraged is the process of casting a ballot with little discussion of where that process fits within the larger academic and political landscapes.

This chapter begins with an overview of the role of higher education in preparing young Americans for civic participation as well as the declining support available for institutions to meet this obligation. I then turn to a discussion of how the intersection of campuses with partner organizations can be understood through research into nonprofit organizations. Having established the importance of including these organizations as any part of an analysis of campus-based civic engagement programming, I explain how the action planning process creates an auditing relationship between partner organizations and campuses before turning to a discourse analysis to assess how these organizations' training materials as well as the campus-based planning they facilitate, frame the act of voting.

CONTEMPORARY CIVIC ENGAGEMENT LANDSCAPE IN HIGHER EDUCATION

While many believe colleges and universities have a role to play in preparing individuals for participatory citizenship in a pluralist democracy, the logic that traditionally underscores this understanding of the role of higher education has, of course, been eroding for quite some time. In *Academic Fault Lines: The Rise of Industry Logic in Public Higher Education* (2019), Patricia J. Gumport traces the declining commitment to what she terms the social institution logic—an understanding of questions of democratic preparedness—with an industry logic. Under the social institution logic, higher education has an "inclusive mandate to fulfill a broad array of functions for society, including contributions that have provided essential continuity and change in democratic, economic, intellectual, and cultural arenas" (p. 9). Under this logic, colleges and universities are understood to improve the lives of individual graduates and do so in ways that "elevat[e] the quality of life for the citizenry" (p. 476). Gumport argues that starting in the late 1970s, however, "a widespread decline of public trust in social (especially public) institutions and increased expectations for higher education to embrace economic priorities, including workforce training and economic development needs, alongside—if not at times overshadowing—human development, socialization, and citizenship functions" (p. 22).

In response, members of the academic community turned first to community service and then service-learning to address the twin threats of a "market-centered approach" and the "political disaffection of America's youth" (Hartley 2009, p. 14). In the late 1990s, Campus Compact issued and over 500 university presidents signed a 'President's Declaration on the Civic Responsibility of Higher Education' explicitly recognizing that "service [was] not leading student to embrace the duties of active citizenship and civic participation" (Ehrlich & Hollander, 1999 as cited in Hartley 2009, p. 22). Over the next decade, various groups issued calls for campuses to recommit themselves to some form of engagement (Hartley 2009, p. 23). One such report, *A Crucible Moment: College Learning and Democracy's Future* (2011), outlined the need to move civic education from an optional to central aspect of postsecondary education with an emphasis on four components: knowledge, skills, values and collective action. *A Crucible Moment* highlighted model programs and offered recommendations on how colleges could "take part in a larger national effort to elevate civic learning and democratic engagement as an animating priority for the nation and an expected part of every college student's academic and campus life experience" (p. 47). Notably, those drafting *A Crucible Moment* held round-tables with a range of actors including one composed of national civic organizations.

Chad Woolard's *Engaging Civic Engagement: Framing the Civic Education Movement in Higher Education* (2017) offers a comprehensive overview of the varied approaches colleges and universities as well as associated professional and educational organizations and institutions take when seeking to incorporate civic education within higher education broadly. Through tracing the discourse produced by the "organizations and scholars who are promoting civic education" (p. 37), Woolard identifies six forms of civic education—service-learning, civic engagement, political engagement, democratic engagement, social justice and antifoundational engagement—and leverages frames analysis in order to distinguish how each form, both explicitly and implicitly, defines the problem and solution that their specific approach to civic education is designed to address (see Table 5.1).

I am particularly interested in the approach Woolard identifies as political engagement. Political engagement builds on the civic engagement form which diagnoses the problem of low engagement as stemming from a "lack of social connectedness; frayed social networks of an individualistic and narcissistic society" as well as the fact that "higher education has moved away from its civic mission" and suggests the solution lies in "repairing lost connections between individuals and the community" through civic

TABLE 5.1 Excerpts from Woolard's Civic Education Framing Matrix (2017)

Signature Frame	Prognostic Frame
Service Learning	Repairing lost connections between individuals and the community through service learning
Civic Engagement	Repairing lost connections between individuals and the community through service learning; universities need to embrace and institutionalize civic engagement
Political Engagement	Universities need to embrace and institutionalize civic engagement; political participation needs to be a focus in higher education to increase low participation
Democratic Engagement	Repairing lost connections between individuals and the community through service learning; universities need to embrace and institutionalize civic engagement; the civic engagement movement needs introspections; many civic engagement programs do not promotion true democratic
Critical Engagement	Resist neoliberalism and the corporatization of higher education
Social Justice	Use the classroom to advocate for social justice; community activism

engagement programming (p. 92). Political engagement adds a need to address "low levels of political participation" through intentional focus on improving political participation rates (p. 92) such as voting. The organizations I outline more in the next section are not considered by Woolard and appear to have been ignored within academic literature on civic engagement.[1] However, they seek to and likely do play a key role in shaping civic engagement programming on many college campuses.

THE RISE OF PARTNER ORGANIZATIONS

Faculty and staff now face twin pressures to provide civic education while working at institutions operating under industry logic and often without the resources—be that time, money or training—that would support a robust civic engagement program. A range of organizations have taken on improving youth voter turnout rates as their central focus and seek to accomplish this goal by organizing at and among institutions of higher education to improve their capacity to support young voters.[2] While campuses have the capacity to implement programming and work directly with young voters, partner organizations offer a wide range of resources including but not limited to funding, credibility, training and materials. And, given this combination of resources as well as the explicit intention to shape how campuses approach voter mobilization work, we need to carefully consider how these organizations direct our attention.

Fundamentally, nonprofits serve to "address a market failure (such as youth development for disadvantaged youth) or they provide supplementary services for which the voting public does not wish to pay (such as a symphony)" (Steinberg, 2006 as cited in Never, 2016, p. 82). These organizations function as part of an overarching market that often includes a wide range of "producers or programs and services and many potential clients who 'consume' the programs and services in different ways—as well as many indirect players and forces such as regulators, suppliers, umbrella groups, credentials, qualifications, reputations, and others" (Gainer, 2016, pp. 369–370).

Nonprofits often find value through collaboration. In "Value Creation through Collaboration" (2016), Austin and Seitanidi argue that understanding the quality of a collaborative relationship among nonprofit organizations requires examining not only who in the collaboration provides what resources but the kinds of resources provided: the degree to which they are "generic" or "organization-specific" and "fill a gap in the other partner's resource portfolio" (p. 440). Ideally, collaborating nonprofits will have "multiple and deep linkages" that reflects a "breadth and depth" of shared interests (p. 440). And, of course, to attract resources, nonprofits must "deliver sufficient value to the providers of those resources—while providing value to the different constituencies that 'consume' those resources" (Gainer, 2016, p. 385).

Ultimately, then, an analysis of political engagement in higher education requires a consideration of the system within which this engagement takes place as well as an awareness of what various organizations offer each other. In the remainder of this paper, I focus on how two specific organizations—ALL IN Campus Democracy Challenge and Students Learn Students Vote—offer resources to college campuses through a credentialing process that requires campuses to craft voter engagement action plans and submit them for evaluation.

The ALL IN Campus Democracy Challenge (ALL IN), a project of Civic Nation established in 2016, "empowers colleges and universities to achieve excellence in nonpartisan student democratic engagement" ("About"). More specifically, the ALL IN model argues that it provides structure through "program design plus accountability," support through "coaching, training, resources, referrals, and networking," and recognition in the form of "national seals and awards" ("ALL IN Theory of Change"). Participating campuses, of which there were more than 850 in 2022, submit a campus plan in advance of the election and agree to also submit the data they receive from the National Study of Learning, Voting, and Engagement (NSLVE). Drawing on NSLVE data, which shows campus-specific voter registration and turnout rates, ALL IN awards campuses that meet certain voter turnout benchmarks receive accolades in the form of seals. ALL IN also runs a number of programs for specific higher education constituencies including athletic conferences and state-based challenges, coaches, presidents, etc. In this paper, I'm particularly interested in how ALL IN facilitates campus action planning and the kinds of documents that result from the process.

Created in 2016, the Students Learn Students Vote Coalition (SLSV) serves as a national clearinghouse of sorts for the higher education student voting space. SLSV seeks to "convene and connect campuses, nonprofit partners, students, and philanthropic leaders with each other, and with resources and programming" and sees change as "rooted in institutionalizing nonpartisan voter engagement within campus cultures and processes" (About Us). Efforts to convene, connect and institutionalize take varied forms including but not limited to organizing monthly coalition meeting, hosting working groups and affinity groups, providing minigrants and writing and distributing one-pagers and training guides on a variety of topics. The coalition has grown significantly since its founding and now includes 400 partners (both campuses and organizations) while working with close to 2,000 campuses overall.

Both organizations frame institutionalization of the voting process within campus operations to be a key step for improving student voting rates and center campus-wide action planning in their work. In 2017, these two organizations, in collaboration with others such as Campus Vote Project, American Democracy Project, NASPA Lead Initiative, and the Democracy Commitment, authored a common action planning guide entitled the *Strengthening American Democracy Guide* (SADG). The SADG is "a tool designed to help faculty, staff, and students write strong action plans to increase civic learning and democratic engagement on college and university campuses" (SADG v. 1). The SADG is now on its third version and the contributing organizations list has expanded to include other major partner organizations including Democracy Works, Student PIRGs and the Andrew Goodman Foundation indicating coalescence around this planning model. Participation in the ALL IN Campus Democracy Challenge requires submitting an action plan; and, said action plan is evaluated using a rubric that aligns with this guide.[3] The guide is published under the auspices of SLSV and regularly promoted by its staff as a key tool campuses should use in developing their programming.

Those of us on campuses select from a range of services provided by these nonprofits (as well as others). For example, staff and faculty members might take advantage of training webinars on writing an action plan, guidance on how to institutionalize voter registration efforts on campus and a national credentialing process that can help push administrators to agree that both staff time and funding should be dedicated to these efforts. At the same time, nonprofits want to turn out young voters and campuses provide access to a significant number of potential young voters in a specific location and with established pathways through which they can be organized. And, nonprofits themselves are dependent on philanthropic funding—funders who have specific end goals they want to see—which influences the work they do on college campuses.[4]

The ALL IN Campus Democracy Challenge offers the guidance of an action planning process as well as, importantly, an opportunity for credentialing as individual campuses effectively receive a stamp of approval for their work by earning specific seal or award from the case of the ALL IN Campus Democracy Challenge. A wide range of planning materials exist to help campuses think through institutionalizing voter engagement work on their campuses. Drawing on this material, campuses create their own action plans which they submit to various entities in order to be eligible for awards or certifications. For the ALL IN Challenge, trained volunteers score submitted plans using a provided rubric. Campuses that pass a certain score threshold receive additional recognition for having a well-developed action plan. Moreover, campuses are actively encouraged to submit their plans at least once prior to the "official" submission to receive a score and feedback on the quality of the plan. The sponsoring organization—ALL IN—also provides materials such as press releases and sample social media posts to help the members of the campus community who head up these efforts gain media attention for their campus' work. Collectively, these programs can help faculty and staff pressure their campuses to elevate voter mobilization efforts as a campus priority while also improving the voter registration and turnout rates among their student body.

To be clear, I think there is value to be found in the system as it has been set up: as the nonprofit literature suggests these organizations provide resources that can absolutely benefit campus actors who need funding, guidance, etc. That said, we ought to think carefully about how these competitions and awards programs may influence campus actors. Offering athletic conference or state-wide competitions and sharing best practices with participants can create useful pressure and put helpful information into the hands of faculty, staff and students. But, because these programs apply a standard metric to all campuses, it might also narrow the range of activities a campus coalition considers undertaking. In particular, the *SADG* which encourages all campuses, regardless of their context, to use a singular process to develop a campus action plan and evaluates that plan against a set rubric sets up an auditing process that awards campuses for a particular approach to civic engagement. As a result, I argue it moves beyond providing a resource into what I see as a form of auditing. I explain this concept in more depth in the next section.

CAMPUS ACTION PLANNING AS AN AUDITING PROCESS

Planning and evaluating our own work with a rigorous eye has value and a variety of credentialing programs can support universities in focusing their efforts on campus priorities.[5] Yet, by offering a program explicitly designed to evaluate action plans, and particularly by evaluating in not just a summative but also a formative way, these organizations essentially audit the civic engagement programming of colleges and universities. The SADG provides specific expectations for what makes a "good" plan, external readers evaluate that plan against a rubric, and campuses receive accolades based on the degree to which their plan meets these external standards. Audits of the kind discussed here are optional, of course, and can absolutely play a valuable role in gaining resources and respect from campus administrators. But, it is also important to acknowledge that participation in these programs incentivizes attention on some activities over others and frames those activities in specific ways.

I use the term "audit" intentionally to highlight how participating in the action planning process may unwittingly shape our approach to civic engagement. Foucault argues that an "Audit is essentially a relationship of power between scrutinizer and observed: the latter are rendered objects of information, never subjects in communication (Foucault 1977: 200)"

(Shore & Wright, 2000, p. 59). As Shore and Write observe in "Coercive Accountability: The Rise of Audit Culture in Higher Education" (2000) the language of audits as driving improvement "rests upon a simultaneous imposition of external control from above and internalization of new norms so that individuals can continuously improve themselves. In short, external subjection and internal subjectification are combined so that individuals conduct themselves in terms of the norms through which they are governed" (p. 62). In response to audits, individuals will shift their "professional, collegial and personal identities" and while audits technically avoid exposing external standards, "audit culture relies upon self-managed hierarchical relationships and coercive practices. The self-directed, self-managed individual is encouraged to identify" with the terms of reference offered by the audit and opportunities to "challenge [sic] the terms of reference" are limited at best (p. 62).

The SADG planning process—a collaborative project that relies on staffing from various organizations in its creation, explicitly seeks to shape how individual campuses and thus individuals plan the civic engagement work on their campuses, is evaluated, etc.—represents an auditing project within the civic engagement space. I'm not necessarily saying the process is a bad one or one that is misapplied. I do, however, think that given the ability of an auditing process to shape individual and organizational priorities and behaviors combined with the fact that campus actors who want to pursue civic engagement programming often believe they need the resources offered by participation in such auditing programming means that we need to consider the degree to which critical questions have or have not been asked about this system and the degree to which it may influence how civic engagement is being framed and promoted in higher education by incentivizing campuses to define civic engagement in particular ways.

Having established the importance of nonprofit organizations within higher education's approach to civic engagement programming, as well as the way in which the action planning process that is central to programming and evaluation constitutes a form of auditing, I now turn to an analysis of a variety of primary documents from these organizations in an effort to identify how they frame voter mobilization efforts for campuses.

SO, WHAT ARE WE COUNTING?

In order to understand how these nonprofits, and particularly the action planning process directs campus' attention, I examined three sets of materials: the *Strengthening American Democracy Guide*, the Democratic Action Plan Rubric, and a set of example campus action plans ALL IN features on its website.

Strengthening American Democracy Guide v.1–3

Given that SADG has been updated for each of the last three election cycles, with new versions released in 2017, 2019, and 2021), its evolution provides a window into shifts in what the coordinating groups view as a priority within a campus plan. To be clear, the bulk of the guide stays the same over these cycles which means the small changes stand out. With regard to process, the guide places considerable emphasis on the process of planning. Prior to presenting guiding questions, the SADG offers specific definitions to help planning groups distinguish among the types of work being done (e.g., civic engagement is distinguished from political engagement) and the values that should guide planning (e.g., it should be continuous, intentional, and innovative). Figure 5.1 offers a visual representation of the nine steps of the planning process outlined in the SADG v. 3 which include

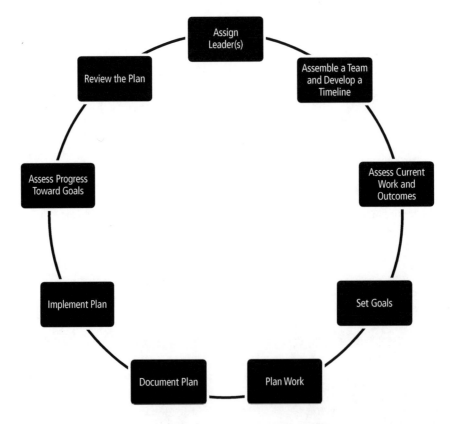

Figure 5.1 Action Planning Process Steps Featured in *Strengthening American Democracy Guide v. 3*

assigning leaders and assembling a team, assessing current work, setting goals, planning work, documenting and implementing the plan and assessing progress.

The one significant evolution across these three versions of the SADG is the shift to indicate that diversity, equity and inclusion should be a part of the planning process. This shift comes out in three areas. First, while the 2017 version of the guide argues that all goals set should be S.M.A.R.T. (specific, measurable, achievable, realistic, and time-bound), the 2019 version not only has the acronym changed to S.M.A.R.T.I.e., (adding inclusive and equitable) but this acronym appears not just in the goals section but as a key term. In the 2019 version, the guiding principles are updated to include the terms "inclusive" and "equitable" with both definitions emphasizing that "goals, strategies, and tactics" of the campaign reflect these principles in order to "bring traditionally excluded individuals and/or groups into processes, activities, and decision/policy making in a way that shares power" (inclusive) and that efforts focus on "campus populations that have historically engaged in civic learning, democratic engagement, and voter participation at lower levels" (equitable).

While these first two shifts focus explicitly on incorporating these values into the planning process, reading the forewords of all three documents suggests a desire to connect to large debates about the future of the United States as a functioning multiracial democracy. All three versions note the collaborating groups share a "common mission of ensuring a more representative democracy" and position the work of colleges and universities to engage students in elections at all levels as key to achieving this end. The first version of the SADG references the need to drive participation in local, state and federal elections arguing that "[h]igher education needs to play a more active role in graduating civically informed and democratically active students—students with the knowledge, skills, and values to solve the country's most pressing problems and who understand that in order to have a strong and truly representative democracy, they need to participate" (2017). In other words, this foreword connects youth participation to having a democratic state that actively works to address significant issues facing the country and do so in a way that is appropriately representative of the population. The second iteration of the SADG (2019) similarly invokes the role of higher education while justifying an emphasis on voting as a "fundamental and measurable" means of assessing engagement and noting the need for action plans to respond to specific campus conditions. The most recent version of the SADG (2021) praises the ability of campuses to innovate in response to the pandemic and puts particular emphasis on "efforts to promote diversity, inclusion and justice, both within the democratic engagement space and among campus populations as a whole" (p. 2).

Democratic Action Plan Rubric

The "Democratic Action Plan Rubric," included in the third volume of SADG (p., 28) facilitates rating plans as undeveloped, emerging, progressing or established on the nine sections offered in the Template and Guiding Questions section of the SADG v.3. Table 5.2 replicates the categories, their definitions, and the requirements for an established rating. As you can see, a rating of "established" in each category requires writing a plan that is quite detailed and does, in looking at the rubric, include some value sets regarding the planning being done on campus.

I identified four value sets within the rubric:

- Wide Scope of Influence: The leadership team, commitment, and strategy must span academic and student affairs as well as including off-campus actors. The importance of including the curricular and co-curricular content is explicitly referenced in the commitment and strategy sections and strongly implied by the evaluation section.
- Information Sharing: In order to receive the highest marks for reporting, campuses must make their "action plan, data, and reports" available both on campus and publicly.
- Data Informed: Campuses are expected to set "special goals" based on an analysis of their NSLVE data. And, the evaluation section requires that campus include an assessment plan that "describes how and what information will be collected and analyzed" that must go beyond "just looking at NSLVE data."

TABLE 5.2 Democratic Action Plan Rubric (2021) Excerpts

Category	Description	Established (Highest Score)
Executive Summary	Overview of the action plan explains: 1) Who developed it 2) The purpose of the plan 3) Where the plan will be implemented 4) The goal(s) of the plan 5) The intended duration of the plan 6) How the plan will be implemented.	Overview of action plan includes responses to all 6 of the suggested guiding questions.
Leadership	Description, including names and titles, of the leadership coalition responsible for improving democratic engagement. 5 categories of participation are encouraged: 1) students 2) faculty 3) student affairs 4) community/national organizations 5) local elections office coordination.	A leadership team of all relevant stakeholders (across 5 categories) exists. The team includes academic affairs, student affairs, and students as well as community partners and/or the local election office. The team includes diverse and marginalized communities.

(continued)

Focusing on How Not Why ▪ 77

TABLE 4.2 Democratic Action Plan Rubric (2021) Excerpts (cont.)

Category	Description	Established (Highest Score)
Commitment	Description of institutional commitment to improving democratic engagement.	According to the plan, institutional commitment is visible and widely communicated—internally and externally. It is woven into the culture of the institution and is clearly reflected in the institution's mission, learning outcomes, curriculum, and co-curriculum.
Landscape	Analysis of student data, campus climate, and current institutional efforts for improving democratic engagement.	The plan communicates a comprehensive understanding of its students, campus efforts, and climate; AND is using this information to inform its strategy.
Goals	Description of institutional short-term (e.g., by next election) and long-term (e.g., in next decade or two election cycles) desired democratic engagement results.	Short-term and long-term democratic engagement goals are described. Goals are also S.M.A.R.T.I.E.: Specific, Measurable, Achievable, Realistic, Time-bound, Inclusive, and Equitable.
National Study of Learning, Voting, and Engagement (NSLVE)	Free report providing campuses with their actual student registration and voting rates.	Summary AND detailed (e.g., demographic) NSLVE data are described and specific goals based on these data are set.
Strategy	Description of institutional efforts to reach desired democratic engagement results.	Strategy includes short-term tactics and long-term strategies. Tactics include a description of multiple voter registration, voter education, and voter turnout activities. Long-term strategies seek to make civic learning and democratic engagement an established part of the institution's curriculum and co-curriculum and go beyond the election.
Reporting	Description of institutional efforts to make plans, data, and reports public.	Action plan, data, and reports are shared on campus AND are publicly available.
Evaluation	Description of institutional efforts to evaluate the action plan, implementation, efforts, and results.	The evaluation strategy describes how and what information will be collected and analyzed as well as how the results will be used to make improvements. Includes more than just looking at NSLVE data. Evaluation happens before, during, and after plan implementation. Evaluation strategy crosses several categories of participation from the Leadership Section.

- Inclusive and Equitable: Earning top marks requires building a team that "includes diverse and marginalized communities" (leadership) as well as setting goals that are not only measurable and achievable, among other criteria, but also inclusive and equitable (goals).

Sample Plans

As part of the resources offered to help campuses in developing their action plans, ALL IN's website includes a page with twenty action plans drawn from four-year institutions, community colleges, and HBCUs that "were determined to be the strongest submitted to date in our 2020 action plan review process" (Action Plan Examples). After reviewing all twenty plans, I discovered many of these campuses have done an excellent job of developing a broad coalition, thinking carefully about their NSLVE data and establishing specific processes to support students through registering and casting a ballot in ways that meet the particular challenges of their campus context. However, many failed to articulate a connection between voting and any larger understanding of citizenship, the democratic process or the responsibilities of living in a pluralist democracy.

However, out of the twenty, only six plans connect voting to a broader understanding of politics, identity or citizenship. When this connection does happen it appears to occur when colleges have a particularly strong understanding of their own mission which can then be connected to voting rather than coming from working through the SADG. For example, Virginia Wesleyan links social responsibility and engaged citizenship to the school's Methodist heritage and argues that solving community issues requires engaging with local and state elections. Two community colleges, the Community College of Philadelphia (CCP) and Delta College, both connect voting to their responsibility as community colleges. CCP not only highlights the connection between voting and protests but argues that given their responsibility to specifically economically disenfranchised populations within Philadelphia, the campus has a particular obligation to "enable them to use their vote as their voice." Delta College's plan emphasizes the need for voting to be situated within a cultural and political context and not discussed as an end in itself. Towson University positions voting as a community commitment that serves not just students but the communities students are from while also arguing that students need "intrinsic motivation and a sense of responsibility" to drive their motivation alongside the logistical support that facilitates successfully casting a ballot. North Carolina A&T explicitly discusses ways they are framing voting as part of a community identity as well as arguing that process barriers are just one of issues with voting rates. It also advocates for bigger conversations about the state of democracy. And, Texas Women's University connects voting to an ethos of public service that already has a strong hold in the study body. These plans indicate a way that campuses can articulate a nonpartisan, specific connection between voting and a larger understanding of higher education's obligation or the role of voting within a multiracial democracy. Perhaps it is not surprising that of these six universities, five have distinct identities be it as a community college, HBCU, religiously affiliated institution, or women's college.

MOVING BEYOND PROCESS

In looking at various planning materials, the SADG rubric, and highlighted action plans, it is clear partner organizations follow through on their commitment to offer resources that emphasize the process of voting. Remember, these groups explicitly argue that low political participation rates with voting stem from barriers in the voter registration and turnout process—some of which face all voters living in a particular state while others are unique to a state's student population. And, this process is important. However, I am dismayed by how little the training documents or rubric have to say about the value of voting as a democratic act or the connection between voting and a broader understanding of citizenship and participatory democracy. To the degree that partner organizations facilitate auditing and thus shape how campuses approach discussing, planning, and executing this work, the limited connections drawn between voting and a broader concept of democratic decision making or citizenship is striking and may well be leading campuses away from engaging on this topic.

There are a number of ways campuses might be encouraged to discuss the value of voting that remains entirely nonpartisan and fits with a variety of campus identities. For example, in *The Duty to Vote* (2019) Julia Maskivker argues citizens have an obligation to vote given that it is a task that requires relatively little of us and yet can be a path toward achieving justice. As she puts it, "a natural duty of justice requires citizens to acquire minimal epistemic competence and vote with a sense of the common good in order to support fair governance" (p. 3). She refers to this understanding of voting as a Good Samaritan approach to voting that recognizes voting as a small act that places a minimal burden on each individual citizen and yet is a way of supporting other members within one's community by voting for policies that can be of value and support to them.

Beyond this moral claim, the literature suggests four additional means of framing the value of voting: instrumental, expressive, individual or collective. First, voting is an instrumental good that can be valued "because of its capacity to further a particular (collective) goal, namely, the goal of improving justice or preventing injustice. In short, we can value elections for (collectively) instrumental reasons" (Maskivker, 2019, p. 49). This form of voting encourages individuals to decide "whether to vote, and for whom, based on whether the voter believes her vote could make a difference in the election" (Perrin, 2014, p. 52). Second, voting has an expressive value as it provides voters an opportunity to "express oneself, to make a point to the public" (Perrin, 2014, p. 53). In both the instrumental and expressive cases, the act of voting connects to other forms of political participation by suggesting that voting is another place to share one's voice (expressive) and by suggesting the voting may be one part of a multi-pronged strategy designed to achieve a particular end (instrumental).

In either case, voting may be framed as an individual or collective activity. Voting is often cast as a particularly private and thus individual act that "says something important about what the voter truly believes and who she is, and it is among the most important things she can do as a citizen" (Perrin, 2014, p. 54). And yet, voting can create a social or collective identity in multiple ways. As individuals are linked to publics "[d]eciding whether to vote, and for whom to vote, and even how to vote (since there are many ways to vote such as in-person early voting, absentee ballot, etc.), are acts that trigger belonging to a social group" (Perrin, 2014, p. 71). Indeed, Maskivikar explicitly argues that "voting is anything but solitary. We must see it as a collective endeavor if it is to mean anything at all for democracy" (p. 12). Her argument casting voting as a moral duty explicitly positions the vote as a collective active act as "the duty to vote as a Good Samaritan is a duty to cooperate with others in bringing about justice" (Maskivker 11).

Finally, for a republic with many individuals with a wide range of views on a wide range of issues, voting provides a strategy for handling conflict through democratic agonism. Notably, under this viewpoint, "democracy is not a system of coming to consensus or agreement, but a system of managing and airing social conflict so that social order does not disintegrate into chaos" (Mouffe as cited in Perrin, p. 91).

To conclude, in a period when allegiance to democratic norms is eroding, I would argue campuses have an obligation to intentionally address why students should value liberal democracy and its primary means of participation. Action planning that does not prompt campuses to investigate and explain their own commitments to a pluralist, liberal democracy, that keeps us focused on how without encouraging explicit considerations of why, may inadvertently direct our attention away from one the key opportunities for higher education to strengthen democracy.

NOTES

1. Specifically, I mean that these organizations have not been the site of research. I found articles where authors note their campus efforts include interns from the Campus Democracy Project or the Andrew Goodman Foundation, for example. But, with the exception of one article critiquing Paul Loeb's work with the Campus Election Engagement Project, I found very little that took these organizations seriously as sites worthy of academic attention.
2. As distinguished from a wide range of organizations that include supporting student vote outreach as part of their work on broader civic engagement programming (e.g. the American Democracy Project, NASPA's CLDE Knowledge Community) or their work with students (e.g. Hillel's MitzVote or the Feminist Majority Foundation's Vote Feminist! Campaign).
3. Campus Vote Projects' Voter Friendly Campus certification, which currently enrolls up to 300 campuses each election year, also uses the Strengthening American Democracy Guide as the base of their action planning process.
4. As this formation suggests, a full understanding of this ecosystem absolutely requires a consideration of the priorities of funders. If funders want to see voter registration numbers rise or vote turnout numbers rise - as opposed to a focus on other softer and harder to assess civic skills - then funders can use their resources (money) to direct the activities of nonprofit organizations which will, in turn, influence the kinds of sources these organizations offer to campuses. While this chapter focuses specifically on the planning documents offered by nonprofit organizations it would be a mistake to assume that these organizations are completely free to make their own choices in deciding what they prioritize in their work with campuses. For more details on the role of philanthropy in this process, please consult Terri Taylor's chapter in this volume.
5. See Caroline Lee's chapter in this volume.

REFERENCES

About. (n.d.). ALL IN Campus Democracy Challenge (n.d.). Retrieved August 1, 2023, from https://allinchallenge.org/about/

About. (n.d.). Campus Vote Project. Retrieved August 1, 2023, from https://www.campusvoteproject.org/about

About us. (n.d.). Students Learn Students Vote Coalition. Retrieved August 1, 2023, from https://slsvcoalition.org/about/

Action Plan Examples. (n.d.). ALL IN Campus Democracy Challenge (n.d.). Retrieved August 1, 2023, from https://allinchallenge.org/resources/action-plan-examples/

Austin, J. E., & Seitanidi, M. M. (2016). Value creation through collaboration. In D. O. Renz & R. D. Herman (Eds.), *The Jossey-Bass handbook of nonprofit leadership and management* (4th ed.; pp. 427–443). John Wiley & Sons, Inc.

Gainer, B. (2016). Marketing for nonprofit organizations. In D.O. Renz & R. D. Herman (Eds.), T*he Jossey-Bass handbook of nonprofit leadership and management* (4th ed.; pp. 366–395). John Wiley & Sons, Inc.

Gumport, P. J. (2019). *Academic fault lines: The rise of industry logic in public higher education*. Johns Hopkins University Press.

Hartley, M. (2009). Reclaiming the democratic purposes of American higher education: Tracing the trajectory of the civic engagement movement. *Learning and Teaching: The International Journal of Higher Education in the Social Sciences, 2*(3), 11–30.

Never, B. (2016). The changing context of nonprofit management in the United States. In D.O. Renz & R. D. Herman (Eds.), *The Jossey-Bass handbook of nonprofit leadership and management* (4th ed.; pp. 80–101). John Wiley & Sons, Inc.

Miskivker, J. (2019). *The duty to vote*. Oxford University Press.

Perrin, A. (2014). *American democracy: From Tocqueville to town halls to Twitter*. Polity Press.

Shore, C., & Write, S. (2000). Coercive accountability: The rise of audit culture in higher education. In M. Strathern (Ed.), *Audit cultures: Anthropological studies in accountability, ethics, and the academy* (pp. 57–89). Routledge.

Students Learn Students Vote Coalition. (2017). *Strengthening American Democracy: A Guide for Developing an Action Plan to Increase Civic Learning, Political Engagement, and Voting Rates Among College Students* (Version 1). Retrieved on August 1, 2023, from https://younginvincibles.org/wp-content/uploads/2017/10/Strengthening-American-Democracy_smaller-1.pdf

Students Learn Students Vote Coalition. (2019). *Strengthening American democracy: A guide for developing an action plan to increase civic learning, political engagement, and voting rates among college students* (Version 2.).

Students Learn Students Vote Coalition. (2021). *Strengthening American democracy: A guide for developing an action plan to increase civic learning, political engagement, and voting rates among college students* (Version 3). Retrieved on August 1, 2023, from https://allinchallenge.org/wp-content/uploads/StrengtheningAmericanDemocracyGuide_VOL3.pdf

The Global Perspective Institute, Inc. and the Association of American Colleges and Universities. (2011). *A crucible moment: College learning and democracy's future*. https://www2.ed.gov/rschstat/research/pubs/college-learning-democracys-future/crucible-moment.pdf.

Theory of Change. (n.d.). ALL IN Campus Democracy Challenge (n.d.). Retrieved August 1, 2023, from https://allinchallenge.org/wp-content/uploads/ALL-IN-Challenge-Theory-of-Change.pdf.

Woolard, C. (2017). *Engaging civic engagement: Framing the civic education movement in higher education*. Rowman & Littlefield.

CHAPTER 6

BRIDGING THE COMPLEXITIES OF HIGHER EDUCATION AND PHILANTHROPY

Teresa Taylor
Lumina Foundation

ABSTRACT

As educators, economic engines, and civic pillars, colleges and universities are essential to the task of responding to rising authoritarianism and reforming democratic institutions to meet the needs of their entire constituencies, especially those who have been historically marginalized. But they must evolve to meet the moment, developing new solutions, engaging new partners, and shrugging off old habits that no longer serve them. In this chapter, I examine higher education and philanthropy as complex adaptive systems. Understanding system dynamics helps explain why philanthropy interested in strengthening democracy largely ignores higher education and why higher education's efforts have atrophied in recent years. Higher education needs strong relationships outside the academy in local communities, with students and other constituents, and in the broader democracy building movements. Philanthropy can help higher education build such relationships, but private foundations are neglecting colleges in most democracy building efforts. The chapter concludes with recommendations for potential collaborative strategies for redesigning and restoring American democracy.

THE OPPORTUNITY AND CHALLENGE BEFORE US

Democracies across the world face twin challenges: responding to rising authoritarianism and reforming themselves to meet the needs of their entire constituencies, especially those who have been historically marginalized. This requires defending the systems we have while also rejecting the status quo and a romanticized version of the past. With new pressure from growing economic inequality, increasing effects of climate change, and deep distrust from the electorate, this is a very tall order for already overstrained systems. But they must evolve to meet the moment, developing new solutions, engaging new partners, and shrugging off old habits that no longer serve them.

As educators, economic engines, and civic pillars, colleges and universities are essential to this task. They annually teach millions of students from across the country and the globe about core subjects of human knowledge, from the arts and humanities to science and engineering to technical trades. Students across disciplines develop skills core to democratic participation, including how to challenge the status quo with new ideas, how to live and learn in diverse communities, how to assess the validity of information, what historical and societal developments led us to the current moment, and what skills and areas of knowledge can have personal and collective impact. They also provide a place for students to create community and personal bonds that hold fast long after graduation—something particularly important in an era where loneliness and social isolation are rising. Colleges' research mission allows for the long-term study of complex problems, debate among scholars on how best to understand and address those problems, and encouragement to publicly share findings. These intertwined teaching and research functions help society as a whole evolve and provide essential independent voices to corroborate or challenge what elected officials present to the public.

Colleges and universities also serve as economic engines that can help people feel that democracy is working for them. Earning credentials has lifted countless graduates and their families into a more secure economic station. As major employers, particularly in less populated areas, colleges provide regional economic security. After all, they are unlikely to relocate or offshore their workforce.

Finally, colleges and universities play key roles as civic pillars. Higher education can illustrate evolving societal values, for example, as they have opened their doors to the whole of society, not just a select few. During election season, they host debates and serve as polling centers. And they serve as special reflections of Americans' constitutional freedoms of speech and assembly. As the Supreme Court observed in *Sweezy v. New Hampshire* (1957), "No one should underestimate the vital role in a democracy that is played by those who guide and train our youth" (p. 250).

But colleges are not yet rising to the urgent challenges of today. Dated civic engagement approaches don't always resonate with the diverse population of today's students or connect to broader democracy movements (Hope 2022). We lack evidence of what students actually learn and experience in college that promotes positive social and civic behavior after graduation, especially for students who are older, come from communities of color, are part-time, and have work and/or caretaking responsibilities (Chittum et al., 2022). Administrators, faculty, and staff do not always know how to respond when hate and extremism show up on campus, whether physically or in online spaces (Polarization & Extremism Research & Innovation Lab, 2022). And, given rising public skepticism and increasing intrusions into academic freedom and public higher education governance, colleges need to recalibrate when to be bold and when to keep out of the political fray (PEN America 2023).

Higher education cannot address these challenges on its own. It needs strong relationships outside the academy in local communities, with students and other constituents, and in the broader democracy building movements. These connections can increase awareness of the public problems that students need to be prepared to address. They also can build trust and demonstrate relevance that may be attractive to prospective students and helpful when the sector needs allies to defend itself. These kinds of relationships, however, are almost always overlooked in the day-to-day challenges of running an American college or university.

Philanthropy can help higher education build such relationships, but private foundations are neglecting colleges in most democracy building efforts. Significant funding supports both higher education and democracy, but in separate pools, limiting higher education's ability to realize its full potential in strengthening and evolving our democracy. In fact, only a handful of people and projects address both higher education and democracy. It's not enough to meet the moment.

So can higher education and philanthropy—two diffuse and diverse sectors—work together to redesign and renew American democracy for the good of everyone? A first step can be defining the parameters of each sector's complexity. This process helps us better understand both higher education and philanthropy, including their strengths and weaknesses. Having spent several years identifying these challenges and opportunities as part of my role at Lumina Foundation, I'm pleased to be able to share my perspective from inside philanthropy and to highlight the work of several of my grantees. My hope is that this article may inspire others in philanthropy and higher education to join in these efforts.

TRACING THE COMPLEXITIES OF AMERICAN PHILANTHROPY AND HIGHER EDUCATION

Since the country's founding, philanthropic organizations have been unique contributors to American social, political, and economic development (Tocqueville, 1840). The sector includes millions of individual donors and hundreds of thousands of organizations, each with their own distinct charitable purposes and approaches to funding.

Private foundations are a uniquely powerful force in the United States, with 60% of assets held by foundations globally—nearly nine times the amount held in the second-ranked country (Johnson 2018). Their giving is growing, up 28.5%, adjusted for inflation, between 2017 and 2021 alone (Giving USA Foundation 2021). At least 127,595 private foundations are recognized by the IRS, with total assets of approximately $1.2 trillion and total annual giving around $90 billion (Candid 2021). Since 1969, they have been subject to significant federal regulatory burdens. As a result, more flexible organizational forms are growing in popularity, including Donor Advised Funds (DAFs) and LLCs, especially with younger philanthropists who made their fortunes in the technology sector.

Education is the top subject area for philanthropic support, receiving more than a quarter of all U.S. philanthropic funding (Candid 2021). Indeed, in FY 2022 alone, America's colleges and universities benefitted from $59.5 billion from private foundations and individual donors (Council for Advancement and Support of Education 2023, p. 6).

Much of this support, however, goes to already wealthy institutions. For example, in 2022, the top five gifts to institutions—all selectives with existing endowments—totaled $2.1 billion (Philanthropy News Digest 2023). These five gifts were nearly ten times the entire amount received by all public associate's institutions that year (Council for Advancement and Support of Education 2023, p. 8–9). Indeed, private Research I institutions receive more than 44 times as much voluntary giving annually as public associate's institutions (Council for Advancement and Support of Education, 2023).

American democracy also receives significant philanthropic support. From 2011–22, 15,864 funders (mostly private foundations) have awarded $15.5 billion in 175,003 grants across 32,043 recipients (Candid n.d.). Of that, $5.3 billion went to "civic participation," defined as "supporting non-election related civic education, leadership development, organizing, engagement, and volunteerism... [including] participation in the political process, as well as mobilization and advocacy around specific issue areas or with specific constituencies" (Candid (n.d.).

But trends in philanthropic funding for democracy open foundations up to critique. For example, funding spiked during the Trump administration, especially in grants for media, government, and campaigns/elections/

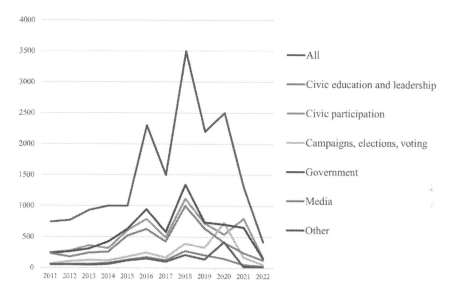

Figure 6.1 Private Foundation Funding for U.S. Democracy 2011–2022. Author illustration based on data from Candid Democracy.

voting, but decreased dramatically after the election of President Biden (Figure 6.1).

This drop prevents sustained democracy-building work between elections that often helps citizens decide whether the system includes them and produces benefits for them. Moreover, it invites complaints like those delivered by J.D. Vance in his successful 2021 Senate Campaign. He argued, "All across our country, we have nonprofits—big foundations—that are effectively social-justice hedge funds... Taken together, they represent well over $1 trillion in wealth, and that wealth is deployed in almost exclusively partisan ways" (GR Editors 2021).

But the most important problem for purposes of this volume is that higher education is largely overlooked by philanthropy interested in supporting democracy in the United States. Only $354.5 million of philanthropic funding for U.S. democracy went to "education"—just 2.2% of the total—and only a portion of that went to colleges and universities (Candid, n.d.). My own experience with democracy funders groups is that higher education is almost never mentioned, except as a possible research partner. What's going on?

The complexity of higher education offers at least a partial explanation. Higher education in the United States includes multiplicities of institution types, missions, roles within the institution, types of students served, and places in which the work takes place. Cohen et al. have gone so far to declare the American college "a prototypic organized anarchy [that] does not know what it is doing" (2022 p. 3). According to the National Center for

Education Statistics (2022), as of the 2020–21 academic year, 5,916 postsecondary institutions were operating in the United States—1,892 public, 1,754 private nonprofit, and 2,270 private for-profit—3,931 of which grant degrees. These institutions serve over 25 million enrolled students, employ nearly 4 million faculty and staff, and offer hundreds of majors and programs (National Center for Education Statistics n.d.a, n.d.e). Revenues exceeded $485 billion for publics, $409 billion for private nonprofits, and $17 billion for private for-profits (National Center for Education Statistics n.d.b, n.d.c, n.d.d).

A major driver of this complexity is the hyper-specialization encouraged among scholars, students, and administrators. Rewards flow to those who stay inside their bubbles and do not poke too much at others' spheres. But hyper-specialization erects barriers that make colleges hard to navigate and can impact enrollment, retention, and attainment rates, especially for students from marginalized groups. It can also dissuade employers, community partners, and governments from engaging because it's never clear who, if anyone, speaks for the institution as a whole. And, because most higher education actors are in their own bubble, they may not be able to see these labyrinths clearly enough to correct them—or may simply not have the incentives to act. One of my grantees has worked with police forces, churches, the federal government, civil right groups, and K–12 schools on effective responses to rising extremism and polarization. For a project focused on higher education that Lumina supported, she told me that her team has never had a harder time nailing down actionable guidance. Why? Because the higher education actors the team interviewed only thought through the lens of their own role and, without guidance targeting that role, they couldn't see what they were supposed to do about the problem.

Hyper-specialization also challenges efforts to work across institutions and even within them. Faculty, administrators, and development staff usually pitch funders on something that the applicant can control within their own sphere of influence that will reflect positively for promotion and tenure, meet institutional fundraising goals, or not disturb the status quo or ruffle too many feathers. A similar "stay in your lane" dynamic also exists within philanthropy, which typically has well-defined funding priorities and teams staffed on specific issue areas. As a result, both sides of a potential funding relationship have disincentives to collaborate. This lack of engagement means that problems and solutions are often defined too narrowly, overly depending on the unique context of a particular college or the priorities of a single funder.

And, because higher education efforts related to democracy are mostly starved for resources, sometimes institutions are happy to get any resources at all, without considering whether the funding opportunity is solving a core problem or helping build essential capacity. Take, for example, student voter registration, which has recently enjoyed notable philanthropic support. But, according to Thomas et al. (2020), student voter registration rates have long been about 75%, mirroring the overall registration rate, so it was not really a problem that needed solving. On the other hand, campuses have very different rates of students *voting* and taking other civic actions. Thomas et al. found that institutions could address these issues by engaging students in robust democratic participation inside and outside the classroom, for example by promoting political discussion, social cohesion, student leadership opportunities, and creating a buzz around election season that didn't end after election day (Thomas et al. 2020). Yet, very little philanthropic funding encourages institutions to support and sustain such efforts over time, thereby exacerbating the problem that funding that is available is focused on a non-issue, rather than on efforts that could make a difference in democratic participation.

Some big gifts with high visibility and budgets have minimal impact on the sector. This can happen with both institution-specific gifts and national efforts. Since 2015, the Kinder Foundation (n.d.) has provided $60 million to establish and grow the Kinder Institute on Constitutional Democracy at the University of Missouri. Its most recent eight-figure gift allowed the university to grow its summer internship program to 40 students. Brian Chesky gave $100 million and worked with President and Mrs. Obama to launch the Voyager Scholarship, a two-year program for juniors and seniors committed to public service (Obama Foundation 2022). That program serves 100 students annually. With more than 18 million undergraduates currently enrolled in American higher education, surely the country would benefit from larger gifts that aim to engage many more students (National Student Clearinghouse Research Center 2023).

MAKING SENSE OF THIS LANDSCAPE WITH COMPLEXITY THEORY

So what are we supposed to do with all of this? What might lead to a more fruitful dynamic between higher education and philanthropy in collaborative efforts to strengthen American democracy? To clarify our task, we need a framework that can handle such complex systems. Enter Complexity Theory. Emerging from sectors as diverse as mathematics, immunology, and healthcare system management, it holds that the world is made up of complex adaptive systems such as the human body, the stock market and the American higher education and philanthropic sectors (Park 2017; Begun et al. 2002; Zimmerman et al. 1998). All complex adaptive systems are massively entangled, self-organizing, dynamic, and resilient (Begun et al. 2002). I will describe each of these in turn and use them to illuminate promising steps to strengthen relationships across higher education and philanthropy in service of renewing American democracy.

Note: Not all philanthropic giving qualifies as being part of a complex adaptive system. This discussion focuses solely on private foundations because they do make up such a system thanks to a shared regulatory system, high visibility of their efforts, and similar organizational types and modes of engagement. Individual donors do not because their giving is much more random, difficult to trace over time, and largely ungoverned.

MASSIVELY ENTANGLED

Complex adaptive systems are made up of interdependent but autonomous parts that rely on networks and relationships to create the whole that goes beyond an aggregation of individual parts (Park 2017). A herd of cats is not a complex adaptive system, but a school of fish is.

Often, system parts are complex adaptive systems themselves. A human body has skeletal, cardiovascular, digestive, and other major systems that are each made up of different cells with unique functions, each a small universe of its own. Damaging one part threatens the whole and forces others to compensate. And strengthening one part helps the other parts to relax and maximize their own function.

Seeing private foundations and higher education as complex adaptive systems illuminates a few key ideas. Both are distinct, autonomous systems. Philanthropy does not exist simply to provide funding for the priorities of others, nor does higher education exist solely to create workers for the economy. Both are their own universes of resources, organizations, communities, ideas, and people.

SELF-ORGANIZING

Actors within complex adaptive systems develop behaviors in response to the interactions made possible through the system's unique conditions that evolve over time. Control is distributed, not centralized, as individual parts of the system learn behaviors and develop habits as they interact with others in the system. Attempts at external control without significant support from within the system, therefore, will probably fail to produce large-scale change.

Take, for example, philanthropic efforts in the early 20th century by industrialists such as Andrew Carnegie and John D. Rockefeller to reform higher education. Their successes included broad adoption of the credit hour system, college preparatory curriculum for K–12, and the four-year course of study for baccalaureate programs. Though many of these specific interventions took hold, the philanthropists' vision for higher education—a system of a small number of elite universities and a large group of vocational and technical programs—never fully came to realization. Indeed, regional publics, small liberal arts colleges, teachers colleges, and land-grant universities only grew in number, despite the reformer philanthropists' lack of support. Ris concluded that these reform-minded philanthropists "had money and a mandate, but ultimately they could only coerce and cajole, not dictate... [especially] for the institutions that they had designated as losers [which] had nothing to lose from defying [them]" (2022 p. 295).

DYNAMIC

Complex adaptive systems exist in a state of continual change, thanks to the many parts, relationships, and external forces at work. This creates continuous learning opportunities that are difficult to trace to any single precipitator. Diversity allows these systems to flourish by introducing new stimuli that helps them learn and adapt to a greater variety of new circumstances. Viewing new conditions as an opportunity, not a threat, may be an important shift in how we frame higher education's role in redesigning and renewing American democracy. After all, over time, the country has grown, become home to an increasingly diverse population, and has taken on new roles domestically and on the global stage. It simply isn't possible to go back to some past version of the American system without extinguishing the parts of the system that have emerged since that past version existed. That doesn't mean that some won't try, though, as shown by recent efforts to roll back racial equity efforts and to promote educational censorship in K–12 and higher education, discussed at length in other chapters in this book.

Even small changes to a complex adaptive system can produce dramatic effects if they impact the "source code" or initial conditions of the system's development (Begun et al. 2002). For example, an increase of two degrees Celsius would be an insignificant temperature change on any given day but, as a permanent temperature change, will wreak havoc on global systems because it fundamentally change core global climate conditions.

The pro-democracy movement within higher education has been less dynamic over the past 20 years due to waning funder attention, competition for resources, and shifting institutional priorities. Many efforts have atrophied, gone stale, or ended altogether. The time has come to let those movements evolve to meet the moment—and that should start by introducing stimuli such as new relationships and ideas. After all, many existing efforts were born in optimistic periods in American history such as the post-war period in the 1950s and the beginning of the 21st century, when democracy was on the rise globally, the American economy was growing, racial equity was not much of a priority, and higher education was not politicized to the degree it is today. Conditions have changed dramatically and so should our strategies for responding to them.

RESILIENT

Complex adaptive systems are strong and durable over time because they have clear system boundaries honed by experience that define the system's identity and what's in and out. This helps systems weather inherent external unpredictability as they adapt to changing dynamics while maintaining system integrity.

This resiliency brings some solace as higher education faces a wave of threats from censorship, governance changes, enrollment drops, and wavering public opinion. Colleges and universities have weathered seasons of change before—and their large number, ubiquity through the United States, and significant number of constituents will make it nearly impossible to stamp them out.

At the same time, with elements of their "source code" now in play, higher education actors must rise to the challenge by becoming more dynamic and responsive to external threats and critiques. One way to do that involves building stronger relationships with allies and potential partners. After all, connections within and across complex adaptive systems make the whole something more than the parts (Slaughter & Garlow 2023). Fostering relationships can introduce new stimuli, add capacity to enhance system functions, and build resilience to ongoing change. For higher education and philanthropy, opportunities for better connection abound. With their resources, convening power, and large networks, private foundations may be among the most important for higher education to engage, but they are often hard to understand. The next section will shed some light on the system boundaries of private foundations.

SYSTEM BOUNDARIES OF PRIVATE FOUNDATIONS

Private foundations can be opaque to those outside the sector. Thus, I hope this analysis based on my own experience will shed light on why private foundations are not good candidates for baseline support for some institutions and social programs but can be essential for other efforts, particularly in a period of change.

Private foundations are not organized around *giving money* but about providing support in service of specific charitable purposes as identified at their founding and approved by the Internal Revenue Service to award tax-exempt status. The philanthropic sector is too often painted with a broad brush, with little awareness of the number and variety of organizations and donors. Most analyses tend to focus on the largest, most visible foundations, which masks significant parts of the landscape and makes too many assumptions that all foundations follow similar tendencies. Many prospective beneficiaries see philanthropic organizations as mere sources of capital—not necessarily partners worthy of deeper relationships. They also tend to conflate what's good for their own context with what's good for all of higher education, let alone the country itself.

Even private foundations with generous endowments and annual giving budgets soon find that their funding doesn't go as far as they would like. Philanthropic spending pales in comparison to governmental spending in the US. For example, education is a top subject area for philanthropic support, receiving about $23.4 billion annually, which is more than a quarter of all US philanthropic funding (Candid 2021). But this was less than a quarter of what the U.S. Department of Education spent ($94 billion in Fiscal Year '23), not to mention states (the predominant funder of public institutions) and other federal agencies (USASpending.gov 2023).

As a result of trying to have impact with limited resources, private foundations change strategy over time as they consider the needs of the day and the results of their prior efforts. Foundations generally retain control over strategic changes in priorities and direction with little public accountability. It can be deeply frustrating to be a grantee when a foundation changes direction, but it's also a key boundary of how private foundations act.

Indeed, a core characteristic of private foundations is their special freedom to act with minimal external friction. They do not need to rely on elections, fundraising, public opinion, or political clout to act. They can change strategy quickly and can take the long view on impact. Jamie Merisotis, President and CEO of Lumina Foundation, has written, "[P]hilanthropic organizations—particularly well-endowed, private foundations such as Lumina—exist for one reason: to use the assets we hold in trust to act as society's risk-takers" (Merisotis 2014).

What does this look like in practice? Foundations regularly support problem definition, solution development and testing, and communications and convening strategies to share lessons learned and implications for others. Ideally, these efforts will elevate marginalized voices, experiment with new ideas, and fill in funding for efforts that public financing can't support. Private foundations can also mobilize funds for unexpected emergencies while also committing to an issue for the long term. These processes can inform how governments, employers, and social movements define and implement larger-scale strategies. For example, foundations have routinely enhanced federal funding opportunities by convening prospective beneficiaries to let them connect with experts, hear from peers, and have space to meet as an applicant team to develop strategies outside their daily grind.

But private foundations' freedom has a downside. The ability to move quickly with a relatively small number of people may mean bypassing the hard, necessary work of creating public buy-in. Many K–12 funders experienced this during the rise and fall of the Common Core State Standards. The Standards were adopted rapidly by most states and endorsed by the federal government, but their ascent came to a halt as teachers and local officials pushed back on what they felt was an agenda imposed on them from above. Moreover, a similar line of critique has been used by autocratic voices to push out foundations and their partners. As Hungarian Prime Minister Viktor Orbán's spokesman observed with regard to pushback against the regime from the nonprofit and philanthropic space, "With all due respect, most of these N.G.O.s are basically following a political idea. The problem is that these N.G.O.s have never been elected. Altogether, they represent a couple of hundred people, without a democratic mandate" (Zerofsky 2019).

CONCLUSION: GETTING STARTED ON STRENGTHENING TIES BETWEEN HIGHER EDUCATION AND PHILANTHROPY

As we have seen, philanthropies give billions annually to democracy and higher education in the United States. These funding flows, however, are separate and not well calibrated to the actions that colleges could take to have the most positive impact on strengthening democracy.

Improved relationships might start by identifying specific issues where higher education needs to evolve its role in democracy. After all, most funding relationships start with the prospective grantee pitching a good idea. Success here may not only improve higher education's ability to attract philanthropic funding for its democracy efforts but also enhance how it defines postsecondary education quality, equity, and relevance to the broader community.

Meanwhile, private foundations should lean into their role as convenors and problem definers to inform how higher education actors develop strategies. As one scholar has observed, this "problem-centered thinking often does not come naturally to scholars who normally derive direction from the internal questions that are debated within disciplines" (Clotfelter 2005, p. 17). Over the past few years, my work at Lumina has involved getting to know the higher education and democracy community and identifying areas where more work is needed. These include:

1. Teaching and learning strategies that promote engagement across difference and attend to the needs of diverse student populations,

particularly students of color, adult learners, and students with work and family responsibilities;
2. Strategies for community and technical colleges that do not merely duplicate what has worked in four-year settings, particularly in how their academic offerings build community and strengthen democracy;
3. Better recognition of the full array of democracy- and community-building behaviors that go beyond voting, including those valued by Gen Z but not usually embraced by older generations (e.g., protest, informal community support);
4. Stronger evidence of the impact of civic and community-based learning opportunities on behavior after graduation; and
5. Connecting teaching and learning approaches to strengthen democracy with effective responses to the climate crisis, the rise of Artificial Intelligence, and other major societal challenges.

More focus on these areas could enhance how individual colleges define their own unique role in the abstract project of democracy. After all, our daily existence takes place in human-sized places where positive work across difference may be more likely because it is less clouded with polarized national dialogue. Colleges are physically part of a wide variety of communities, while also being well-networked through membership organizations and other collaborative efforts. This makes higher education a potentially powerful scaling partner for democracy-building strategies.

In so doing, colleges may help provide understanding of an underexplored area in the democracy movement. Most democracy-building efforts focus on individual- or systems-level change—think get-out-the-vote campaigns and ranked choice voting proposals—but neglect the spaces where people come together in community. These places have diminished in number and evolved into entirely different forms (e.g., online communities and social media). Colleges both represent these types of collective settings—and are one of the few that purposely draw people from many different backgrounds and put them into classrooms, dorms, clubs, and stadiums to accomplish something with people they may never have met otherwise (More in Common & SNF Agora Institute, 2023).

To meet these opportunities, higher education does not necessarily need to launch a lot of new initiatives, but first look for existing capacity and potential connections with other reform movements, even if they don't have "democracy" in the title. One particularly promising connection could bridge colleges' democracy-building efforts with attainment and student success movements. Over the last two decades, private foundations like Lumina have been committed to building capacity in higher education to support access, retention, and completion. Most funding in these areas has turned away from institutions themselves and toward national and regional intermediary organizations as scale and policy change became dominant concerns (Haddad 2021). Key areas include data collection and analysis, attending to the full range of student needs (financial, personal, health, and academic), policy incentives and accountability measures, structural academic reform to the credit hour and general education requirements, and the promotion of coherent program pathways.

Civic and community-based learning efforts could connect more overtly here, given strong evidence that these experiences support retention and completion (Chittum et al. 2022). Moreover, the student success movement could provide insight for designing civic interventions more attentive to race, gender, socioeconomic status, age, and other elements of student identity. After all, a macroanalysis of the last decade of research on civic and community-based learning practices found that only about a fifth of studies with generalizable findings address outcomes for historically underserved groups; those that do focus almost exclusively on retention and graduation outcomes (Chittum et al. 2022, p. 23).

Working together, higher education and philanthropy could break important new ground in democracy movements. Higher education, at its best, can shape millions of students' ability to make meaning and have impact in the world. Colleges can serve as anchors for their communities, offering expertise, physical space, and a promise to stay put (something few other employers can do). Campuses stretch from coast to coast, into nearly every community in the country. Philanthropy, at its best, can use its flexibility and freedom to foster new ideas, coalitions, and evidence to create the conditions for American democracy to deliver for its people today. It can point toward the opportunities for growth, for addressing past wrongs, and for establishing a shared vision about who we are as a country, as communities, and as individuals. Together, they could refine what modern democracy movements need from their citizens to thrive and develop a wide variety of teaching and learning approaches to meet that need in thousands of different American communities. It will be hard work to get started, even harder to keep going, but this labor will produce innumerable benefits for students, faculty, and the country as a whole.

REFERENCES

Begun, J. W., Zimmerman, B., & Dooley, K (2002). *Health care organizations as complex adaptive systems.* https://www.napcrg.org/media/1278/beginner-complexity-science-module.pdf

Candid. (2021). *Key facts on U.S. nonprofits and foundations.* https://www.issuelab.org/resources/38265/38265.pdf

Candid. (n.d.). *Philanthropy and democracy dashboard.* https://democracy.candid.org/dashboard/

Chittum, J. R., Enke, K. A. E., & Finley, A. P. (2022). *The effects of community-based engagement in higher education: What we know and questions that remain.* Association of American Colleges and Universities. https://www.aacu.org/research/the-effects-of-community-based-engagement-in-higher-education

Clotfelter, C. T. (2005). *Patron or bully? The role of foundations in higher education.* Terry Sanford Institute of Public Policy at Duke University, Working Papers Series SAN05-09. Retrieved from: https://files.eric.ed.gov/fulltext/ED493390.pdf

Cohen, M. D., & March, J. G. (1974). *Leadership and ambiguity: The American college president.*

Council for Advancement and Support of Education. (2023). *CASE insights on voluntary support of education (United States): 2022 key findings.* https://www.case.org/system/files/media/inline/VSE%202022%20Key%20Findings.pdf

Giving USA Foundation. (2021). *2021 giving overview: Tableau visualization.* https://givingusa.org/giving-usa-limited-data-tableau-visualization/

GR Editors. (2021, May 20). Conservative author and venture capitalist J. D. Vance: eliminate all special tax privileges for foundations. *The Giving Review.* https://www.thegivingreview.com/conservative-author-and-venture-capitalist-j-d-vance-eliminate-all-special-tax-privileges-for-foundations/

Haddad, N. (2021). Philanthropic foundations and higher education: The politics of intermediary organizations. *The Journal of Higher Education, 92*(6), 897–926. https://doi.org/10.1080/00221546.2021.1888635

Hope, E. C. (2022). *Rethinking civic engagement.* Brennan Center for Justice. https://www.brennancenter.org/our-work/research-reports/rethinking-civic-engagement

Johnson, P. D. (2018). *Global philanthropy report: Perspectives on the global foundation sector.* Harvard Kennedy School, Center for Public Leadership. Retrieved from https://cpl.hks.harvard.edu/files/cpl/files/global_philanthropy_report_final_april_2018.pdf

Kinder Foundation. (n.d.). *Kinder Institute on constitutional democracy.* http://kinderfoundation.org/major-gifts/education/kinder-institute-on-constitutional-democracy/

Merisotis, J (2014). *A leadership model of philanthropy for student success.* Lumina Foundation. https://www.luminafoundation.org/wp-content/uploads/2014/05/leadership-model-of-philanthropy.pdf

More In Common & SNF Agora Institute. (2023). *Searching for a new paradigm: Collective settings.* https://snfagora.jhu.edu/wp-content/uploads/2023/12/SNF-Agora-Institute_MIC_Collective-Settings_12.5.23.pdf

National Center for Education Statistics. (2022). *Fast facts: Educational institutions.* Retrieved April 25, 2023, from https://nces.ed.gov/fastfacts/display.asp?id=1122

National Center for Education Statistics. (n.d.). *IPEDS trend generator—Employees and instructional staff.* Retrieved April 25, 2023, from https://nces.ed.gov/ipeds/TrendGenerator/app/answer/5/30

National Center for Education Statistics. (n.d.). *IPEDS trend generator—Institutional revenues: What are the revenues (in thousands) of public postsecondary institutions using GASB standards?* Retrieved April 25, 2023, from https://nces.ed.gov/ipeds/TrendGenerator/app/answer/6/13;

National Center for Education Statistics. (n.d.). *IPEDS trend generator—Institutional revenues: What are the revenues (in thousands) of private not-for-profit postsecondary institutions using FASB standards?* Retrieved April 25, 2023, from https://nces.ed.gov/ipeds/TrendGenerator/app/answer/6/15

National Center for Education Statistics. (n.d.). *IPEDS trend generator—Institutional revenues: What are the revenues (in thousands) of private for-profit postsecondary institutions using FASB standards?* Retrieved April 25, 2023, from https://nces.ed.gov/ipeds/TrendGenerator/app/answer/6/17

National Center for Education Statistics. (n.d.). *IPEDS trend generator—Student enrollment.* Retrieved April 25, 2023, from https://nces.ed.gov/ipeds/TrendGenerator/app/answer/2/2

National Student Clearinghouse Research Center. (2023, February 2). *Current term enrollment estimates—Spring 2022.* https://nscresearchcenter.org/current-term-enrollment-estimates/

Obama Foundation. (2022, September 13). *The Obamas and Brian Chesky announce the inaugural cohort of Voyager Scholarship recipients.* https://www.obama.org/updates/the-obamas-and-brian-chesky-announce-the-inaugural-cohort-of-voyager-scholarship-recipients/

Park, J. (2017, October 8). An introduction to complexity theory. *Medium.* https://medium.com/@junp01/an-introduction-to-complexity-theory-3c20695725f8

PEN America. (2023). *Champions of higher education.* https://pen.org/champions/

Philanthropy News Digest. (2023, January 6). Large gifts to universities totaled nearly $4 billion in 2022. Candid. *Philanthropy News Digest.* https://philanthropynewsdigest.org/news/large-gifts-to-universities-totaled-nearly-4-billion-in-2022

Polarization & Extremism Research & Innovation Lab. (2022). *Building resilient & inclusive communities of knowledge.* https://perilresearch.com/resource/brick-building-resilient-inclusive-communities-of-knowledge/administrators/overview/

Ris, E. W (2022). *Other people's colleges: The origins of American higher education reform.*

Slaughter, A., & Garlow, E (2023, March 28). Beyond industrial policy. *Diplomatic Courier.* https://www.diplomaticourier.com/posts/beyond-industrial-policy

Sweezy v. New Hampshire, 354 U.S. 234 (1957)

Tocqueville, A. (1840). *Democracy in America: Volume II* (H. Reeve, Trans.). Project Gutenberg. Retrieved from: https://www.gutenberg.org/files/816/816-h/816-h.htm#link2HCH0026

Thomas, N., Gismondi, A., Gautam, T., & Brinker, D. (2020). *Democracy counts: A report on U.S. election vulnerabilities.* Institute for Democracy & Higher Education. Retrieved from https://tufts.app.box.com/v/democracy-counts-2020

USASpending.gov. (2023). *Agency profile: Department of Education (ED).* https://www.usaspending.gov/agency/department-of-education?fy=2023

Zerofsky, E. (2019, January 7). Viktor Orbán's far-right vision for Europe. *The New Yorker.* https://www.newyorker.com/magazine/2019/01/14/viktor-orbans-far-right-vision-for-europe

Zimmerman, B., Lindberg, C., & Plsek, P. (1998). *Edgeware: Lessons from complexity science for health care leaders.* VHA Inc.

SECTION II

BUILDING INSTITUTIONAL AND ADMINISTRATIVE
CAPACITY FOR POLITICAL LEARNING AND
DEMOCRATIC ENGAGEMENT

CHAPTER 7

FOSTERING CAMPUS CULTURES THAT ARE ALL IN FOR NONPARTISAN DEMOCRATIC ENGAGEMENT

Stephanie King
ALL IN Campus Democracy Challenge at Civic Nation

Jennifer Domagal-Goldman
ALL IN Campus Democracy Challenge at Civic Nation

ABSTRACT

In the last 10 years, the higher education sector has experienced a growing number of nonprofit partners and programs intended to foster and support nonpartisan college student civic learning, political engagement, and voter participation efforts. The Students Learn Students Vote Coalition maintains a list of over 300 nonpartisan student voting related and campus-based partners connected to civic engagement in higher education (Students Learn Students Vote Coalition, 2023). One such program that works to institutionalize nonpartisan democratic engagement efforts with colleges and universities is the ALL IN Campus Democracy Challenge (ALL IN). The ALL IN program

Leaning Into Politics, pages 101–119
Copyright © 2024 by Information Age Publishing
www.infoagepub.com
All rights of reproduction in any form reserved.

was founded in 2016 as a nonpartisan initiative of the 501(c)(3) Civic Nation. To date, ALL IN supports a network of more than 1,000 campuses in all 50 states and the District of Columbia through their theory of change, which is designed to offer structure, support, and recognition to higher education institutions. The article discusses emergent data from ALL IN's program and community of practice initiative. The data will focus on evidence from ALL IN's campus action plan analysis, surveys, and assessment of national voter registration and turnout rates compared to program objectives. Based on evidence from ALL IN's campus action plan analysis, surveys, and assessment of national voter registration and turnout rates compared to program objectives, the authors make recommendations for what steps campuses and practitioners can take to institutionalize their efforts to ensure students graduate prepared to be politically engaged in their communities and our democracy.

This chapter explores the impact of the ALL IN Campus Democracy Challenge program by way of quantitative and qualitative data related to nonpartisan campus democratic engagement action planning, as well as college student voter registration and turnout efforts in midterm and general elections. Specifically, it highlights campus data by institution type (e.g., Minority Serving-Institutions, Hispanic-Serving Institutions, Historically Black College and Universities, community colleges) connected with program engagement, especially emergent data from ALL IN's community of practice program. Based on evidence from ALL IN's campus action plan analysis, surveys, and assessment of national voter registration and turnout rates compared to program objectives, the authors make recommendations for what steps campuses and practitioners can take to institutionalize their efforts to ensure students graduate prepared to be politically engaged in their communities and our democracy.

In 2012, the National Task Force on Civic Learning and Democratic Engagement released the report *A Crucible Moment: College Learning and Democracy's Future*. The *Crucible Moment* report was commissioned by the U.S. Department of Education, in response to national discourse that effectively limited the mission of higher education to workforce preparation and training, while marginalizing learning that is fundamental to democracy. Since then, the higher education sector has experienced a growing number of nonprofit partners and programs intended to uplift and support nonpartisan college student civic learning, political engagement, and voter participation efforts (see, for example, Students Learn Students Vote, 2023; American Political Science Association, 2023).

Many of the organizations invested in supporting nonpartisan student democratic engagement are guided by a framework presented in the Task Force's (2012, p. 30) national call to action; the framework poses five essential actions to prepare students with the knowledge and skills necessary for informed civic responsibility and action. The five actions are:

1. Reclaim and reinvest in the fundamental civic and democratic mission of schools and of all sectors within higher education.
2. Enlarge the current national narrative to promote civic aims and civic literacy as educational priorities contributing to social, intellectual, and economic capital.
3. Advance a contemporary, comprehensive framework for civic learning—embracing U.S. and global interdependence—that includes historic and modern understandings of democratic values, capacities to engage diverse perspectives and people, and commitment to collective civic problem solving.
4. Capitalize upon the interdependent responsibilities of K–12 and higher education to foster progressively higher levels of civic knowledge, skills, values, and action as expectations for every student.
5. Expand the number of robust, generative civic partnerships and alliances locally, nationally, and globally to address common problems, empower people to act, strengthen communities and nations, and generate new frontiers of knowledge.

Many nonpartisan and democratically-focused nonprofit organizations responded to this call by stepping up to support students, campuses, and communities with establishing voter engagement plans as well as to deepen community engagement (e.g., the Students Learn Students Vote SLSV Coalition, the American Democracy Project at the American Association of State Colleges and Universities, NASPA and the Fair Election Center's Campus Vote Project. On SLSV, see Murray in this volume; on Campus Vote Project, see Kappus in this volume). One program that aspires to support each of the five proposed actions from a higher education context is the ALL IN Campus Democracy Challenge (https://allinchallenge.org/).

Beginning in 2013, colleges and universities were first eligible to receive comprehensive National Study of Learning, Voting, and Engagement (NSLVE) campus voting reports from the Institute for Democracy and Higher Education (IDHE). Data from IDHE's (2012) NSLVE analysis showed that only 45% of college students voted in the presidential election, compared to an estimated 57.5% of eligible citizens who voted that same year (Bipartisan Policy Center, 2012). These new data indicated that college *students* were neither registering to vote nor turning out to vote at the rates of college *graduates*, long known to register and vote at higher rates than the general population (Ahearn, Brand, & Zhou, 2023). Simultaneously, Ideas 42, a social and behavioral science firm, issued their (Neri, Leifer, & Barrows, 2016) report, *Graduating Students into Voters*. The combination of dismal national student voter engagement rates combined with new social science research identifying barriers to college student participation in the electoral process, and offering suggestions for ways to counteract these barriers, inspired the creation of the ALL IN Campus Democracy Challenge. This data gap pointed to a need and provided an opportunity for the ALL IN program to offer structure, support, and recognition to colleges and universities prioritizing the institutionalization of nonpartisan democratic engagement efforts and resources.

Neri and colleagues (2016), in the *Graduating Students into Voters* report, organized the barriers to college student voter engagement into three buckets: 1) new voters, not youth voters; 2) identity and self-expression; and 3) psychological distance. Table 7.1 explores the multiple expressions of each of these barriers explored further in the report.

Identifying the behavioral insights about the barriers to student political engagement from the Ideas 42 report offered a roadmap for campuses looking to change campus culture, breakdown stigmas and difficulties related to voting, and to ultimately increase student voter participation as one form of political engagement.

Further, as many institutional stakeholders explore the behavioral barriers for electoral participation by students, they are also mandated to make a "good faith" effort to register eligible students to vote through Section 487(a)(23) of the Higher Education Act of 1965 that references the National Voter Registration Act of 1993 (NVRA). The Higher Education Act requires that institutions in 44 States and the District of Columbia (Idaho, Minnesota, New Hampshire, North Dakota, Wisconsin, and Wyoming are exempt from the NVRA) distribute voter registration information and/or forms to students. However, defining what makes a good faith effort and mapping how to tie this to student-learning is not clearly articulated. This is where having a campus roadmap like ALL IN's theory of change (see Figure 7.1; *Higher Ed Insight*, September 2019) and steps for participating

TABLE 7.1 Graduating Students Into Voters–Barriers

1: New Voters, Not Youth Voters	2: Identity and Self-Expression	3: Psychological Distance
1a. Students are uncertain about the details and implications of registering and voting	2a. Most students do not view themselves as "voters"	3a. Students do not think concretely enough about voting
1b. Students are insecure about their level of political knowledge	2b. Students may be uncomfortable registering at school and unsure how to register at home	3b. Students do not link political participation and their everyday experiences
1c. Students overestimate the difficulty of registration and voting	2c. Voting is not visible on campus, so students don't think it's common	

Source: Neri, Leifer, & Barrows, 2016

campuses are helpful to institutional leaders. For instance, campuses that take the actions to participate in NSLVE, drafting and implementing robust, data-informed campus democratic engagement plans—combined with understanding core learning areas for students—can provide a more robust and sound guide to deepen the engagement of their students (see Miles et al., & Murray in this volume). Ultimately, allowing the campus culture to change to be one that includes a civic ethos.

HISTORY AND PRESENT OF ALL IN CAMPUS DEMOCRACY CHALLENGE

ALL IN empowers colleges and universities to achieve excellence in nonpartisan (meaning ALL IN does not support or oppose candidates for public office or take a stand for or against any political party) student democratic engagement, which it defines as including civic learning, political engagement, and voter participation. ALL IN encourages institutions of higher education to help students form the habits of active and informed citizenship, as well as to institutionalize democratic engagement activities and programs—making them a defining feature of campus life. ALL IN works with a variety of other nonprofits, nonpartisan organizations and efforts that together create an ecosystem intended to catalyze and support colleges and universities in their efforts to ensure students are informed and engaged participants in all aspects of our democracy.

ALL IN has grown to include more than 1,000 participating colleges and universities across all 50 states and Washington, D.C. These institutions include two-year and four-year, public and private colleges and universities, and enroll almost 10 million students. ALL IN's participating campuses include more than 250 community colleges and 265 minority-serving institutions (MSIs) composed of nearly 200 Hispanic Serving Institutions (HSIs) and 50 Historically Black Colleges and Universities (HBCUs). Collectively, participating campuses are at the forefront of this work and are helping to institutionalize and scale important efforts to ensure that nonpartisan civic learning and democratic engagement play a central role in student learning and development.

ALL IN'S THEORY OF CHANGE AND HOW IT WORKS

ALL IN strives to work with colleges and universities to improve civic learning, political engagement, and voter participation, collectively defined as democratic engagement. To best understand the ways in which ALL IN could differentiate itself within the nonpartisan student voting space and

106 ▪ S. KING and J. DOMAGAL-GOLDMAN

Figure 7.1 ALL IN theory of change (2022).

best support colleges and universities with institutionalizing nonpartisan democratic engagement, the ALL IN program went through a thorough external analysis with Higher Ed Insight (HEI) to yield a theory of change (HEI, September 2019).

ALL IN's theory of change (Figure 7.1) posits that the structure (program design and accountability), support (consultation, training, resources, and networking), and recognition (awards and accolades) that the ALL IN team provides to colleges and universities assists participating campuses to take a series of actions that help advance cultures of democratic engagement. The theory of change suggests that these actions result in higher education playing a significant role in fostering more engaged and inclusive democracy in the United States (HEI, September 2019).

Unlike traditional political organizing programs that focus on improving participation by directly registering voters, removing barriers to participation, making public service announcements, or implementing turnout tactics, ALL IN focuses on education, culture change, and long-term, sustainable impact. ALL IN is unique and innovative in that it seeks to not just have an impact on one specific election, but a residual effect on all following elections, as well as engagement between elections. ALL IN's program design provides structure so that an institution can assess where it is at, where it wants to go, and how it is going to get there. The institution first makes a public commitment to improvement and then unites siloed efforts through the formation of a campus-wide working group. The working group then participates in the continuous process of improvement using the structure of *Strengthening American Democracy: A Guide for Developing an Action Plan to Increase Civic Learning, Political Engagement, and Voting Rates Among College Students* (Students Learn Students Vote Coalition Partners, 2023) to set goals and document strategy in an action plan (for discussion on how such planning and structure directs attention of campuses, see Rank in this volume). Participating campuses are provided with ongoing support from ALL IN staff and fellows through consultations, trainings, educational webinars, reports, conference presentations, and communities of practice. These communities of practice have grown to include cohorts of campuses across athletic conferences, by cities, within states, as well as by institutional type.

Recognition is the final component of ALL IN's theory of change. The ALL IN Campus Democracy Challenge hosts a biennial awards ceremony in odd-numbered years to recognize campuses, campus voting coalitions, and individuals working to increase nonpartisan college student democratic engagement. Additional opportunities for recognition are built into our programming year-round including the annual Student Voting Honor Roll, Highly Established Action Plan Seal, and Most Engaged Campus recognition. Recognition is considered a key component of change management—in this case, the change being the setting of campus goals and strategy for nonpartisan voter engagement as demonstrated by participation in ALL IN and the development of campus action plans (see for example: Kezar & Eckel, 2022; Eckel, Hill, Green, & Mallon, 1999; and Kotter, 1995). Campus stakeholders reported in the initial and subsequent surveys that they found the recognition of campus efforts important to broader campus or buy-in and growth (HEI, 2020; see also Kedrowski in this volume).

ALL IN CAMPUS DEMOCRACY CHALLENGE PROGRAM MODEL

Campuses join ALL IN, complete a set of steps, are recognized for their commitment, and earn national seals and awards for exemplary efforts. Any accredited, degree-granting, post-secondary institution may participate and there is no cost to participate. To get started with ALL IN, campuses are asked to take the following actions (ALL IN Campus Democracy Challenge, 2023):

- *Make a Commitment.* Campuses make a public commitment to foster nonpartisan democratic engagement on campus. By joining with the other participating campuses, they send a collective message that this work is important.
- *Assemble a Coalition.* Campuses form a campus-wide working group or coalition composed of a diverse group of stakeholders including student affairs educators, faculty, administrators, students, and external nonpartisan partners. Campuses are especially encouraged to partner with local elections officials as an avenue to connect the campus more deeply to the governing process. Working with local election officials provides the campus direct access to any voting regulations students may need to abide by when casting a ballot and registering to vote. (see also Kedrowski, Miles & Murray in this volume.)
- *Plan.* The coalition develops and implements a nonpartisan campus democratic action plan using data from the National Study of Learning, Voting, and Engagement (NSLVE), administered by Tufts University's Tisch College (as of 2023, previously administered by IDHE), and by considering their campus' unique mission, demographics, and culture.
- *Share.* Campuses share their action plans and campus NSLVE reports with ALL IN. All action plans are shared online so that campuses can learn from one another. Campuses are also encouraged to publicly share their NSLVE reports.
- *Be Recognized.* All participating campuses are recognized for joining ALL IN and making a commitment to increasing student voting

rates and helping students form the habits of active and engaged citizenship. Campuses with student voting rates of over 20% in midterm elections and 50% in presidential elections also earn seals. Campuses and individuals leading work on campuses are also eligible for awards.

By completing these steps, campuses are *ideally* increasing their strategic capacity—the ability of institutional leaders to manage the resources available (e.g., budget, personnel, programming) to them in order to effectively institutionalize nonpartisan democratic engagement (Booth-Tobin, Munis, K.; Smithson-Stanley, L.; & Han, 2021). More specifically, when campus representatives create an action plan, they are thoughtfully mapping out the institution's ability to manage its resources and capabilities in pursuit of nonpartisan engagement being a part of the campus's culture. In asking an institution to *Make a Commitment,* the institution appoints a primary contact and joins ALL IN, and also the commitment is further emphasized when a senior leader signs on the ALL IN Presidents' Commitment. The Presidents' Commitment, while not an explicit ALL IN program requirement, was adopted in 2020 as a way for presidents, provosts, and chancellors to publicly express their support of their respective institution's dedication to advancing a campus civic ethos by doing more than the minimum requirements of the 1998 Reauthorization of the Higher Education Act of 1965 (ALL IN Presidents' Commitment, 2020).

Another component of a campus's strategic capacity is related to *Assembling a Coalition* of individuals to take part in these efforts with the buy-in from senior leadership. Having relevant stakeholders on an institution's voting coalition in a more formalized way has in some cases led to the creation of nonpartisan student voting groups, cross-campus collaborations, and working across sectors. The campus coalition takes ownership of documenting a campus's efforts to support year-round voter registration, education, turnout, and access in an action plan. When a campus creates a plan and shares it with their campus coalition, an institution is better positioned to implement specific strategies for starting new programs and initiatives or improving existing ones. The action plan process also takes goals and breaks them down into steps so that desired results can be achieved (Students Learn Students Vote Coalition Partners, 2023). The strength of the ALL IN program is that it provides campuses with structure, support, and recognition that holds them accountable to themselves and others and fosters long-term culture change that centers democratic learning and engagement as part of the collegiate experience. Later in this chapter we explore the correlations of action planning, voting coalitions, and senior leader engagement on voter registration and turnout with participating ALL IN campuses.

ALL IN ultimately seeks to help shift culture in three places: at the campus level, at the student level, and across the higher education sector (see right-hand column in Figure 7.1). The ALL IN program shifts culture at the campus level, by working with college and university senior leaders, faculty, staff, and campus voting coalitions to incorporate education for civic learning, political engagement, and voter participation into the ethos of an institution. ALL IN also supports campus culture at the student level, by instilling the value of lifelong participation in our country's democracy. Across the higher education sector, ALL IN works with a council of presidents and an array of higher education organizations, Secretaries of State, and other nonpartisan partners (i.e., through our participation in the Students Learn Students Vote Coalition). Taken together, ALL IN believes that our work to support students, campuses, and cross-cutting national efforts through conferences and partnerships helps to shape a more robust and inclusive democracy in which college students are informed and engaged.

CONTEXT OF HIGHER EDUCATION

All of the work that ALL IN and participating campuses do to foster cultures of nonpartisan democratic engagement on college campuses is done within a broader context of higher education and democracy in the United States. ALL IN works to advance student and institutional engagement across the curriculum and co-curriculum while nurturing and engaging with a broader national network of colleges and universities, higher education associations, and other partners. Taken all together, this work to ensure that college students have the experiences necessary to develop the knowledge, skills, attitudes, and behaviors needed for informed participation in our political sphere by fostering robust civic cultures on campuses will ideally result in a more robust, inclusive, and representative American democracy rom greater inclusion of college student voters and actors in our political sphere.

That said, the ALL IN program must be adaptable to many campus contexts to ensure the lived experiences of students at participating institutions can have an equitable opportunity to participate in the electoral process. As ALL IN introduces structure and support to its participating campuses, these are often built with the understanding that the needs of all campuses are not the same. For instance, the 2017 report, *MSI Vote: Ensuring Democracy and Promoting Voting through the Power of Minority Serving Institutions,* outlined the key issues that affect student and racial and ethnic minority turnout in elections across the nation (Hallmark & Martinez, 2017). This report stated that while various factors may influence an individual's ability to participate in the electoral process, higher education institutions that are minority-serving, should consider the distance to polling sites, the time it takes to get to those sites, and why these factors disproportionately affect students, especially those from minoritized groups. Hallmark and Martinez (2017) also examined the effects of various policies that perpetuate voter suppression at MSIs. To that end, ALL IN takes these factors into consideration and has created additional layers of support for MSIs, particularly Historically Black Colleges and Universities (HBCUs) and Hispanic-Serving Institutions (HSIs), by addressing the barriers proposed in the MSI Vote report.

One such effort to address barriers to students at MSIs is ALL IN's Community of Practice program. The community of practice model is based upon a foundational framework, whereby practitioners from similar communities have the opportunity to reflect in real time on their unique contexts and share promising practices (Lave & Wenger, 1991). ALL IN's community of practice model gathers stakeholders from campuses in cohorts by state, athletic conference, or campus type to convene regularly to share ideas, resources, and best practices for advancing nonpartisan democratic engagement on their individual campuses and across their cohort of campuses. ALL IN staff and campus fellows provide additional coaching, convening, and resources to these cohorts above and beyond what is provided for all participating campuses. ALL IN's approach with communities of practice is institutional in nature, goes beyond any one election cycle, and is resource-intensive.

METHODS

We established a two-pronged approach to collecting and evaluating the impact of the ALL IN program through an external evaluation by Higher Education Insight. First, we administer an annual survey of participating institutions in late fall (first conducted in 2019 by Higher Ed Insight). Completed by a campus' primary contact (a faculty member or administrator with responsibility for nonpartisan voter registration and engagement on campus), the results of the survey help us better understand how the initiative is strengthening practice and shifting culture on college campuses, as well as which aspects of ALL IN most facilitate transformative change. Second, we facilitate a quantitative analysis of changes in student voting rates at participating ALL IN campuses and make comparisons to non-participating campuses through a partnership with NSLVE facilitators and by comparing voting rates of ALL IN campuses with the national average.

EVIDENCE OF IMPACT

ALL IN's first survey of campus stakeholders—specifically the faculty, staff, and administrators responsible for nonpartisan voter engagement efforts on campus and serving as primary contacts to ALL IN staff—was administered by Higher Ed Insights (HEI) in 2019. Initial findings included that campuses believed that participation in ALL IN is having an impact on advancing nonpartisan college student voter registration, education, and turnout. Stakeholders also reported that access to resources—particularly campus staff time—was central to a campus's student democratic engagement work and to the level of engagement with ALL IN. HEI also found that participating campuses were taking steps to increase nonpartisan student democratic engagement and assessed their progress as moderately effective. Campus voting outcomes (e.g., registration and turnout) were closely tied to reported campus investment in increasing student democratic engagement (HEI, 2020).

From ALL IN's early, external quantitative evaluation by the Institute for Democracy and Higher Education (IDHE), ALL IN campuses experienced larger voting rate changes from 2014 to 2018 than non-participating campuses. The difference—1.7 percentage points—was statistically significant (IDHE, 2021). The change in the voting rates analysis demonstrates that the increase between 2014–2018 was largely attributable to an increase in yield rates (i.e., higher proportions of registered voters turning out to vote) at ALL IN-participating campuses. This is consistent with ALL IN's commitment to a more holistic student engagement philosophy than simply focusing on registration efforts. By comparing average reported college student voting rates provided by the NSLVE for the 2018 and 2020 elections with average rates of engaged ALL IN campuses, we determined that ALL IN-participation was associated with a mean turnout 2.2 percentage points higher than non-participating campuses in 2018 and that this trend persisted through the 2020 election (ALL IN, 2022a).

A comparison of the voter turnout and voter registration rates of institutions participating in ALL IN to the overall college rates shows that partnering with ALL IN makes a tangible impact on a campus's voting and voter registration rates. In fact, ALL IN's Impact Report (2022a) indicates:

- In 2018, campuses participating in ALL IN outperformed nonparticipating campuses by an average of 2.2 percentage points based on an external analysis of the election results.
- In 2020, campuses participating in ALL IN outperformed the national college student voting average of 66% by an average of 2.2 percentage points, a 16.2 point increase over 2016.

These differences in voting and registration rates demonstrate a clear, measurable impact of participation in the ALL IN program. On top of campuses that work with ALL IN generally, campuses that participate in State or City Voting Challenges or Athletic Conference Voting Challenges have the added benefit of operating as a community of practice, receiving customized support and resources, and garnering even better results. This community of practice model is already producing exciting results. In fact, campuses participating in an ALL IN organized community of practice cohort are outpacing other ALL IN campuses. Specifically, the ALL IN Impact Report (2022a) shows:

- ALL IN campuses participating in one of our State or City Campus Voting Challenges outperformed the national average by a full three percentage points.
- ALL IN campuses participating in one of our Athletic Conference Voting Challenges outperformed the national average by a full five percentage points.
- Campuses participating in a State, City, or Athletic Conference Voting Challenge are more likely to submit an action plan and submit a National Study of Learning, Voting, and Engagement (NSLVE) report to ALL IN showing deeper levels of program engagement from campuses in these cohorts.
- Additionally, early data indicate the promise of our HBCU community of practice, as participating campuses had higher than average levels of voter registration in 2020 (see more below).

This model suggests that participation in these types of cohorts results in higher engagement, registration, and turnout rates.

Through our comparison of average voter registration and turnout rate comparisons of campuses participating in both NSLVE and the ALL IN program and those that are participating in NSLVE but not ALL IN, we determined that ALL IN participating HBCUs outperformed the national average by 2.4 percentage points; ALL IN participating community colleges outperformed the national average by 3.5 percentage points, and ALL IN participating Hispanic Serving Institutions (HSIs) outperformed the national average by 7 percentage points. ALL IN seeks to engage more institutions of these respective types to increase their voter registration and turnout rates in 2022 and beyond, through participation in the ALL IN program and in-depth support through our communities of practice program.

In 2022, the ALL IN team expanded our communities of practice model to support more campuses by way of adding additional communities of practice for HSIs and community colleges in hopes of increasing student voter registration and turnout rates in future elections. ALL IN was able to hire seven Community of Practice Fellows—faculty and/or administrators at participating community colleges or Minority-Serving Institutions—to convene and coach cohorts of these types of campuses. ALL IN also provided financial support for institutions just beginning their nonpartisan democratic engagement efforts and worked to increase efforts to identify the tactics that enable these campuses to increase their student voter registration and turnout rates while infusing civic engagement into their campus cultures. ALL IN's focus is on recruiting and supporting new MSIs (especially HBCUs and HSIs) and community colleges as these campuses are generally the most under-resourced campuses.

ALL IN compared the average voter registration and turnout rates from the 500+ 2020 NSLVE reports that campuses provided directly to ALL IN as of January 2022 and compared them to published campus rates in *Democracy Counts 2020: Record-breaking Student Turnout and Resiliency* (Thomas, Gismondi, Gautam, & Brinker, 2021). Based on these comparisons, campuses actively engaged in ALL IN:

- had a voting rate of 68.2%, 2.2 percentage points higher than the average campus voting rate for the 1,200 campuses participating in NSLVE;
- had a registration rate of 83.8%, 0.8 points higher than the NSLVE average of 83.0%;
- that participate in an Athletic Conference Voting Challenge had an average voter turnout rate of 71.1% compared to 66% for all NSLVE campuses, a 5.1 point difference; and
- that participate in a State or City Voting Challenge campuses had an average voter turnout rate of 69% compared to 66% for all NSLVE campuses, a 3 point difference.

Overall, more engaged and committed campuses are seeing greater increases in student voting. We expect to have updated evaluation and impact data following our analysis of 2022 NSLVE data for ALL IN participating campuses in 2024.

CHALLENGES WITH INSTITUTIONALIZE NONPARTISAN ENGAGEMENT WITHIN THE HIGHER EDUCATION SECTOR

In examining the barriers to institutionalizing nonpartisan voter engagement in higher education, the ever-changing landscape of higher education and voting regulations are the primary obstacles to college student voting. For instance, while ALL IN works with nearly 1,000 campuses, the number of participating institutions wanes as colleges and universities close or merge. At least 44 public or nonprofit colleges have closed, merged, or announced closures or mergers since March 2020 (Castillo & Welding, 2023). In addition, the higher education sector has been experiencing a decline in enrollment for years. In Spring 2022, there was a 3.1% drop in enrollment compared to the year previous (Schwartz, 2023). While the decline began to slow in 2023 with only a 0.5% year over year decline, the overall trend in lack of enrollment in higher education institutions impacts an institution's ability to maintain staff, programs and services related to the student experience [i.e., nonpartisan voter engagement] (Lederman, 2023). While budget cuts due to dropping enrollment impact programmatic offerings of an institution, one of the biggest impacts to the ALL IN program is staff transitions.

Given the volume of staff transitions, many institutions struggle to maintain their nonpartisan voter engagement work and few, if any, have succession plans in place for when a personnel responsible for civic learning and democratic engagement leaves a campus. As reported in the 2022 ALL IN Nonpartisan Campus Democratic Engagement Action Plan Report (2023) only 31% of campuses that submitted a 2022 action plan had a full or partial leadership succession plan, though that number is up compared to 15% in 2020. In addition, 165 ALL IN campuses that joined the program before 2022 changed their ALL IN primary contact in 2022. These transitions in campus leadership make it challenging for campuses to complete the ALL IN program steps and to submit responses to self or institution reported surveys.

ALL IN continues to build relationships with the primary contact as transitions occur at participating institutions and as new campuses join the ALL IN program, the same can be said for the breadth of work ALL IN does in partnership with senior leaders (e.g., provost, presidents, chancellors). While ALL IN has continued to see growing interest from senior leaders regarding our nonpartisan efforts, it has become increasingly challenging to manage these relationships and related research projects due to a variety of factors. For instance, the turnover rate in senior leaders since the inception of the Presidents' Commitment in 2020 is staggering (Zackal, 2022). The COVID-19 pandemic exacerbated a longer-term trend of high turnover rates (Melidona, Cecil, Cassell, & Chessman, 2017) as more presidents delayed retirement when the pandemic hit (Zackal, 2022).

With the increased turnover, many senior leaders who have stepped into the president or chancellor position are either not the original signatory to the Presidents' Commitment for the institution or they are less familiar with the ALL IN program overall. Given the difficulties within the higher education sector related to staff transitions—at all levels—coupled with enrollment drops and budget cuts, institutionalizing nonpartisan democratic engagement is a challenge for many institutions. Further complicating the matter is the increase in legislation that impedes access to voting for young people (Guzman, Medina, & Siegel-Stechler, 2023). A prime example impacting the higher education sector is whether or not college IDs with quality as a form of identification in order to vote. In 2023, at least five states have either proposed or passed laws that would prohibit students from using their college-issued IDs to vote (Alonso, 2023). The inability to use a student ID as a form of identification for voting is a complex issue in that it is the only form of ID a college-age student has. As reported by the American Civil Liberties Union (2021) many Americans do not have one of the forms of identification states accept for voting. In fact, the ACLU describes Voter ID laws like the inability to use a campus ID as a form of ID as a legislative practice that deprives many voters of their right to vote. Therefore, asking campus personnel to manage internal obstacles in conjunction with legislative changes creates a challenging environment for campuses to regularly and effectively participate in the ALL IN program.

EMERGENT QUESTIONS AND WHAT'S NEXT

Throughout this chapter, we explored an example of a nonpartisan democratically focused organization working to support campuses with preparing Americans and all students for civic responsibility through higher education as defined through the National Task Force on Civic Learning and Democratic Engagement's 2012 report's call to action. While the framework of the ALL IN program considers the psychological barriers to student voting, and the difficulties for various institution types (e.g., Minority-Serving Institutions), there is much to be learned about institutionalizing democratic practice into the collegiate experience. There are four areas we think should be explored further to support campus stakeholders with the prioritization of nonpartisan democratic engagement. These areas include: 1) Campus action planning; 2) leadership succession planning; 3) the role of senior leaders; and 4) the work of nonpartisan student voting groups. We outline each of these priority areas and recommendations for future exploration.

- **Campus action planning**: Campuses are developing strategic capacity as they draft, implement, and improve data-informed campus action plans for nonpartisan college student civic learning, political engagement, and voter participation. It would be helpful for more nonpartisan organizations focused on civic engagement to work in collaboration with programs like ALL IN to help more campuses create campus voter coalitions and draft data-informed action plans earlier in the action planning cycle, allowing for plans to be improved and implemented in a timely manner. (For more on action planning, see Rank in this volume.)
- **Leadership succession planning**: With the immense turnover rates in faculty, staff and leadership on college and university campuses, groups like ALL IN are experiencing first-hand how important it is that nonpartisan voter engagement work belongs somewhere on

campus, such as embedding the work in the function of an office. We also recommend that colleges and universities identify at least one person's job description to include political engagement and that there is planning in place for that work to continue beyond the tenure of the specific individual.
- **Senior leadership**: While the peer-to-peer student efforts are essential to this work, increasingly we see that the commitment and buy-in of senior leaders across higher education—presidents/chancellors, system heads, provosts, and deans—matters in creating robust cultures of nonpartisan democratic engagement on campuses as well as ensuring sufficient financial and other resources for this work.
- **Student voting groups**: The proliferation of nonpartisan campus voting groups, especially those connected with broader coalitions of faculty, staff and local stakeholders (including local elections officials/offices), is fast becoming an important tactic in this work. These groups become personal to students on campus, respond to needs specific to local campus ecosystems, and ensure student input from the campus to the national level.

For further exploration, we implore all higher education stakeholders to consider these four key areas of an institution's strategic capacity to manage its resources and capabilities in pursuit of the institutionalization of nonpartisan democratic engagement.

REFERENCES

Ahearn, C. E., Brand, J. E., & Zhou, X. (2023). How, and for whom, does higher education increase voting? *Research in Higher Education, 64*, 574–597. https://doi.org/10.1007/s11162-022-09717-4

ALL IN Campus Democracy Challenge. (March 2023). *2022 ALL IN annual report.* https://allinchallenge.org/wp-content/uploads/2022-ALL-IN-Annual-Report.pdf

ALL IN Campus Democracy Challenge. (2023a). *How does the challenge work?* https://allinchallenge.org/challenge/how-work/

ALL IN Campus Democracy Challenge. (2023b). *2022 ALL IN Nonpartisan campus democratic engagement action plan report.* https://allinchallenge.org/wp-content/uploads/2022-ALL-IN-Nonpartisan-Campus-Democratic-Engagement-Action-Plan-Report.pdf

ALL IN Campus Democracy Challenge. (2022a). *Impact report.* https://allinchallenge.org/wp-content/uploads/ALL-IN-Impact-Report-Final_2022.pdf

ALL IN Campus Democracy Challenge. (September 2022b). *Theory of change.* https://allinchallenge.org/wp-content/uploads/ALL-IN-Challenge-Theory-of-Change.pdf

ALL IN Campus Democracy Challenge. (2020). *Presidents' commitment.* https://allin challenge.org/presidents-commitment-background/

Alonso, J. (2023, July 7). State voter ID laws in flux, Student IDs in question. *Inside Higher Ed.* https://www.insidehighered.com/news/students/free-speech/2023/07/07/bans-student-ids-voting-proposed-five-states

American Civil Liberties Union. (2021) *Fact sheet on voter ID laws.* https://www.aclu.org/documents/oppose-voter-id-legislation-fact-sheet

American Political Science Association. (2023, July 15). *Civic engagement groups.* https://connect.apsanet.org/raisethevote/civic-engagement-groups/

Bipartisan Policy Center. (2012): *2012 voter turnout report.* https://bipartisanpolicy.org/report/2012-voter-turnout/

Booth-Tobin, J., Munis, K., Smithson-Stanley, L., & Han, L. (2021). *Understanding strategic capacity in constituency-based organizations.* Baltimore, MD: P3 Labs at Johns Hopkins University. https://drive.google.com/file/d/1AOkvH0yB2S66QBI2Bs4lXiIu7O57m3z7/view

Eckel, P., Hill, B., Green, M., & Mallon, B. (1999). *Reports from the road: Insights on institutional change.* Washington, DC: American Council on Education (ACE).

Gagliardi, J. S., Espinosa, L. L., Turk, J. M., & Taylor, M. (2017). *American college president study.* American Council on Education.

Guzman, P., Medina, A., & Siegel-Stechler, K. (2023, March 22). *Voting laws and other access issues shaped the youth vote in 2022.* CIRCLE https://circle.tufts.edu/latest-research/voting-laws-and-other-access-issues-shaped-youth-vote-2022

Hallmark, T., & Martinez, A. (2017). *MSI vote: Ensuring democracy and promoting voting through the power of minority serving institutions.* Rutgers University Center for Minority Serving Institutions. https://cmsi.gse.rutgers.edu/sites/default/files/MSIvote.pdf

Higher education act of 1965 section-by-section analysis. (1965). U.S. Department of Health, Education, and Welfare, Office of Education.

Higher Ed Insight. (Spring 2020). *ALL IN Campus Democracy Challenge survey of participating campuses, Fall 2019.* https://allinchallenge.org/wp-content/uploads/ALL-IN-HEI-Member-Survey-Report_Spring-2020-Final.pdf

Higher Ed Insight. (September 2019). *ALL IN Challenge: Model of transformative change.* https://allinchallenge.org/wp-content/uploads/ALL-IN-Challenge-Report_HEI_September-2019.pdf

Institute for Democracy & Higher Education. (2012): *2012 NSLVE Findings.* https://idhe.tufts.edu/resources/2012-nslve-findings

Institute for Democracy and Higher Education. (January 2021). Evaluation of Civic Nation's ALL IN Campus Democracy Challenge. https://allinchallenge.org/wp-content/uploads/2021-IDHE-ALL-IN-Evaluation-Report.pdf

Kezar, A., & Eckel, P. (2002). Examining the institutional transformation process: The importance of sensemaking, interrelated strategies, and balance. *Research in Higher Education, 43*(3).

Kotter, J. P. (March-April 1995). Leading change: Why transformation efforts fail. *Harvard Business Review.*

Lave, J., & Wenger, E. (1991). *Situated learning: Legitimate peripheral participation.* Cambridge: Cambridge University Press. http://dx.doi.org/10.1017/CBO9780511815355

Lederman, D. (2023, October 2). *Citing significant budget deficits, several colleges face cuts.* Inside Higher Ed. https://www.insidehighered.com/news/business/cost-cutting/2023/10/02/several-colleges-plan-cuts-address-significant-financial-woes

Melidona, D., Cecil, B., Cassell, A., & Chessman, H. M. (2023). *The American college president: 2023 edition.* American Council on Education. https://www.acenet.edu/Documents/American-College-President-IX-2023.pdf

National Task Force on Civic Learning and Democratic Engagement. (2012). *A crucible moment: College learning and democracy's future.* Association of American Colleges and Universities.

Neri, D. J., Leifer, J., & Barrows, A. (2016) *Graduating students into voters: Overcoming the psychological barriers faced by student voters, A behavioral science approach.* Ideas 42. https://www.ideas42.org/wp-content/uploads/2017/05/Students_into_Voters.pdf

Schwartz, N. (2023, June 5). *These 5 charts break down spring enrollment trends.* Higher Ed Dive. https://www.highereddive.com/news/these-5-charts-break-down-spring-enrollment-trends/651951/

Students Learn Students Vote Coalition Partners. (2023). *Strengthening American democracy: A guide for developing an action plan to increase civic learning, political engagement, and voting rates among college students* (4th Ed.). ALLINChallenge.org. https://allinchallenge.org/wp-content/uploads/StrengtheningAmericanDemocracyGuideVOL4.pdf

Students Learn Students Vote Coalition. (2023, October 1). *Partner directory.* https://slsvcoalition.org/partner-directory/

Thomas, N., Gismondi, A., Gautam, P., & Brinker, D. (2019). *Democracy counts 2018: An analysis of student participation.* Institute for Democracy and Higher Education, Tufts University's Jonathan M. Tisch College of Civic Life. https://tufts.app.box.com/v/idhe-democracy-counts-2018

Thomas, N., Gismondi, A., Gautam, P., & Brinker, D. (2021). *Democracy counts 2020: Record-breaking turnout and student resiliency.* Institute for Democracy and Higher Education, Tufts University's Jonathan M. Tisch College of Civic Life. https://tufts.app.box.com/v/democracy-counts-2020

Zackal, J. (2022). *Riding the wave of college presidential turnover.* HigherEdJobs. https://www.higheredjobs.com/Articles/articleDisplay.cfm?ID=3013

CHAPTER 8

HOW AMERICA'S COMMUNITY COLLEGES SUPPORT DEMOCRACY

Belinda S. Miles
SUNY Westchester Community College

George Keteku
SUNY Westchester Community College

Tiago Machado
SUNY Westchester Community College

Glenetta Phillips
SUNY Westchester Community College

Rinardo Reddick
SUNY Westchester Community College

ABSTRACT

This chapter illuminates how the State University of New York's Westchester Community College (SUNY WCC) and other community colleges contribute to building and strengthening America's Democracy. Using theoretical,

---

Leaning Into Politics, pages 121–139
Copyright © 2024 by Information Age Publishing
www.infoagepub.com
All rights of reproduction in any form reserved.

historical, and practitioner frameworks, the authors explore the distinctive role of community colleges in providing opportunities to learn and practice aspects of democracy.

Curriculum, policy, and programmatic activities at many U.S. community colleges align in ways that demonstrate institutional commitment to preparing individuals for participation in a democratic republic. The general education curriculum standard at community colleges is typically designed to broaden understanding of self, others, and society (O'Banion, 2016). Many co- and extracurricular activities at community colleges provide opportunities for students to engage in activities that build skills such as advocacy, collaboration, and managing divergent perspectives, which are useful for civic engagement in a democracy. Policies established by college administrators and Boards of Trustees often reflect democratic ideals such as inclusion, equity, and fairness. Even campus structures can serve as artifacts of institutional culture that support or inhibit democracy learning and engagement.

Chapter authors represent diverse institutional perspectives providing readers with insight and authenticity based on observations as well as lived experiences.

Higher education has long played a role in helping to shape American democracy. The Morrill Act of 1862 (Morrill Act, 1862) that created Land Grant colleges and universities at once expanded and foreshadowed the enduring connection between public higher education and the practice of democracy. The first unambiguous evidence of this was the second Morrill Act that followed in 1890 (Morrill Act, 1890). Although it took 28 years to address the glaring flaw of excluding African Americans, the updated version in 1890 was an affirmation that a thriving democracy must provide universal access to higher education for all its population. President Truman's move to establish a Commission on Higher Education and the report it issued in 1947 (Zook, 1947) supporting the establishment of nationwide public community colleges further solidified the relationship between higher education and the practice of democracy. Among other things, the report reserved a vital role for community colleges with a substantial charge to meet the educational as well as workforce development needs of returning veterans and an expanding population.

Two important realities were at the heart of these twin national policies that spanned the nineteenth and the twentieth centuries. First, to consolidate American democracy and bolster a nation on the rise to a superpower status, it was an indispensable condition to provide universal access to postsecondary education. Second, to have a robust and thriving democracy, the nation's youth must be a big part of all civic engagements and, thus, make them ready to render service to country and community.

A year before the Truman Commission issued its report, the State University of New York's Westchester Community College (SUNY WCC) was founded. The impetus and the mandate for establishing SUNY WCC were not dissimilar to the drivers behind the Morrill Act in 1862 and 1890. In all these cases, the motivation and the assumptions were that a national democratic dispensation is aligned with the provision of affordable, quality higher education in the local community.

Having entered the landscape long after the founding of American higher education during the colonial era, community colleges have been considered a "disruptive innovation in academia that fosters an equitable and inclusive democracy" (Miles, 2019) since they made higher education more accessible and affordable, welcoming many more students who had limited access due to cost, location, and other restrictive barriers. Community colleges opened the door to more women, adult learners, veterans, first generation scholars, people of color, and other historically excluded or marginalized groups (Nora, 2000). Access to democracy learning was thus expanded to the droves of new enrollees, currently numbering nearly 12 million (AACC, 2023).

Now a thriving institution federally designated as both a Hispanic Serving Institution (HSI) and Minority Serving Institution (MSI) and serving more than 20,000 students annually, SUNY WCC is among the more than 1,000 U.S. community colleges that contribute to building and strengthening the nation's democracy through their curriculum, policies, and programmatic activities. These elements at American community colleges intersect in ways that reveal institutional commitment to preparing individuals for participation in a democratic republic. The general education curriculum, which is standard at community colleges, is typically designed to broaden understanding of self, others, and society (O'Banion, 2016). The co-curricular and extracurricular activities at community colleges extend this learning through opportunities for students to engage in activities that build skills such as advocacy, collaboration, and managing divergent perspectives—all useful for civic engagement in a democracy. Further, policies established by college administrators and Boards of Trustees often reflect democratic ideals such as inclusion, equity, and fairness. Even campus structures can serve as artifacts of institutional culture that support or inhibit democracy learning and engagement.

MISSION AND PURPOSE

The overarching mission and purpose of community colleges reflects and upholds democratic principles. The 1947 report of the Truman Commission describes community colleges as places that help "remove economic and geographic barriers to educational opportunity (Truman Commission Report, 1947, p. 67)." The report also implored colleges and universities to educate for the purpose of achieving a "fuller realization of democracy" (p. 1).

World wars depicted how once great democracies could succumb to totalitarian regimes. According to Harbour (2016), "this history showed that democratic institutions were fallible, and their failure could be catastrophic." The Truman Commission Report guidance to colleges and universities to instill in students "... self-discipline and self-reliance... ethical principles as a guide for conduct... sensitivity to injustice and inequality... [and] the spirit of democratic compromise and cooperation (p. 10)" signaled strong intent to counter such fallibility.

New York State Education law (2023) that governs community colleges including SUNY WCC emphasizes inclusion and the "open door" concept specifying even how "college facilities must be available for use in the late afternoon, evening, and summer to afford an educational opportunity for both full-time and part-time students and to assure maximum utilization of available physical resources." Beyond access, the state law also promotes roles for "community service and economic and workforce development programs and services" (Sec. 601.2).

With the purpose of providing citizens with equal access to higher education and to opportunities that completing a college education creates, Ronan (2012) describes both land-grant colleges and community colleges as "democracy's colleges." The Truman Commission Report (1947) elaborates: "The social role of education in a democratic society is at once to ensure equal liberty and equal opportunity to differing individuals and groups, and to enable the citizens to understand, appraise, and redirect forces, men, and events as these tend to strengthen or to weaken their liberties."

CURRICULUM

The community college general education curriculum serves, in part, to promote skills needed for participation in democracy. In "Now Is the Time: Civic Learning for a Strong Democracy," Hurtado (2019) states that "engaged citizenship requires development of college students' capacities and habits of mind that include knowledge, skills, and values to counter misinformation, negotiate conflict, and identify threats to a pluralistic democracy" and that "how and what we teach the next generation is critical to building a hopeful vision of an American society that is more equitable, sustainable, and economically stable, and is governed by a strong democracy."

At the very core of many community college missions is the commitment to prepare students for transfer to baccalaureate granting institutions or for entry to the workforce. The transfer curriculum is assumed to be the first two years of baccalaureate study inclusive of arts, humanities, social sciences, and liberal arts—often called the general education curriculum. It is broadly accepted that curricular areas in the general education clusters expand cognitive and critical thinking abilities valued in democratic society (Wynn & Ziff, 2023). Recognizing the substantial numbers of students completing such courses at community colleges and even in dual enrollment high school programs, the National Endowment for the Humanities (NEH) endowed funds to support faculty development and enriched curriculum at these institutions to ensure quality (Townsend, 2019).

SUNY policy on general education requirements makes provisions "for students concurrently enrolled and successfully completing SUNY credit courses designated as meeting SUNY General Education in the high school." The policy allows for granting SUNY General Education credit for those courses regardless of the term of matriculation and/or the general education program being completed (SUNY, 2021).

A robust example of relevant cross-disciplinary learning at SUNY WCC is how faculty members incorporated real world themes such as food and the environment into the general education curriculum to promote understanding "from multiple points-of-view" and "exploring relevant impacts within society"—desired skills for democratic engagement. Beginning in 2016, the Faculty Senate General Education Committee conducted the Integrative Learning Project (ILP) involving as many as 80 faculty who integrated selected themes into their teaching and explorations alongside cross-curricular and cross-departmental campus events (e.g., club activities, movie presentations, campus symposiums, etc.) connected to the themes. While the initiative was interrupted by the shift to remote learning in Spring 2020 due to the urgent health, family, and social concerns the college faced caused by a global pandemic, the experience was immersive and heightened the opportunity for broader learning and empathy. The Faculty Senate General Education Committee plans to resume this work in the future (personal communication, Rajan Shaun, October 5, 2021).

Studies looking at civic engagement among students attending community colleges highlight a handful of challenges that particularly confront these two-year institutions. Although these challenges are not considered insurmountable barriers, the literature tends to characterize them as especially embedded in the structural makeup of two-year colleges. For instance, a robust and positively linear relationship exists between the number of hours students spend outside the classroom on college campuses with increased civic and community engagement (Newell, 2014). This is particularly challenging for most community colleges because residential options are not part of the setup at inception or would not come to fruition in the near term. At any rate, the time students spend before and after classes for extracurricular activities are often severely constrained by several factors. SUNY WCC falls in this category of non-residential campuses, with most of its diverse student body commuting from home by bus, cars, and trains to the main campus and other off-campus sites. To turn this potential limitation into an advantage, the curriculum facilitates an upward and sturdy slope to civic engagement through the general education curriculum.

All matriculated students in each of SUNY WCC's four schools must complete as many as 30 credits of general education courses out of 60–64 credits required to earn an Associate of Arts or Science (A.A., or A.S.) degree or an Associate degree in Applied Science (A.A.S.). This is irrespective of whether a student's educational pathway leads straight to the workforce into "middle skills" jobs; well-paying work that requires more than a high school credential but not the bachelor degree (JPMorganChase, 2016) or to a four-year institution to earn a baccalaureate degree in the arts, humanities, natural science, social science, or in any of the areas in STEM. Preparation for direct employment typically occurs in Associate of Applied Study degrees that provide career and technical education that often leads to licensing and/or certification required for job entry. Nursing, Emergency Medical Technicians, and Respiratory Therapists are examples of such curricular areas. Although to a lesser extent than Associate of Arts or Associate of Science degrees, these occupationally focused degree programs include a general education component that ensures access to learning in the social sciences, humanities, and liberal arts.

For example, a student at SUNY WCC with the ambition of entering the police academy to become a law enforcement officer, or completing degree requirements to work as a radiology technician would be required to take 15 to 21 credits in humanities and social sciences. General education courses such as American History or Government, in Economics, or on the Native Peoples of America and so on, would invariably prepare and equip the student to think critically and engage effectively in supporting or defending democratic principles. Same goes for students transferring to pursue a pre-medicine or engineering degree in higher education.

Many community colleges also offer vocational training for skilled labor development through their workforce and community education units. These short-term non-degree programs often lead to industry specific certifications. However, they are not typically designed to promote skills development for democracy.

SUNY WCC is working to enhance its infrastructure for Applied Learning and Career Education to expand student engagement in hands-on real-world activities and solutions to all academic disciplines. Internships, job shadowing, and other work-based learning experiences leverage classroom learning extending it to the community and engaging stakeholders in mutually beneficial partnerships. These experiences expose students to diverse viewpoints and encourage understanding of cultural, socioeconomic, racial, emotional, interfaith, and gender differences—all of which have the potential to improve living in a democratic society.

Micro-credential badges are a related recent trend for community college offerings to help employers fill talent gaps with workers referred to as STARS; "skilled through alternative routes (McKinsey, 2022)." Designed to respond to quickly changing workforce needs, these credentials provide specific skills training and serve as an alternative or addition to traditional college degrees. A recent EdResearcher "study considered 25,891 survey responses from learners who started the courses between February 2017 and September 2021. The courses covered topics related to business, marketing, professional advancement, finance and data science (D'Agostino, 2023)." Programs like Braver Angels and Unify America referenced in the report encourage civic engagement and civil discourse by promoting skills like talking civilly and respectfully with people who have opposing views, listening deeply, and being open to a wide range of viewpoints. Awarding microcredentials in these areas could prepare students for rewarding service-learning, community engagement, and social justice projects as well as career (Mlyn, 2022).

SUNY WCC Service Information Leadership Badges (SUNY WCC Leadership and Service, n.d.) are given through the Department of Student Involvement for new and transfer students going to four-year colleges. The Leadership Badges include building skills to provide transferable skills in 20 hours of elective sessions from each of the six focus areas; the badges are self-paced, self-guided, and completed in one semester. Students commit to understanding Service-Learning and Servant Leadership. The six focus areas are 1) Employability, 2) Leadership skill building, 3) Theory, 4) Understanding Diversity, Equity, and Inclusion, 5) Health and Wellness, and 6) Service-Learning and Civic Engagement where students complete 10 hours of community service and provide a reflection on their experiences.

SUNY WCC's Commit to Change program is another service information program designed to allow students to participate in becoming change agents on campus building on their civic-rich duties towards belonging to the fabric of the college in supporting each other in leadership actions. This program reinforces learning and creates the social change necessary to reduce inequities and disparities within our campus community to try to ensure that scholars are actively implementing new and innovative models of leadership, civic engagement, conflict resolution, values and ethics, social change model, and power and privilege for the campus and the community.

This program is a cross-disciplinary connection for our students within their semesters. Commit to Change participants range from liberal arts to trucking, electricians, healthcare services, computers, culinary arts, and many more diverse training skilled labor careers. Commit to Change is a 12-week leadership development series. The overall premise of the program is to engage students in their development as leaders while working on a project that promotes positive social change within our college community and in the broader Westchester County community. The experience incorporates a SharkTank-style model for students to present initial project concepts, with faculty members serving as panelists to hear the groups and select projects and to serve as consultants or leads during the remainder of the session. Additional credentials students can achieve include: Mindful Warriors, LatinXcellance, Student Government Association (SGA), Orientation Leadership Program, and Alternative Spring Break Program.

Partially funded by the National Endowment of the Humanities (NEH), the Humanities Institute at SUNY WCC engages students with "humanities themes and ideas throughout their educational experience...encouraging critical thinking and cultural understanding while also reflecting the concerns of many of its community members. It provides them with the opportunity to consider their experiences and those of family members while learning more about the immigrant communities that together make up Westchester County (NEH for All, n.d.)." These activities provide more exposure and sensitivity to foster democratic ideals amid SUNY WCC and Westchester County's increasing diversity.

SUNY WCC is also committed to culturally responsive teaching methodologies (Patton, 2022) that "focus on students' assets rather than their deficits" to enhance engagement and learning. This asset-oriented pedagogy was developed by researchers at Arizona State University's Center for Broadening Participation in STEM (Arizona State University, 2023). SUNY WCC was recently awarded a $3 million grant from the National Science Foundation (NSF) to expand this work by increasing the recruitment, retention and graduation rates of students pursuing degrees in STEM, with a focus on serving Hispanic students. Through the grant, SUNY WCC leverages prior work with NSF Advanced Technology Education partner Mentor-Connect (2023)—a project that mentors community colleges in NSF grantsmanship—to establish a Hispanic-serving Institution resource hub (HSI-Hub). The HUB will serve as a catalyst for initiatives at 14 regional SUNY and CUNY community colleges to enable them to more effectively serve the HSI community and its stakeholders (Whissemore, 2023).

The grounds for the effectiveness of culturally responsive teaching methodologies have been prepared by continuous tweaking of extant practices common to community colleges. One of these is in developmental education, which was initially designed to develop the reading, writing or math skills of students who are deemed—usually through standardized tests—underprepared for college-level courses. Interestingly, developmental education programs, once an innovative plank designed to bridge the gap between high school and college readiness evolved to be a structural barrier to student success (Cullinan and Lewy, 2021) and, consequently, a potential inhibitor to democracy learning and engagement. Developmental education became a high obstacle for far too many students on the pathway to degree completion. Infused with the nation's democratic ethos and seeking to meet its goals of building minds and futures, SUNY WCC introduced steps that have nearly phased out the holding place the developmental education program had become.

Using alternative placement methods, SUNY WCC reduced placements in remedial math by 24.7 percentage points and remedial English by 24.8 percentage points for all new first-time degree-seeking students when comparing Fall 2015 and Fall 2022 SUNY WCC Institutional Research, Planning, and Effectiveness (2023). Alternative placements involve using multiple measures (Cullinan & Lewy, 2021) of prior academic performance and a co-requisite support course model to replace "high stakes" exams that placed inordinate numbers of students in remedial coursework. Similarly, SUNY WCC's Viking ROADS (Resources for Obtaining Associate Degree) program, a replication of the CUNY Accelerated Study in Associates Programs (ASAP) program, provides mandatory wrap-around supports to help students navigate coursework contributing to doubling the college's three-year graduation rate (Weissman, 2022; Weissman 2023). This type of program navigation improvement means increased exposure to curriculum and other experiences that increase awareness and practice with principles and ideals that support democracy learning.

This work is not without its challenges. The college continues to open its doors to candidates drawn from the entire Westchester region and its environs. The enduring intention to equip students with the ability to realize their full potential is still confronted with students poorly prepared for college work and having financial as well as other constraints of life. Innovations have been the way out of such constraints. SUNY WCC's Academic Support Center (https://www.sunywcc.edu/academics/asc) provides resources for all kinds of learners and actively works with faculty to help students improve their work. The College's Center for Teaching and Learning (WCC Center For Teaching and Learning, 2023) also supports faculty professional development to expand capacity to optimally support student learning.

Despite these challenges, skills acquired through general education are both iterative and cumulative. Bloom's taxonomy (Tabrizi & Rideout, 2017) is a frequently used rubric that assesses progression with increasingly complex cognitive learning abilities. Successive or higher-level skills such as judgment, analysis and synthesis described in Bloom's framework correlate with skills useful for democratic engagement. The Council of Europe's Competences for Democratic Culture (2023) also provides useful insight into skills that can be taught to prepare individuals to participate in democracy.

As scholars on higher education and civic engagement increasingly turn their attention to community college students, new insights are coming to the fore (Rosenbaum, 2020; Harbour, 2018; Turner, 2016; Newell, 2014;

Prentice, 2011). For instance, leadership commitment to civic engagement builds a culture of tolerance, that in turn, leads to the development of "students who could lead a cause (Harbour, pp. 37)."

CO-CURRICULAR AND EXTRACURRICULAR ACTIVITIES

Community colleges provide co-curricular and extracurricular activities that promote participation in democracy. SUNY WCC's participation in the National Study of Learning, Voting, and Engagement research initiative advances democratic learning and nonpartisan capacity building at community colleges (Harris et al., 2023). By providing campuses with disaggregated data around their distinct voting population, the study helps campus coalitions make data driven decisions in the development of their civic engagement strategic plans (see Leah Murray's chapter in this volume). In 2020, their national data included more than 1.8 million students from 265 community colleges. This report indicated that "in 2020, the rate of registered students who then voted hit 80%, an important milestone and signal that they are vested in their own futures and the health of democracy (Thomas et al., 2021)."

SUNY WCC was designated a "Voter Friendly Campus" which is administered through a partnership between the Fair Election Center's Campus Vote Project and NASPA. The designation is based on a campus plan to register, educate, and turnout student voters, by facilitating voter engagement efforts on campus, and through a final analysis of these efforts (including in the face of the upheaval caused by a global pandemic in 2020). The mission of the Voter Friendly Campus designation is to bolster efforts that help students overcome barriers to participating in the political process. As part of the effort to be designated a voter friendly campus, SUNY WCC helped 920 students register to vote in 2020. Due to the creative work of the campus coalition of faculty, staff and students, students were able to attend various virtual events aimed at informing voters on local, state, and federal issues. SUNY WCC fully embraces the civic mission of higher education to prepare students to be engaged participants in our democracy and is excited to continue engaging students in this essential work (SUNY WCC Strategic Plan, 2023).

Having signed on to the Presidents' Commitment in the All-In Democracy Challenge (2023), SUNY WCC's leadership supports and encourages education, action, and advocacy for the institution. Annual funding cycles typically unite faculty, students, staff, trustees, and other supporters in seeking support to sustain and grow the college. Additionally, New York Law (2023) requires the State's higher education institutions SUNY and CUNY (City University of New York) to provide voter resources and communicate registration information to all students. The State University Student Assembly also participates in Higher Education Advocacy Days.

Among on-campus voter coalitions that give students hands-on involvement in practicing democracy are: Student Government Association Standing Committee for Civic Engagement; the MotiVote software (Motivote, 2023) which gamifies civic engagement practices to encourage student participation; and a multi-tiered communication plan that includes emails, interactive social media posts and direct mail. Additionally, SUNY WCC partners with local community organizations including the League of Women Voters and the County Board of Elections.

Shared governance, one of the hallmarks of academia, is another way students and community college members engage in democracy practice. The American Association for Colleges and Universities states that "democratic principles should... be reflected in the way higher education institutions are governed, with the civic and democratic agenda influencing the institutional mission and vision and with all relevant stakeholders encouraged to participate in decision-making processes of the institution... This type of participation encourages the acquisition of practical knowledge of, and trust in, democratic and participative processes" (Gallagher, 2021). Changing student cohorts could make student engagement in shared governance seem volatile while taking "time to acknowledge, hear, and react to new groups of students honors their perspectives and promotes an atmosphere of mutual and respectful engagement in the collaborative decision-making process" (Miles et al., 2020)—desirable qualities for democracy.

Another significant caveat regarding student participation in extracurricular activities is that many students cite the problem of limited time and financial support as barriers to engagement (Thomas & Jones, 2017). Financial support they receive from programs like SUNY WCC's Viking ROADS or campus work-study jobs can alleviate this burden and spurn participation.

COLLEGE POLICIES

Community college policies offer another way to support democratic ideals. It is standard for college policies to underpin federal and state laws regarding protected classes, non-discrimination and other mandates for equality. Many higher learning institutions have evolved policies to embrace principles of diversity, equity, and inclusion more directly thus promoting fairness, participation, and belonging. SUNY Chancellor Dr. John B. King, Jr. recently asserted that, "at SUNY, our resolve to provide opportunity for all has never been stronger. The commitment to diversity, equity, and inclusion will continue to be a factor in every goal we pursue, every program we create, every policy we promulgate, and every decision we make" (SUNY News, 2023).

This commitment to inclusion is reflected in the designated "safe" spaces available to students according to affinity groups at SUNY WCC. SUNY Westbury's DEI webpage includes Holley and Steiner's (2005) description of safe spaces as "any physical space that allows students to feel secure enough to take risks, honestly express their views, and explore their knowledge, attitudes, and behaviors" without fear of retribution. Such spaces may also take the form of specialized First-year Orientation programs and seminars, English as a second language groups, adult learners, and more.

Safe spaces, as part of any institutional environment and places where those feeling particularly vulnerable can withdraw to, date to the 1960s. In the political atmosphere of that era, women on campuses especially fought for a place for an individual or a group retreat (Harris, 2015). In the heated political and social atmosphere of 2016 and beyond in America, these spatial arrangements triggered vociferous reactions, first, against a charge of overprotecting students, and later, on the grounds that safe spaces potentially undermine free speech rights on college campuses (Boyer, 2016; Franks, 2020; Grieve 2016; Jordan, 2017). While these two characterizations may or may not apply to many higher education institutions, especially community colleges, the mission of SUNY WCC nudges it to find ways to assist the diverse students who join the college community every academic year. With its open-door admission policy, SUNY WCC onboards generations of young people, most who are first in their families to gain access to higher education. The college's open gates provide access for well-prepared high school graduates as well as those in need of intense and targeted academic support. Added to the mix are international and non-traditional students who are embracing new opportunities for learning and career advancement.

The dividends for the college, Westchester County, New York State, and certainly the country, are enormous when the college succeeds in incorporating democratic ideals such as inclusion and belonging to support the success of each student. Above all, building minds and futures of students drawn from different affinity groups and designating places that reflect the national demographic composition is work done well by a community and in a holistic fashion (Jackson, 2021). At SUNY WCC, one of the many threats to student success and retention is students' ability to cope and deal with the relentless stress that accompanies rites of passage, transition from one way of life to another, financial difficulties, and many other issues that impact mental health. The college's response in understanding what students need and including safe spaces for individuals and/or groups to address and alleviate some of this angst helps students develop success strategies that keep them on track toward their goals.

Through the mission and goals set up for its Department of Mental Health and Counseling (DMHC), SUNY WCC pursues a holistic care for the students that goes beyond academics (Brown & Mangan, 2016; Harpalani,

2017). Thus, the DMHC mission is to create "a campus environment that is safe, growth fostering, and prioritizes the psychological, social, and emotional well-being of our community." The David Swope Student Center where the DMHC offices are located, also houses multiple services students (Counseling, Student Involvement, Student Government, cafeteria) and includes spaces for relaxation, meditation and devotion, and personal retreat (www.sunywcc.edu/student-services/mental-health-services/). All in all, SUNY WCC's safe spaces are important cogs in the drive to prepare students for civic engagement and democratic participation. In the end, healthy, vibrant students weather all storms and persist in their studies till they 'walk' at commencement (Harpalani, 2017) and into their futures.

CHALLENGES AND OPPORTUNITIES

In supporting democracy learning, community colleges and all institutions of higher education may find themselves facing challenges that often are at odds with the mission of engaging and supporting democratic ideals such as academic freedom and free speech. These challenges are complicated, often embroiled in the politicization of democracy as part of the local communities in which these institutions serve or the national context surrounding such communities. Among the struggles that institutions of higher learning may face as they attempt to strengthen democracy learning are political polarization, issues of free speech and academic freedom, and globalization and diversity.

Ziblatt (2023) notes that, "while some partisan polarization is healthy for democracy, one of the key drivers of democratic decay in new and established democracies is intense polarization, where political opponents begin to regard each other as existential enemies, allowing incumbents to justify abuses of democratic norms to restrain the opposition, and encouraging the opposition to use "any means necessary" to (re)gain power." Like any other organization in our society, higher education institutions are not immune to the perils of political polarization and controversies that may dominate discourse. Many may struggle to navigate and address the deep divisions of diverse perspectives, political ideologies, free speech, academic freedom, inclusivity, and lived experiences. This creates challenges to maintain a balanced and inclusive approach in advocating and supporting democracy.

According to West (2022), "One of the overlooked ingredients of democracy is a vibrant civil society with a knowledge sector that is free of political interference and the ability to train students in independent analysis and critical thinking." Higher education strives to embrace and provide an environment that engages in the principles of academic freedom and free speech as core and foundational values. Consequently, balancing these values with the responsibility to foster an inclusive, welcoming, civil environment can be challenging. Controversial or sensitive topics are bound to happen as part of the academic discourse in the classroom or on campus, leading to debates about the boundaries and challenges of free speech and academic freedom. Institutions constantly are working to be agile in finding ways to navigate these challenges, ensuring that all voices are heard and have a seat at the table. Hence, the goal is to encourage and facilitate support for democratic values and foster an inclusive and respectful environment that is grounded in engagement and celebration of the core values of freedom of expression, freedom of speech, and freedom of academic thought.

Former AAC&U President Carol Geary Schneider (2022) laments that "democracy faces monumental problems, both at home and in a global era of rising authoritarianism. Those challenges—health, poverty, hunger, housing, the inequitable education system, climate, social distrust and more—are daily realities for many students." Institutions of higher education are often microcosms of the larger communities, which may be diverse and global in nature. This is because the students, faculty and staff are from diverse backgrounds, perspectives and lived experiences. Each person brings the intersectionality of who they are to the table, which enriches the engagement on a multitude of levels. While diversity, equity, inclusion, and belonging are a strength, it can also present challenges in supporting democracy. Differences in cultural and social norms, values, ideologies, and lived experiences often lead to conflicts or misinterpretations. Creating spaces for open dialogue, engagement, civil discourse, and creating a sense of belonging nurtures a democratic environment where diverse perspectives are respected, valued, celebrated, and welcomed.

CONCLUSION

A vigorous and healthy democracy requires an informed, engaged, and active society, and higher education has a critical role to play in educating students to sharpen their knowledge, skills, and values necessary for democratic participation. Specifically, "a liberal education provides the foundational knowledge and skills that empower students to advance the common good through responsible and engaged citizenship in local, national, and global contexts (AACU, 2023)."

The Democracy Commitment states that "colleges and universities have an obligation to educate about democracy, to engage students in both an understanding of civic institutions and the practical experience of acting in the public arena. The American community colleges share this mission of educating about democracy, not least because we are the gateway to higher education for millions who might not otherwise get a post-secondary education. More critically, we are rooted deeply in local communities who desperately need the civic leadership and practical democratic capacity of our students for their own political and social health" (Ronan, 2012). However, underrepresentation of... community colleges in voter participation is a concern. The All-In Campus Democracy Challenge (2022) reported that voter participation by community college students remains underrepresented despite an increase in voting by that demographic, signaling that there is more work to do to engage these students more actively. Recent scores on the National Assessment of Educational Progress (2022) show marked declines in civic and history learning in recent years by eighth graders potentially foreshadowing a pipeline of students ill-prepared for democracy learning and participation when they arrive to college campuses.

The consequences of inertia are severe. In her compelling note regarding inaction to defend liberal education, AAC&U President Lynn Pasquerella (2023) brilliantly states that, "without immediate collective action, liberal education and the democracy it serves stand to lose everything, everywhere, all at once." Therefore, "we the people," must act and act quickly. The American Association of Colleges and Universities (2022) warns that "if our higher educational institutions continue to sit on the sidelines of democracy as a whole and play a minuscule part in transforming a better union, we are all at fault." Higher education plays an extraordinary position in democracy, the community, civic engagement, social justice, and in reaching people globally to enhance humanity. "Academia and civil society play an important role in promoting and cultivating democratic interests throughout the world" (Blessinger et al, 2023).

The initial conditions for robust democratic citizenship, as embodied in the debates among America's founders, are procedural (Scigliano, 2000). That is, participation in democratic societies starts with the right to vote, the acceptance of choices made by the majority, the institutionalization of minority protection mechanisms and all the freedoms guaranteed in the national constitution. The more advanced conditions are embodied in the substantial definition of democracy. Individuals are not only guaranteed rights of citizenship, but they are offered myriad opportunities including years of higher education to acquire and improve their skills. In their work inside and beyond the classroom to prepare students for the labor market and future learning, community colleges are well positioned to support and expand acquisition of democratic competencies.

REFERENCES

All-In Democracy Challenge. (2023). https://allinchallenge.org/presidents-commitment/

American Association of Colleges and Universities. (2022). *Educating for democracy.* American Association of Colleges and Universities. Aacu.org/trending-topics/educating-for-democracy

American Association of Community Colleges. (2022). *About us.* American Association of Community Colleges. Aacc.nche.edu/about-us/

Arizona State University Center for Broadening Participation in STEM. (2023). Stemcenter.asu.edu

Blessinger, P., Khodabocus, F., Panait, M., & Giridharan, B. (2023). Universities' role in supporting democracy—And the SDGs. Universityworldnes.com/post.php?story.

Boyer, J. (2016). *Academic freedom and the modern university.* https://news.uchicago.edu/sites/default/files/attachments/Academic_Freedom_V1.pdf

Brown S., & Mangan K. (2016). What 'safe spaces' really look like on college campuses, 63 CHRON. HIGHER EDUC., (summarizing responses to Dean Ellison's letter).

Community College Regulations, N.Y. Educ. (2023). Law.Suny.edu/media/suny/content-assets

Council of Europe. (n.d.). "Competences for democratic culture." coe.int/en/web/education/competences-for-democratic-culture

Cullinan, D., & Lewy, E. B. (2021). A better way to place students: what colleges need to know about multiple measures assessment. mdrc.org/sites/MMABrief

D'Agostino, S. (2023). Microcredentials confuse employers, colleges and learners, Inside Higher Ed.

European Union. (2023).Reference Framework of Competencies for Democratic Culture. coe.int/en/web/education

Franks. M. A. (2020). The second amendment's safe space, or the constitutionalization of fragility. *Law and Contemporary Problems, 83*(3), 137–.

Gallagher, T. (2021). The democratic imperative for higher education: Empowering students to become active citizens. *Liberal Education.* aacu.org/liberaleducation

Grieve, P. (2016). *University to freshmen: Don't expect safe spaces or trigger warnings.* CHI. https://www.chicagomaroon.com/2016/08/24/university-to-freshmen-dont-expect-safe-spaces-or-trigger-warnings/

Harbour, C. (2016). *Community colleges and democracy as problem solving.* Office of Community College Research and Leadership. occrl.illinois.edu/docs. https://occrl.illinois.edu/docs/librariesprovider2/news/occrl/community-colleges-and-democracy-as-problem-solving.pdf.

Harpalani. (2017). "Safe Spaces" and the Educational Benefits of Diversity. *Duke Journal of Constitutional Law & Public Policy., 13*(1).

Harris, C., Jorgensen, C. Lovett, L. Oakomolafe, S, Thomas, N., & Trogden, B. (2023). Five things you should know about connecting democracy and the curriculum.

Holley & Steiner. (2005). *Campus safe spaces.* oldwestbury.edu/division/diversity

Hurtado, S. (2019). "Now is the time": Civic learning for a strong democracy. *Dedalus, the Journal of the American Academy of Arts & Sciences, 148*(4), 94–107. https://www.amacad.org/publication/now-time-civic-learning-strong-democracy

Jackson, M. (2021). Unmasking the fragility of trigger warnings, safe spaces, and code-switching on campus. *Educational Theory, 71*(2), 247–266. https://doi.org/10.1111/edth.12474

Jordan, J. (2017). *Challenges to freedom of speech on college campuses: Joint hearing before the Subcommittee on Healthcare, Benefits and Administrative Rules and the Subcommittee on Intergovernmental Affairs of the Committee on Oversight and Government Reform, House of Representatives, One Hundred Fifteenth Congress.* U.S. Government Publishing Office.

JPMorgan Chase & Co., SUNY Westchester Community College, NYC Labor Market Information Service. (2016). *Connecting to promising careers: middle-skill jobs in the lower hudson valley—A collaboration of education, business, and government.* https://www.gc.cuny.edu/sites/default/files/2021-07/Connect%20to%20Promising%20Careers%20mid.%20skill%20jobs%20in%20lower%20hudson%20valley.pdf

McKinsey. (2022). *Tearing the 'paper ceiling': McKinsey supports effort driving upward mobility for millions of workers.* https://www.mckinsey.com/about-us/new-at-mckinsey-blog/tearing-the-paper-ceiling-mckinsey-supports-movement-for-upward-mobility-of-millions-of-workers

Mentor Connect. (2023). https://www.mentor-connect.org/https://www.mentor-connect.org/mentor-connect/program-overview

Miles, B., Wood, C., & Young, K. (2020). Valuing each other and achieving more together. In S. Cramer & P. Knuepfer (Eds.), *Shared governance in higher education—Vitality and continuity in times of change* (vol. 3.9, pp. 25–40). State University of New York Press.

Miles, B. (2019). *Excellence revealed—Again—April 26, 2019.* https://www.sunywcc.edu/about/president/presidents-weekly-messages/message-from-dr-belinda-s-miles-excellence-revealed-again-april-26-2019/

Mlyn, E. (2022). "Our house is burning." *Inside Higher Ed.* Insidehighered.com/views

Morrill Act of July 2, 1862 (1862). Public Law 37-108, 07/02/1862; Enrolled Acts and Resolutions of Congress, 1789–1996; Record Group 11; General Records of the United States Government; National Archives.

Morrill Act of August 30, 1890. (1890). ch. 841, 26 Stat. 417, 7 U.S.C.

MotiVote. (2023). https://motivote.us/

NEH for All. (2023). Supporting Humanities Programming in Westchester County. nehforall.org/projects/humanities-westchester-community-college

National Assessment of Educational Progress. (2023). nationsreportcard.gov/highlights/civics

National Study of Learning, Voting, and Engagement at Community Colleges. (2023). idhe.tufts.edu/nslve

Newell, A. M. (2014). America's democracy colleges: The civic engagement of community college students. *Community College Journal of Research and Practice, 38*(9), 794–810. https://doi.org/10.1080/10668926.2012.720862

New York State Law. elections.ny.gov/NYSBOE. https://system.suny.edu/media/suny/content-assets/documents/communitycolleges/CC-Regulations.pdf

Nora, A. (2000). Reexamining the community college mission. New expeditions: Charting the second century of community colleges. *Issues Paper No. 2.*

Association of Community Coll. Trustees. American Association of Community Colleges, Washington, DC.Kellogg Foundation, Battle Creek, MI.2000-00-009p.

O'Banion, T. (2016). A brief history of general education. *Community College Journal of Research and Practice, 40,* 1–8. 10.1080/10668926.2015.1117996

Pasquerella, L. (2023). Transformative power: We must push back against the attacks on higher ed and democracy. *Liberal Education.* aacu.org/liberaleducation/articles

Patton, M. (2022). Adding culturally responsive strategies into STEM. *Community College Daily.*

Prentice, M. (2011). Civic engagement among community college students through service learning, *Community College Journal of Research and Practices, 35*(11), 842–854. https://doi.org/1080/1066892080/2205014

Rajan, S. (2021). Dr. Shaun Rajan. https://www.sunywcc.edu/academics/school-of-mathematics-science-and-engineering/dr-shaun-rajan/

Ronan, B. (2012). Community colleges and the work of democracy. *Connections.* Kettering.org

Rosenbaum, J. E. (2021). Associations between civic engagement and community college completion in a nationally representative sample of young adults. *Community College Journal of Research and Practice, 45*(7), 479–497. https://doi.org/1080/10668926.2020.1724574

Schneider, C. G. (2022). *All in? Or just some?* Inside Higher Ed. https://www.insidehighered.com/views/2022/01/10/higher-eds-role-civic-learning-and-democracy%E2%80%99s-future-opinion

Scigliano, R. (Ed.). (2000). *The federalist: A commentary on the Constitution of the United States.* The Modern Library.

SUNY News. (2023). SOTUS Affirmative Action. https://www.suny.edu/suny-news/press-releases/6-23/6-29-23/

SUNY Procedural Guidance for General Education (2021). https://system.suny.edu/academic-affairs/acaproplan/general-education/suny-ge/

SUNY WCC Center for Teaching and Learning. (2023). https://www.sunywcc.edu/contact/center-for-learning-resources-library-media-and-instructional-technology/

SUNY WCC Institutional Research, Planning, and Effectiveness. (2023). https://www.sunywcc.edu/about/ir/

SUNY WCC Leadership and Service. (2023). https://www.sunywcc.edu/student-services/getinvolved/leadership/

SUNY WCC Strategic Plan. (2023). https://www.sunywcc.edu/about/strategic-plan/mission/

SUNY WCC Viking ROADS. (2023). sunywcc.edu/student-services

Tabrizi, S., & Rideout, G. (2017). Active learning: Using Bloom's taxonomy to support critical pedagogy. *International Journal for Cross-Disciplinary Subjects in Education, 8*(3), 3202–3209.

Thomas, N., Dismondi, A., Guatum, P., & Brinker, D. (2021). Democracy counts 2020: Record breaking turnout and student resiliency. Institute for Democracy and Higher Education. National Study of Learning, Voting, and Engagement. Tufts.app.box.com.

Thomas, L., & Jones, R. (2017). Student engagement in the context of commuter students. *London: The Student Engagement Partnership (TSEP). Listhomas.co.uk*
Tisch, J. (2021). All-In Democracy Challenge. tufts.app.box.com.
Townsend, R. B. (2019). *Rediscovering humanities education in community colleges.* Spring Bulletin.
Turner. (2016). *Community colleges and democracy as problem solving community college research and leadership.* occrl.illinois.edu/docs. https://occrl.illinois.edu/docs/librariesprovider2/news/occrl/community-colleges-and-democracy-as-problem-solving.pdf
Truman. (1947). Truman Commission on Higher Education P. 67
Vaughan, G. (2000). *The community college story* (2nd ed.). Community College Press.
Weissman, S, (2022), *Community College Student Support Program Yields Results.* Inside Higher Ed. Insidehighered.com.
Wesissman, S. (2023). *SUNY Expands Academic Support Program.* https://www.suny wcc.edu/student-services/opportunity-programs/viking-roads/
West, D. (2022). *Why academic freedom challenges area dangerous for democracy.* Darrell M. West. Why academic freedom challenges are dangerous for democracy | Brookings.
Whissemore, T. (2023). Funding RoundUp. AACC Community College Daily. October 4, 2023.
West, D. (2022, September 8). Why academic freedom challenges are dangerous for democracy. *Brown Center Chalkboard.* Brookings.edu
Wynn, C., & Ziff, E. (2023). General education classes strengthen democracy. *The Progressive Magazine.* https://progressive.org/op-eds/general-education-classes-strengthen-democracy-wynn-ziff-230907/
Ziblatt, D. (2023). *Challenges to democracy.* harvard.edu/dziblatt/challenges-democracy
Zook, G. F. (1947). The President's Commission on Higher Education. *Bulletin of the American Association of University Professors (1915–1955), 33*(1), 10–28.

CHAPTER 9

EMBRACING THE POLITICS OF THE POSSIBLE

Voter Engagement at an R1 Institution

Karen M. Kedrowski
Iowa State University

ABSTRACT

This chapter describes and analyzes the author's work to expand voter engagement efforts at a Research Intensive (R1) public institution. While the institution historically provided civic education and engagement opportunities in various places on campus, there had not been coordinated work on voter engagement. Initially, these efforts were met with skepticism and indifference. Through participation in national voter engagement programs, the institution accrued awards that established the credibility of the initiative and of the author. In addition, the author worked with key stakeholders across campus units to build trust and create personal relationships that, in time, led to breakthroughs. The chapter ends with some takeaways for others working on voter engagement at R1 institutions.

Leaning Into Politics, pages 141–155
Copyright © 2024 by Information Age Publishing
www.infoagepub.com
All rights of reproduction in any form reserved.

Civic engagement professionals have decried the decline in civic knowledge, political participation, and faith in American institutions for decades. Charles Quigley (1999) of the American Bar Association traced the beginning of civic education as a desire to socialize the waves of European immigrants arriving in the late 19th century. Quigley traced the decline in civic knowledge to the Vietnam War, the counterculture movement and the critiques of civics education by the civil rights movement. The decline in civic knowledge corresponded with declining voter turnout rates and particularly low voter turnout among young people (aged 18–24; U.S. Census Bureau, 2015). Fast forward a quarter century, American democracy still faces threats, among them poor civic knowledge (Annenberg Public Policy Center, 2022), low faith in government institutions (Gallup Poll, n.d.), distrust of the mass media (Brenan, 2022), deep divisions over the significance of the January 6, 2021 insurrection (Galston, 2023), and increasing barriers to voting nationwide (Singh & Carter, 2023).

Various scholars and advocates have called upon higher education institutions to recommit themselves to their civic missions. For instance, in 1999, Boyte and Hollander called upon US research universities to return to their civic missions to help stem Americans' growing disengagement from civic life (Boyte & Hollander, 1999). Similarly, *A Crucible Moment* (2012) also challenged higher education to return to its civic roots and integrate civic education and engagement in all dimensions of campus life. Soria et al. (2016) renewed this call, stating that few students planned to vote, nor saw themselves as community leaders or showed little growth in their political or social involvement (pp. 7–8). Brunner et al. (2016) argued that land-grant universities need to return to their civic education roots and Cruzado (2019) maintained that land-grant institutions "are called upon to raise up Americans to a better standard of living and greater participation in our democracy through education" (p. 229).

This literature, however, was published before the mob violence at the U.S. Capitol on January 6, 2021. These protesters were very politically engaged; many saw themselves as patriotic Americans defending their president against what they believed was a stolen election. These events led to renewed calls for increased civic education and engagement with the intention of restoring popular sovereignty and faith in American institutions and elections (see for example Davenport, 2021; Hunt & Meyer, 2021; Luke, 2021).

This chapter is a case study of the author's efforts to answer these calls by building upon existing civic engagement work and expanding voter engagement at a Midwestern, public, land-grant R1 institution. This institution has a STEM focus and the liberal arts, where civic education normally resides, occupy a secondary position. Previous civic engagement efforts were diffuse and uncoordinated. The administration, sensitive to concerns from external audiences, was leery of political engagement. This chapter provides a case study of the politics of the possible, through the slow process of building allies and trust and concludes with take-aways colleagues at land-grant institutions (and perhaps others) can consider in their own efforts.

BACKGROUND

I spent more than two decades at a public regional, teaching institution in the South, where I led civic engagement and education efforts for a decade, with significant support from the administration. We had generous funding from a donor and community partners. In retrospect, mine was a privileged position. When civic engagement work is led by a dean and a vice president, people show up, help plan and do the work. It also did not hurt that there was no on-site university counsel and the state legislature usually ignored the institution.

In January 2019, I transitioned to a new role at a R1 institution, as Director of the Carrie Chapman Catt Center for Women and Politics at Iowa State University (ISU). I was hired as a full professor with tenure. Civic engagement, including voting engagement, was a long-standing part of the Catt Center's mission; however, it was a peripheral rather than a central activity. I was excited to bring my civic engagement experience to a larger institution with greater resources and equally eager to meet people and find allies.

Existing Infrastructure

When I arrived, I followed the Campus Vote Project's recommendations for "Making Your Campus Voter Friendly" (Campus Vote Project, n.d.) by learning about existing programming through conversations and email outreach.

Catt Center Initiatives: My new office was the home of several civic engagement efforts, including voter registration and sponsoring at least two endowed lectures each year. In addition, ISU—through the Catt Center—already participated in several national voting initiatives. The first was the National Study of Learning, Voting, and Engagement (NSLVE), which provides reports on student voter turnout in presidential and midterm elections (NSLVE, n.d.). Second, the Catt Center had an existing relationship with the voting advocacy group, the Andrew Goodman Foundation (AGF), which provided funding to pay student voting ambassadors and expenses for voter engagement work. Third, the Catt Center also hosted a Campus Election Engagement Project Fellow who did voter engagement work. This intern was available because ISU was a member of Iowa Campus Compact, which provided civic engagement resources, networking, and professional development opportunities to member institutions.

Relevant Curriculum: The undergraduate general education program requires all students to take one course in U.S. Diversity and one course in International Perspectives, which comprise the University's civic education curriculum. Courses in American Government and/or U.S. History are not required per se, although they could be used to meet other requirements in Social Sciences or Humanities.

Similarly, various academic programs have internships, which may involve working with a local nonprofit or other civic group, and service-learning opportunities and/or requirements. Both provide work experience and opportunities to collaborate with community organizations. In addition, the University Lectures program, housed in Academic Affairs, sponsors dozens of public events each year, including candidate forums and lectures on current affairs.

ISU's slogan is "Innovate at Iowa State," and the University opened an $85 million Student Innovation Center (SIC) building in August 2020, with meeting space and support staff. While much of the SIC's focus is geared to business and engineering, its mission also includes civic innovation.

Co-Curricular Activities: Several campus organizations have civic or political activism missions; about 30 are listed in the "political and activism" category on the student affairs website (https://www.stuorg.iastate.edu/organizations/17/type). There was also interest in voter engagement by various student groups, especially College Democrats and student government. They provided human and financial resources to support civic engagement and had the ability to reach students from all corners of campus. In addition, all fraternities and sororities have a designated charity for which they raise money, which also promotes civic engagement. However, these community engagement activities may or may not be connected to civic education or political engagement. In 2020, a year after my arrival, the NCAA began to emphasize civic engagement for college athletes (Nevis, 2023).

Community Partners: The League of Women Voters of Ames/Story County also does substantial programming and voter engagement work. The Story County Auditor, who administers elections, also developed resources for students on Iowa voting law. In addition, the County Auditor placed several polling places on or near campus to serve precincts that included on-campus housing, nearby fraternities and sororities and countless rental apartments and homes. The Auditor also scheduled satellite (early voting) locations on campus to serve the Ames population.

Likewise, the 2020 Iowa Caucuses would provide for students to engage with the political process through presidential candidate visits, student employment, internship, volunteer opportunities and news media coverage. In addition, Iowa also has same-day registration, which would boost student voter registration and turnout rates.

In the process of discovering the existing civic engagement landscape on campus, I learned interest in voter engagement was existent, though scattered and uncoordinated. Thus, I identified voter engagement activities as an area where I could make significant contributions.

Challenges

There were significant challenges as well. First, there was the institutional culture. Iowa State University, as an R1 institution, focuses primarily on the "research of discovery" (Boyer, 1990) whereas student development outside the classroom or lab is left primarily to student affairs personnel. However, no student affairs personnel are dedicated to civic or voter engagement and there is no central office for community engagement or service-learning. As such, Iowa State is typical of research institutions that have fewer staff (per 1,000 students) dedicated to civic engagement than private and liberal arts colleges (Evans, Marsicano & Lennartz, 2019). Second, while there was interest in voter engagement on the part of student groups, these efforts were uncoordinated and often at cross purposes. For example, in 2019, three different student organizations hosted voter registration tables on National Voter Registration Day—simultaneously and in the same location.

Third, there was a combination of disinterest and even suspicion from university leadership. For instance, many STEM faculty and students hold and convey a "culture of disengagement," in which they see social problems as largely irrelevant to their work (Nguyen 2021). Similarly, the then-vice president of student affairs was uninterested in student voter engagement because the staff were already overcommitted, although he paid lip service to it.

In addition, after the 2016 presidential election, with President Donald Trump's win that "surprised" many, students and parents complained that many professors talked about the election, even in science and engineering courses, where the topic was not germane. There were also complaints that some outside organizations sought to register students during class time and promoted partisan or ideological agendas in the process. These complaints led the administration to worry the state legislature might act on these complaints.

In August 2020, the campus was embroiled in a controversy about an English instructor's syllabus, which barred students from writing about "any topic that takes at its base that one side doesn't deserve the same basic human rights as you do (i.e.: no arguments against gay marriage, abortion, Black Lives Matter, etc.)" (Sequiera & Gehr, 2020). This statement was a clear violation of students' freedom of expression and led to scrutiny and outrage from, variously, the Board of Regents, state legislators, donors, and the conservative national media. Many stakeholders called for ISU to discipline or dismiss the instructor. The controversy led to a mandatory syllabus statement on free speech (Wikert, 2020), mandatory free speech training for all employees and students (Free speech, n.d.), and more concern about bringing politics into the classroom.

These events and worries led to the conscious enforcement of the University's "germaneness" policy, which stipulates that material presented in class must be germane to the subject matter (ISU Faculty Handbook, 2021). The provost also banned any faculty from using class time for student voter registration. In addition, he cautioned against discussing the election or communicating their own preferences to students during class time. These directives were issued campus wide via email and the employee newsletter, *Inside Iowa State* (Roepke, 2022). This list of "do nots" had a significant chilling effect. Many instructors were reluctant to do anything related to politics and elections, even those activities consistent with the policy.

In addition, the Registrar's office was skeptical of sharing race and ethnicity data for the National Survey of Learning, Voting, and Engagement (NSLVE) reports, which provide detailed information about student voter turnout. This concern stemmed from the ISU student body profile, which is 75% White. Registration officials were worried that with detailed breakdowns, some students might be identifiable.

Similarly, the Trademark Office refused permission to use the word "Cyclones" or any trademarked images in voter engagement efforts, consistent with a strict policy policing the use of trademarked words and symbols by student organizations. This policy resulted from a lawsuit involving a t-shirt distributed by a student chapter of NORML, the National Organization for the Reform of Marijuana Laws, that featured the mascot, "Cy," and a marijuana leaf (Connor, 2016). The inability to use university marks handicapped the Catt Center's efforts to market voter engagement efforts in a recognizable way.

At the same time, the Catt Center lost some of its existing voter engagement resources. ISU dropped its membership in Iowa Campus Compact in 2019 after a round of budget cuts. This also ended its relationship with CEEP. There was an immediate loss of human resources (the CEEP fellow) as well as a lost opportunity to use the networking and other resources offered by Iowa Campus Compact. The next year, the AGF reduced its support to its member campuses, providing only enough for small stipends to two student ambassadors (rather than three) and none for supplies.

Another challenge stemmed from George Floyd's murder at the hands of Minneapolis police officer Derek Chauvin in May 2020. This tragedy led to a nationwide reckoning on the state of race relations. It also rekindled a decades-old campus controversy about Carrie Chapman Catt, a famous alumna whom some believe was racist (other stakeholders, notably, do not share this opinion) (See for example Cox, 2020; Looft et al., 2020) and a movement to change the name of Catt Hall. Since the Carrie Chapman Catt Center was leading student voter engagement efforts, this controversy complicated matters. Some offices were unresponsive to the Catt Center's overtures, and some individuals were hostile. Even the then-vice president for diversity, equity, and inclusion (DEI) kept his distance from the Catt Center, despite the fact that the Catt Center was one of ISU's first DEI initiatives.

EXPANDING VOTER ENGAGEMENT

Initial 2020 Efforts

Given this uneven landscape, in 2020 I followed the Campus Vote Project's (n.d.) recommendations to "find support" and build a coalition. I reached out to numerous student organizations and offices on campus inviting them to join a coalition, which met with mixed responses. There are substantial benefits to a coalition: building a campus network, sharing responsibilities, access to resources and legitimacy for the work. Coalitions also help build a collective identity and benefits of working toward shared goals (see for example Enriquez, 2014). Coalition members included the local League of Women Voters, the College Democrats, Residence Life, and University Lectures Program among others. However, many student organizations and student affairs offices shied away.

At the same time, I became involved with national initiatives, like the ALL IN Campus Democracy Challenge (ALL IN, n.d.) and the Voter Friendly Campus initiative (Voter Friendly Campus, n.d.). These organizations provided best practice documents and networking resources lost by ending ISU's membership in Iowa Campus Compact and they also provided national recognitions that would publicize and legitimate the Catt Center's voter engagement efforts. Publicity and national recognition were especially valuable considering the Catt Hall controversy. As a result of the Catt controversy, I built a personal relationship with the president, Wendy Wintersteen, who agreed to sign the President's Commitment and make me the campus contact. This also helped establish ISU's standing in the ALL IN community.

Wintersteen also agreed to recruit other Big XII athletic conference presidents to sign the President's Commitment and engage with the Big XII Votes Challenge, which provides support, friendly competition, and opportunities to collaborate between the conference members. Once all Big XII campuses agreed to participate, Big XII administrators would then allow us to use the Big XII logo. I then became the co-coordinator of the Big XII Votes Challenge and represented Iowa State in the Iowa Votes Challenge.

Again, these affiliations provided human and financial resources and recognition that further legitimated the Catt Center's voter engagement activities on campus.

As the designated ALL IN campus contact, I shamelessly promoted myself as the president's designated leader for student voting engagement as I approached potential partners. Consequently, some offices were willing to meet and work with me. For example, the County Auditor happily worked with me as the point person for arranging on-campus polling places and promoting student outreach. I worked with a member of the student government to distribute voting information to residence halls and with the League of Women Voters to reach out to the Greek community. I also adapted and circulated the Ask Every Student (AES) Canvas (online learning management system) Module, which was downloaded over 200 times. This is about twice the number of downloads of this module at other Canvas campuses.

I also applied for, and received, a grant from AES to support voter engagement work. With these funds and AGF's support, I hired five student interns to work on voter engagement efforts. They earned academic credit and stipends. The AES Grant also paid for CyRide (local bus system) bus ads advertising the early voting opportunities. Finally, I developed and sent a series of all student emails with information about voting, candidates, and deadlines. These tactics were employed again—in some fashion—in 2022.

Accolades Build Visibility and Credibility

The Catt Center earned numerous recognitions through AGF, ALL IN and the Voter Friendly Campus Initiative for its 2020 work. Each recognition was shared with administrative leaders and publicized through social media and news outlets. Moreover, the ISU regularly publishes announcements of grants and awards received and I made sure the voting recognitions and AES grants were included. In 2022, I was named AGF Campus Champion of the Year, an award that I added to my signature block. These accolades provided the Catt Center's voter engagement work with visibility, positive exposure, legitimacy, and credibility. This legitimacy was important to counter some of the reluctance to engage in political engagement from various corners of the institution.

Furthermore, the recognition broke some logjams by 2022. The Registrar, after assurances from Tufts University, the institution that hosts the NSLVE reports agreed to provide racial and ethnic breakdowns for the NSLVE reports. This information helps us identify additional low turnout groups for targeted efforts. The Trademark Office granted the Catt Center permission to use the "Cyclones Vote" moniker, #CyclonesVote hashtag, and an image of the University mascot in its branding. The Trademark

Office granted the request when it came from a university office (the Catt Center) rather than a student organization and with reassurances that the moniker would only be used for nonpartisan voter engagement. Finally, the Catt Center also hired the mascot, Cy, to pose with voting messages around campus and these images were used in our voter outreach efforts in 2022.

New Allies and Partners

For the 2022 election, I sought to develop new allies and partners to expand voter engagement on campus. In 2021, the Catt Center and the Political Science department worked with the SIC to hire a student team to develop student voter outreach strategies for the 2022 election. This "Innovation Dash" was featured by President Wintersteen in a meeting with campus leadership. The students' ideas from this Dash were the blueprint for student engagement strategies in 2022, which were also planned through the SIC. Employing and training students as voter advocates helps students to develop civic habits and peer-to-peer advocacy is an effective voter engagement strategy (Clay et al., 2018).

In addition, between 2020 and 2022, the vice presidents of DEI and student affairs resigned. Because of the simmering controversy, the president enlisted me to brief each new campus leader on Carrie Chapman Catt's biography and the Catt Center's activities. These meetings built personal relationships with each leader who then in turn, supported the Catt Center's work. This included financial support and publicity, but also, importantly, ensured the cooperation of their subordinates. Emails were exchanged, videoconferences scheduled, and collaboration happened.

In 2021, I was elected to the Faculty Senate. I developed a resolution calling upon faculty to refrain from scheduling exams and to be flexible with attendance requirements on Election Day. This resolution was passed by the Student Government, the Graduate and Professional Student Senate and the Faculty Senate (Kedrowski, 2022a). The Graduate School Office was also very helpful in reaching the postdoc population, which would otherwise not receive messages targeted to students.

Finally, by 2022, I was able to counter the provost's negative messaging around elections with a list of "dos" to accompany the provost's list of "don'ts." This statement, having been vetted by University Counsel and the Provost's Office, described activities that faculty could do with students to encourage them to research issues and to vote (Kedrowski, 2022b).

By the end of the 2022 election, the Catt Center was recognized as the campus leader for student voter engagement. The external accolades were met with praise and thanks from internal audiences and campus leaders. Certain challenges remain, of course. Nonetheless, there is much to celebrate.

TAKEAWAYS

What advice can I provide to someone who wishes to undertake a similar effort at an R1? Here are some takeaways:

Understand the Faculty Rewards System

The tenure and promotion criteria at an R1 is centered on research, which might preclude one from undertaking civic engagement activities. I was hired as a tenured full professor, so I could engage in this work with little risk. In addition, the ISU faculty review system is based on a "personal responsibility statement" (PRS) that is adaptable and can include many initiatives, as long as—for tenure stream faculty—research comes first. Arguably one could negotiate a PRS that includes civic and voter engagement so it can be recognized and rewarded. Moreover, ISU's *Faculty Handbook* requires that publications in the scholarship of teaching and learning (SoTL) be evaluated the same as any other publications. Thus, publications stemming from civic and voter engagement work would "count" toward tenure, promotion, and merit raises.

However, if one's institution uses "one size fits all" faculty review criteria, undertaking civic engagement work is considerably riskier, especially if it is (mis)characterized as "service" and if SoTL publications are discounted or not counted at all. Arguably, undertaking such work at any R1 might be easier for a non-tenure-stream faculty member whose primary responsibility is teaching and student development. However, an untenured faculty member may be particularly vulnerable to attacks from displeased donors or state legislators.

One of my civic engagement colleagues opines that one barrier to bringing minoritized faculty to civic and voter engagement initiatives is because this work is not typically recognized and valued by political science departments to the same degree as the scholarship of inquiry (Boyer, 1990). Once a faculty member has earned tenure and promotion, it's difficult to switch to civic and voter engagement work. I think this is true. None of my political science colleagues, professionally socialized at (an) R1 institution(s), had done any civic engagement work prior to, or subsequent to, my arrival. However, political scientists who make their careers from studying power and systems of government are best positioned to participate in civic engagement because we understand the stakes.

Embrace the Politics of the Possible and Build Trust

Higher education institutions of any Carnegie classification—whether public or private—operate in constrained environments. In this case, constraints include state and federal law, university policy, and a degree of scrutiny from lawmakers, the press, and donors that was greater than what I experienced previously. Frustrating though they are, I work with the University Counsel and Provost to distribute messages consistent with these parameters. This strategy had the added benefit of building trust.

The willingness to work with the Provost, the Registrar, and University Counsel built trust. They learned that the Catt Center was careful not to put the university at risk. Reaching out to the College Republicans, Young Americans for Freedom and Turning Point USA chapters also enhanced the Catt Center's reputation for inclusiveness and nonpartisanship. This also led to the opportunity to build personal relationships in these key offices so there is someone I can contact as needed. Even the simmering controversy about Carrie Chapman Catt resulted in personal relationships with key campus leaders that enhanced the Catt Center's credibility and resulted in fruitful collaborations.

Rethink the Coalition

Iowa State has numerous offices that collaborate with the Catt Center on voter engagement; however, this group is not a coalition in the sense that I had at my previous institution. The group does not meet and does not share in decision making. However, each member of the coalition makes a particular contribution to the voter engagement effort at the direction of the Catt Center. Given the workload each organization faces and the unwieldy size of the group, meetings would not be fruitful. Instead, I work with students on developing and implementing voter engagement strategies and facilitating outreach to campus stakeholders.

Emphasize Nonpartisanship and Neutrality

Some of the administration's reticence stems from concerns that voter registration and engagement efforts were driven by partisanship or ideology, a valid concern based on prior experience. Therefore, I quickly learned that I needed to emphasize that the Catt Center's civic engagement work is strictly nonpartisan. Similarly, when hosting candidate visits or forums, be sure to invite everyone who is running and to publicize all events identically. Moreover, in the communications, be sure to indicate that all candidates were invited and include a neutrality statement.

Drop What Doesn't Work

Civic and voter engagement can easily turn into a huge task with each year or election cycle leading to more and more activities. However, the odd-numbered years between election cycles may offer an opportunity to evaluate activities and to eliminate strategies that do not work. This same tactic can be used for any civic engagement activities. For instance, in 2022, we did not attempt to have separate social media channels for voter outreach but chose to use existing ones with the #CyclonesVote hashtag.

Expect Challenges and Celebrate Breakthroughs

One abiding concern at ISU is that STEM students have significantly lower voter turnout rates than students in other fields. Engaging with them, and their faculty and staff mentors, remains challenging. Even the Faculty Senate resolution was not passed unanimously, with opponents expressing concern that the statement would be perceived as partisan, or that asking faculty to accommodate students' voting was inappropriate. Expect challenges and figure out how to address or work around them. In the meantime, celebrate victories. For all the badges, shields, and certificates ISU has received in the last four years, my two greatest points of pride are the faculty "can do" list published in *Inside Iowa State* and permission to use "Cyclones Vote."

CONCLUSION

This experience at Iowa State shows that expanding voter engagement at an R1 institution happens in fits and starts. It requires care, determination, commitment and patience. Most importantly, civic engagement professionals need to build trust: trust that one isn't going to embarrass the institution; trust that one will follow the university's policies; and trust that one knows what they are doing. While one's enthusiasm for student civic and voter engagement may be infectious, the infection's spread is slow and uneven. Nonetheless, the work is valuable and important and helps these institutions to fulfill their land grant and higher education missions to create an educated and engaged citizenry.

REFERENCES

ALL IN Campus Democracy Challenge. (n.d.). *Home.* https://allinchallenge.org/

Annenberg Public Policy Center. (2022, September 13). *Americans' civic knowledge drops on First Amendment and branches of government.* News release. https://www.annenbergpublicpolicycenter.org/americans-civics-knowledge-drops-on-first-amendment-and-branches-of-government

Boyer, E. L. (1990). *Scholarship reconsidered: Priorities of the professorate.* Carnegie Foundation for the Advancement of Teaching. https://www.umces.edu/sites/default/files/al/pdfs/BoyerScholarshipReconsidered.pdf.

Boyte, H., & Hollander E. (1999). Wingspan declaration on renewing the civic mission of the American research university. *Civic Engagement, 8.* https://digitalcommons.unomaha.edu/slcceciviceng/8.

Brenan, M. (2022, October 18). *American's trust in media remains near record low.* Gallup Poll. https://news.gallup.com/poll/403166/americans-trust-media-remains-near-record-low.aspx.

Brunner, B. R. (Ed.). (2016). *Creating citizens: Liberal arts, civic engagement, and the land-grant tradition.* University of Alabama Press.

Campus Vote Project. (n.d.). *Student voter engagement handbook.* https://www.campusvoteproject.org/resources.

Clay, R., Lombardi, D., Burns, M., & Muthig, K. (2018, March). *Institutionalizing voter engagement: A guide to developing and adopting handbook language.* Campus Vote Project. https://www.campusvoteproject.org/_files/ugd/85cfb4_3c41f44b5a844f2eb2e2c7e361035861.pdf.

Connor A. (2016, February 4). NORML ISU wins lawsuit after four-year battle. *Iowa State Daily.* https://iowastatedaily.com/71002/news/norml-isu-wins-lawsuit-after-four-year-battle/.

Cox, J. (2020, July 1). Letter: Carrie Chapman Catt is not a racist. *Iowa State Daily.* https://iowastatedaily.com/236306/opinion-letters/letter-carrie-chapman-catt-is-not-a-racist/

Cruzado, W. (2019). Renewing the promise of land-grant universities. In W. V. Flores & K. S. Rogers (Eds). *Democracy, civic engagement, and citizenship in higher education: Reclaiming our civic purpose* (pp. 217–224). Lexington Books.

Davenport, D. (2021). Wanted: Informed patriots: The January riot on Capitol Hill was a shocking example of civic ignorance and disrespect—and proof that our schools must teach civics again. *Hoover Digest, 2*(Spring), 84. *Gale Academic OneFile,* link.gale.com/apps/doc/A661724988/AONE?u=iastu_main&sid=googleScholar&xid=0bd6e27a.

Enriquez, L. (2014.) "Undocumented and citizen students unite:" Building a cross-status coalition through shared ideology. *Social Problems, 61*(2), 155–174. https://doi.org/10.1525/sp.2014.12032

Evans B. J., Marsicano, C. R., & Lennartz, C.T. (2019). Cracks in the bedrock of American democracy: Differences in civic engagement across institutions of higher education. *Educational Researcher, 48*(1), 31–44. https://doi.org/10.3102/0013189X18809053

"Free Speech" (n.d.). https://freespeech.iastate.edu/

Galston, W. A. (2023, January 6). *Polls show Americans are divided on the significance of January 6.* Brookings Institution. https://www.brookings.edu/articles/polls-show-americans-are-divided-on-the-significance-of-january-6/.

Iowa State University faculty handbook. (2021). Section 7.2.1.2: Scholarly discourse and germaneness. p. 106. https://www.provost.iastate.edu/sites/default/files/wdclientcss/Faculty/Policies/Faculty%20Handbook%20-%20August%202021%20-%20final.pdf

Gallup Poll (n.d.) *Confidence in institutions*. https://news.gallup.com/poll/1597/confidence-institutions.aspx

Hunt, S. K., & Meyer, K. R. (2021). Making the case for a pedagogy of civic engagement, antiextremism, and antiracism: A response to forum essays. *Communication Education, 70*(4), 451–457. https://doi.org/10.1080/03634523.2021.1958239

Kedrowski, K. M. (2022a). *Resolution to support student voting on election day*. https://www.facsen.iastate.edu/sites/default/files/uploads/21-22%20Docket%20Calendar/21-20%20-a%20Resolution%20to%20Support%20Student%20Voting%20on%20Election%20Day.pdf.

Kedrowski, K. M. (2022b, September 22). How can faculty encourage students to vote? *Inside Iowa State*. https://www.inside.iastate.edu/article/2022/09/22/vote

Looft, R., Mookerje, R., & Schaal, M. (2020, July 6). Letter: Collective statement calling for changing the name of Catt Hall. *Iowa State Daily*. https://iowastatedaily.com/235933/opinion/letter-collective-statement-calling-for-changing-the-name-of-catt-hall/.

Luke, T. W. (2021). Democracy under threat after 2020 national elections in the USA: "Stop the steal" or "give more to the grifter-in-chief?" *Educational Philosophy and Theory, 55*(5), 551–557. https://doi.org/10.1080/00131857.2021.1889327

National Study of Learning, Voting, and Engagement. (n.d.). *Home*. https://idhe.tufts.edu/

(The) National Task Force on Civic Learning and Democratic Engagement. (2012). *A crucible moment: College learning & democracy's future*. Association of American Colleges and Universities. https://www.aacu.org/publication/a-crucible-moment-college-learning-democracys-future.

Nevins, D. L. (2023, October 16). College athletes support civic engagement. *The Fulcrum*. https://thefulcrum.us/college-athletes-support-civic-engagement.

Nguyen, L. M. (2021). Engineering a culture of public engagement in the Trump era—Challenging the status quo. *International Journal of Engineering, Social Justice, and Peace, 8*(1), 78–85. https://doi.org/10.24908/ijesjp.v8il.14211

Quigley, C. N. (1999, February 25–26). *Civic education: Recent history, current status, and the future*. American Bar Association. https://www.civiced.org/papers/papers_quigley99.html

Roepke, D. (2022, September 22). As Election Day nears, a review of political expression guidelines. *Inside Iowa State*. https://www.inside.iastate.edu/article/2022/09/22/activity

Sequiera, R., & Gehr, D. (2020, August 24). Iowa State responds after professor's syllabus bars opposition to Black Lives Matter, gay marriage, abortion. *Ames Tribune*. https://www.amestrib.com/story/news/2020/08/24/iowa-state-university-professor-controversial-syllabus-black-lives-matter/5626650002/#:~:text=Iowa%20State%20University%20has%20taken,said%20in%20a%20statement%20Friday.

Singh, J., & Carter, S. (2023, June 23). States have added nearly 100 restrictive laws since SCOTUS gutted the Voting Rights Act 10 years ago. Brennan Center for

Justice. https://www.brennancenter.org/our-work/analysis-opinion/states-have-added-nearly-100-restrictive-laws-scotus-gutted-voting-rights

Soria, K. M., & Mitchells, T. D. (Eds.). (2016). *Civic engagement and community service at research universities.* Palgrave McMillan.

United States Census Bureau. (2015). *Historical reported voting rates.* https://www.census.gov/library/visualizations/time-series/demo/voting-historical-time-series.html

Voter Friendly Campus. (n.d.). *About us.* https://www.voterfriendlycampus.org/

Wikert, J. (2020, November 11). *New required syllabus statement on free expression.* https://www.provost.iastate.edu/academic-programs/policies/new-required-syllabus-statement-on-free-expression

CHAPTER 10

WHO'S IN THE ROOM WHEN IT HAPPENS?

Use of Data Driven Analysis and Power Mapping to Build an Inclusive Political Engagement Coalition

Leah A. Murray
Weber State University

ABSTRACT

At least as far back as de Tocqueville (1838), the idea of the importance of associational life has been central to considering how democratic societies function. Building from that observation, scholars have shown that social capital matters for building a democratic structure that can withstand attacks against its principles. Democracy flourishes because of social bonds. Higher education is made up of very diverse people, all of whom can play a role in advancing political learning and civic engagement on campuses. An active and inclusive campus coalition can broker social connections across diverse and disconnected segments by building trust. I explain in replicable detail the work we did at Weber State University to build a more inclusive coalition for political learning, how we continuously use data to inform who is in the room when we make our plans, and present a power mapping exercise I created as part of the Students Learn Students Vote Ask Every Student co-designer cohort. This chapter provides a roadmap to build a politically inclusive coalition and provides access to important resources to deploy in that effort.

At least as far back as de Tocqueville (1838), the idea of the importance of associational life has been central to considering how democratic societies function. Building from that observation, scholars have shown that social capital matters for building a democratic structure that can withstand attacks against its principles. In the work of higher education, when we are creating a culture on a campus that embraces democratic principles, it is "through shared action, the process can become one of transforming those older assumptions into new values and assumptions of an inclusive nature" (McMaster, 2013). As McMaster demonstrates in his work on building an inclusive campus, culture change depends upon building a community to defend it; it cannot exist at the whim of a provost. Additionally, democracy is not a final product, but a dynamic iterative journey. So too should be coalition building, in which we create "place(s) for informal exchange of experiences and opinions and knowledge among people who are both connected with each other, so that they are inclined to listen, and different from each other, so that they are exposed to diverse ideas and experiences" (Estlund, 2003, as cited in Allen, 2004). Campuses convene diverse interlocutors to build social capital among a community of actors who will be the core of democracy on campus.

Scholars interested in how social capital and democracy are connected have often posited two possible theories: social capital is a necessary precondition for democracy to thrive (Putnam 2000) or that social capital and democracy have a reciprocal relationship such that as you build democracy you foster social capital, and as you foster social capital you build democracy (Paxton, 2002; Sides, 1999; Tavits, 2006). Other scholars have found that it is the trust that is built that fosters both democracy and social capital (Newton, 2001; Sides, 1999; Uslaner, 1999). Regardless of the causal direction, the research all points to the fact that democracy flourishes in the building of relationships and social bonds. An active and inclusive campus coalition can broker connections across diverse and disconnected segments (Burt, 2001), which builds the social trust necessary for democracy to thrive. As Uslaner argues, "while the effects of social trust on collective action are not always—or even usually—large, they are consistent. No other variable affects as many types of collective action as generalized trust" (Uslaner, 1999, p. 130). Thus, the campus coalition models what higher education needs to build democracy by becoming a reciprocal democratic unit itself.

INITIAL WEBER STATE UNIVERSITY COALITION

Perhaps the best way to assess political learning on a campus is to work with the Institute for Democracy and Higher Education (IDHE) on a campus climate study (Thomas & Brower, 2017), which is what we did at Weber State University in 2018. IDHE researchers met with six student focus groups, four faculty focus groups, one focus group with the Deans of the various colleges, one staff focus group, one focus group with administrators in diverse positions, one focus group with a coalition of faculty and staff who were committed to political learning and conducted elite interviews with six executive level administrators. Following the intervention, IDHE delivered an eight-page report highlighting Weber State University's strengths and weaknesses. For example, Weber State learned from the study that it had a student-centered environment with strong student-faculty relationships with some infrastructure for political learning, but that there were no habits of discussion about controversial issues and a pervasive culture of politeness. Our campus has used the study as a baseline for all its political engagement work since (Murray, 2024).

The study was part of a larger national project in which 12 AASCU college campuses spent a few years together working on assessing the political learning on their campuses (Copeland, et.al., 2021) to see "what structures, norms, human characteristics, and political forces promote campus climates for political learning and engagement in democracy" (Connors, et.al., 2018, p. 2). Some commonalities emerged from the findings across campuses. For example, political learning is highly dependent on individuals and personalities and if someone left their position then the work would stall. Personality-led political engagement programming creates vulnerabilities for campuses and more importantly, for democracy. Of note was that if senior administrators were no longer interested, people would stop doing the work on campus. If we are going to meet the challenge of building the democracy we need, campuses need to consistently provide a political engagement program that draws students in and builds their civic knowledge, skills and agency. In this chapter, I argue that the best way to defend against administrators no longer being interested or leaving the campus is to institutionalize the work through intentional coalition building, ensuring that everyone who needs to be in the room to invite students to the work of building this democracy is in the room.

Specifically for the 2018 study with IDHE, Weber State University was asked to put together a coalition to ensure that we had students, faculty, staff, and administrators from across the campus to participate. For many campuses, when a request comes in to do civic engagement work, the university finds the person with the most appropriate job title and assigns that person the work. In our case, the director of the Center for Community

Engaged Learning was assigned as the liaison for this project; this person was not a political scientist, was not particularly interested in politics, and generally thought of civic work as depoliticized community service. This reflects the common experience at universities where the definition of civic engagement has focused more on community service (Jacoby, 2009). At Weber State, like at campuses across the nation, "service-learning soared to prominence... integrated into academic courses and majors as well as into initiatives" (Jacoby, 2009, p. 13). When a request for civic engagement assessment was made to the university, the administration would only allow the study to happen if the CCEL director was in charge. I was able to successfully argue that I should be a voice in the coalition and put myself in that space. Meanwhile, the CCEL director put together a coalition of people she had worked with, which was focused more on community service than on political engagement, resulting in a very specific group of people leading on the research project.

Another issue with the way in which campuses approach this work is that people often do the work based on relationships they already have. In the case of Weber State, between the study and receiving the report, the CCEL director had left the university. The new director decided not to lead on the project and delegated to a staff member in the center, who I have worked closely with on other projects. Because of that relationship, I moved into a position of leadership on the political engagement coalition, thus centering political science in the work of civic engagement.

On the face of it, I immediately felt that there was a problem with the constitution of the coalition as many of the people in the room were not necessarily interested in politics but had been selected because of their connection to the CCEL's previous director. Weber State has over 500 faculty and over 1000 staff members. The people who were in the room were all people who knew someone in the CCEL; it was a very tight knit group, and quite frankly, of similar political views and backgrounds. Given what I knew of their politics, I also believed the group was politically out of step with the Utah state legislature and the community in which Weber State University lives.

The first thing Weber State University did once I was in a position of leadership was convene the coalition to review the results of the IDHE campus climate report. Generally, IDHE analyzed campuses through four frames: structural—policies, departments, programs, and physical spaces; political—internal and external factors that shape institutional governance and decision-making; cultural—shared norms, values and principles, history, symbols, and symbolic events; and human—composition, behaviors, competencies, and knowledge (Thomas & Brower, 2017). Broadly, campuses were found to have an institutionalized commitment to civic engagement that was apolitical in nature—specifically there was more support for service-learning or community service than for political engagement (Murray et al., forthcoming). IDHE also found that the 2016 election had made discussing politics very difficult, with two groups of students complaining they were not welcome on campus: conservative students and students from historically marginalized groups (Murray et al., forthcoming). Finally, faculty at the campuses in the study were not prepared to facilitate political discussions in their classrooms (Murray et al., forthcoming). The specific findings for Weber State were similar to other campuses and the political engagement coalition that had been convened was particularly vulnerable to these challenges.

In advance of reviewing the findings, I asked all the members of the coalition to take the Four Quads political diagnostic tool created by Patrick Dolenc and Kimberly Schmidl-Gagne (Cooke et al., 2018). Four Quads[1] is a political diagnostic tool that asks respondents to rate their position on policies—both in what policy they are most attracted to and how much they care. Respondents choose a policy position from among four options, each reflecting one of four ideological positions: modern liberal, classical liberal, radical, and conservative. Then respondents indicate how strongly they hold their belief along a spectrum of no opinion to strong. Respondents are then placed along an x-axis from equality to hierarchy and a y-axis from individual to community. Everyone in the coalition identified to one side of the ideological spectrum. To provide a frame of reference, I have conducted the Four Quads survey with students over the years and generally, Weber State students identify more broadly across the spectrum. The diagnostic helped to demonstrate the need for greater inclusion in programming and decision making so that they would be more reflective of the students and community members we were trying to reach and who had felt especially isolated in the 2016 election and its aftermath.

Weber State University also learned from the IDHE study that there was a divide between students who were members of the dominant faith group in Utah, The Church of Jesus Christ of Latter-Day Saints, and other students. We also learned that students who live in housing, who are mostly from out of state, felt they did not have much in common with students who were local. We learned that some students felt they could not speak out due to the ideological orientation, real or perceived, of faculty grading them, and faculty felt they were unable to speak due to the political orientation of the Utah State legislature that may be monitoring them. In each of these cases, people in these groups felt alienated from the campus political community at large, which resulted in Weber State not being a space where anyone could meet the challenges of democracy, much less students learning how to do so. The default position from people was that they should not speak, everyone was reporting they were silenced, and conversations that are vital to a healthy democracy were not happening.

One of the coincidences of our report was our assessment happened during a year when the campuswide Engaged Learning Series led by the Center for Community Engaged Learning focused on civility. Across campus were signs telling students to be civil when discussing hard topics. Civility as a topic was my idea as I thought given the hostility in the political world in 2018, we needed to teach our students to be more civil in their conversations. Our Politics 365 report found that our students were already too polite. Layering civility admonishments on top of already timid dispositions did not help and in fact probably chilled political speech on our campus more. The study showed that hard political conversations were not happening in classrooms and that students from different groups only saw each other in classes; faculty were too afraid to have political conversations in their classes or were convinced their content area was not about politics and thus would not give any time to current controversial topics. Where, then, would dialogue happen? How, then, would students learn what they needed to know to become fully engaged citizens of their communities? The campuswide politeness chilling effect led to a culture of not engaging. The problem of not building habits of discussion about political issues are compounding: if campuses are not introducing students to dialogue, they are not learning politically and are ill-prepared for democracy and society when they graduate. If not on campus, when and where will people learn how to engage across differences?

WEBER STATE UNIVERSITY COALITION BUILDING

Persuading faculty to pivot in their classrooms is a monumental task and given that faculty were reporting they did not want to discuss political issues (Murray, et.al., pending), to meet the more urgent challenge to get students ready to be fully engaged citizens Weber State realized that the only space where hard political conversations would possibly happen was in co-curricular programming on campus. Our biggest obstacle to making that happen was the need to diversify people involved in organizing programming. I also began deliberately inviting people to the table who met a specific gap in our connections. For example, I reached out to the LDS Institute on campus and invited them to a conversation about what we had learned and asked them to be a part of our coalition going forward. I am not a member of the dominant faith and do not necessarily understand the reference points of those students. To best understand them, considering they are a major part of our student body and that the Church is a dominant cue-giver in Utah, I needed a staff member from that Institute at the table. We reached out to residential life to make sure that we had programming that made sense in housing. Again, faculty do not usually conduct programming in residence halls and to a certain extent it has been almost thirty years since I lived in one, so I needed their staff at the table to help make that possible.

Due to these efforts our coalition began to grow from a small one of like-minded individuals who already did a lot of work together to a larger, more inclusive, cross-campus one that represented pockets of students we needed to reach to make our political engagement happen. Once we had our coalition closer to reflecting the political diversity of the campus as well as leveraging our co-curricular space, we turned our attention to our National Study of Learning, Voting, and Engagement (NSLVE) data. This data is integral to understanding what is happening on a campus with regard to voter registration and voter turnout. It matches enrollment records submitted to the National Student Clearinghouse to publicly available voting files collected by Catalist (NSLVE, n.d., about). Data are sub-aggregated by voting method, age group, education level, enrollment status, gender, race/ethnicity, and program of society. Many campuses use NSLVE data as a reporting tool of the percentage of the student population who votes. Weber State University had used its NSLVE data that way as well, but it began to use it as a periodic self-assessment tool to see who was still missing from the voting population. Students who were missing, reflected in our voter registration and voter turnout rates, may be so due to the university not knowing how to speak to them. Immediately two more important vulnerabilities became obvious.

First, Weber State University is 74.7% White, which means it is a predominantly White institution. It is trying to become a Hispanic Serving Institution, 12.1% of students fall in that racial-ethnic demographic category, and is deliberately reaching out to that community. The NSLVE data showed that White students registered to vote and then voted at higher rates than students of color. Weber State needed a more inclusive political engagement coalition that could develop outreach and messages that might resonate with the 25% students of color. Political engagement work can be particularly exclusive to students of color because the entire political system already alienates them. Imagine yourself as a member of a minoritized population on a predominantly White campus being told you had to talk about important political topics of the day. If White religious students were feeling chilled, then it must be the case that Weber State students of color were feeling that more so. We needed to find trusted messengers and on our campus at that time there were two places where our students of color could be found: in athletics and in multicultural centers, neither of which had staff who were represented on the coalition.

We were sensitive to the fact that staff from our multicultural centers are already asked to do a disproportionate amount of work on campuses. Yet, we knew anecdotally from our Hispanic students that the people they trusted most on campus were staff in those centers. Our campus only has 1.6% Black students, and they are over-represented in athletics. When we asked our student-athletes what it would take to make them get involved in politics and register to vote, they told us the people on campus they trusted most were their coaches. Athletics staff was harder to bring into the work because they are wary of politics and due to NCAA rules, they are kept separate from faculty. But no one in our coalition was going to be a trusted messenger for students of color and if we were going to invite those students, we had to know their coaches. We connected with our Senior Women's Administrator who helped us map out which coaches were the most interested in our work. She also helped us understand the reference points for our student athletes and how they are often out-of-state students, identified earlier as feeling disconnected from local students, and the athletics department was working to build them a community. To a certain extent, working with athletics helped us meet two of our gaps: Black students and out of state students. I reciprocated the work by serving on the Student Athletic Advisory Committee. Thus, building a diverse and engaged coalition can also help campuses address challenges of disproportionate work loads.

Second, Weber State University students in the STEM fields did not vote at the rates that students did in the Social Sciences and the Arts and Humanities. This trend is similar to campuses across the country that have shared NSLVE data. For Weber State, the top three voting fields were History, Foreign Languages, and English and most of the majors with top rates were in the broader areas of social sciences and arts and humanities. For the most part, STEM areas of studies had voting rates in the 30s, except for Math (43.2%). Interestingly, the IDHE report indicated that one math professor was teaching a course about the math of redistricting, which may have led to math students feeling some connection to politics. It is also an example of how fields of study can bring their own expertise to civic engagement work. But generally, science students reported that politics was not something that would ever be discussed in their classes. Again, this reflects national trends as well. We needed to have some scientists in the room. Using our NSLVE data, I visited faculty in colleges that had those fields of study and asked who would be interested in building our democracy.

INSTITUTIONALIZING THE ROOM WHERE IT HAPPENS

To be clear, Weber State's evolution was an organic process. For our civic work to lean into politics and meet the challenges of building the democracy we need, we need to be intentional about who is in the room when planning is happening. We need to foster reciprocal trusting relationships among our stakeholders so that we can protect the vulnerable groups in our student populations; by institutionalizing the work we create a system that works for them. To that end, I worked on a project[2] through an Ask Every Student co-designer grant to create a more systematic approach to Weber State's campus coalition and work. Ask Every Student is a "national joint initiative that facilitates collaboration between campus leaders and nonprofit partners to help campuses ask every student to participate in the democratic process and achieve full student voter registration" (Studentvoting, 2023). The initiative provided funds for people to design resources that would help campuses to conduct their voter engagement work. As part of the grant, we developed a power mapping tool and workshop activity to assist any campus to find and develop a coalition of the people who help the work thrive.

First, a campus should identify the partners for the coalition—who are the representatives of the disconnected segments we need to invite in? Four questions inform this work: (1) what is the purpose of your coalition?; (2) what is the scope of the work of your coalition?; (3) what are the gaps in your coalition?; and (4) what are any other considerations regarding your coalition? These guiding questions can help a campus that is new to the work as well as help disrupt the path-dependence of campuses who have done political engagement one way for a long time. The first two questions help to center the conversation. For example, at Weber State University, our coalition is a political engagement coalition operating during the fall semesters of even years, focused on voter registration, voter education, and voter mobilization. Because we have an institute that does the broader civic engagement work, members of the coalition know they have a limited, but intense, commitment during election season. But some campus coalitions may have broader or narrower scopes. Some campuses only operate during presidential election years. The third question speaks very directly to what we learned by accident: who is missing from the room? Finally, every campus lives in a political ecosystem and the fourth question helps flesh out that landscape. In Utah, for example, we are a Republican state and all the work we do is closely watched by our state legislature, which funds us. Every coalition must be very mindful of being non-partisan, but will also have to consider how their work is perceived.

Based on the answers to these guiding questions, campuses create a list of partners who should be in the room while planning political engagement. These partners will be the individuals who can help foster trust with other partners to build a healthy democratic system. For each partner, campuses should also determine what skills, connections and capacities or "superpowers" that partner brings. For example, as I highlighted earlier, at Weber State University we knew that students of color registered to vote and voted at lower rates than our White students. Narrowing in, we knew that our Black students, who only comprise 1.6% of students, were over-represented in our student-athlete population. In our partner identification activity, we noted that we needed to have coaches as partners, and we listed their superpower as being people that student-athletes respect. No one in our coalition was a coach and thus we did not have the best people to carry that message to those students, so we needed to identify a partner who specifically would be a trusted information broker for them. When those trusted messengers became involved, our student-athletes started participating and in 2020 we received national coverage from ESPN for their work volunteering as poll workers for the local County Clerk. The messaging for student athletes reached all our student-athletes generally but had the effect of connecting us to our Black students as well.

Partner identification should also be done regularly in conjunction with any new data about a campus. To be thoughtful about where the coalition meets gaps in your programming, be vigilant about seeing those gaps. Campus cultures are dynamic, and we need to always revisit how we are meeting the challenges. For example, as we built our coalition, we uncovered other places where students exclusively got information. We learned that some students only get information at campus entry points, and they were more likely to pay attention when they were on campus. Therefore, we needed to have staff from advising, parking, etc. also in our coalition. All places we might not immediately think of as being integral to a robust political engagement plan, but all have been very helpful in moving our work forward.

Once a campus identifies partners, create a map[3] of those partners based on two variables: the amount of support for the work and the amount of power they have on campus. Score each partner on campus on a scale from one to five, where one is opposed or a barrier to the work and five is actively supportive of the work; and on a scale from one to five, where one is not helpful for reaching the goals and five is essential for reaching the goals. The amount of support is then graphed on the x axis and the power of the partner is graphed on the y axis. This practice of power mapping allows people on campus to discuss who is most important, why they are most important, which can inform the understanding of civic engagement and how a campus defines it. The process also allows campus members to see who is vital and missing from the coalition and who may need more convincing to be involved.

Optimally, partners are in the top right quadrant: highly essential for reaching goals and super supportive of them. But democracy is never an optimal situation and campuses are microcosms of democracy. When you create a power map, you can see very quickly what you need and how much bandwidth it will require. In Weber State University's example, we needed athletics on board because coaches were trusted messengers to student-athletes. Yet there are obstacles to athletics participating because of NCAA guidelines that keep faculty away from coaches. Furthermore, given the divisive politics of the era, athletics did not want anything political at their sporting events. We were not allowed to conduct voter registration at football games for years because the whole idea was just too scary for the athletics department. Here is where knowing the superpower of people on campus is helpful. When we connected with our Senior Women's Administrator, we were able to make the argument that we should become part of their community. We worked with the interested coaches specifically and asked them who were the right people to reach out to. By the end of the process, Weber State's political engagement coalition has a strong relationship with powerful information brokers to student athletes resulting in a 100% voter registration among seven of our teams and dozens of student athletes volunteering as poll workers on Election Day in 2020 and 2022. Weber State also built, in conjunction with All In, a Big Sky Votes conference wide mobilization effort.

CONCLUSION

Since we deployed a coalition style of voter engagement leadership, our programming has reached more students across campus. In 2022, a midterm election year, we had over 900 students connect using our voter registration portal, which for a regional comprehensive university, most of our students are local and were registered in their high school, is a major accomplishment. It also approached the 1100 voter registrations we had in 2020, a presidential election year. The increase is also a far cry from the first voter registration drive the political science department conducted in 2002, which reached 78 students.

Once we identified who student athletes would listen to and brought the Athletics Division, their coaches and other key messengers into our coalition, Weber State had a 20-point jump in Black student voting from 2016 to 2020. Other racial demographics also increased in voter turnout: Asian student voting increased by six percentage points; American Indian/Alaska Native by five percentage point; Hispanic students increased by five percentage points; Native Hawaiian/Pacific Islanders increased 3 percentage points; students of more than one race increased by 13 percentage points; and White students by four percentage points from 2016 to 2020. All the boats rose with the tide and Weber State University closed previous racial gaps in voting.

In 2023, Weber State University hosted an event that challenged our legislature trying to ban diversity, equity, and inclusion on campuses by bringing the legislator who authored the bill as well as two legislators who kept it from passing to a panel discussion. 250 students showed up in silent and powerful protest holding signs saying they deserved to be seen. I can draw a line from the people in Weber State's coalition who are trustworthy to our students of color to the sign making activities that happened on campus prior to the event to the students knowing they could trust me enough to know that I was hosting something they could protest and would honor their right to do so. That event was one of the best attended political co-curricular events we have had on campus, and it was in large part possible due to the work of fostering trust among stakeholders through intentional coalition building at Weber State University.

In order to meet the needs of all students, Weber State University had to build a political engagement coalition with trusted messengers and information brokers. Using different studies and assessments described in this chapter, Weber State was able to identify gaps and needs and find the right campus leaders to mobilize different populations of students with the right messages.

NOTES

1. Four Quads is available for anyone to use at https://www.4quads.org/
2. This activity is part of the Coalition Building Curriculum in the *Ask Every Student* Toolkit and was developed in collaboration with the SLSV Coalition Resources & Support Subcommittee as part of the *Ask Every Student* 2022 Codesigner Cohort.
3. An example of the power map is accessible at https://www.studentvoting.org/institutional-partnerships

REFERENCES

Allen, B. (2004). Working together: How workplace bonds strengthen a diverse democracy. *Perspectives on Politics, 2*(3), 568–569. https://doi.org/10.1017/S153759270425037X

Ask Every Student. (n.d.). *About.* https://www.studentvoting.org/. Accessed 29 September 2023.

Burt, R. (2001). Structural holes versus network closure as social capital. In R. Burt (Ed.), *Social capital: Theory and research* (pp. 31–56). Aldine de Gruyter.

Connors, I. C., Domagal-Goldman, J., Hunt, S., Thomas, N., & Upchurch, K. (2018). *Weber state university: An IDHE campus climate report.* Institute for Democracy & Higher Education.

Cooke, O., Dolenc, P., & Schmidl-Gagne, K. (2018). Beyond left-right: teaching inequality with four ideological lenses. *International Journal of Pluralism and Economic Education, 9*(1/2). Retrieved from https://ideas.repec.org/a/ids/ijplur/v9y2018i1-2p18-35.html

Institute for Democracy & Higher Education. (n.d.) *The National Study of Learning, Voting, and Engagement.* https://idhe.tufts.edu/nslve, accessed 28 September 2023.

Jacoby, B. (2009). Civic engagement in today's higher education: An overview. In *Civic engagement in higher education: Concepts and practices.* John Wiley & Sons, Inc.

McMaster, C. (2013). Building inclusion from the ground up: A review of whole school re-culturing programmes for sustaining inclusive change. *International Journal of Whole Schooling, 9*(2).

Murray, L., Upchurch, K., & Thomas, N. (in press). Assessing campus climates for politically charged times. *JHOE.*

Murray, L. (2024). Is the engagement working? Assessing political engagement across multiple departments. In L. Bell, C. Ong Whaley, & A.D. Rank (Eds.). *Civic pedagogy: Teaching engagement in an era of divisive politics.*

Newton, K. (2001). Trust, social capital, civil society, and democracy. *International Political Science Review, 22*(2), 201–214. https://doi.org/10.1177/0192512101222004

Paxton, P. (2002). Social capital and democracy: An interdependent relationship. *American Sociological Review, 67*(2), 254–277. https://doi.org/10.2307/3088895

Putnam, R. D. (2000). *Bowling alone: The collapse and revival of American community.* Simon & Schuster.

Sides, J. (1999). *It takes two: The reciprocal relationship between social capital and democracy.* UC Berkeley: Institute of Governmental Studies. Retrieved from https://escholarship.org/uc/item/2z6534q2

Students Learn Students Vote Coalition. (n.d.). *Building equitable, diverse, and inclusive campus coalitions for full participation.* https://www.studentvoting.org/institutional-partnerships. Accessed 11 September 2023.

Tavits, M. (2006). Making democracy work more? Exploring the linkage between social capital and government performance. *Political Research Quarterly, 59*(2), 211–225. https://doi.org/10.1177/106591290605900204

Thomas, N., & Brower, M. (2017). Politics 365: Fostering campus climates for student political learning and engagement. In E. C. Matto, A. R. M. McCartney, E. A. Bennion, & D. Simpson (Eds.), *Teaching civic engagement across the disciplines* (pp. 361–374). American Political Science Association.

Thomas, N., Copeland, C., Murray, L. A., & Upchurch, K. (2021). Assessing and improving political learning and engagement on college campuses. *eJournal of Public Affairs, 10*(3). https://bearworks.missouristate.edu/ejopa/vol10/iss3/10/

Tocqueville, A. d. (1838). *Democracy in America.* G. Dearborn & Co.

Uslaner, E. M. (1999). Democracy and social capital. In M. E. Warren (Ed.), *Democracy and trust* (pp. 121–150). Cambridge University Press. https://doi.org/10.1017/CBO9780511659959.005

CHAPTER 11

OPENING THE "POD" DOORS

The Public Intellectual in an Age of Democratic Decline

Saladin Ambar
Rutgers University

ABSTRACT

This chapter is a reflection on my experiences as the host of the Eagleton Institute of Politics at Rutgers University's podcast, This Moment in Democracy. The podcast, begun in 2022, focuses on topics and individuals tied to important political questions facing the nation, with the "Moment" portion of the podcast's title reflecting the present and precarious state of American democracy. My short stint as host to date has led me to consider a number of early lessons that point to how public intellectuals working on university campuses and engaging in new and increasingly varied media formats, may be part of the solution to reinvigorating American democracy—albeit not without first addressing a number of important risks.

In the summer of 2022, I was asked if I'd be interested in hosting a podcast for the institute of politics I'm affiliated with at Rutgers University. The

Eagleton Institute of Politics has a long and distinguished history as the State of New Jersey's leading institution where the practice of politics—the world of government and politicians (not to be confused with the world of its more abstract cousin, political science)—is taught. Working at such an institution was and is a special kind of experience, as many of my colleagues in political science do not always share a love of politics. At Eagleton, it is nearly a prerequisite. Taking on the role of podcast host was really a no-brainer for me, given my own interests, and my deep affinity for the values and mission of Eagleton.

What I've learned from the experience may be of some use to those who fashion themselves public intellectuals, a somewhat bloated and overused term, but one that nevertheless has not found its better. To be clear, a public intellectual as I define it here, is someone whose scholarship is intended to speak to those outside academia, as much as it is intended for those in one's discipline. This is not only a matter of language choices one makes (eschewing vainglorious academic terminology, for example), as it is one of subject matter. A public intellectual is going to not only speak from the vantagepoint of the broader public, but also explore topics of particular interest and relevance to it as well. Within these parameters reside a good deal of diversity in terms of individuals, subjects, and methodological approaches for reaching the general public.

By way of example, I would consider the historian and economist Thomas Piketty and the political scientist Danielle S. Allen, to be trafficking in the same field in this regard, even though they offer rather different respective approaches in doing so. Both scholars employ innovative and yet familiar tools in their methodological approaches. For Allen, her work on racial segregation in the United States centers the theme of friendship in her narrative, while Piketty's work on wealth inequality uses historical novels to assist in his comparative historical analysis (see, e.g., Allen, 2004; Piketty, 2017). Both works are rich in analytical depth and their respective efforts to make difficult conceptual arguments more accessible is the definition of public-facing scholarship.

What I hope to do in this short chapter is offer some considerations for those engaged in this kind of work—or hoping to (perhaps in some "post-tenured world," as many tell it, usually with a weighty aspirational sigh). Having been a blogger (Huffington Post), commentator (PBS New York and New Jersey's MetroFocus), and columnist (NJ Spotlight), among other public-oriented endeavors, I can say that the world of podcasting is not all that much different. Each of these kinds of projects ask their protagonists to adopt a handful of roles, all juggled at the same time, that will undoubtedly test how one feels about what they're doing, and whether they wish to continue doing it at all.

This gauging of one's satisfaction in the role of public intellectual has arguably become more intense in recent years, if for no other reason than American democracy has been strained to something approaching a breaking point. And that makes the choices we entertain as academics intentionally speaking to fellow-citizens all the more consequential. In the next pages I will address the "multiple personalities" embedded in the life of a public intellectual—especially those charged with taking upon themselves tasks that go beyond one's more prosaic role as scholar and instructor. Indeed, there are at least four such personalities that I have had to reflect on since hosting "This Moment in Democracy." They include my responsibility to the *forum* itself—in this case a brand-new undertaking by the Institute, one whose mission and purpose are ipso facto, greater than my own.

The second "personality" to be juggled is that of the larger university and how one's work reflects upon not only the forum (a podcast in my case), but also the entity beyond (Rutgers). Former National Football League Commissioner Pete Rozelle would often describe his primary job as protecting the "shield," by which he meant the NFL insignia, i.e., its brand. There is a kind of "shield cognizance" at play in the life of the public intellectual who has to be mindful of the *institution* they are working for. In addition, there is that other, occasionally forgotten party, the *self*. In other words, one must cultivate an awareness and sense of responsibility for representing, let's say, a podcast, and then a university, while being mindful of how approaching a particular topic may challenge your personal, political, and perhaps even moral sensibilities.

Finally, there is the dirty little secret that while most colleges and universities say they value "public-facing" faculty, the truth of the matter is that most simply value publicity, and at the micro-level, departments reward *scholarship* above and beyond anything else. This sword cuts two ways in that all research-oriented institutions place a premium on publishing, but not all value the type of scholarship public intellectuals produce. Might I add, that this latter reality often serves as a convenient cloak to shroud a greater or lesser antipathy to the work of scholars of color and other more marginalized members of the academic community. *That* is for another book—but there it is. The work of a public intellectual in academia has to be considered in this somewhat shaded light where outwardly directed scholarship is praised and encouraged, but all too often ignored, and at times, punished. Certainly, taking unpopular or controversial opinions can lead to difficulties in advancing one' career; but the more subtle impediment can be found in employing qualitative methodologies, particularly in the service of public-facing work. When I first heard "I don't know what to think about this 'American Political Development,'" from a senior colleague as I did in my first job, it proved to be less about unfamiliarity with a fairly well-entrenched methodological approach within political science (historical institutionalism) than it was an admonition against public oriented work. Needless to say, by Thanksgiving I was looking for another job.

Is that enough to dissuade you from accepting that position as host, columnist, cable television contributor, and overall "face" of your university outside Hickman Hall or wherever you teach? I hope not. I hope not because as self-serving as it sounds, the country needs you. There has not been a more important time for public intellectuals in the United States. After sharing my own experiences with these four faces of the public intellectual—*forum leader, institutional representative, individual,* and *scholar*—perhaps you will rethink taking on the task of continuing or joining the ranks of public intellectuals. Don't let the admittedly pretentious sounding quality of the term fool you. There is, after all, little more pretentious than thinking one's own work, however "private" or "academic," does not have its own set of consequences for the broader public as well. So, let us choose among pretensions. I sincerely hope you choose the former. Here are the four variables for you to consider.

THE FORUM

The moment you accept an offer to attach yourself to a venue in the service of the broader public, you relinquish a bit of yourself. Most academics know this—your university press of choice is going to edit your work; it will be sent out for review, and your ideas will be refashioned, even in the slightest degree. Most of us write this off as the democratization of ideas and we extoll the virtues of a vigorous peer-review process. That said, speaking for myself, I don't "like" it as such. Six books into my career I still longingly await the email from my editor informing me that my "manuscript has been accepted as is—amazing job!" I'm not holding my breath.

Of course, this is the most basic example of what attaching oneself to public spaces is like for the would-be public intellectual. Giving a talk at the 92nd Street Y? Guess what—their expectations, culture, audience, and implicit demands are going to be different than the ones at, say, the Schomburg Center for Research in Black Culture, or Powell's Books. Learning these subtle differences is important—and each venue will ask you to abide by the cultural norms they've come to be known by. When I began hosting the podcast in 2022, I was in a sense responsible for helping to establish what these norms and expectations would be for "This Moment in Democracy." In what is anticipated as a perennial virtual venue for Eagleton, a basic understanding, not spoken aloud, but there all the same, is that I should be effective enough as a host to go unnoticed. This virtue allows for an interchangeability of the role sufficient to account for the changes wrought by life as an academic: sickness, death, and outside offers. Anyone—well perhaps not *anyone*, but lots of people—should be able to step in and fill your role in the event any of the aforementioned should occur.

This means keeping a hint of space between one's full personality and beliefs and the sanctity of the forum's burgeoning identity. In a word, you ain't Marc Maron. Or whomever your favorite podcast host, columnist, cable contributor, or vlogger is. One of the oddities and challenges for gauging success can be found in the clever interplay between venue and personality that offers just enough intrigue from the latter, without drowning out the vibrancy of the former. If you have watched an episode of "Inside the Actors Studio" after James Lipton stepped down, then bully for you. I suspect you are in a distinct minority.

The public intellectual's venue—and there will likely be many over the course of a career—is to be respected and its format honored. This is true whether or not you are responsible for its growth or merely a visitor. If you are charged with representing the venue in some way, or at the very least, upholding its values, then learning what those interests and values are before engaging, goes without saying. I've known a number of progressive colleagues, who for example, have approached the invitation to appear on FOX News rather differently. The same is true for friends asked to appear on RT television, Russia's news outlet. If you agree to go on, then be prepared to play by the rules they've established. And remember, that old adage "no person steps into the same river twice" applies. Any forum you engage is bound to change you, even if it's just the public's perception of you. How great or small a change is indeterminate—but accept that some change is likely to occur. More on this later.

Finally, one more trite aphorism: there are horses for courses. Be sure the forum you decide to share your knowledge with the public from is a good fit for your goals, values, and sense of self-worth. In a sense, being a public intellectual calls for the managing of your academic career in new and often unclear ways. If you have not thought about how writing, appearing, or speaking somewhere will enhance your effectiveness as said public intellectual, then please do. It is better to do well in those venues that are in keeping with who you are—or at least aspire to be—in the public imagination, than those that poorly fit, though opportune. To wit, I leave you with the reminder that when asked about how he felt about being typecast as a tough guy, Humphrey Bogart (1954) responded: "I think [typecasting] makes stars out of people." Nobody will become a Bogart or Bacall from the perch of a political science department, but if you wish to maximize your effectiveness as a public intellectual, like Bogey, learn what you do best—and who you are at your core—and hew closely to that.

YOUR INSTITUTION

My work as podcast host has provided me the opportunity to engage with some well-known and intriguing political personalities. And yet, their engagement is as much with the university as it is with me. It's important to remember that by agreeing to be interviewed, they are also seeking something—promoting a new book, or political idea—or maybe just building their "personal brand," as it were. They are doing so, not because I'm the host, but because Rutgers University provides the social currency they're looking for. Moreover, that institutional affiliation is also a reminder that how I personally interact with guests reflects upon the university.

Unless you are operating under your own banner, you will have to weigh how your podcast, lecture, television appearance, and the like reflect not only upon you, but also your institution. How much this reflection shapes your actions is a personal decision, but you'd be unwise not to consider it. Are there any number of directions during interviews I would have liked to have traveled with guests that I've shied away from? Absolutely. I can recall one interview with a former New Jersey politician where I personally would have liked to revisit an episode from their career that was challenging, to say the least. While I've never been told what not to ask or cover, it has been fairly easy for me to intuit that certain questions are best asked by journalists rather than me. Again, it comes down to understanding the mission of the institution, the venue, and as I will discuss next, what you can personally abide. Journalists are expected to adopt a somewhat pointed, if not adversarial stance, when interviewing people—it is the essence of the "softball" question critique. In academia, on the other hand, an interview with a campus (or virtual) guest typically involves a relationship the institution wishes to cultivate or improve. To date myself here, "Sam Donaldsoning" your way through a campus interview with a guest may score you points—but not the kind you want (if you can't ask your grandparents about this style of journalism see, Donaldson, 1987).

If you and your institution—the one creating the financial and creative support for what you're doing—agree that your purpose is to upend the status quo or "speak truth to power" in your forum, then by all means, go there. Personally, I see this better fulfilled in my role as scholar and teacher. It is in these latter two roles that I am as unapologetically "me" as anyone can be. I'll have a few things to say about scholarship shortly, but the point here is to remember that your journey as a public intellectual involves myriad roles: scholar, teacher, mentor, adviser, public speaker, and so forth. Each of these incarnations calls for slightly different presentations of oneself. You should never compromise your fundamental values for anyone or any place; but prudence dictates judging where the expression of those values is best offered. Going on your college's radio station to rant about your president's or department chair's, or provost's *godawful* policies may be in keeping with "who you are," but I'd suggest a thoughtful opinion piece somewhere in lieu of this.

Dare I say, in the age of social media the ability of public intellectuals to "let it fly" has been seriously curtailed. Some deliciously irreverent insights have undoubtedly been lost these past few decades. But so have some deeply offensive, and fairly goofy commentaries. Knowing that one's words carry an immortal tail that follows you online—think of it as an unforgiving Haley's Comet—we are well past the age of Buckley-Vidal verbal fisticuffs (Gordon, 2015). Is this partly the result of the deepening corporatization of universities, media, and intellectuals, themselves? Certainly (Andrews & Catropa, 2013). We all are teaching and learning in a far more sanitized cultural milieu than our forebears. Some of this lost behavior has thankfully been confined to the ashbin of history. Some of it was damned necessary and profoundly intriguing. My word of advice on this front: let your scholarship first, and your teaching, second, be the avenues by which your irreverence shines. When your name and public persona is attached to something else—PBS, MSNBC, Chautauqua, or whatever—the carpenter's rule applies. Measure twice, cut once, lest you be the one cut.

YOU

I would not interview Donald Trump. At least not as our podcast is currently convened—a nonpartisan, information gathering and disseminating venue for political and policy enthusiasts. It is not my role to "go after" our guests. I could not in good conscience abide this role in the case of former President Trump. And I imagine, there are other prospective guests who fit this bill as well. At the very least such a decision on my part would require a rethinking of our format if even for this one interview. Perhaps that moment will arise with other future guests. I do not mean to raise a straw man argument. There has been the very occasional guest whose language or approach has caused us to revisit what we are willing to memorialize under the Eagleton Institute's banner. So, the avowed White nationalist and insurrectionist alone doesn't present this problem. But such a hypothetical case does raise the question of how to manage potential gulfs between host and guest with respect to political divides.

At the time of this writing there are guests on the horizon that raise such dilemmas for me. While none rise to the level of Trump, I find myself currently weighing what kinds of questions I simply cannot *not* ask. This is where the Venn diagram's center containing the interests of the podcast and my own becomes somewhat hazy. And by interests here, I mean my personal integrity—what I do not wish to face in the mirror the next morning.

In the end, your role as commentator, podcast host, lecturer and the rest ought not be bigger than your most important relationship: the one with yourself. One doesn't make a very good public intellectual—or even podcast host—if one can hide behind that persona when convenient.

All of this may ring as somewhat pretentious, but if you're reading this then more likely than not you are in a profession where standing, writing, and yes, pontificating, before the public is your job description. We may not wish to think of it as such, but even the most democratic of classrooms let alone articles or books are dependent upon the premise that you are the expert assigned to share your worldview. Or at least a slice of it. Given we are in a moment where American democracy faces a host of unique vulnerabilities, the role of public intellectual has never been more important. This means the exercising of wisdom in that role—choosing one's battles carefully while not running from those that call for all the courage you can muster—is essential. Don't sell your visibility, however great or small, short. If you find yourself in a place where your personal moral compass is compromised by engaging with a forum, institution, or individual be prepared to walk away. Or, if you must, be willing to let the face behind the microphone or lectern to be fully exposed. Allowing your work to be edited is one thing; allowing *yourself* to be edited is something entirely different.

SCHOLARSHIP

A final caveat about working as a public intellectual in this moment of enormous flux. Democratic decline be damned. Most colleges and universities want you to publish and will not, despite their full-throated proclamations to the contrary, reward you for your work in the public arena. Those opinion pieces, radio appearances, and television spots notwithstanding, the prestige of the realm has changed little over the years: it's still publish or perish. So, be sure before embarking on this important venture of bringing your research and expertise before the public that you have established a level of publication that inoculates you from the put-downs sure to come, that your work is vanity based or less "rigorous" than your colleagues. Nothing quite smarts like the rebuke that your work is "not political science" (though in time this may come to be a great compliment for you). Make it smart less by having a record that makes such rebukes look like what they generally are: petty. At the end of the day, universities are in the business of promoting themselves before promoting public discourse. When the two ends are in harmony, all is well. When they are not, be sure to have established a good rapport with your school's media relations person.

There is a kind of allure to building a public persona I've seen lead to considerable problems for friends and those less familiar to me over the years. My lamentations about this usually conclude with the proviso: "If only Icarus had published!" Stay in academia long enough and you're likely to get burned. But your scholarly record and reputation does afford you some protective covering for those who for whatever reason, don't like, grasp, or appreciate your work, and wish to let the world know it. This is especially true for racial minorities and women in the profession who all too often have to depend on external letters to advance within their home institutions. Of my 15 years as a professor, only one of them was spent where I was not the only Black male in the department, and that was my first. Remember, your scholarly flag is harder to dismiss than your article in the *Washington Post's* Monkey Cage. Therefore, build as strong a scholarly edifice as possible, dear public intellectual, especially if you are a member of a scholarly community that has had to produce twice as much to be taken half as seriously. Even this is no guarantee, but you will have done all you could.

Ultimately, the best public intellectuals have a scholarly track record that goes before them, lending credibility and hard-earned insights that enrich their communication. Coupled with an appreciation that not everyone has read Thomas Kuhn, one can generate real interest and understanding of the world we live in—no small feat in a most confusing time. Now that you have been armed with this bit of coffee-table book wisdom, I'll share some thoughts about where you—and we—go from here.

CONCLUSION: THE FUTURE OF THE PUBLIC INTELLECTUAL

My favorite book in my youth from a public intellectual was written by someone not trained in the academy. Harold Cruse's complex, searing, and at times maddening 1967 tome, *The Crisis of the Negro Intellectual*, opened a world of insights to me as someone just beginning to ponder his place in the world of ideas (Cruse, 2005). Undoubtedly Cruse's position as an outsider was critical to his ability to generate novel and penetrating insights into the world of Black political and cultural life in the 1960s. Cruse's lack of a PhD didn't hurt him from making an enormous impact on the discourse on race and American democracy. It was an era of autodidacts and polymaths who, steeped in a world of books, travel, and meaningful intellectual battles, garnered their share of the marketplace of ideas.

Sadly, the intellectual battles of our era are being defined by Twitter-Takedowns and tiresome rejoinders on cable television. Tik Tok has seemingly become but the latest fad passing for the cutting edge of political discourse. From the 1950s to late 1980s, everyone knew who the great public intellectuals were. Today, people don't even read the *New Yorker* for the cartoons.

This is all the more reason to embrace the effort, though a vain one it may be. Part of the restoration project in American democracy must be the reconvening of public intellectuals—people reading serious books with important things to say without talking down to people. There are, of course, notable exceptions and they can't do it by themselves. Academia should continue to be the great nursery for bringing these great minds to the public. That means doing our part to make sure professors are free to enter the enterprise without fear of tainted tenure files or being pressured by statewide elected leaders for having done so. The relationship between public political thinkers and democracy has always been integral to the health of the polity. Where there's atrophy in one, there is atrophy in the other.

No, your podcast, column, commentary, or lecture won't "save democracy." That's asking too much. But every venture forward expands the thinking space of our fellow Americans—the *demos* of our democracy. And if it is a failed venture, at least you'll have retained your conscience, dare I say, your soul. So, sleep tight as Shakespeare's Brutus slept, knowing (Shakespeare, 2023):

> I shall have glory by this losing day
> More than Octavius and Mark Antony
> By this vile conquest shall attain unto.

REFERENCES

Allen, D. S. (2004). *Talking to strangers: Anxieties of citizenship since* Brown v. Board of Education. University of Chicago Press.

Andrews, M., & Catropa, D. (2013, February 8). Bemoaning the corporatization of higher education. *Inside Higher Ed.* https://www.insidehighered.com/blogs/stratedgy/bemoaning-corporatization-higher-education

Cruse, H. (2005). *The crisis of the Negro intellectual.* New York Review of Books Classics.

Donaldson, S. (1987). *Hold on, Mr. President!* Random House.

Mowat, B. A., & Werstein, P. (Eds.). (2023). *The tragedy of Julius Caesar.* Folger Library.

Piketty, T. (2017). *Capital in the twenty-first century.* Belknap Press.

Gordon, R. (2015, August 4). The fight that changed political TV forever. *Politico.* https://www.politico.com/magazine/story/2015/08/04/william-buckley-gore-vidal-debates-1968-121009/

SECTION III

STRENGTHENING STUDENT VOICE AND ENHANCING CIVIC SKILLS AND DISPOSITIONS

CHAPTER 12

DEVELOPING EMPOWERED CITIZENS

How Universities Help Build Efficacy

Laurie L. Rice
Southern Illinois University Edwardsville

Kenneth Moffett
Southern Illinois University Edwardsville

ABSTRACT

For many students who start college immediately after completing high school, a college education overlaps the period in which they move from being ineligible to vote in elections to having the chance to vote in their first presidential election. Yet, neither reaching the age of enfranchisement nor enrolling in a university guarantee that young people feel empowered to participate, nor that they see the importance of voting in a democracy. Using data from surveys of students at Southern Illinois University Edwardsville in 2016, we test whether taking classes on government and being encouraged by anyone to vote in that election are connected with changes in political efficacy. We discover that taking a class on government and politics is connected with higher perceptions of being better informed about politics than others, and that being encouraged to vote in the 2016 presidential election is associated with a decrease in the perception that one's vote does not matter.

Colleges and universities are commonly viewed as important for democracy.[1] Preparing students to participate in democracy was part of the founding mission of many universities, regardless of current institutional mission (Checkoway, 2001). Yet, while education level consistently predicts voting and other forms of political participation (see, e.g., Campbell et al., 1960; Rosenstone & Hansen, 1993; Verba et al., 1995) several recent studies have found limited impact of a university education on voting and other forms of political participation (Berkinsky & Lenz, 2011; Kam & Palmer, 2008, 2011; Niemi & Klinger, 2012).[2] For example, Kam and Palmer (2008, 2011) found that once experiences prior to college are considered, no difference in participation exists between those who attend and complete college versus those who do not attend.[3]

More worrisome, Niemi and Klinger (2012) examined participation rates among 18 to 24-year-olds and found that those who did not attend college had significantly higher levels of political participation than university students. The few studies that found a positive impact of education on participation focus more narrowly on specific elements of a college education like one's number of credits in the social sciences (Hillygus, 2005), or whether one has taken a political science course (Moffett & Rice, 2015). In sum, Persson (2015, p. 699) states that, "The literature provides a frustrating, divided picture and we are left without a clear answer as to whether education causes political participation."

The lack of a clear, consistent causal link between a college education and participation in democracy could be linked to the activities that universities do or do not undertake to advance their civic mission. After all, even those universities that focus on civic engagement often limit their efforts to community engagement and avoid the democratic dimensions of civic engagement (Saltmarsh & Harley, 2011). Thus, the evidence to date is mixed with respect to whether universities are fulfilling their civic mission. In a challenging and polarized political environment, the absence of clear evidence likely creates difficulties for universities in supporting the nonpartisan activities needed to help students engage with the political process. After all, explicitly nonpartisan activities are still interpreted by some as suspect and partisan, especially in areas where increased voting rates among traditionally aged college students, who lean leftward politically (Pew Research Center, 2020), might influence election outcomes. Without evidence to support the value of these activities, and under heightened scrutiny, more universities may hesitate to engage in activities that could help strengthen democracy.

In this chapter, we speak indirectly to this debate by focusing on how colleges and universities can facilitate beliefs crucial for sustaining and strengthening democracy through developing attitudes conducive to active citizenship. We begin by discussing the role of political efficacy, and why developing this is important for young people. We then test whether taking courses on government and politics, and encouraging people to vote in the presidential election are connected with changes in political efficacy. These results can help universities who are beginning to focus on their civic mission identify effective actions they can take to help promote engaged citizens. Also, these results furnish concrete evidence of these actions' value for those institutions whose efforts are more developed but face heightened scrutiny.

THE IMPORTANCE OF EFFICACY

Like the links between education level, voter turnout and political participation, political efficacy has regularly predicted many forms of political participation, including voting (See e.g., Campbell et al., 1960; Oser et al., 2022; Rosenstone & Hansen, 1993; Verba et al., 1995). Political efficacy has multiple dimensions including "the effectiveness the individual feels in his relation to politics" (Campbell et al., 1960, p. 104) and "a sense of personal competence in one's ability to understand politics and to participate in politics (what political scientists call internal efficacy) as well as a sense that one's political activities can influence what the government actually does (external efficacy)" (Rosenstone & Hansen, 1993, p. 15). While educational attainment predicts political efficacy (Campbell et al., 1960; Jackson, 1995), little attention has been paid to the extent to which higher education facilitates or develops political efficacy.

This potential link between higher education and political efficacy is important to explore because many young adults may arrive at college lacking the efficacy necessary to participate. Frequently, those entering college directly from high school experience their first opportunity to participate in a presidential election during their undergraduate experience. After years of not being old enough to vote, young adults may not automatically possess a strong sense of political efficacy. While successful participation enhances efficacy (Valentino et al., 2009), young adults who receive their first opportunity to vote in an election cannot draw upon prior experience in successfully participating in elections. Condon and Holleque (2013) suggest that young people's efficacy at this stage is instead developed from observing family members' participation. A self-concept of political competence in early adulthood is connected with being more likely to vote and engage in an array of political activities (Krampen, 2000).

To the extent that young adults' efficacy is determined by their home life and socioeconomic status, education might reinforce participatory inequality (Paulsen, 1991) rather than help young people who previously lacked efficacy develop it. Yet, several studies indicate universities can play a valuable role in helping students develop efficacy. Beaumont (2011) found that being part of a politically active community as an undergraduate and participating in a program that emphasized political action skills mitigates this efficacy gap. While students began with varying efficacy levels which were heavily influenced by their socioeconomic status, program participation helped reduce the influence of socioeconomic status on efficacy (Beaumont, 2011). Colby et al (2007) studied 21 courses and cocurricular programs focused on political engagement and found significant increases in participants' internal efficacy levels. Yet, the programs that Beaumont (2011) and Colby et al (2007) studied were not available university-wide, but rather were available to a limited number of students. Might other simple and more widely accessible activities also contribute to students' efficacy levels?

The most common reasons college students gave for not voting include perceptions that they don't know enough about politics, or that their vote doesn't matter (Booth et al., 2023; DelleVolpe, 2023). We hear these sentiments in our classrooms, and they are supported by survey research (Booth et al., 2023; DelleVolpe, 2023).[4] Both reasons are tied to a lack of political efficacy, with the former concern more closely aligned with a lack of internal efficacy and the latter more consistent with a lack of external efficacy. Colleges and universities can potentially help students overcome deficits in both types of political efficacy through activities that help equip students with political knowledge and demonstrate to students the value of voting.

DEVELOPING EFFICACY

We examine how colleges and universities can help students develop the dispositions on which a sense of civic agency depends by offering classes on government and encouraging students to vote in elections. Classes on government educate students on governmental institutions, political behavior, current politics and other topics relevant to elections. These courses should help students feel better informed about government and politics and counter feelings that they lack enough knowledge to participate. Taking a class about government and politics may also help reduce feelings that one's vote does not matter, but we would not expect having been encouraged by someone to vote to increase perceptions of one's political knowledge. Meanwhile, encouragements to vote, whether from faculty, student organizations, university officials or other students can counter perceptions that one's vote does not matter. These encouragements may counter perceptions explicitly, by offering arguments regarding the value of voting. Or, they may occur implicitly by providing signals from trusted voices that voting is important. In either event, Holbein and Hillygus (2020) note that activities like taking a class and being encouraged to vote may help students overcome personal barriers and follow through on an intent to vote. Thus, we expect that taking a class about government and politics and having been encouraged by someone to vote is connected with changes in different aspects of efficacy.

To assess these links, we rely on online survey data of students between the ages of 18 and 25 at a specific university, Southern Illinois University Edwardsville (SIUE).[5] This sample was gathered in October 2016 prior to the election. Right after the 2016 general election, there was a follow up survey sent to students who responded to the pre-election survey. The pre-election survey had a response rate of approximately 9.7% (Rice and Moffett, 2019). While this raises questions about generalizability, this university represents the populations of many similar universities in many respects (see Moffett & Rice, 2016). However, part of this University's mission is to provide social and economic mobility through an affordable, high-quality education, having one of the lowest tuition rates in its state, and admitting the vast majority of its first-time freshmen and transfer applicants (SIUE, 2023).

Because of its institutional focus, it serves many students unlikely to come to college with high levels of political efficacy due to the link between high socioeconomic status and heightened political efficacy. This provides a good test case for the potential of college activities to help increase students' efficacy. The other advantage of focusing on a single university is we can compare the democratic agency and internal efficacy of otherwise similar students who have experienced specific interventions like taking a class on government[6,7] or being encouraged to vote to those who have not had these experiences. Before discussing our matching methodology and results, we identify known shapers of efficacy that we consider in the analysis as matching covariates, along with how we measure them.

Personal Characteristics

Students' efficacy levels are likely related to their personal characteristics, including their choice of major, strength of partisanship and demographic characteristics such as race or ethnicity and gender. Beaumont (2011) found that political science majors have higher levels of efficacy compared to students of other majors. Some studies also link other social science majors to higher participation levels (e.g., Hillygus. 2005) and because efficacy predicts participation, this may suggest other social science majors also possess higher levels of efficacy compared to students majoring in other subjects. We use two binaries for political science and other social science majors based on answers to a question in which we asked about each student's major. More information about the question wording for each item, summary statistics, matching balance statistics, robustness checks, and reverse causality checks is available in the Online Appendix.

In a two-party system, the strength of attachment with a major political party is likely to also shape perceptions of efficacy, including the value of one's vote. Previous research demonstrates that strength of partisanship is associated with higher levels of both internal and external efficacy (Jackson, 1995). By using a series of questions, we construct a binary for those who self-identify as strong partisans.

Gender is associated with political efficacy. On the one hand, Beaumont (2011) reports that gender is a significant predictor of college students' initial efficacy levels, with men having higher efficacy levels. Jackson (2005) also finds men have higher internal efficacy levels, but there is not a gender gap for external political efficacy. However, Zhou and Pinkleton (2012) found female students had higher levels of external political efficacy. To consider the potential impact of gender, we asked each respondent for their sex and used a binary for females.

Similarly, race or ethnicity is also connected with efficacy, with contradictory findings about this relationship as well. Paulsen (1991) found that those who are members of racial minority groups have lower levels of efficacy and Beaumont (2011) found that White students had higher initial levels of efficacy. Conversely, Jackson (1995) found that Black students had higher levels of internal efficacy, but lower levels of external efficacy.[8] To account for the potential impact of race or ethnicity, we asked each respondent for their race and ethnicity.

Past Experiences With Politics

Past political activity, like voting, can increase one's efficacy especially if that person sees it as successful (Valentino et al., 2009). Students who were eligible to vote in a previous election and chose to do so are likely to have higher levels of efficacy than students considering voting for the first time. While 18-to-25-year-olds have only been eligible to participate in zero to two presidential elections, depending on their age, those with past experience with voting likely have higher efficacy. Each respondent was asked whether they had voted in elections prior to this election.

Yet, other experiences with politics besides voting may also shape students' efficacy. These include students' levels of political information consumption and their online political expression. Zhou and Pinkleton (2012) found that online news consumption was associated with heightened political efficacy among young adults. While Zhou and Pinkleton (2012) did not find a direct link between online political expression and political efficacy, others have. Lane et al (2019, p. 63) uncovered that "... the more respondents felt motivated to present themselves as politically active on social media, the more they viewed themselves as politically interested, efficacious, and active." Further posting political opinions or sharing political material on Facebook have been found to increase political interest (Lane et al., 2019). Thus, students who consume political information online or share political content or opinions are likely to also have higher efficacy.

We use several indicators to operationalize these constructs. We measure the effects of internet news readership and reading blogs about politics based on responses to two questions about these items with five-point response options ranging from not at all to very often. To consider the effects of online political participation on political efficacy, we use an index of four different items that include expressing one's views online in several ways and sharing images or webpages about politics, candidates, or interest groups ($\alpha = .86$). We also employ a two-item index that comprises watching videos on the internet and reading social media feeds about politics to measure the effects of social media exposure on efficacy ($\alpha = .77$).

Political Engagement of Parents and Friends

For young people who lack experience with voting, the political experiences of one's family may influence one's own efficacy levels (Condon & Holleque, 2013). Beaumont (2011) found that political discussion at home before coming to college was a significant predictor of college students' initial efficacy levels. We use three five-point indicators ranging from strongly disagree to strongly agree to measure the effects of parents' political participation: the extent to which they regularly vote in elections, encourage the respondent to express their own opinions about politics even if they differ from their parents and discussing politics at home when growing up. These indicators were reported by students and not their parents, as parents were not surveyed.

Similarly, the political activity of young people's friends can also be an important influence on political activity among young people (Quintelier et al., 2012; Moffett & Rice, 2016). We use a three-item index to measure the effects of peer civic engagement, including friends being active in volunteer work in their community, voting in elections, and encouraging the respondent to express their opinions about politics even if they differ from the peer group ($\alpha = .68$).

College Activities

Our dependent variables focus on two forms of efficacy that young adults frequently lack. We use one indicator of internal efficacy and a different one of external efficacy. We asked each respondent on a five-point scale about the extent to which they felt that they were better informed about politics and government than most people (internal efficacy) and the extent to which they believe that their vote doesn't matter (external efficacy). The response options ranged from agree strongly to disagree strongly.

We use two binary variables to measure the effects of taking a class on government, politics or civics, and being encouraged by anyone to vote in the 2016 presidential election. We expect a positive sign for taking a class on government and politics for our measure of internal efficacy, as these classes should help increase students' knowledge about government and politics. We also anticipate that there may be a negative sign for taking a class on government and politics for our measure of external efficacy, as some classes on government and politics emphasize the importance of voting. A negative sign would indicate that the class led them to disagree that their vote did not matter. Meanwhile, we anticipate a negative relationship between having been encouraged to vote and our indicator of external efficacy, as encouragements to vote should decrease perceptions that one's vote does not matter. However, we do not anticipate having been encouraged to vote will have a significant impact on our indicator of internal efficacy, as these encouragements to vote were not typically paired with information about candidates or political issues.

Matching Method

We utilize one-to-one genetic matching with replacement to execute our analyses (Diamond & Sekhon, 2013; Sekhon, 2011). We incorporate a propensity score into the analysis, as having knowledge of this score's estimated values improves the accuracy of this method (Diamond & Sekhon, 2013). Matching in this manner allows us to compare observations that are otherwise similar on an array of covariates, but have received different treatments. This analysis is performed with replacement, as matching discrepancies are reduced because we can use untreated units as a match more than once (see Abadie & Imbens, 2006). Our matching routines include a bias correction to eliminate any bias that comes about due to our choice of a matching estimator without impacting the variance of that estimator (Abadie & Imbens, 2016).

This technique improves upon an ordered logistic regression in two ways. First, matching allows us to estimate an average treatment effect on the treated (ATT) while an ordered logistic regression does not. Second, matching allows us to estimate what would have happened in the absence of taking classes on government and politics, or on being encouraged to vote. This happens by utilizing the existing dataset to generate a dataset that includes observations that are as similar as possible based on the values of the matching covariates (Stuart, 2010). This allows us to estimate what would have happened in the absence of taking courses on government and politics, or on being encouraged to vote. Thus, we can estimate the effects of taking a course on government and politics, and on being encouraged to vote on political efficacy.

RESULTS

Before we analyze the results, we must investigate the extent to which the control and treatment groups are similar to one another (King et al., 2017). If these groups are dissimilar, then we cannot use matching to estimate an ATT because we cannot discern the difference between our effect and our matching covariates. The imbalance statistics are provided in Appendix B of the Online Appendix. In 83.33% of cases, the Kolmogorov-Smirnov (KS) tests are not significant after matching has happened. Further, the variance ratio for all variables is consistent with well-behaved matching results after matching has occurred as all variance ratios are below two (see Zhang et al., 2019, p. 5). Finally, the mean EQQ differences are reduced after matching in 73.21% of cases (see Diamond & Sekhon, 2013; Sekhon, 2011). Thus, we are confident that we have reduced imbalance and that the control and treatment groups are sufficiently similar to one another. Consequently, any remaining differences across the varying levels of our treatment variables can be attributed to the effect of the activities and not to preexisting differences (Eggers & Hainmueller, 2009).

Table 12.1 contains our results for both of our dependent variables. The results indicate that taking a class in political science is connected with a .357-point increase in perceptions that one is better informed about politics than most people. Moreover, being encouraged to vote is associated with a .7-point decrease in the perception that one's vote does not matter. These results align with our theoretical expectations, as taking a course in political science is linked with increased internal political efficacy. Additionally, being encouraged to vote is connected with a reduced perception that one's vote does not matter.

While these results are promising, it is possible that they are an artifact of two known statistical concerns: p-hacking and reverse causality. To verify whether our results are model-dependent or are specified in a way that conveniently confirms a researcher's theoretical expectations, we removed one

TABLE 12.1 Effects of Taking a Class and Being Encouraged to Vote

	Believes Better Informed About Politics Than Most People		Perception That One's Vote Doesn't Matter	
	Taken a Class	Encouraged to Vote	Taken a Class	Encouraged to Vote
Effect on Being Better Informed about Politics	.357	.098	—	—
Effect on Perception that One's Vote Doesn't Matter	—	—	–.301	–.700
Abadie-Imbens Standard Error	.184	.248	.225	.395
95% Confidence Interval Lower Bound	–.006	–.390	–.746	–1.477
95% Confidence Interval Upper Bound	.720	.586	.144	.077
T-Statistic	1.945	.395	–1.339	–1.769
P-Value (Two-Tailed)	.052	.693	.181	.077
P-Value (One-Tailed)	.026	.347	.091	.039
N	162	333	154	321

Notes: In this table, those who have taken a class on government and politics at a university or have been encouraged by anyone to vote in the 2016 election are compared with those who have not had these experiences. Second, the covariates on which the matching is based are described in the text. Third, the effects on being better informed about politics are the average treatment effect for the treated (ATT). Finally, the matching results are from 1:1 genetic matching with post-matching bias adjustment. Thus, the N represents the matched number of observations.

matching covariate at a time while retaining all others (Head et al., 2015; Ho et al., 2007). The results are contained in Appendices C and D of the Online Appendix and display 56 different functional forms. Of these, 47 (or 83.93%) are identical in terms of the signs and significance patterns as those displayed in Table 12.1. The remaining nine results that differ from those in Table 12.1 do not exhibit any systematic patterning that would undermine our conclusions.

We have also examined whether reverse causality is present in our results, as it is possible that feeling better informed about politics causes one to take a class in political science, or that the perception that one's vote does not matter is connected to changes in being encouraged to vote in the 2016 election. Overall, reverse causality is present in five of sixteen (or 31.25%) instances. Yet, only one of those concerns the connection between the perception that one's vote does not matter and either of our treatment variables. However, four of them center around perceptions that one is better informed about politics than others. Thus, feeling better informed about politics can also lead one to take a class on government and politics.

DISCUSSION AND CONCLUSION

Simple actions by colleges and universities can make a big impact on students' sense of democratic agency, even when controlling for other important factors like the extent to which one's parents and friends encourage political activity. Yet, activities have differential impacts on the beliefs necessary to support a democracy in which young people participate. The results suggest taking a multifaceted approach is important to counter common beliefs young people hold that make them hesitant to participate, like believing that their vote does not matter. These multifaceted approaches may help students develop skills and undertake strategies that will help them follow through on an intent to vote (see Holbein & Hillygus, 2020).

Some might question whether students with higher preexisting efficacy levels are more likely to take classes on government. Reverse causality tests suggest this is quite likely. Yet, because we match based on a variety of factors known to influence efficacy, it is unlikely that these results are solely the product of reverse causality. Because students at this university have a significant choice over whether they take a class on government, the causal arrow likely points both ways for this activity. However, students have little control over whether someone encourages them to vote. We find evidence that both types of activities shape efficacy.

Others may question whether the effect that we discover is due to activities within the university (like taking a class or being encouraged to vote), or whether those effects are due to messaging from outside of the university. Many college students have moved recently and are unlikely to appear on campaign contact lists (Squire et al., 1987). Yet, they may have been exposed to more general GOTV ads on local media. To test this, we would need data on media exposure at either an individual-level or at the designated market area-level to make this connection (see e.g., Denison et al., 2023). Even if we had access to this data, though, most respondents would have been concentrated in the St. Louis media market as this was a survey of a single set of students at one university. Thus, this limitation is not something that we can test with the research design that we employed. However, it can be mitigated by investigating these findings in other contexts.

Beyond the positive effects we uncover, universities can also influence several of the variables we controlled for in our analysis: politically active friends and online political expression. Facilitating spaces where students can discuss politics and make friends with others who are politically active can have positive impacts on efficacy (Beaumont, 2011; Colby et al., 2007).

Encouraging online political expression can also foster heightened efficacy levels among students (Zhou & Pinkleton, 2012). Yet, these activities require universities to wade more directly into political activities.

Offering classes on government and encouraging students to take them and encouraging students to vote have positive effects on students' political efficacy and sense of democratic agency. These results should help universities just beginning to focus on their civic mission identify simple yet effective actions they can take to help promote engaged citizens, and give institutions whose efforts are more developed, but also facing heightened scrutiny, concrete evidence of the value of these actions.

NOTES

1. Jacoby (2009) and Checkoway (2001) provide overviews of the history of the civic mission of universities.
2. This is even after one controls for an array of other factors, including one's socioeconomic status.
3. These experiences prior to college include one's high school experience and home life.
4. However, fewer members of Gen Z than Millennials who did not vote said they chose not to do so because they thought their vote did not matter (Booth et al., 2023).
5. The questions that we used are available in the Online Appendix, available at http://www.kenmoffett.net/research.
6. A course on government and politics is not required for students to graduate. Some states have such requirements, and this invites further exploration in those contexts.
7. We do not investigate the impact of variations in how these courses are taught, but we do note that faculty at SIUE use many approaches in these classes.
8. Higher socioeconomic status is also a predictor of higher levels of efficacy (Paulsen, 1991), with income predicting external efficacy but not internal efficacy (Jackson, 1995). Our survey did not ask about income or other indicators of socioeconomic status, however we do control directly for parents' political involvement as reported by students (which is related to socioeconomic status), as income influences political participation (see, e.g., Verba et al, 1995). However, parents' political involvement is an imperfect proxy for the effects of income.

REFERENCES

Abadie, A., & Imbens, G. W. (2006). Large sample properties of matching estimators for average treatment effects. *Econometrica, 74*(1), 235–267. https://doi.org/10.1111/j.1468-0262.2006.00655.x

Abadie, A., & Imbens, G. W. (2016). Matching on the estimated propensity score. *Econometrica, 84*(2), 781–807. https://doi.org/10.3982/ECTA11293

Beaumont, E. (2011). Promoting political agency, addressing political inequality: A multilevel model of internal political efficacy. *Journal of Politics, 73*(1), 216–231. https://doi.org/10.1017/S0022381610000976

Berinsky, A. J., &. Lenz, G. S. (2011). Education and political participation: Exploring the causal link. *Political Behavior, 33*(3), 357–373. https://doi.org/10.1007/s11109-010-9134-9

Booth, R. B., Medina, A. & Suzuki, S. (2023). *Gen Z, aware of its power, wants to have impact on a wide range of issues.* Center for Information & Research on Civic Learning and Engagement. https://circle.tufts.edu/latest-research/gen-z-aware-its-power-wants-have-impact-wide-range-issues

Campbell, A., Converse, P. E., Miller, W. E., & Stokes, D. E. (1960). *The American Voter.* John Wiley & Sons.

Checkoway, B. (2001). Renewing the civic mission of the american research university. *The Journal of Higher Education, 72*(2),125–147. https://doi.org/10.1080/00221546.2001.11778875

Colby, A., Beaumont, E., Ehrlich, T., & Corngold, J. (2007). *Educating for democracy: Preparing undergraduates for responsible political engagement.* The Carnegie Foundation for the Advancement of Teaching. Jossey-Bass.

Condon, M., & Holleque, M. (2013). Entering politics: General self-efficacy and voting behavior among young people. *Political Psychology, 34*(2), 167–181. https://doi.org/10.1111/pops.12019

DellaVolpe, J. (2023). *Understanding the Gen Z vote: Post-election research project.* Murmuration, Walton Family Foundation, https://murmuration.org/guest/publication/14?s=39

Denison, B., Dahlen, H., Kim, J-E. C., Williams, C., Kranzler, E., Luchman, J. N., Trigger, S., Bennett, M., Nighbor, T., Vines, M., Petrun Sayers, E. L., Kurti, A. N., Weinberg, J., Hoffman, L., & Peck, J. (2023). Evaluation of the "We Can Do This" campaign paid media and COVID-19 vaccination uptake, United States, December 2020–January 2022. *Journal of Health Communication, 28*(9), 573–584. https://doi.org/10.1080/10810730.2023.2236976

Diamond, A., & Sekhon, J. J. (2013). Genetic matching for estimating causal effects: A general multivariate matching method for achieving balance in observational studies. *Review of Economics and Statistics, 95*(3), 932–945. https://doi.org/10.1162/REST_a_00318

Eggers, A. C., & Hainmueller, J. (2009). MPs for sale? Returns to office in postwar British politics. *American Political Science Review, 103*(4), 513–533. https://doi.org/10.1017/S0003055409990190

Head, M. L., Holman, L., Lanfear, R., Kahn, A. T., & Jennions, M. D. (2015). The extent and consequences of p-hacking in science. *PLoS Biology, 13*(3), e1002106. https://doi.org/10.1371/journal.pbio.1002106

Hillygus, D. S. (2005). The missing link: Exploring the relationship between higher education and political engagement. *Political Behavior, 27*(1), 25–47. https://doi.org/10.1007/s11109-005-3075-8

Ho, D. E., Imai, K., King, G., & Stuart, E. A. (2007). Matching as nonparametric preprocessing for reducing model dependence in parametric causal inference. *Political Analysis, 15*(3), 199–236. https://doi.org/10.1093/pan/mpl013

Holbein, J.B. and Hillygus, D.S. 2020. *Making young voters: Converting civic attitudes into civic action.* Cambridge University Press.

Jackson, R. A. (1995). Clarifying the relationship between education and turnout. *American Politics Research, 23*(3), 279–99. https://doi.org/10.1177/1532673X9502300302

Jacoby, B. (2009). Civic engagement in today's higher education: An overview in *Civic engagement in higher education: Concepts and practices.* Jossey Bass.

Kam, C. D., & Palmer, C. L. (2008). Reconsidering the effects of education on political participation. *Journal of Politics, 70*(3), 612–631. https://doi.org/10.1017/S0022381608080651

Kam, C. D., & Palmer, C. L. (2011). Rejoinder: Reinvestigating the causal relationship between higher education and political participation. *Journal of Politics, 73*(3), 659–663. https://doi.org/10.1017/S0022381611000363

King, G., Lucas, C., & Nielsen, R. A. (2017). The balance-sample size frontier in matching methods for causal inference. *American Journal of Political Science, 61*(2), 473–489. https://doi.org/10.1111/ajps.12272

Krampen, G. (2000). Transition of adolescent political action orientations to voting behavior in early adulthood in view of a social-cognitive action theory model of personality. *Political Psychology, 21*(2), 277–297. https://doi.org/10.1111/0162-895X.00188

Lane, D. S., Lee, S. S., Liang, F., Kim, D. H., Shen, L., Weeks, B. E., & Kwak, N. (2019). Social media expression and the political self. *Journal of Communication, 69*(1), 49–72. https://doi.org/10.1093/joc/jqy064

Moffett, K. W., & Rice, L. L. (2015). Taking college-level political science courses and civic activity. In S. M. Chod, W. J. Much, & S. M. Calindo (Eds.), *Technology and civic engagement in the college classroom: Engaging the unengaged.* (pp. 13–48). Palgrave Macmillan.

Moffett, K. W., & Rice, L. L. (2016). *Web 2.0 and the political mobilization of college students.* Lexington Books.

Niemi, R. G., & Klinger, J. D. (2012). The development of political attitudes and behaviour among young adults. *Australian Journal of Political Science, 47*(1), 31–54. https://doi.org/10.1080/10361146.2011.643167

Oser, J., Grinson, A., Boulianne, S., & Halperin, E. (2022). How political efficacy relates to online and offline political participation:A multilevel meta-analysis. *Political Communication, 39*(0), 607–633. https://doi.org/10.1080/10584609.2022.2086329

Paulsen, R. (1991). Education, social class, and participation in collective action. *Sociology of Education, 64*(2), 96–110. https://doi.org/10.2307/2112881

Persson, M. (2015). Education and political participation. *British Journal of Political Science, 45*(3), 689–703. https://doi.org/10.1017/S0007123413000409

Pew Research Center. (2020). *On the cusp of adulthood and facing an uncertain future: What we know about Gen Z so far.* https://www.pewresearch.org/social-trends/2020/05/14/on-the-cusp-of-adulthood-and-facing-an-uncertain-future-what-we-know-about-gen-z-so-far-2/

Quintelier, E., Stolle, D., & Harell, A. (2012). Politics in peer groups: Exploring the causal relationship between network diversity and political participation. *Political Research Quarterly,* 65(4), 868–881. https://doi.org/10.1177/1065912911411099

Rice, L.L., & Moffett, K.W. (2019). Snapchat and civic engagement among college students. *Journal of Information Technology & Politics,* 16(2), 87–104. https://doi.org/10.1080/19331681.2019.1574249

Rosenstone, S. J., & Hansen, J. M. (1993). *Mobilization, participation, and democracy in America.* Macmillan Publishing Company.

Saltmarsh, J., & Hartley, M. (2011). Democratic Engagement. In Saltmarsh, J. and Hartley, M. (Eds.), *'To serve a larger purpose': Engagement for democracy and the transformation of higher education.* (pp. 2–12). Temple University Press.

Southern Illinois University Edwardsville. (2023). *Factbook.* Institutional Research and Studies. https://www.siue.edu/inrs/factbook/pdf/FbCurrent.pdf

Squire, P., Wolfinger, R. E., & Glass, D. P. (1987). Residential Mobility and Voter Turnout. *American Political Science Review,* 81(1), 45–65.

Stuart, E. A. (2010). Matching methods for causal inference: A review and a look forward. *Statistical Science,* 25(1), 1–21. https://doi.org/10.1214/09-STS313

Valentino, N. A., Gregorowicz, K., & Groenendyk, E. W. (2009). Efficacy, emotions and the habit of participation. *Political Behavior,* 31(3), 307–330. https://doi.org/10.1007/s11109-008-9076-7

Verba, S., Schlozman, K. L., & Brady, H. E. (1995). *Voice and equality: Civic voluntarism in American politics.* Harvard University Press.

Zhang, Z., Kim, H. J., Lonjon, G., & Zhu, Y. (2019). Balance diagnostics after propensity score matching. *Annals of Translational Medicine,* 7(1), 1–11. https://doi.org/10.21037/atm.2018.12.10

Zhou, Y., & Pinkleton, B. E. (2012). Modeling the effects of political information source use and online expression on young adults' political efficacy. *Mass Communication and Society,* 15(6), 813–830. https://doi.org/10.1080/15205436.2011.622064

CHAPTER 13

POLITICAL SOCIALIZATION IN CAMPUS LIFE

Can Student Organizations Replicate Civic Learning in Tocqueville's Voluntary Associations?

J. Cherie Strachan
The University of Akron

Michael R. Wolf
Purdue University Fort Wayne

Elizabeth A. Bennion
Indiana University South Bend

ABSTRACT

Insights from scholars of associational life suggest student organizations have the potential to serve as the most robust source of civic learning on campus. To assess political socialization in campus life, the co-founders of a consortium to facilitate cross-campus data collection developed and fielded the National

Survey of Student Leaders (NSSL) on 35 U.S. campuses. Respondents included student officers representing 5,567 registered student organizations. Findings indicate student organizations serve as a source of significant political socialization for college students. Disappointingly, however, the full potential of campus life remains untapped. As in the broader public sphere, civil society on campus failed to fully compensate for the participation-suppressing effects of traditional gender-role socialization on women or for Asian and Hispanic students' low levels of political engagement relative to White student leaders. Further, too few groups on campus cultivated an intrinsic civic identity that extends expectations beyond volunteering to include participation in overtly political acts. Most troubling, some student organizations including varsity and intramural sports teams as well as some low-activity academic and service-oriented clubs, were correlated with lower student political engagement and voting, likely by channeling their time and effort into alternative activities.

For the past several decades, scholars and policy makers associated with the civic engagement movement have called for higher education institutions to cultivate healthy civic and political engagement among college students (Bok 2006; Boyer 1987; Carnegie Corporation of New York 2003; Colby et al. 2003; Colby et al. 2007; Ehrlich et al. 2000; Galston 2001). While such calls were initially triggered by declining civic and political participation among young people (Lawless & Fox 2015; Ostrom 1998; Shames 2017; Wattenberg 2012; Zukin et al , 2006) today's advocates must focus on how to help current college cohorts overcome barriers that make engagement in public life more difficult, including rising voter suppression, civil unrest, partisan polarization, democratic backsliding, rudeness, threats, and political violence (Anderson 2018; Brown, Block, & Stout 2021; Boatright et al 2019; Kalmoe & Mason 2022). Given that early levels of civic and political interest and participation help to predict long-term adult engagement, it is increasingly important to identify effective ways to provide college students with political socialization robust enough to help them overcome these obstacles and to prepare them for the type of public-spirited participation required to sustain democracy.

Faculty who respond to such concerns are likely to focus on the substantive content of their courses as a way to shape student awareness of civic and political obligations. Such efforts make considerable sense, as academics have a great deal of control over curriculum, but little over what happens elsewhere on campus. This approach overlooks that early political observers did not attribute average Americans' ability to establish and sustain a democratic form of government to formal education, but to their participation in an exceptional civic infrastructure characterized by an overlapping array of voluntary associations. Membership in these organizations, which were more apt to address social, civic, and philanthropic endeavors than overt political agendas, were famously described by Alexis de Tocqueville as the "schools of democracy" where Americans' learned both the art of organizing and self-interest rightly understood (Tocqueville 1845).

Scholars continued to praise the US' exemplary levels of civic voluntarism, describing Americans as a "nation of joiners" up through the 1950s and 1960s (Almond and Verba 1963; Schlesinger 1944). Seminal political behavior research in the 1990s confirmed civic voluntarism as by far the best predictor of civic and political participation throughout adulthood (Verba, Scholzman and Brady 1995). Despite praise for all types of voluntary associations, ranging from bridge clubs to bowling leagues (Putnam 2000), not all membership organizations are equally beneficial, including those with exclusionary membership policies and especially those founded to advance nativist, racist, and xenophobic agendas detrimental to pluralism and inclusion (Rosenbaum 2000).

Beyond membership policies, organizational features matter as affiliation with many contemporary voluntary associations requires little more than paying dues. Others involve members in a full array of ongoing activities ranging from serving in elected leadership positions, coordinating nomination and electoral processes, following by-laws, chairing committees, managing budgets, attending meetings, participating in deliberation, casting ballots, and implementing programming. Clearly the latter, as well as associations that overtly socialize members to embrace civic and political obligations, are much better at cultivating the knowledge, skills, and dispositions required for public-spirited participation in democracy (Skocpol 2003, 2011). Despite these insights into ideal versions of associational life that sustain democracy, political scientists have conducted little applied research to understand the structure of civil society on our very own campuses. This research attempts to remedy our oversight.

THE NATIONAL SURVEY OF STUDENT LEADERS

The National Survey of Student Leaders (NSSL) was the inaugural project of a consortium that served as a precursor to the Bliss Institute's Consortium for Applied Civic Engagement Studies (ACES), which sponsors multi-campus data collection for civic engagement and pedagogy research. The NSSL was designed to explore whether student organizations provide an on-campus version of civil society that offers an effective means of political socialization. Given the need to develop an accurate, detailed account of organizational policies and activities, a questionnaire was emailed to the president of each of the 5,567 student organizations registered on 35 participating campuses in the spring of 2015. These 35 colleges and universities included community colleges, regional public universities, small liberal arts colleges, and large research-intensive universities, across every major geographical region of the continental United States. An initial request to participate and two reminder prompts were e-mailed to these presidents, yielding 1,896 responses. When the president of an organization failed to respond to an invitation, two reminder prompts were sent to a secondary contact (typically a vice president or a treasurer). This follow-up effort yielded an additional 297 responses. Of the initial sample of student officers (a president, a vice president, or a treasurer) affiliated with one of these 5,567 student organizations, 2,193 answered the questionnaire, for an overall response rate of 39.3%.

Reflecting gender-based patterns of student engagement on college campuses, more student leaders identified as women (62%) than men (38%). With an average age of 22, only 15.4% of the student leaders were nontraditional students. Not surprisingly, student leaders were more apt to be juniors, seniors, or graduate students, at 88.3%, than freshman or sophomores. They were also more like to be White (70%) than Asian or Pacific Islander (10%), Black (7%), Hispanic (7%) or Native American (less than 1%). Finally, nearly 6% of respondents identified as multi-racial or other when asked to report their racial and ethnic identities.[1]

PROPOSITIONS, DATA AND MEASURES

Dependent Variables

Given that the goal of this study focuses on promoting participation through robust political socialization, student officials were asked to self-report their attitudes and anticipated behaviors on a number of civic and political outcomes. The design of this research does not allow us to assess the effect of participation in student organizations on members. However, it seems likely that student officials would experience more robust political socialization than members. If leadership experiences do not boost political socialization and desired political outcomes, it is far less likely that participation would have an effect on members. Hence our political outcome variables include student officials': political interest, anticipated political participation overall, anticipated participation in voting, anticipated participation in high-intensity political acts, anticipated civic participation, political efficacy, and collective efficacy.

Political interest was measured by asking officials to self-report their level of political interest in state/local, national, and international politics on a 4-point scale ranging from Not at All to Very Interested. As factor analysis supported treating these items as a single variable, scores on all items were added to create an index of political interest.

Anticipated political participation was measured by asking officials to self-report their likelihood of participating in an array of civic (engaging in community problem solving, volunteering) and political activities (voting in local elections, voting in national elections, persuading others to vote, signing petitions, attending rallies, contacting elected officials, donating money, or working for a party/candidate). These items were assessed with a four-point scale ranging from Not at All to Very Likely. Responses were used to create several indices to measure anticipated participation. The first of these was a measure of Overall Participation that summed scores on all items. Factor analysis indicated these items measured three distinct types of participation, which clustered around voting, time and resource intense acts, and civic acts. Therefore, we also constructed a measure of Voter Participation that summarized scores on vote-related items (voting in national and voting in local elections); a measure of Intense Political Participation that summed scores on time and commitment to intense activities (persuading others, attending rallies, contacting elected officials, donating or working for a candidate/party, signing a petition); and a measure of Civic Participation that summed scores on community problem solving and volunteering.

Political Efficacy was measured with standard political science items including: People like me don't have a say about what government does; Sometimes politics and government can seem so complicated that a person like me can't really understand what is going on; Public officers don't care much what people like me think; and It would be difficult for someone like me to make a real difference in politics or government. As factor analysis supported treating these items as a single variable, scores on these items, measured on a four-point scale ranging from Strongly Agree to Strongly Disagree, were summed for an overall measure of Political Efficacy.

Given that participation in organizations might create faith in the effectiveness of collective action not captured by traditional political efficacy items, several questions attempted to tap officials' sense of Collective Efficacy. The items tapped views on whether: Politicians respond to citizens if enough people demand change; Most people are willing to work together toward a common goal; and If you want to get things done as a citizen, working with others is the best way. Factor analysis supported treating these items as a single variable. Hence scores on these items, measured on a four-point scale ranging from Strongly Agree to Strongly Disagree, were summed for an overall measure of collective efficacy.

Independent Variables

The key independent variables measured student officials' experiences within their respective organizations. First, an organization's purpose could not only affect officials' self-selection into particular groups but might also continue to shape their attitudes and anticipated behaviors after joining. One would expect clubs with an explicitly political agenda to correlate with higher levels of political interest, political participation, and political efficacy. Meanwhile those with a service focus should correlate not only with higher levels of political interest, but also with civic participation and collective efficacy. Beyond these hypotheses, it is possible that other types of groups could affect our outcomes of interest. Lawless and Fox (2013), for example, find that playing competitive sports boosts women's political ambition, suggesting that being a member of an intramural or varsity sports club might have a similar effect. Research on Greek organizations associate them with higher campus activity levels that should bolster civic skills and with interpersonal growth (Gallup 2014; Pike 2000; Routon and Walker 2014). Given that Skocpol (2003) describes the robust political socialization provided by fraternal organizations (with a federated structure, an active service agenda, formal deliberative processes, and tightly bonded members), we might anticipate that presiding over Greek fraternities and sororities, which are some of the last remaining campus organizations to match this description, could also bolster individual political outcomes. As a result, Organizational Type was measured by asking student officials to select from a list that ranged from academic, professional, and service clubs, to Greek, multicultural, LGBTQ, and religious organizations. Officers were also offered an "other" category, although none of the clubs listed under "other" coalesced into a single, coherent organizational type.

In addition to Organizational Type, the array of activities and decision-making practices that an organization undertakes may also provide student officials with the opportunity to hone their civic and political skills, which should boost performance on our civic and political outcome variables. Student officials were asked to report how frequently they undertook an array of different activities, by selecting from an eight-point scale that ranged from Less than Once a Year or Never to Once a Week or More. Factor analysis indicated these items measured five distinct types of participation, which clustered around the frequency of holding meetings, sponsoring events, promoting shared values and obligations to internal and external audiences, relying on the executive board or advisors to make decisions, or relying on group deliberation to make decisions.

Accordingly, several indices reflecting different types of activities were created. These included Meeting, which summed scores on items measuring the frequency of holding meetings (for all members, for the executive board, and for committees/subcommittees); Eventing, which summed scores on items measuring the frequency of sponsoring or co-sponsoring an array of events (educational events, social activities, fundraising for the organization, and fundraising for charity); Proselytizing, which summed scores on items related to frequency of promoting shared values and participatory obligations to internal and external audiences (via hosting ceremonies/rituals, giving speeches, and distributing materials that relied on epideictic rhetoric to extol shared commitment to philanthropic or public policy outcomes, along with desired actions to advance desired outcomes); Executive Deciding, which summarized scores on items measuring hierarchical decision-making (relying on the executive board or on a faculty advisor to make decisions); and Deliberating, which summarized scores on items measuring use of formal, deliberative decision-making (by referring to a constitution/by-laws, engaging members in deliberation, using formal rules, and negotiating compromises among members).

Control Variables

Several demographic variables that affect the broader electorates' attitudes toward and participation in politics were included in this study. Student officials were asked to self-report their age, year in college, race/ethnic identity, and sex.[2] We anticipated that older, more advanced, and male student officials would be more interested in politics, would anticipate higher levels of overall and high-intensity political participation, and would have higher levels of traditional political efficacy. We predicted that older, more advanced, and women students would report higher levels of civic participation and would report higher levels of collective efficacy. We anticipated that students with racial/ethnic identities associated with lower levels of political engagement in the broader electorate, such as Hispanic and Asian student leaders, would report lower forecasts of political participation and efficacy.

REGRESSION ANALYSIS AND FINDINGS

We ran a series of regression models for each of the dependent variables described above. The first series of regression models include the type of student organization along with the student officials' demographics as control variables, while the second series of regression models also incorporate the type of organizational activity and decision-making that respondents have experienced.

Political Interest

Two regression analyses (see Table 13.1) were run to identify effects on political interest. In the first model, several demographic and organizational

TABLE 13.1 Regression of Student Leader Demographics, Type of Group, and Group Activity on Political Interest (Interest in International, National, and Local Politics)

	Overall Political Interest		Activities of Group: Overall Political Interest	
	Coefficient	Std Error	Coefficient	Std Error
Other Ethnicity	0.474**	0.186	0.461**	0.197
Hispanic	−0.228	0.185	−0.256	0.200
Black	−0.206	0.194	−0.142	0.209
Asian	−0.181	0.168	−0.179	0.179
Male	0.250**	0.098	0.197*	0.103
Class Level	0.001	0.058	0.007	0.061
Age	0.033***	0.013	0.038***	0.013
Honor Society	0.236	0.241	0.198	0.251
Academic	−0.209	0.159	−0.148	0.170
Residence Life	0.138	0.528	0.038	0.620
Intramural Sport	−0.799***	0.249	−0.639**	0.271
Varsity Sport	−0.428	0.485	−0.437	0.487
Fraternity	0.486*	0.288	0.457	0.314
Sorority	−0.310	0.265	−0.308	0.286
Cultural/Ethnicity	−0.063	0.216	−0.034	0.228
LGBTQ	0.051	0.455	0.084	0.473
Religious	0.133	0.216	0.109	0.238
Service	−0.024	0.189	−0.132	0.201
Professional	−0.087	0.167	−0.133	0.182
Political	1.588***	0.290	1.594***	0.302
Special Interest	0.146	0.171	0.136	0.181
Eventing			0.073	0.058
Proselytize			0.072	0.050
Executive Decision			−0.020	0.058
Group Meetings			−0.539	0.055
Group Deliberation			0.004	0.008
_cons	5.432***	0.345	5.042***	0.328

* $p < -.10$, ** $p \leq .05$, *** $p \leq .01$

Note: Comparison groups are White & "Other" type of group.

traits are associated with an increase in student officials' levels of political interest. Older male students who belongs to either a fraternity or a political organization were associated with increased political interest. Students who selected "other"—where students selected this label to any of the more specific racial/ethnic categories offered—as their ethnic identity were associated with increased political interest. Meanwhile, playing an intramural sport was consistently associated with suppressed political interest. Interestingly, none of the organizational activity or decision-making features contributed to an up-tick in overall political interest, although adding them to the model does reduce the influence of belonging to a fraternity.

Overall Participation

Two regression analyses (see Table 13.2) were run to identify effects on overall political participation. Only one demographic trait, being older, was associated with increased political participation in either model, while self-identifying as Hispanic or Asian was associated with suppressed overall participation in both models relative to those who self-identified as White.[3] In the first model, several types of organizations were associated with higher levels of overall political participation, including fraternities and honor societies, as well as LGBTQ, political, and special interest organizations. In the second model, political and LGBTQ student groups were the only specific types of clubs that were associated with promoting overall participation.

Voter Participation

Two regression analyses (see Table 13.2) were run to identify effects on voting. Few variables increase students' likelihood of voting in either model. The first reveals that, as we would expect, belonging to a political organization is associated with greater intention to cast a ballot in the future. The second reveals that belonging to an organization that sponsors more events is also associated with greater intention to cast a ballot in the future. Meanwhile, several demographic variables and organizational traits are consistently associated with lower anticipated voter turn-out. These include being Asian or Hispanic (as opposed to being White), as well as playing intramural sports or participating in residence life organizations. In the second model, residence life's associated negative effect on voting is mitigated by event-sponsoring. Belonging to a cultural/ethnic organization, however, is also associated with a lower likelihood of voting.

Civic Participation

Given that the social desirability of voting may result in over-reporting an intention to undertake this particular political act, student officials'

TABLE 13.2 Regression of Student Leader Demographics, Type of Group, and Group Activity on Voter Participation and Overall Participation: Voter, Civic, and High Intensity (Persuade Others, Work for or Donate to Campaign, Contact Elected Official, Attend Rally or Sign Petitions)

	Overall Participation		Activities of Group: Overall Participation		Voter Participation		Activities of Group: Voter Participation	
	Coefficient	Std Error	Coefficient	Std Error	Coefficient	Std Error	Coefficient	Std Error
Other Ethnicity	0.639	0.666	0.590	0.701	−0.025	0.202	0.006	0.214
Hispanic	−1.718***	0.664	−2.099***	0.703	−0.933***	0.201	−0.965***	0.215
Black	0.715	0.694	0.611	0.729	−0.233	0.211	−0.182	0.223
Asian	−1.908***	0.595	−2.070***	0.628	−1.185***	0.182	−1.189***	0.194
Male	−0.227	0.348	−0.467	0.364	0.076	0.106	0.061	0.111
Class Level	−0.235	0.208	−0.329	0.220	0.044	0.063	0.015	0.066
Age	0.087*	0.046	0.118**	0.048	0.013	0.014	0.016	0.014
Honor Society	1.883**	0.857	1.455	0.888	0.156	0.262	0.027	0.273
Academic	−0.815	0.569	−0.804	0.606	−0.056	0.173	−0.118	0.186
Residence Life	−0.840	1.850	−0.221	2.154	−0.954*	0.567	−0.430	0.664
Intramural Sport	−2.077**	0.887	−1.480	0.961	−0.536**	0.271	−0.464	0.296
Varsity Sport	−2.014	1.763	−2.219	1.176	0.228	0.540	0.181	0.542
Fraternity	2.564**	1.020	1.111	1.107	0.034	0.312	−0.084	0.341
Sorority	0.656	0.947	−0.160	1.014	0.102	0.288	0.173	0.310

(continued)

Political Socialization in Campus Life • 209

TABLE 13.2 Regression of Student Leader Demographics, Type of Group, and Group Activity on Voter Participation and Overall Participation: Voter, Civic, and High Intensity (Persuade Others, Work for or Donate to Campaign, Contact Elected Official, Attend Rally or Sign Petitions). (continued)

	Overall Participation		Activities of Group: Overall Participation		Voter Participation		Activities of Group: Voter Participation	
	Coefficient	Std Error	Coefficient	Std Error	Coefficient	Std Error	Coefficient	Std Error
Cultural/Ethnicity	0.752	0.770	0.795	0.802	−0.342	0.235	−0.438*	0.246
LGBTQ	3.882**	1.594	3.786**	1.643	0.564	0.489	0.504	0.506
Religious	−0.197	0.768	−0.308	0.841	−0.086	0.233	−0.206	0.256
Service	0.315	1.594	−0.284	0.710	0.002	0.204	−0.171	0.217
Professional	−0.287	0.592	−0.615	0.639	0.055	0.181	−0.081	0.196
Political	6.949***	1.027	7.106***	1.053	0.824***	0.308	0.721**	0.321
Special Interest	1.255**	0.609	0.995	0.640	0.032	0.185	−0.047	0.196
Eventing			0.884***	0.203			0.146**	0.062
Proselytize			0.303*	0.193			0.011	0.054
Executive Decision			−0.300	0.206			−0.068	0.063
Group Meetings			−0.191	0.193			−0.081	0.059
Group Deliberation			0.042	0.028			0.002	0.009
_cons	21.552***	1.059	18.973***		6.143***	0.319	6.204***	0.413

* $p < -.10$, ** $p \leq .05$, *** $p \leq .01$

Note: Comparison groups are White & "Other" type of group.

anticipated participation in other civic acts or higher-intensity political acts may provide a better indicator of the variables that facilitate political engagement. A wide array of organizations facilitate civic participation, and, unlike in the case of voting, there is little evidence that organizational membership and activities are negatively correlated with other forms of civic participation (see Table 13.3). In the first and second model of civic participation in Table 13.3, only the demographic trait of being male is associated with suppressed civic participation. Meanwhile, belonging to a fraternity or a sorority, as well as to cultural/ethnic, religious, service, professional, political, or special interest organization is associated with higher levels of civic voluntarism and community problem-solving. In the second model, the list of organizations associated with higher levels of participation is almost identical, except that honor societies are associated with higher levels, while sororities and professional clubs are associated with lower levels. Organizations that host frequent events and proselytize by encouraging members to embrace shared values and commitments are also associated with higher levels of student officials' reported civic engagement.

High-Intensity Participation

Higher intensity participation beyond voting, like persuading others, working for or donating to campaigns, contacting elected officials, or attending rallies/signing petitions, also are associated with a broader pattern of group membership and demographic backgrounds relative to both voting and civic participation. Two regression analyses (see Table 13.3) were run to identify effects on willingness to engage in more intense forms of political participation. In the first model, being older—along with belonging to a fraternity, honor society, political, special interest or LGBTQ organization are all correlated with higher anticipated participation in politics. Meanwhile, self-identifying as Hispanic relative to identifying as White, and advanced class standing, along with participating in academic organizations or playing either intramural or varsity sports were associated with lower levels of high intensity political participation.

In the second model that includes group activities, age and belonging to a political or an LGBTQ organization are still significant. When organizations that regularly sponsor events are included in the model, fraternities and special interest groups lose their independent statistical significance, suggesting that it is these organizations' active role in event planning and sponsorship, rather than their unique status as Greek organizations, that drives the association between membership and high-intensity political activity. Meanwhile, the list of variables associated with lower political participation includes not only being Hispanic, having advanced class standing,

Political Socialization in Campus Life • 211

TABLE 13.3 Regression of Student Leader Demographics, Type of Group, & Group Activity on Civic Participation and High Intensity Participation (Persuade Others, Work for/Donate to Campaign, Contact Elected Official, Attend Rally or Sign Petitions)

	Civic Participation		Activities of Group: Civic Participation		High Intensity Participation		Activities of Group: High Intensity Participation	
	Coefficient	Std Error	Coefficient	Std Error	Coefficient	Std Error	Coefficient	Std Error
Other Ethnicity	0.239	0.174	0.171	0.178	0.422	0.451	0.443	0.478
Hispanic	0.004	0.172	-0.036	0.179	-0.792*	0.449	-1.116**	0.477
Black	0.284	0.181	0.150	0.186	0.722	0.474	0.700	0.501
Asian	-0.240	0.156	-0.329	0.161	-0.417	0.405	-0.519	0.432
Male	-0.430***	0.091	-0.495***	0.093	0.127	0.236	-0.007	0.249
Class Level	-0.001	0.054	-0.008	0.055	-0.278**	0.141	-0.329**	0.150
Age	-0.013	0.012	-0.008	0.012	0.081***	0.031	0.104***	0.033
Honor Society	0.629	0.224	0.563**	0.226	1.012*	0.581	0.827	0.606
Academic	0.062	0.149	0.134	0.155	-0.778**	0.386	-0.752*	0.414
Residence Life	0.355	0.487	0.048	0.552	-0.240	1.264	0.159	1.481
Intramural Sport	-0.160	0.233	0.102	0.246	-1.374**	0.605	-1.089*	0.660
Varsity Sport	0.271	0.464	0.213	0.451	-2.500**	1.204	-2.587**	1.208
Fraternity	1.038***	0.268	0.556**	0.284	1.512**	0.696	0.617	0.760
Sorority	0.602**	0.247	0.310	0.258	-0.139	0.464	-0.755	0.697

(continued)

TABLE 13.3 Regression of Student Leader Demographics, Type of Group, & Group Activity on Civic Participation and High Intensity Participation (Persuade Others, Work for/Donate to Campaign, Contact Elected Official, Attend Rally or Sign Petitions). (continued)

	Civic Participation		Activities of Group: Civic Participation		High Intensity Participation		Activities of Group: High Intensity Participation	
	Coefficient	Std Error	Coefficient	Std Error	Coefficient	Std Error	Coefficient	Std Error
Cultural/Ethnicity	0.521***	0.201	0.567***	0.204	0.558	0.522	0.608	0.548
LGBTQ	0.423	0.419	0.360	0.421	2.912***	1.089	2.944***	1.130
Religious	0.502**	0.201	0.541**	0.214	-0.558	0.521	-0.533	0.574
Service	0.997***	0.175	0.830***	0.181	-0.624	0.458	-0.884*	0.487
Professional	0.315**	0.155	0.151	0.163	-0.630	0.403	-0.650	0.437
Political	1.034***	0.264	1.006***	0.267	5.200***	0.701	5.470***	0.723
Special Interest	0.498***	0.159	0.464***	0.164	0.726*	0.413	0.609	0.438
Eventing			0.224***	0.052			0.508***	0.139
Proselytize			0.140***	0.045			0.149	0.120
Executive Decision			0.024	0.053			-0.244*	0.141
Group Meetings			-0.323	0.049			-0.055	0.132
Group Deliberation			0.011	0.007			0.030	0.019
_cons	6.121***	0.275	4.999***	0.345	9.398***	0.718	7.750***	0.926

* $p < -.10$, ** $p \leq .05$, *** $p \leq .01$

Note: Comparison groups are White & "Other" type of group.

participating in sports, or belonging to an academic organization, but also belonging to organizations dedicated to facilitating community service. The latter is unfortunate, but not entirely surprising, given the complex role of volunteerism in higher education's civic engagement movement. A commitment to volunteerism and community engagement does not automatically translate into a commitment to other forms of active citizenship, including political engagement (Wattenberg 2012; McCartney, Bennion, and Simpson 2013). Belonging to an organization that relies heavily on hierarchical, executive decision-making is also associated with lower anticipated participation in time-consuming political activities.

Political Efficacy

Two regression analyses were run to identify effects on standard measures of political efficacy. Given that many of the skills learned while leading student organizations are transferrable to political settings, experiences within many types of student organizations should have the potential to increase student officials' levels of political efficacy. In both models (See Table 13.4), several variables were associated with student officials' assessments of their own political efficacy (indicated with negative coefficients). In the first model, being older and Black (as opposed to being White), along with leading an honors, fraternal, service, or political organization were associated with higher levels of political efficacy. All of these demographic traits and organizational variables remain significant in the second model, with the addition of joining a cultural/ethnic organization. Meanwhile, being Asian as opposed to identifying as White is associated with lower levels of traditional political efficacy in both models.

Collective Efficacy

Similarly, participating in all types of student organizations could, potentially, bolster student officials' sense of collective efficacy. Two regression models (See Table 13.4) were run to identify effects on collective efficacy. They reveal that only a few experiences in student life were associated with increased levels of student officials' sense of collective efficacy (here with positive coefficients). In the first model, these experiences include describing one's ethnicity as "other," along with participating in honors, fraternity, cultural/ethnic, and political organizations. In the second model, being Black as opposed to identifying as White, as well as belonging to a student organization focused on community service or on LGBTQ identity were also associated with higher levels of student officials' sense of collective

TABLE 13.4 Regression of Student Leader Demographics, Type of Group, & Group Activity on Efficacy (Internal & External) & Collective Efficacy (Politicians Respond to Demands, People Willing to Work Together, Work with Others if you Want to Get Things Done)

	Efficacy Coefficient	Efficacy Std Error	Activities of Group: Efficacy Coefficient	Activities of Group: Efficacy Std Error	Collective Efficacy Coefficient	Collective Efficacy Std Error	Activities of Group: Collective Efficacy Coefficient	Activities of Group: Collective Efficacy Std Error
Other Ethnicity	-0.209	0.253	-0.317	0.178	0.551***	0.212	0.651***	0.221
Hispanic	-0.095	0.249	0.062	0.179	0.263	0.208	0.137	0.221
Black	-0.760***	0.261	-0.763***	0.186	0.339	0.219	0.463**	0.232
Asian	0.469**	0.231	0.487*	0.161	0.001	0.191	-0.027	0.200
Male	0.192	0.131	0.214	0.093	-0.001	0.109	-0.012	0.113
Class Level	0.063	0.077	0.082	0.055	-0.098	0.064	-0.095	0.067
Age	-0.046***	0.017	-0.049***	0.012	0.017	0.014	0.022	0.014
Honor Society	-0.911***	0.329	-0.913***	0.226	0.724***	0.271	0.666***	0.280
Academic	0.013	0.214	-0.007	0.155	-0.060	0.178	-0.026	0.189
Residence Life	-0.655	0.718	-0.832	0.552	0.552	0.598	0.081	0.709
Intramural Sport	-0.509	0.342	-0.599	0.246	0.030	0.282	0.270	0.304
Varsity Sport	-0.588	0.681	-0.610	0.451	-0.492	0.568	-0.491	0.565
Fraternity	-0.959**	0.387	-1.148***	0.284	0.623*	0.322	0.623*	0.349
Sorority	-0.196	0.358	-0.193	0.258	0.182	0.300	0.131	0.318

(continued)

TABLE 13.4 Regression of Student Leader Demographics, Type of Group, & Group Activity on Efficacy (Internal & External) & Collective Efficacy (Politicians Respond to Demands, People Willing to Work Together, Work with Others if you Want to Get Things Done). (continued)

	Efficacy		Activities of Group: Efficacy		Collective Efficacy		Activities of Group: Collective Efficacy	
	Coefficient	Std Error	Coefficient	Std Error	Coefficient	Std Error	Coefficient	Std Error
Cultural/Ethnicity	−0.433	0.289	−0.518*	0.204	0.447*	0.240	0.585**	0.250
LGBTQ	0.539	0.592	0.617	0.421	0.790	0.493	0.866*	0.507
Religious	−0.257	0.289	−0.294	0.214	0.250	0.243	0.383	0.261
Service	−0.525**	0.552	−0.523*	0.181	0.311	0.209	0.400*	0.221
Professional	−0.259	0.223	−0.338	0.163	0.048	0.186	0.163	0.200
Political	−1.941***	0.382	−2.047***	0.267	0.827*	0.318	0.757**	0.329
Special Interest	−0.072	0.228	−0.063	0.164	0.254	0.190	0.166	0.199
Eventing			−0.053	0.052			0.024	0.064
Proselytize			−0.029	0.045			0.005	0.055
Executive Decision			−0.092	0.053			−0.043	0.065
Group Meetings			0.072	0.049			0.065	0.060
Group Deliberation			0.003	0.007			0.003	0.009
_cons	10.112***	0.391	10.293***	0.345	12.126***	0.328	11.844***	0.421

* $p < -.10$, ** $p \leq .05$, *** $p \leq .01$

Note: Comparison groups are White & "Other" type of group.

efficacy, as were being a member of the honor society, fraternity, cultural/ethnic, and political organizations.

DISCUSSION

A number of important patterns emerge from our regression analyses. First, while playing sports may be linked to political ambition among a narrow subset of college women who are already interested in politics (Lawless and Fox 2013), our findings suggest that playing sports in college was consistently associated with lower levels of political interest, lower levels of anticipated voting, and lower levels of anticipated high intensity political acts. Indeed, it is the most significant experience that students have on campus associated with lower levels of anticipated voting, as all other variables related to lower voter turnout are linked to being a member of a low-propensity demographic group (Hispanic and Asian) or a student organization that represents such a demographic group. The questions posed in our questionnaire do not allow us to determine whether intramural and varsity athletes are simply too busy to participate in politics, whether avoiding voting and politics reflects self-selection onto sports teams, or whether avoiding voting and politics is cultivated within their teams. The finding that more advanced students, who are busier with their academic careers, also predicts less frequent participation in high intensity political acts, however, suggests that feeling strapped for time may be at the core of this correlation. Similarly, the finding that residential hall organizations are associated with lower voter turnout unless they regularly sponsor events suggests that active organizations may be able to remedy disinterest by more purposefully organizing a group into political activities. Future research, however, should explore the connections with lower levels of political engagement in order to develop effective interventions.

Second, participation in several types of organizations beyond sports teams are associated with lowering the likelihood of participating in more intense political acts. Academic and service-oriented student organizations, which the Civic Voluntarism Model (Verba, Schlozman, & Brady 1995) suggests should hone transferrable civic skills and pull people into public life, may actually lower such participation—unless such organizations frequently sponsor their own social, educational, and fundraising events. It appears that when these types of organizations have low activity levels, they may encourage students to supplant political activism with alternative activities such as studying or volunteering. Redirecting this tendency may require more purposeful efforts to connect students' academic and community service interests to the government policies and programs that affect them.

Third, the findings that relative to White students, Hispanic and Asian students are typically less likely to participate in future political acts and the finding that Asian students are likely to have lower levels of political efficacy reflects broader patterns and is not surprising (Krogstad, 2014a, 2014b). However, these findings do suggest that colleges and universities will need to find more effective strategies for reaching different types of students. A contrasting finding about racial and ethnic identity is that Black officers had higher levels of both political and collective efficacy and that those who selected "other" in response to the racial demographic prompt also had higher levels of political interest and collective efficacy. Black students may have higher levels of political efficacy in response to the historic contemporaneous presidency of Barack Obama, and of collective efficacy because of the Black Lives Matter movement's presence on many of their campuses. Meanwhile students who identify as "other" may have developed a more precise or nuanced answer about their racial and ethnic identity than the census categories provided—with careful construction of this identity triggering group consciousness, along with political interest and collective efficacy.

Fourth, these regression analyses suggest that participation in student organizations on campus may do little to disrupt traditional gender role socialization's effect on women's political attitudes and behavior. That male students' had generally heightened political interest is not surprising as it reflects patterns in political behavior among the electorate (Atkeson & Rapoport 2003; Wolok & McDevitt 2011). What is surprising, however, is that participation in Greek organizations—which meet so many of Skocpol's (2003) best practices for voluntary associations—consistently are associated with higher levels of fraternity officials', but not sorority officials', political interest, political participation, and political efficacy. Fraternities' ability to pull men into public life is further exemplified by the finding that belonging to a fraternity over-compensates for low male civic participation—as well as by the finding that participation in Greek life is associated with fraternity officials' greater levels of collective efficacy, but not sorority leaders. This finding is somewhat troubling, as participation in a fraternity over time has been associated with higher levels of symbolic racism and sexism (Bleeker & Murnen 2005; Boeringer 1999; Sidanius, VanLaar, & Sears 2008; Syrett 2009). Given that Greek officials regardless of their gender identity lead organizations with equally robust opportunities to participate in skill building activities and deliberations (Strachan & Bennion 2016), future research should explore ways to encourage sorority leaders to realize that learning experiences within sororities have prepared them for leadership roles in civic and especially in political life. Identifying best practices for all-female groups is especially important, given the role that women's organizations historically played (and continue to play) in facilitating women's participation in politics (Sanbonmatsu & Walsh 2009). Furthermore, more attention is due to African American sororities, which anecdotal accounts indicate are much more effective at bolstering members' political engagement (Johnson 2015).

Fifth, aside from age, the variables associated student officials' more explicit political participation appear to appeal to students' narrow self-interest rather than a broader sense of civic duty or obligation. Students who join and belong to LGBTQ organizations, for example, are apt to have strong group consciousness and to recognize that on-going legislative debates, executive orders, and court decisions will affect their lives in profound ways. Political organizations and special interest groups may also appeal to students through self-interest. Yet healthy democratic systems benefit from more regular and mundane participation by those who share a sense of civic duty (Campbell 2006). Throughout American history, voluntary associations focused on social, civic, and philanthropic endeavors also often exhorted members to fulfill public-spirited obligations by paying attention to public issues and voting in elections. Such practices sustained high levels of political participation without resorting to polarizing issues or inflammatory political rhetoric (Skocpol 2003). Further research should explore ways to encourage apolitical student organizations to adopt similar public-spirited commitments.

Finally, organizational activities and decision-making styles were influential in different ways than anticipated. Given the emphasis on deliberation, not only because it teaches transferable political skills and parallels government processes (Skocpol 2003), but also because it bolsters civic identity (Campbell 2006), we suspected that exposure to deliberation would increase civic and political engagement. It was not significant in any of the models. This finding may reflect the fact that our respondents held leadership roles and influenced group decisions via their positions, even without access to deliberative decision-making. Exposure to deliberation may have been a significant variable if we had surveyed student organization members at large rather than officers. Given the finding that heavier reliance on executive decisions suppresses high-intensity political participation, future efforts should more fully explore the potential effects of organizational decision-making on political engagement.

Meanwhile, organizational activities are relevant, as hosting frequent events is associated with all versions of anticipated political and civic participation, while those engaged in proselytizing facilitated civic engagement. Organizations with robust activity levels and a clear mission connected to civic and political life appear to provide better political socialization than others. Understanding the type of educational and social activities typically undertaken by these clubs, as well as the values communicated to internal and external audiences, will provide further insight into best practices for political socialization within student organizations.

CONCLUSION AND RECOMMENDATIONS

Our findings indicate that student organizations could provide a source of significant political socialization for college students, in the same way that voluntary associations function in political science's Civic Voluntarism Model. Yet this research also suggests that even before significant obstacles to college students' political engagement—including rising voter suppression, partisan polarization, democratic backsliding, rudeness, threats, and political violence—the full potential of campus life remained untapped. As in the broader public sphere, the structure of civil society on campus struggles to mitigate the lower participation from traditional gender role socialization on women or to fully address the needs of minoritized students with low levels of political engagement. Further, given that proselytizing was only associated with civic participation, it appears that too few groups on campus focused on cultivating an intrinsic public-spirited civic identity that encompassed participation in political acts like voting. Yet it is precisely this sense of civic duty that predicts consistent, ongoing political participation throughout adulthood (Campbell 2006).

Moreover, some student organizations including sports teams, and some low-activity academic and service-oriented clubs, suppressed students' political engagement, likely by channeling their time and effort into alternative activities. Our findings suggest political socialization in student organizations could be improved if more groups helped students to hone civic and political skills by actively engaging them in planning and hosting campus events including activities that explicitly promote and facilitate civic and political participation.

Based on these findings, political socialization in student organizations could be improved with the following recommendations:

- Encourage student organizations to sponsor and implement a wide array of activities, to ensure members are engaged in public life on campus and have ample opportunity to hone important civic skills. Although it is beyond the scope of our questionnaire, there may be additional civic skill development when democratic values are directly connected to such work, as the Rank chapter in this volume, finds.
- Require student organizations to rely on elected officers, frequent meetings, deliberative processes, and by-laws to increase members' familiarity with the basics of democratic decision-making, which

may provide an important foundation for lifelong active political participation.
- Develop appropriate interventions to ensure students from demographic groups with low levels of civic and political participation have ample opportunity to contribute to the on-campus public sphere and receive robust political socialization tailored to their specific lived experiences (See Poloni-Staudinger and Strachan 2020.)
- Provide incentives for apolitical student groups focused on social, civic, and philanthropic agendas to incorporate messages about the importance of public-spirited participation in democracy, such as paying attention to public issues and voting.

So much has changed, and is changing, on college campuses, that updates are essential to determine how many of these patterns still hold. Has participation in campus activities bounced back now that students have returned to campus, or are student organizations struggling with the basic task of recruiting members? Since 2015, many student athletes became prominent BLM activists, while professional athletes sponsored voter registration drives. Have these activities mitigated the correlation between intramural sports and low levels of political engagement? Similarly, has the further politicization of women's issues and the recent spike in young women's political participation after the Dobbs decision mitigated the effects of traditional gender role socialization in student organizations more broadly and in Greek organizations more specifically? Perhaps most pressing, do students need to learn an entirely different set of civic skills grounded in civil resistance (Chenowith, 2021) to respond to voter suppression, democratic backsliding, and increased political violence?

Answering these questions—and more—can help to ensure that as many students as possible have access to robust political socialization through well-designed extracurricular activities in campus life. Hence the Bliss Institute's ACES consortium intends to facilitate future waves of the NSSL, along with qualitative interviews and focus groups. The goal is to better understand how to best cultivate our students' civic and political engagement through participation in student organizations, as well as to provide campuses that prioritize higher education's civic mission with regular campus updates that help to benchmark their performance.

APPENDIX
Participating Institutions, Characteristics, and Response Rates

Institution	Location	Type	Student Organizations	Response Rate
Arkansas Tech University	Russellville, AR	Public	98	42.8%
California State University, Chico	Chico, CA	Public	173	40.5%
Centre College	Danville, KY	Private	60	41.7%
Dickinson State University	Dickinson, ND	Public	19	68.4%
Eastern Illinois University	Charleston, IL	Public	206	47.6%
Emory University	Atlanta, GA	Private	348	45.4%
Emporia State University	Emporia, KS	Public	130	43.8%
Flagler College	St. Augustine, FL	Private	32	53.1%
Harper College	Palatine, IL	Public	30	53.3%
Indiana University, Bloomington	Bloomington, IN	Public	560	30.5%
Indiana University, South Bend	South Bend, IN	Public	88	39.8%
Iona College	New Rochelle, NY	Private	71	60.6%
Lake Superior State University	Sault Ste. Marie, MI	Public	67	58.2%
Manchester University	N Manchester, IN	Private	57	72.0%
Merrimack College	North Andover, MA	Private	40	82.5%
Miami University	Oxford, OH	Public	160	32.1%
Morehead State University	Morehead, KY	Public	107	62.6%
Northeastern Illinois University	Chicago, IL	Public	75	50.7%
Northwest Missouri State University	Maryville, MS	Public	119	54.6%

(continued)

APPENDIX
Participating Institutions, Characteristics, and Response Rates (continued)

Institution	Location	Type	Student Organizations	Response Rate
Piedmont Virginia Comm College	Charlottesville, VA	Public	33	33.3%
Queens University of Charlotte	Charlotte, NC	Private	53	54.7%
Rosemont College	Bryn Mawr, PA	Private	8	75.0%
Salem State University	Salem, MA	Public	55	61.8%
Susquehanna University	Selinsgrove, PA	Private	113	48.7%
The College of Wooster	Wooster, OH	Private	107	66.4%
University of California, San Diego	San Diego, CA	Public	512	19.7%
University of Tampa	Tampa, FL	Private	122	45.1%
Univ of Tennessee at Chattanooga	Chattanooga, TN	Public	134	37.6%
University of Wisconsin, Madison	Madison, WI	Public	850	38.6%
Utah Valley University	Orem, UT	Public	136	36.8%
Washington College	Chestertown, MD	Private	74	46.0%
Weber State	Ogden, UT	Public	131	36.6%
West Texas A&M University	Canyon, TX	Public	124	29.8%
Salve Regina College	Newport, RI	Private	53	50.9%
Towson University	Baltimore, MD	Public	204	23.5%

NOTES

1. While the pool of campus leadership positions may reflect the sociodemographic campus composition of our participating institutions, there are certainly systematic self-selection in the types of students who seek out, or who are encouraged to seek out, leadership positions on campus that may not entirely reflect the sociodemographic composition of the student body. The relative background of leaders is likely not directly comparable to the campus composition, though disentangling the structural incentives, ambitions, and demographic pressures that drive different patterns of leadership backgrounds is not the direct focus of this piece. That said, participating Consortium members received a campus-specific report, where they were encouraged to compare the demographic identities of their student officials to their overall student body—and to develop a plan to recruit minoritized students if they were underrepresented in leadership roles. At least one campus followed this advice to increase the number of Hispanic students serving in this capacity.
2. Given that the questionnaire was administered in 2015, our response categories for this item did not include the full array of gender identity options that we would offer in a contemporary version. As a result, we are unable to report the percentage of student leaders who identified as transgender or nonbinary.
3. We recognize the distinction between the terms Hispanic and Latinx, as well as debate over which term is appropriate. Our questionnaire item offered students the option of identifying as Hispanic rather than Latinx to provide a broader category and to include students whose origins are outside South America. Given time constraints, we did not offer Latinx as an additional response option.

REFERENCES

Almond, G. A., & Verba, S. (1963). *The civic culture: Political attitudes and democracy in five nations*. Princeton University Press.

Anderson, C. (2018). *On person no vote, How voter suppression is destroying our democracy*. Bloomsbury Publishing.

Atkeson, L. R., & Rapoport, R. B. (2003). The more things change the more they stay the same: Examining gender differences in political attitude expression, 1952–2000. *Public Opinion Quarterly, 67*(4), 495–521.

Bleeker, E. T., & Murnen, S. K. (2005). Fraternity membership, the display of degrading sexual images of women, and rape myth acceptance. *Sex Roles, 53*(7–8), 487–493.

Boatright, R. G., Schaffer, T., Sobieraj, S., & Young, D. G. (Eds). (2019). *A crisis of civility? Political discourse and its discontents*. Routledge.

Boeringer, S. B. (1999). Associations of rape supportive attitudes with fraternities and athletic participation. *Violence Against Women, 5*(1), 81–90.

Bok, D. (2006). *Our underachieving colleges*. Princeton University Press.

Boyer, E. L. (1987). *College: The undergraduate experience in America*. Carnegie Foundation for the Advancement of Teaching.

Brown, N., Block, R., & Stout, C. (2021). *The politics of protest.* Routledge.
Campbell, D. E. (2006). *Why we vote: How schools and communities shape our civic life.* Princeton University Press.
Carnegie Corporation of New York and CIRCLE. (2003). *The civic mission of schools.*
Chenowith, E. (2021). *Civil resistance, What everyone needs to know.* Oxford University Press.
Colby, A., Ehrlich, T, Beaumont, E., & Stephens, J. (2003). *Educating citizens: Preparing undergraduates for lives of civic and moral responsibility.* Jossey-Bass.
Colby, A., Beaumont, E., Ehrlich, T., & Corngold, J. (Eds.) (2007). *Educating for democracy: Preparing undergraduates for responsible political engagement.* Jossey-Bass.
Edwards, M. (2014). *Civil society* (3rd ed.). Polity Press.
Ehrlich, T, (Ed). (2000). *Civic responsibility and higher education.* The American Council on Education and Oryx Press.
Gallup. (2014). *Fraternities and sororities: Understanding life outcomes.*
Galston, W. A. (2001). Political knowledge, political engagement, and civic education. *Annual Review of Political Science, 4,* 217–234.
Johnson. T. (April 26, 2015). The political power of the Black sorority. *The Atlantic.* Retrieved from http://www.theatlantic.com/politics/archive/2015/04/loretta-lynch-and-the-political-power-of-the-black-sorority/391385/
Kalmoe, N. P., & Mason, L. (2022). *Radical American partisanship, Mapping violent hostility and the consequences for democracy.* University of Chicago Press.
Krogstad, J. M. (April 2, 2014a). *Hispanics punch below their weight in midterm elections.* Pew Research Center. http://www.pewresearch.org/fact-tank/2014/04/02/hispanics-punch-below-their-weight-in-midterm-elections/
Krogstad, J. M. (April 9 2014b). *Asian American voter turnout lags behind other groups; some non-voters say they're 'too busy.'* Pew Research Center. http://www.pewresearch.org/fact-tank/2014/04/09/asian-american-voter-turnout-lags-behind-other-groups-some-non-voters-say-theyre-too-busy/
Lawless, J. L., & Fox, R. L. (2013). *Girls just wanna not run, The gender gap in young Americans' political ambition.* Women & Politics Institute.
Lawless, J. L., & Fox, R. L. (2015). *Running from office: Why young Americans are turned off to politics.* Oxford University Press.
McCartney, A. R. M., Bennion, E. B., & Simpson, D. (2013). *Teaching civic engagement: from student to active citizen.* American Political Science Association.
McFarland, D., & Thomas, R. (2006). Bowling young: How youth voluntary associations influence adult political participation. *American Sociological Review, 71,* 401–425.
Ostrom, E., & the American Political Science Association Task Force on Civic Education in the 21st Century. (1998). Expanded articulation statement: A call for reactions and contributions, *PS: Political Science & Politics, 31*(3), 636–638.
Pike, G. R. (2000). The influence of fraternity and sorority membership on college experiences and cognitive development. *Research in Higher Education, 41*(1), 117–139.
Poloni-Staudinger, L. M., & Strachan, J. C. (2020). TLC keynote: Democracy is more important than a p-value: Embracing political science's civic mission through intersectional engaged learning. *PS Political Science & Politics, 53*(3), 569–574.

Putnam, R. D. (2000). *Bowling alone: The collapse and revival of American community.* Simon & Schuster.

Routon, P. W., & Walker, J. K. (2014). The impact of Greek organization membership on collegiate outcomes: Evidence from a national survey. *Journal of Behavioral and Experimental Economics, 49,* 63–70.

Sanbonmatsu, K., Carroll, S. J., & Walsh, D. (2009). *Poised to run: Women's pathways to the state legislatures.* Center for American Women and Politics.

Schlesinger, A. M., Sr. (1944). Biography of a nation of joiners. *American Historical Review, 50*(1), 1–25.

Shames, S. (2017). *Out of the running: Why millennials reject political careers and why it matters.* New York University Press.

Sidanius, J., Levin, S., Van Laar, C., & Sears, D. O. (2008). *The diversity challenge: Social identity and intergroup relations on the college campus.* Russell Sage.

Skocpol, T. 2003. *Diminished democracy, from membership to management in American civil life.* The University of Oklahoma Press.

Skocpol, T. (2011). Civil society in the United States. In M. Edwards (Ed.), *The Oxford handbook of civil society.* Oxford University Press

Strachan, J. C. and Bennion, E. A. (2016). *Revolutionizing the role of student organizations: Gender and political leadership.* Paper presented at the Annual Meeting of the Midwest Political Science Association, April, Chicago, IL.

Syrett, N. (2009). *The company he keeps, A history of white college fraternities.* The University of North Carolina Press.

Tocqueville, Alexis De, & Henry Reeve. (1845). *Democracy in America.* ed by Spencer, John C., & H.G. Langley.

Verba, S., Schlozman, K. L., & Brady, H. E. (1995). *Voice and equality, Civic voluntarism in American politics.* Harvard University Press.

Wattenberg, M. P. (2012). *Is voting for young people?, 3rd ed.* Pearson.

Wolak, J., & McDevitt, M. (2011). The roots of the gender gap in political knowledge in adolescence. *Political Behavior, 33*(3), 505–533.

Zukin, C., Keeter, S. A., Jenkins, K., & Delli Carpini, M. X. (2006). *A new engagement? Political participation, civic life and the changing American citizen.* Oxford University Press.

CHAPTER 14

FOSTERING CIVIC RESILIENCE

A Framework for Campus Misinformation Reduction

Ryan W. Flynn
University of Illinois Springfield

Elora A. Agsten
The College of Wooster

ABSTRACT

While misinformation and its effects on news consumption and civic participation have been discussed at length, frequently missing from these discussions are misinformation's complicated social dimensions. While much misinformation is spread online due to technical or monetary factors, individuals are often more susceptible to misinformation when it is situated around a community. Once an individual believes an ideology situated around misinformation, showing that person "the facts" is usually not enough to convince them to stop believing misinformation. Institutions of higher education, however, have the potential to disrupt this dynamic for our students. As both living and learning environments, colleges and universities can instruct students in critical information literacy and critical civic engagement, provide space for conversation, and facilitate a sense of belonging. This chapter presents a new framework to help colleges and universities build their students' resilience towards misinformation and begin finding their civic identity.

While not new or an exclusively twenty-first-century problem, misinformation and its effects on voting habits gained heightened attention in many academic disciplines since the US presidential election and the Brexit referendum of 2016 (Soll, 2016). For the purpose of this chapter, the general term "misinformation" will be used to encompass all forms of misinformation, disinformation, or propaganda, whether intentional on the part of the user or not (see Lewandowsky et al. [2012] for more discussion on forms of political false belief). Despite these discussions, the problem of misinformation is persistent, particularly online. When algorithms of social networking sites (SNS) promote posts with higher amounts of "engagement," monetary incentives for misinformation often overshadow other concerns. Misinformation then becomes part of a larger brand strategy, politicians rely on it to influence public opinion and technology companies can liquidate departments dedicated to its prevention (Birchall, 2021; Folkenflik, 2023; Hagey and Horwitz, 2021; Myers and Grant, 2023).

Higher education has not ignored the threat of misinformation. Teaching librarians have misinformation awareness in their information literacy curricula, civic engagement offices address misinformation in election programming, and instructors of many disciplines discuss misinformation within their classrooms. While all of these strategies are needed, such efforts to date generally have not addressed the community nature of the problem. Individuals are not usually persuaded to abandon misinformation beliefs by simply being shown "the facts" (Marwick, 2018). Rather, our social networks, in both "real life" and online, help us define what we believe to be true (Brashier & Marsh, 2020; Munn, 2018; Restrepo et al. 2021). As both living and learning communities, college and university campuses are in a unique position to provide a necessary community for their students, as well as pedagogical practices and dialogue spaces to encourage deliberative civic discourse. With this confluence of resources, what would a community-focused approach to misinformation reduction look like on our campuses?

This chapter presents a theoretical framework with which to combine existing resources to confront the misinformation problem in a higher education setting. The first section is a brief literature review discussing research on misinformation prevention efforts. In the second section, we create a theoretical framework based on existing literature. In order to educate students to address misinformation, an institution must 1) give students the tools to tackle misinformation through critical information literacy instruction; 2) prioritize critical civic literacy and engagement as a means to instill a sense of action in students; and 3) facilitate and devote space for deliberative dialogue and provide opportunities for students to build their own agency. Above all, an institution must 4) employ strategies that build a sense of belonging at the institution itself. Together, these strategies seek to build a community of learners engaged with the democratic process, their communities, and a critical understanding of how information is created and used. While these skills are useful throughout a student's time in college and beyond, the intent of this framework is to give administrators, faculty, staff, and librarians another tool to help prevent radicalization due to misinformation by providing other outlets for community building, critical questioning, and political discussion.

MACRO, INDIVIDUAL, AND COMMUNITY IDEAS ON PREVENTING MISINFORMATION

The macro-level approach to misinformation prevention has focused almost exclusively on content moderation on SNS, or, less frequently, legislative action (Bak-Coleman et al., 2022; Funke & Flamini, 2019). Research suggests that content moderation alone does not effectively lead to a reduction in misinformation. Rather, as Bak-Coleman et al. (2022) find, a combination of factors including account banning, reducing the speed at which viral misinformation can travel via algorithmic recommendation systems, and "nudging" users to re-consider whether they wish to share a questionable post could provide a macro-level framework for reducing misinformation. However, all of these methods are left to the discretion of corporations to make decisions on what qualifies as misinformation, what strategies they wish to implement, and how transparent they wish to be about their algorithmic recommendation systems. Instead, as Gillett and Suzor (2018) state in their paper on incels- involuntary celibates, a misogynist Internet subculture- and "quarantining" of incel rhetoric on the site Reddit, "the problem with incels is incels." Once a community is situated around a hateful or radicalizing ideology, content moderation is not enough to de-radicalize individuals or prevent the rhetoric and subsequent misinformation from spreading further. Due to the monetization of content and advertising inherent to most SNSes, there is consistently a monetary incentive to allow misinformation to proceed, until it reaches a point where it hurts advertising capabilities (Global Disinformation Index, 2022; Maheshwari, 2016).

An individual approach to misinformation prevention borrowed from information literacy instruction is common in education and libraries. Information literacy is defined by the Association of College and Research Libraries (2015) as "the set of integrated abilities encompassing the reflective discovery of information, the understanding of how information is produced and valued, and the use of information in creating new knowledge and participating ethically in communities of learning." Academic librarians have been teaching information literacy skills to undergraduate students for decades (Ariew, 2014). Librarians widely teach information evaluation to students using a heuristic model, such as Blakeslee's (2004) CRAAP test or Caulfield's (2019) SIFT method. These methods teach students to evaluate a source for bias with information found within the potential source itself (the CRAAP test) or to perform lateral reading (the SIFT method) by examining what other sources have to say about its trustworthiness. While both methods encourage students to make decisions about the reliability of a source before using it, these methods do not take into account outside factors that influence how users interact with misinformation, such as algorithmic bias or community influence (Lewandowsky et al., 2012; Noble, 2018; Pennycook & Rand, 2020; Restrepo et al., 2022).

There are several logistical reasons for this adoption. Academic teaching librarians are usually the main instructors of information literacy on campuses, and that instruction is often only available at the invitation of the regular classroom instructor. While some institutions do have for-credit information literacy courses, most teaching librarians will only interact with a group of students for one class period, leaving no time for major scaffolding of concepts without prior support from the main instructor. Given these limitations, we fully recognize the pedagogical necessity of these individual-based misinformation prevention methods. They are easy to teach and for students to understand; we use them in our own instruction. However, these checklist methods have several ideological limitations (Bull et al., 2021; Meola, 2004) and they largely put the responsibility of misinformation prevention on the decisions of the individual student and their initial emotional response to that misinformation (particularly with Caulfield's SIFT), ignoring community or social influence.

A student's individual critical reasoning, however, is not infallible and often subjective to the prior beliefs of that person (Lewandowsky et al. 2012; Pennycook & Rand, 2020; Tripodi, 2022). Psychology research has also demonstrated that showing someone "the facts" is generally not enough to prevent them from believing in falsehoods (Marwick, 2018). The number of times a person hears a claim also contributes to whether or not they believe it to be true. Hasher, Goldstein, and Toppino (1977) first documented this "Illusory Truth Effect," and its effect on misinformation belief was further confirmed by Hassan and Barber (2021). This is especially concerning for SNS users, where algorithms often amplify similar content, creating "filter bubbles" where claims are consistently repeated (Pariser, 2012). Other cognitive biases contribute to this. In Brashier and Marsh's (2020) review of psychological literature, individuals often construct their truths based on previous knowledge. If the new knowledge matches their previous perception, they are more likely to accept it. This is also compounded by group influence. Cohen's (2003) multiple-study article shows that when individuals are aware of partisan support of a policy or piece of legislation, they will adopt the position of their political party, regardless of the actual content of said policy. These psychological factors challenge the idea that a student merely needs to "evaluate" their way out of misinformation; cognitive biases do not always allow this to be the case.

A community-based approach to misinformation is currently understudied in the context of higher education. Rather, this idea has been studied most frequently within epidemiology, due to the COVID-19 pandemic. From a technical perspective, Restrepo et al. (2021) noted how many parenting communities on Facebook were drawn to misinformation about vaccines during the pandemic due to misinformation postings of "core" members of the group. Facebook's attempts to "nudge" users away from this misinformation–generally by adding warnings to posts containing certain words–proved to be mostly ineffective (Restrepo et al. 2021). Epidemiologists and other public health officials also worked within community structures during the COVID-19 pandemic to prevent further spread of misinformation, often utilizing community influencers and groups to encourage vaccination and responsible practices surrounding COVID prevention (Korin et al., 2022; Ssanyu et al., 2022). This paired with teaching health or information literacy provides a two-pronged approach to misinformation prevention: both individual and community (Austin et al., 2021). It must also be noted that communities of color are at particular risk for misinformation, because of pre-existing campaigns attempting to politically disenfranchise those communities (Austin et al., 2021). Lessons from this body of research can therefore be applied to our campus communities: strengthening existing community groups can both strengthen a campus and help make it less susceptible to misinformation attempts.

INSTITUTIONAL FOCUS AREAS FOR MISINFORMATION EDUCATION

To address these issues, we present a framework for misinformation education that is a combination of strategies that many higher education institutions are already employing, although not always with that intended purpose or through a specific step-by-step system (see Figure 14.1). This framework is also connected to other efforts supporting higher education's civic mission, as the challenges inherent in combating misinformation are often similar to the challenges of promoting political learning and engagement (Thomas & Brower, 2017). These strategies are not exhaustive and are meant as a starting point for campus stakeholders. It can and should be adapted to meet the needs of the institution employing it.

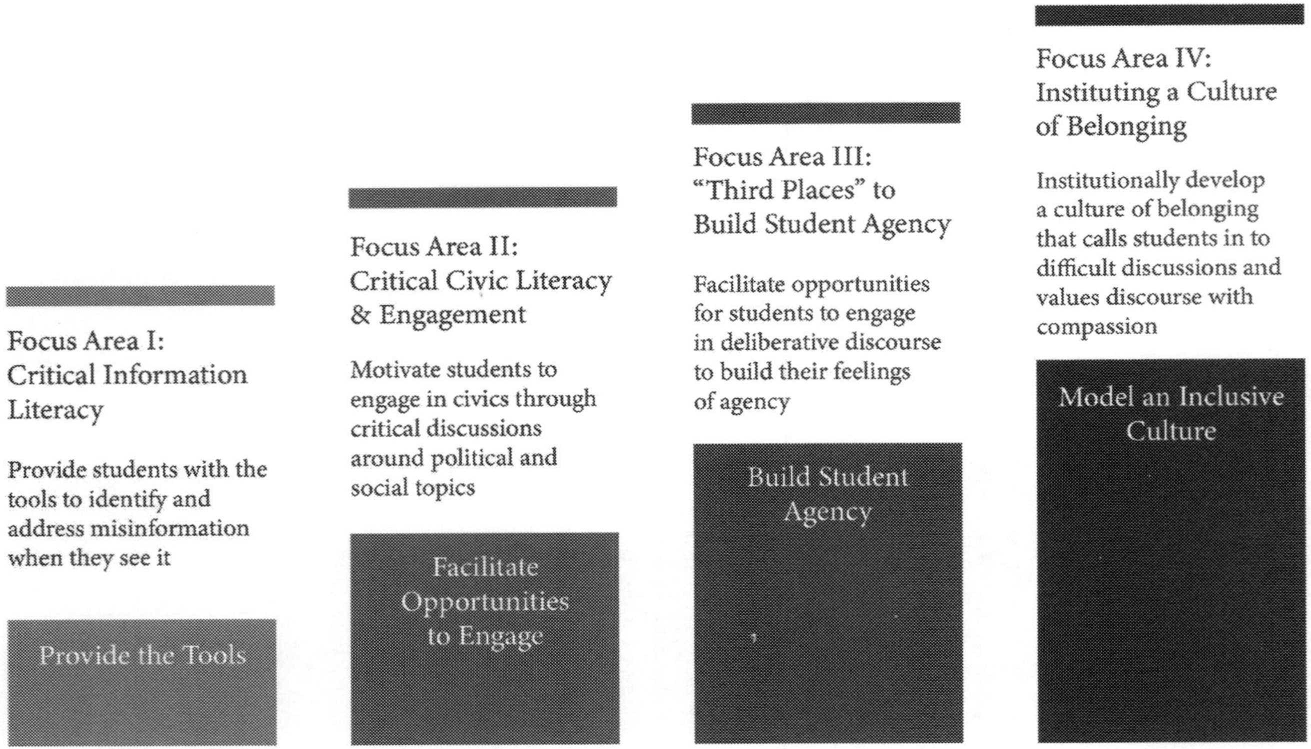

Focus Area I: Critical Information Literacy

Provide students with the tools to identify and address misinformation when they see it

Provide the Tools

Focus Area II: Critical Civic Literacy & Engagement

Motivate students to engage in civics through critical discussions around political and social topics

Facilitate Opportunities to Engage

Focus Area III: "Third Places" to Build Student Agency

Facilitate opportunities for students to engage in deliberative discourse to build their feelings of agency

Build Student Agency

Focus Area IV: Instituting a Culture of Belonging

Institutionally develop a culture of belonging that calls students in to difficult discussions and values discourse with compassion

Model an Inclusive Culture

Figure 14.1 Institutional Focus Areas for Campus Misinformaion Education. Focus Area I: Critical information literacy. Focus Area II: Critical civic literacy and engagement. Focus Area III: "Third Places" to build student agency. Focus Area IV: Instituting a culture of belonging.

FOCUS AREA I: CRITICAL INFORMATION LITERACY

Critical pedagogy provides a valuable ideological lens through which to view community-engaged methods of misinformation prevention. Brazilian education theorist Paulo Freire's *Pedagogy of the Oppressed* (1968) states that the purpose of education is to create a critical consciousness in learners. Learners are therefore encouraged to trust their full ability to reason and to use that reasoning to question the norms of their society and governance, ultimately leading to transformative actions (Freire 1968). However, this work cannot be done alone. Rather, Freire encouraged learners to work in "fellowship and solidarity" to achieve this praxis (Freire 1968, p. 86). Lessons from this critical pedagogy can be translated into critical information literacy by taking "into consideration the social, political, economic, and corporate systems that have power and influence over information production, dissemination, access, and consumption" (Gregory and Higgins, 2013, p. 4). Exposing students to these ideas can be a form of consciousness-raising, as students are not passive consumers of information, but active participants (and targets) in an entire ecosystem of ideas. When students understand that misinformation is part of a larger information system, they can begin to question its persistence and what other factors are at play for its creation and dissemination. As discussed previously, showing someone "the facts" is not enough to pull them away from political misinformation. Rather than maligning someone who falls for misinformation, as campus administrators, staff, and faculty, we must react compassionately and use this opportunity for dialogue to help build critical consciousness with the student.

While this type of instruction is gaining popularity in academic libraries, helping students understand the ways in which information systems are formed and how misinformation creators benefit is important to both their information and civic education. Some examples include discussing ad revenue generated from misinformation, how using partisan-coded keywords generates partisan results in Google searches (thus enhancing cognitive bias) (Tripodi, 2022), or having students reflect on their own SNS use. Additionally, lateral reading—the ability to evaluate a source's reliability by checking its reputation against other sources—is a popular instruction method for both disciplines. Caulfield's (2019) SIFT method is the most famous version of this idea. While lateral reading is an individual-focused information literacy strategy, it can become more critically engaged when framed within a larger conversation about the monetary and power incentives attached to misinformation creation.

Lastly, libraries, as a center of resources on campus, must continue providing civic resources to help students navigate political life in their communities. However, librarians must also provide access to resources about how these facets of their identity, such as race, gender, sexuality, and social class, intersect with political and civic identity. These identity-focused resources not only enhance student research but also contribute to a student's sense of belonging within the library space and the campus community (Chomintra, 2022; Morales et al., 2014; Welburn, 2010). If students do not feel comfortable with their library, they will not engage with it, which has large implications for both their academic success and sense of belonging on campus. Though it is becoming increasingly controversial in many states to do so, library workers have a professional mandate to provide their patrons with diverse resources and must uphold their historic commitment to intellectual freedom, and thus, democratic thought (American Library Association, 2019). When collecting diverse physical items is not possible, due to legal restrictions in areas with conservative governments, we encourage librarians to connect students with online resources whenever possible. While very far from a perfect solution, this can still provide students with some necessary resources.

FOCUS AREA II: CRITICAL CIVIC LITERACY AND ENGAGEMENT

The second institutional focus area combines critical civic literacy and civic engagement practices. While civic literacy is being well-versed in social and political happenings, discussions, and perspectives (Teitelbaum, 2010), civic engagement aims to encourage active democratic participation through engagement in civic institutions and governance (Dewey, 1916, 1927; Jones & Gaventa, 2002). Civic literacy and engagement within higher education can take many forms. This can include voter registration and education, volunteering and service-learning, workshops on organizing and deliberative dialogue, and discussions on social justice and political topics either through classes or campus events and speakers. These initiatives may also be student-led. Programming can also be passive with debate watch parties, email or text reminders to vote or flyers around campus or in residence halls encouraging civic participation.

While these examples are all forms of civic literacy and engagement, we assert that this work must also take a critical stance when discussing the topic of misinformation in this current hyper-partisan political climate. As Teitelbaum explains, "adopting a critical stance means not taking for granted what is known and in place, instead rigorously and wholeheartedly questioning the assumptions that undergird current ideas, practices, policies, and structures" (2011, p. 12). In a political atmosphere where institutions and democratic norms are up for interpretation and revision, higher education must be involved in the discussion. This can take the form of critical pedagogy by encouraging students to ask critical questions about the current political climate and hosting discussions about compassion, equity, and justice.

One example of how this critical pedagogy can take shape in civic engagement practices is through adopting and funding more critical forms of service-learning. Service-learning is a course-based, typically credit-bearing experience that requires students to commit to a volunteer project that benefits the local community and connects back to course content (Bringle & Steinberg, 2010). However, service-learning is not without its challenges. These include the often short-term nature of service-learning (Tryon et al, 2008) and its potential to reinforce saviorism and colonialism (Bocci, 2015; Green, 2003), when the service project is performed for the emotional and academic benefit of the students and is not conscious of the needs of the community they are intending to serve. As Randy Stoecker posits, traditional service-learning—or institutionalized service-learning—allows students to engage in service that is only acceptable and supported by higher education institutions, often shunning more political forms of engagement such as community organizing and protesting (Stoecker, 2016). While service-learning has been pushed as a form of accessible civic engagement and students are more likely today to engage in community service than in the past, this has not moved the needle on political engagement (Harker, 2014; Koliba, 2004; Reinke, 2003; Stoecker, 2016). By liberating service-learning through critical education, we are better able to meet the needs of students and their growth as civically-engaged citizens, as well as the communities we partner with. This includes community allyship for social change, sharing in the production of knowledge, as well as support for community organizing (Stoecker, 2016).

Short-term and long-term outcomes for students engaging in more critical forms of civic engagement show gains in civic identity development (Mitchell, 2015), perspectives and desires to disrupt harmful social systems (Catlett & Proweller, 2011), and mitigating potential harms during that service experience (Santiago-Ortiz, 2019; Straubhaar, 2015; Tryon & Madden, 2019). By challenging students to learn and practice both civic literacy and civic engagement with a critical lens, we are giving them the opportunity to gain perspective into the nuance that many societal structures are built upon—and what misinformation thrives on. Moving towards more critical approaches, we are giving students space to ask tough questions, challenge assumptions, and advocate for changes.

FOCUS AREA III: "THIRD PLACES" TO BUILD STUDENT AGENCY

This institutional focus area emphasizes physical spaces and outlets for student expression in order to build personal agency. Institutions must devote space for students to practice the skills and engage in the opportunities developed in the first two focus areas. We propose doing this through the creation of "third places." As defined by Ray Oldenburg in his book *The Great Good Place* (1989), "third places" are physical locations outside of the home (first place) and work (second place), and provide an opportunity for citizens to engage with each other in face-to-face conversations—not always political conversations either. Oldenburg asserts that "third places" should 1) be neutral ground, where all feel welcome and comfortable, 2) act as an equalizer, specifically in terms of social standing, class, and profession, and 3) uphold conversation as the main activity. Accessible and available campus spaces provide students with an outlet to engage with their peers, ask questions, and feel safe expressing their opinions. While much of the early hype about social media being the new town square has faded and been replaced by more pessimistic outlooks (Klein, 2022), conversations on issues of social and political importance occur on SNS platforms daily. This is unlikely to change; though the limitations of this model of discourse, as well as general discontent with it, are well-documented (Pew Research Center, 2016) and reinforce the need for physical "third places."

"Third places" can take many forms on campus, even if not for the specific purpose of encouraging deliberative dialogue. These spaces may take the form of residence hall common areas, library spaces, meeting rooms, and outdoor patio areas around campus. Academic libraries also provide an example of a "third place." In the past two decades, academic libraries have moved towards more active participation by offering space for public discourse and directly participating in civic programming. Libraries are well positioned to not only provide tools and the expertise needed to train students to better recognize and reduce misinformation but also offer spaces to encourage in-person dialogue. However, librarians will need training and institutional support to do this work effectively (Kranich, 2019).

Spaces encouraging deliberative dialogue and public discourse are not only physical rooms either, as highlighted by Indiana University-Purdue University Indianapolis's (IUPUI) Democracy Plaza (Bonilla & Brown, 2019). The Democracy Plaza includes several chalkboards outside the IUPUI Campus Center and several dry-erase boards inside. This program is led by student leaders called Democracy Plaza Scholars, which also provides a sense of student agency. Each week, a new question is posted on the boards and students may respond to the question or their peers' comments. As the space is dedicated to free speech, staff, and student workers will only remove responses if they directly target an individual. Additional support is provided by the Social Justice Education Department to remediate, including other dialogue-based programs that are not anonymous and where concerns can be exchanged (Bonilla & Brown, 2019). This example shows a critical space for public discourse on social and political issues and helps students realize agency in its dialogue and management.

FOCUS AREA IV: INSTITUTING A SENSE OF BELONGING

Misinformation education from a community-based approach requires students to have the agency to share in the solution and see themselves as equal partners of the campus community. For this to happen, students must feel a sense of belonging within this campus community. Belonging is characterized as a subjective feeling of deep connection with our surroundings and others (Allen, et al, 2021). While many colleges and universities approach belonging as simply a retention issue, belonging also plays a role in encouraging students to use information thoughtfully and engage with civic and community life on campus. Instituting a sense of belonging places the ownership of the success or failure on the institution, not on the student. This dichotomy is key, as it tasks campus administrators, staff, and faculty to create change within their institutions. The work also cannot be placed solely in one office within the institution. Instituting a sense of belonging often requires a change in organizational culture.

As part of this organizational culture shift, institutions need to provide space for students to have opportunities for engagement across lines of difference—such as race, gender, sexual orientation, partisan affiliation, religion, or social class—with the goal of reducing stigma between and among groups of students (Malott et al, 2019). Colleges and universities must also recognize and confront that all students will attend college with already developed assumptions and biases from the consumption of partisan news and parental perspectives. Students being in proximity to peers that may come from different social, economic or racial groups than they do offers important socialization benefits beyond structured programs (Berryman-Fink, 2006; Hudson, 2022; Todd et al, 2011). These interventions take many forms, including institutionally-supported interventions such as deliberative dialogue, "third place" promotion, and mentoring programs.

This work on belonging should operate in tandem with diversity, equity, and inclusion (DEI) initiatives that focus on campus life for marginalized students. This work often goes unsupported, financially constrained, and siloed in one office on campus (rather than a campus-wide initiative). Furthermore, there are growing attacks against DEI initiatives at colleges and universities in a number of states, posing additional challenges for this strategy, but also further emphasizing the importance of DEI initiatives that facilitate belonging (Charles, 2023; Diep & Pettit, 2023). We recognize that this can be a radical and difficult task, specifically at public institutions in states with conservative supermajorities. In these instances, additional care will be needed in crafting language and appropriating funding in order to balance the needs of students and demands from forces outside the institution's control. In such a fraught political moment, it's even more important for institutions of higher education to model compassionate leadership and facilitate the culture shift needed so that all can feel supported and belong. By supporting these changes, institutions impact the virality of misinformation on campus- especially weaponized misinformation that may be targeting specific, marginalized groups (Austin et al., 2021; Osmundsen et al, 2021; Pizzolato and Lee, 2023).

CONCLUSION AND FURTHER WORK

Using a campus community framework to address misinformation is a slow fix to a fast-moving problem. Our framework will not prevent every instance of misinformation on a campus; that is an impossible task. There is also no "one size fits all" solution to misinformation and many of the factors of its spread are outside the scope of a campus community. Though based on research, this framework is theoretical, and quantitative data is needed to support the use of these principles. However, by providing students with the tools, the motivation, and the opportunity to engage in misinformation education, we are providing a cultural shift for campuses to utilize to effect long-term change. When institutions can prioritize these important shifts, while also shifting culture to one that supports belonging and compassionate engagement, we are providing a means for students to take these lessons into their social groups and online spaces, which can begin having an impact on misinformation spread. As both living and learning communities, colleges and universities already have the resources and expertise to implement this shift. This represents progress towards a long-term goal of reducing students' susceptibility to misinformation and providing them with the support—educational, emotional, and physical—to grow as informed participants in the democratic experiment.

REFERENCES

Allen, K. A., Kern, M. L., Rozek, C. S., McInereney, D., & Slavich, G. M. (2021). Belonging: A review of conceptual issues, an integrative framework, and directions for future research. *Australian Journal of Psychology*, 73(1), 87–102. https://doi.org/10.1080/00049530.2021.1883409

American Library Association. (2019, June 24). *Diverse collections: An interpretation of the Library Bill of Rights*. http://www.ala.org/advocacy/intfreedom/librarybill/interpretations/diversecollections/

Ariew, S. (2014). How we got here: A historical look at the academic teaching library and the role of the teaching librarian. *Communications in Information Literacy, 8*(2), 208–224.

Austin, E. W., Borah, P., & Domgaard, S. (2021). COVID-19 disinformation and political engagement among communities of color: The role of media literacy. *Harvard Kennedy School (HKS) Misinformation Review.* https://doi.org/10.37016/mr-2020-58

Association of College and Research Libraries. (2015, February 9). *Framework for information literacy for higher education.* American Library Association. http://www.ala.org/acrl/standards/ilframework

Bak-Coleman, J. B., Kennedy, I., Wack, M., Beers, A., Schafer, J. S., Spiro, E. S., Starbird, K., & West, J. D. (2022). Combining interventions to reduce the spread of viral misinformation. *Nature Human Behaviour, 6*(10), 1372–1380. https://doi.org/10.1038/s41562-022-01388-6

Berryman-Fink, C. (2006). Reducing prejudice on campus: The role of intergroup contact in diversity education. *College Student Journal, 40*(3), 511–516.

Blakeslee, S. (2004). The CRAAP test. *LOEX Quarterly, 31*(3), 6–7.

Bocci, M. (2015). Service-learning and White normativity: Racial representation in service-learning's historical narrative. *Michigan Journal of Community Service Learning, 22*(1), 5–17.

Bonilla, A. L., & Brown, L. A. (2019). Democracy Plaza at IUPUI. In N. V. Longo & T. J. Shaffer (Eds.), *Creating space for democracy: A primer on dialogue and deliberation in higher education* (pp. 193–198). Stylus Publishing.

Birchall, C. (2021). The paranoid style for sale: Conspiracy entrepreneurs, marketplace bots, and surveillance capitalism. *Symploke, 29*(1–2), 97–121. https://doi.org/10.1353/sym.2021.0006

Brashier, N. M., & Marsh, E. J. (2020). Judging truth. *Annual Review of Psychology, 71,* 499–515. https://doi.org/10.1146/annurev-psych-010419-050807

Bringle, R., & Steinberg, K. (2010). Educating for informed community involvement. *American Journal of Community Psychology, 46,* 428–441.

Bull, A. C., MacMillan, M., & Head, A. (2021, July 21). *Dismantling the evaluation framework.* In the Library with the Lead Pipe. https://www.inthelibrarywiththeleadpipe.org/2021/dismantling-evaluation/

Catlett, B. S., & Proweller, A. (2011). College students' negotiation of privilege in a community-based violence prevention project. *Michigan Journal of Community Service Learning, 34*–48.

Caulfield, M. (2019, June 19). *SIFT (The four moves).* Hapgood. https://hapgood.us/2019/06/19/sift-the-four-moves/

Charles, J. B. (2023, April 18). *At gathering of DEI officers, fear, anger, joy, and solidarity.* The Chronicle of Higher Education. https://www.chronicle.com/article/at-gathering-of-dei-officers-fear-anger-joy-and-solidarity

Chomintra, M. (2022). Reflecting on critical DEI practices in spatial collection development, metadata, and instruction. *Journal of Map & Geography Libraries, 18*(1/2), 68–86. https://doi.org/10.1080/15420353.2022.2128971

Cohen, G. L. (2003). Party over policy: The dominating impact of group influence on political beliefs. *Journal of Personality and Social Psychology, 85*(5), 808–822. https://doi.org/10.1037/0022-3514.85.5.808

Dewey, J. (1916). *Democracy and education: An introduction to the philosophy of education.* Macmillan Publishers.

Dewey, J. (1927). *The public and its problems.* Holt Publishers.

Diep, F., & Pettit, E. (2023, January 19). *DeSantis asked Florida universities to detail their diversity spending. Here's how they answered.* The Chronicle of Higher Education. https://www.chronicle.com/article/desantis-asked-florida-universities-to-detail-their-diversity-spending-heres-how-they-answered

Evans, C., & Robertson, W. (2020). The four phases of the digital natives debate. *Human Behavior & Emerging Technologies, 2*(3), 269–277. https://doi.org/10.1002/hbe2.196

Folkenflik, D. (2023, February 16). *Off the air, Fox News stars blasted the election fraud claims they peddled.* NPR. https://www.npr.org/2023/02/16/1157558299/fox-news-stars-false-claims-trump-election-2020

Freire, P. (2018). *Pedagogy of the pppressed.* (50th anniversary ed.; Ramos, M. B., Trans.). Bloomsbury Academic. (Original work published 1968)

Funke, D., & Flamini, D. (2019, August 13). *A guide to anti-misinformation actions around the world.* Poynter Institute. https://www.poynter.org/ifcn/anti-misinformation-actions/

Gillett, R., & Suzor, N. (2022). Incels on Reddit: A study in social norms and decentralised moderation. *First Monday, 27*(6). https://doi.org/10.5210/fm.v27i6.12575

Global Disinformation Index (2022, November 8). *Ad-funded Elections Integrity Disinformation.* https://www.disinformationindex.org/research/2022-11-08-ad-funded-elections-integrity-disinformation/

Green, A. E. (2003). Difficult stories: Service-learning, race, class, and Whiteness. *College Composition and Communication, 55*(2), 276–301.

Gregory, L., & Higgins, S. (Eds.). (2013). *Information literacy and social justice: Radical professional praxis.* Library Juice Press. http://site.ebrary.com/id/10894599

Hagey, K., & Horwitz, J. (2021, September 15). *Facebook tried to make its platform a healthier place. It got angrier instead.* The Wall Street Journal. https://www.wsj.com/articles/facebook-algorithm-change-zuckerberg-11631654215

Harker, D. (2014). Ideology, policy, and engagement: What role can service learning play in a changing democracy? In A. J. Trevino & K. M. McCormack (Eds.), *Service sociology and academic engagement in social problems* (pp. 61–82). Ashgate.

Hasher, L., Goldstein, D., & Toppino, T. (1977). Frequency and the conference of referential validity. *Journal of Verbal Learning and Verbal Behavior, 16*(1), 107–112. https://doi.org/10.1016/S0022-5371(77)80012-1

Hassan, A., & Barber, S. J. (2021). The effects of repetition frequency on the illusory truth effect. *Cognitive Research: Principles and Implications, 6*(1), 38. https://doi.org/10.1186/s41235-021-00301-5

Hudson, T. D. (2022). Interpersonalizing cultural difference: A grounded theory of the process of interracial friendship development and sustainment among college students. *Journal of Diversity in Higher Education, 15*(3), 267–287. https://doi.org/10.1037/dhe0000287

Jones, E., & Gaventa, J. (2002). Concepts of citizenship: A review. *IDS development bibliography* No. 19, Brighton: Institute of Development Studies.

Klein, E. (2022, December 11). *The Great delusion behind Twitter*. The New York Times. https://www.nytimes.com/2022/12/11/opinion/what-twitter-can-learn-from-quakers.html

Koliba, C. J. (2004). Service-learning and the downsizing of democracy: Learning our way out. *Michigan Journal of Community Service Learning, 10*(2), 57–68.

Korin, M. R., Araya, F., Idris, M. Y., Brown, H., & Claudio, L. (2022). Community-based organizations as effective partners in the battle against misinformation. *Frontiers in Public Health*. https://doi.org/10.3389/fpubh.2022.853736

Kranich, N. (2019). Academic libraries as civic agents. In N. V. Longo & T. J. Shaffer (Eds.), *Creating space for democracy: A primer on dialogue and deliberation in higher education* (pp. 199–208). Stylus Publishing.

Lewandowsky, S., Ecker, U. K. H., Seifert, C. M., Schwarz, N., & Cook, J. (2012). Misinformation and its correction: Continued influence and successful debiasing. *Psychological Science in the Public Interest, 13*(3), 106–131. https://doi.org/10.1177/1529100612451018

Maheshwari, S. (2016, December 26). Advertising's moral struggle: Is online reach worth the hurt? *The New York Times*. https://www.nytimes.com/2016/12/26/business/media/advertising-online-ads-fake-news-google.html

Malott, K., Wahesh, E., & Crawford, E. (2019). Anxieties toward outgroup members: Use of an (elaborated) imagined contact intervention with undergraduate students. *Innovative Higher Education, 44*, 133–147.

Marwick, A. E. (2018, March 22). Why do people share fake news? A sociotechnical model of media effects. *The Georgetown Law Technology Review, 2*(2), 474.

Meola, M. (2004). Chucking the checklist: A contextual approach to teaching undergraduates web-site evaluation. *Portal: Libraries and the Academy, 4*(3), 331–344. https://doi.org/10.1353/pla.2004.0055

Mitchell, T. D. (2015). Using a critical service-learning approach to facilitate civic identity development. *Theory Into Practice, 54*, 20–28.

Morales, M., Knowles, E. C., & Bourg, C. (2014). Diversity, social justice, and the future of libraries. *Portal: Libraries & the Academy, 14*(3), 439–451.

Munn, L. (2019). Alt-right pipeline: Individual journeys to extremism online. *First Monday, 24*(6). https://doi.org/10.5210/fm.v24i6.10108

Myers, S. L., & Grant, N. (2023, February 14). Combating disinformation wanes at social media giants. *The New York Times*. https://www.nytimes.com/2023/02/14/technology/disinformation-moderation-social-media.html

Noble, S. U. (2018). *Algorithms of oppression: How search engines reinforce racism*. New York University Press. https://doi.org/10.18574/9781479833641

Oldenburg, R. (1989). *The great good place*. Marlowe & Company.

Osmundsen, M., Bor, A., Vahlstrup, P., Bechman, A., & Petersen, M. (2021). Partisan polarization is the primary psychological motivation behind political fake news sharing on Twitter. *American Political Science Review, 115*(3), 999–1015. https://doi.org/10.1017/S0003055421000290

Pariser, E. (2012). *The filter bubble: How the new personalized web is changing what we read and how we think*. Penguin Books.

Pennycook, G., & Rand, D. G. (2020). Who falls for fake news? The roles of bullshit receptivity, overclaiming, familiarity, and analytic thinking. *Journal of Personality, 88*(2), 185–200. https://doi.org/10.1111/jopy.12476

Pizzolato, J., & Lee, J. J. (2023). Beyond the numbers: How focusing on compositional diversity downplays anti-Asian racism. *Change: The Magazine of Higher Learning, 55*(1), 47–53. https://doi.org/10.1080/00091383.2023.2151808

Pew Research Center. (2016). *The political environment on social media.*

Reinke, S. J. (2003). Making a difference: Does service-learning promote civic engagement in MPA students? *Journal of Public Affairs Education, 9,* 129–157.

Restrepo, N.J., Illari, L., Leahy, R., Sear, R. F., Lupu, Y., & Johnson, N.F.. (2022). How social media machinery pulled mainstream parenting communities closer to extremes and their misinformation during Covid-19. *IEEE Access, 10,* 2330–2344. https://doi.org/10.1109/ACCESS.2021.3138982

Santiago-Ortiz, A. (2019). From critical to decolonizing service-learning: Limits and possibilities of social justice-based approaches to community service-learning. *Michigan Journal of Community Service Learning,* 43–54.

Soll, J. (2016, December 18). The long and brutal history of fake news. *POLITICO Magazine.* http://politi.co/2FaV5W9

Ssanyu, J.N., Kiguba, R., Olum, R., Kiguli, J., Kitut, F. E. (2022). Using community influencer groups to address COVID-19 misinformation and vaccine hesitancy in Uganda: a protocol for a prospective quasi-experimental study. *BMJ Open, 12*(8). http://dx.doi.org/10.1136/bmjopen-2021-057994

Stoecker, R.(2016). *Liberating service learning and the rest of higher education civic engagement.* Temple University Press.

Straubhaar, R. (2015). The stark reality of the "White Saviour" complex and the need for critical consciousness: A document analysis of the early journals of a Freirean educator. *Compare: A Journal Of Comparative And International Education, 45*(3), 381–400.

Teitelbaum, K. (2011). Critical civic literacy in schools: Adolescents seeking to understand and improve the(ir) world. In J. L. DeVitis (Ed.), *Critical civic literacy: A reader* (pp. 11–26). Peter Lang Publishing.

Thomas, N., & Brower, M. (2017). *Politics 365: Fostering campus climates for student political learning & engagement.* Institute For Democracy & Higher Education Report.

Todd, N. R., Spanierman, L. B., & Poteat, V. P. (2011). Longitudinal examination of the psychosocial costs of racism to Whites across the college experience. *Journal of Counseling Psychology, 58*(4), 508–521.

Tripodi, F. (2022). *The propagandists' playbook: How conservative elites manipulate search and threaten democracy.* Yale University Press.

Tryon, E., & Madden, H. (2019). Actualizing critical commitments for community engagement professionals. *Journal of Higher Education Outreach and Engagement, 23*(1), 57–79.

Tryon, E., Stoecker, R., Martin, A., Seblonka, K., Hilgendorf, A., & Nellis, M. (2008). The challenge of short-term service-learning. *Michigan Journal of Community Service Learning,* 16–26.

Welburn, W. C. (2010). Creating inclusive communities: diversity and the responses of academic libraries. *Portal: Libraries & the Academy, 10*(3), 355–363.

CHAPTER 15

INDOCTRINATION, EDUCATION, AND DELIBERATIVE DEMOCRACY

A DEI Case Study

David Moshman
University of Nebraska-Lincoln

ABSTRACT

A major purpose of education should be to promote deliberative democracy—a form of liberal democracy that takes as its ideal the achievement of consensus through rational processes of argumentation. Beginning with a case study of indoctrination in an employee training program concerning matters of diversity, equity, and inclusion (DEI), I suggest that the opposite of indoctrination is education for rationality, which prepares students for deliberative democracy. What we see in education for rationality and in deliberative democracy, but not in cases of indoctrination, are: (1) respect for reasons, (2) respect for persons, (3) respect for truth, and (4) intellectual freedom.

Leaning Into Politics, pages 243–258
Copyright © 2024 by Information Age Publishing
www.infoagepub.com
All rights of reproduction in any form reserved.

A host addresses three contestants on a TV show called "Facts Don't Matter!": "Sorry Arthur, your answer was actually correct, but Paul shouted his opinion louder so he gets the point. And Sue gets a bonus point for being offended by your answer."

This scenario is adapted from a political cartoon (Dator, 2017), not a real TV show, but it illustrates the idea that our society is now "post-truth," caring so little about truth that being loud or offended now counts for more than being correct. Many (especially on the left) see Donald Trump as the poster boy of saying whatever serves your purposes, without regard to truth, as often and as loudly as it needs to be said. Many (especially on the right) fear that educational institutions, which should be all about seeking and teaching the truth, have become centers of "woke indoctrination" in which leftist political ideas about matters related to diversity, equity, and inclusion are taught as unquestionable truth, with alternative ideas rejected out of hand as too offensive even to be spoken. Many believe these problems have been institutionalized administratively in what have come to be known as DEI (Diversity, Equity, and Inclusion) offices and training programs. This has led to legislation in many states banning DEI programs and restricting teaching and learning about matters related to diversity, including laws that apply to higher education (Brint, 2023; PEN America, 2023; Vivian, 2023; Whittington, 2023).

My focus here is on the latter set of claims. Is there evidence of woke indoctrination? As a developmental and educational psychologist concerned with the role of intellectual freedom in learning and development, I have been following these matters closely since the 1980s (Moshman, 1989, 2009, 2017), when what is now dismissed as "wokeness" began to be derided as "political correctness." What I have seen ever since, and still see today, is that what critics call indoctrination is usually nothing more than the teaching of ideas they dislike or disagree with. I have not seen any systematic evidence of woke indoctrination in K–12 or college education, and even anecdotal evidence is generally limited to isolated incidents (cf. Vivian, 2023).

Recently, however, I came across what seems to me strong evidence of indoctrination in a DEI training program mandated for employees of a government agency. Without making any broader claims about the prevalence of woke indoctrination, I present what I found as a case study of how not to teach. I then propose (a) education for rationality as the educational alternative to indoctrination and (b) deliberative democracy as the ideal form of governance. What we see in both education for rationality and deliberative democracy, in contrast to indoctrination, are (1) respect for reasons, (2) respect for persons, (3) respect for truth, and (4) intellectual freedom. Rather than indoctrinate captive audiences in DEI ideologies, we should educate students, employees, and others about matters of diversity, equity, and inclusion in ways that promote rationality and deliberative democracy.

INDOCTRINATION IN DEI: A CASE STUDY

In January 2022, I was asked by Vermont attorney Deborah Bucknam to testify as an expert witness on behalf of her client Benjamin Morley, a vocational rehabilitation counselor at the Vermont Division of Vocational Rehabilitation, who was charging in federal district court that the state of Vermont violated his First Amendment rights by requiring employees to participate in a series of mandatory DEI training sessions that he deemed to be indoctrination (Morley v. State of Vermont, 2022). The sessions were organized and taught by Mirna Valerio, a professional diversity trainer.

I was initially skeptical about the case because people throw around loose charges of indoctrination all the time, especially concerning diversity and related matters. After reading a transcript of the training sessions, however, I was appalled. I quickly agreed to testify, based on my expertise on matters of intellectual freedom in education, that the training was indeed indoctrination. The attorney drafted a list of questions and I provided written answers in preparation for my deposition (I was paid for my time). Several days before the deposition, however, the attorney told me that her client had decided, under pressure, to drop the case. That left me free to transform my prepared deposition testimony into the present case study (the prepared testimony in full is available from the author, as is the training transcript, which is a public record, though the part I quote from does not seem to be available online).

What is indoctrination? Indoctrination is most literally the imposition of a doctrine. Although there is no legally definitive definition, scholarly discussions of indoctrination in philosophy of education and related fields suggest that it generally comes in two forms, one related to curriculum (what is taught) and the other related to instruction (how it is taught). Curricular indoctrination is teaching a curriculum devised on the basis of political, religious, or other ideological commitments rather than on academic grounds. Instructional indoctrination is teaching in a manner that coerces belief and limits dissent rather than convincing students through evidence and argument in a context that encourages critical thinking and free discussion (Moshman, 2017).

How does education differ from indoctrination? The root of the term "education" is "educe," which means to draw out. Education respects students as people with their own beliefs and values and aims to promote progress in conceptual understanding and rational competencies. Indoctrination aims to instill the instructor's beliefs, values, and doctrines without regard to student autonomy (Callan & Arena, 2009; Moshman, 2017, 2021; Siegel, 1988).

With these definitions in mind, what the Vermont DEI training transcript shows is indoctrination with respect to both the curriculum and the manner of instruction. With respect to curriculum, the instructor repeatedly makes unjustified and sometimes false assertions, apparently motivated by ideology rather than evidence, thus violating the right of students (even if they are employees in a training session) to a curriculum devised on academic (or other defensible) grounds. With respect to instruction, the instructor teaches in a manner that undermines students' intellectual autonomy by sharply restricting academic discussion and banning dissent.

Does it matter that this is *training*? How is that related to education and indoctrination? It can be argued that questions of indoctrination do not apply to training because training, unlike education, is just a matter of inculcating basic skills and facts. It is true that intellectual freedom may have little relevance in training employees to follow standard office procedures or making sure they understand and adhere to organizational policies or legal requirements related to their jobs. To the extent that training focuses on basic skills, rules, and objective facts, there is no question of doctrine and thus no indoctrination. As will become apparent, however, the present "training" goes far beyond skills, rules, and facts into concepts, ideas, interpretations, explanations, and theories. In that context, the lack of respect for evidence, argument, and intellectual freedom makes this a program of indoctrination.

Here's an example:

> Before we delve into the work, I'd love to hear from everyone as far as how you're feeling emotionally and physically. Where are you in your body? [Much more about this, culminating in students sharing feelings via chat.]
>
> All right, great. Thank you. Again, get used to that. We are going to be doing a lot of sharing. That is part of doing this work. I'd love to share a little bit about the format and my, sort of, question protocol for this workshop. In terms of questions, I do not take real-time questions. We have a lot to cover. If this were a weeklong workshop and I were with you on site, it would be a different dynamic, but we're trying to squish a lot of content into a short time. The other reason I don't take real-time questions is that it very often serves to derail the work, and what I mean by that is sometimes the questions are very self-serving, and they don't necessarily serve the entire group. And then other times, questions—people ask questions to stop the progress of the group, or to argue, and so that, it's a self-protective measure. I've had lots and lots and lots of workshops where that has happened, and so we're just not going to do it today. (transcript of Zoom session).

This sets a framework in which students are expected to be actively and emotionally involved but are forbidden to question the teacher or engage in academic discussion or argumentation (with repeated reminders of these restrictions later). I did not find anything anywhere in the transcript to suggest that there was ever any critical thinking or serious argumentation about any of the ideas presented in these sessions, although many of them are conceptually complex or controversial, and some are false.

Here's another example. The instructor tells students that the goal of the training is "to lead people to the work and to push them into a new realization." She explains that "the work" includes "dismantling all kinds of isms" and "unlearning harmful ideologies that we, as a society, have both internalized and perpetuated."

How does this demonstrate indoctrination? The idea of "leading" people to "the work" and "pushing" them into the associated ideology does not respect the autonomy of those being led and pushed. In the context of the introduction, it seems clear that the instructor will have sole authority to determine what ideologies are harmful and, because the ideologies are internalized, the instructor is free to delve into students' personal and emotional lives to get students to "unlearn" whatever ideologies are deemed "harmful." Students who are uncomfortable with all this should "simply sit with that discomfort." The extraordinary lack of respect for student autonomy makes this indoctrination rather than education in that, quoting from the above definition of instructional indoctrination, it "coerces belief and limits dissent rather than convincing students through evidence and argument in a context that encourages critical thinking and free discussion."

Here's a third example. A PowerPoint slide of "Community engagement guidelines" (devised without student input) is presented. The guidelines begin with "This is not the time for arguing for argument's sake." They exhort students to "Listen with ears and heart" and "Give your full attention," and specify that "Although silence is a valid way of participating in other situations, your vocal participation is crucial here." Again we see that students are expected to engage actively but not critically. Argumentation is dismissed as "arguing for argument's sake," failing to recognize the crucial role of argumentation in testing ideas, considering alternatives, and promoting student understanding and reasoning. The "community engagement guidelines" reinforce the earlier message to students that this DEI training is an environment in which dissent will not be tolerated.

A fourth example:

> So the first thing is that we are going to acknowledge that racism is real. It's not an opinion. It's real. It is baked into the very fabric of this society. Slavery would not have existed without racism, and without this hierarchy, this racial hierarchy, created by human beings, right? So there's that.
>
> As I said, earlier, we're not going to argue for argument's sake. It really takes away from the work.
>
> ...You listen with your entire body, if you can, all right? Be engaged. Very often, we might listen to respond, which actually means we're not listening.

We see here a quick list of strong claims about race, racism, society, slavery, and history, followed by strong warnings to students that they should be emotionally engaged but cognitively passive, accepting whatever they are told as "real" and thus beyond dispute. The claims are vaguely stated, with no explanation or justification, which are presumably deemed unnecessary because students are required to accept, emotionally, whatever they are told.

For example, consider this claim, which is presented as unquestionably true: "Slavery would not have existed without racism, and without this hierarchy, this racial hierarchy, created by human beings." It's certainly true that racial hierarchies are created by human beings and have served to justify slavery. And I think it's likely true that the creation of a system of racial hierarchy was a necessary condition for chattel slavery as seen in the United States prior to the Civil War. But we can never be certain what would have happened in history under a different set of conditions. Slavery has been common in human societies since antiquity, long before modern conceptions of race. In places like ancient Athens it was not based on anything like race. So a claim that slavery cannot exist without racial hierarchy might be an interesting starting point for discussion but is highly indoctrinative when presented as a statement of unquestionable truth, as it is here, followed by a reminder that argumentation will not be permitted because it undermines "the work."

There are also claims that are just plain false.

> And perhaps most importantly, is to realize that your intent is very different from the impact of your actions. I like to say that nobody cares about your intent, no one cares. It is how you make somebody feel through your words, your actions, your attitudes, the stereotypes that you are reacting to, that's what matters. All right? You can have the best intent in the world; no one cares. It is the impact of your actions. All right? Cool.

Of course we should be concerned with the impact of our actions, but as a matter of psychology, morality, and law, most of this statement is false. People routinely distinguish intentional harm from accidents and commonly assign degrees of responsibility in cases of negligence. Such distinctions are recognized as important by virtually all moral theories and by legal systems in the United States and elsewhere. Developmental research since Piaget (1932/1965) has shown that very young children may judge actions on the basis of impact alone but by age 7 or 8 years, if not earlier, the moral relevance of intent is universally recognized.

Here's another example of false claims:

> And race is a socially constructed category of identity based—created to produce a hierarchy of skin colors. All right? Biologically, we are not very different from each other, so you know, we might have—there might be environmental factors that factor into our skin color and our facial shape, like the

bone shape, but biologically, we are absolutely similar. So there is no scientific basis for the category of race to actually exist.

The instructor is entirely correct that race is a social construct and a matter of identity (Andersen, 2022; Moshman, 2011a). Contrary to 19th-century biological theories of race, which persisted well into the 20th century, there is now a scientific consensus that the biological diversity of the human species cannot be understood by classifying everyone into some small number of racial categories (Graves, 2001). No matter how such categories are constructed, there is more biological variability within them than across them, making their boundaries biologically arbitrary. The invention and persistence of particular "racial" categories is thus more a matter of culture and politics than of biology.

Rather than explaining and justifying her opening assertion, however, the instructor goes on to make unjustified claims that, biologically, people are "absolutely similar," with any individual differences in skin color, facial shape, or bone shape due mostly to "environmental factors." In fact, as a matter of elementary biology, there is substantial genetic diversity in all species, including the human species, and this includes genetic diversity in skin color and other anatomical features such as facial or bone shape, which are determined mostly by heredity, not by the environment we grow up or live in. The evidence that undermined biological theories of race over the course of the 20th century is not evidence against genetic diversity in the human species or the importance of heredity in human development. The casualness about facts, here and elsewhere, suggests a curriculum driven largely by ideology. That by itself is indoctrination, but the violation of student rights is compounded by the indoctrinative manner of instruction, in which students are forbidden to question what is presented.

EDUCATION FOR RATIONALITY

The opposite of indoctrination is education for rationality, which respects and promotes the rational agency of students (Siegel, 1988). Education for rationality respects students as rational agents and promotes their rationality by providing reasons for what is taught and encouraging critical thinking, which requires an educational context of intellectual freedom. In sharp contrast to the training just analyzed, here is a statement on students' academic freedom from the first page of the syllabus for my course in adolescent psychology, which I taught regularly until I retired from teaching:

> The study of adolescence raises controversial issues. Topics addressed in this course include race, gender, culture, religion, morality, sexuality, and violence. You have a right to believe whatever you believe and are encouraged to

express your views on matters relevant to the course, even if others in the class may be offended or upset by those views. You also have a right to express your disagreement with anything you hear or read and a right to decide whether to maintain or modify your views. Your grade in the class will be based on your understanding and reasoning, not on your opinions.

My adolescent psychology course included most of the topics addressed in the DEI training (see Moshman, 2011a, the text I developed for this course). I also taught about these topics in other courses, including a regular doctoral seminar on developmental psychobiology that highlighted evolutionary theorizing. These courses differed dramatically from the DEI training just described in four ways central to education for rationality: respect for reasons, respect for persons, respect for truth, and intellectual freedom.

Before I elaborate on this virtuous tetrad, however, let me extend the discussion to issues of governance at a societal level. I will argue that a form of liberal democracy known as deliberative democracy shares with education for rationality those same four values and commitments.

DELIBERATIVE DEMOCRACY

Democracy is commonly seen as a form of governance based on respect for the will of the people. But if people disagree with each other, how do we establish the will of the people? Respect for persons suggests each person should count equally, which suggests majority rule. But what if the majority chooses to oppress minorities? Political majorities may ban dissent. Religious majorities may outlaw minority religious practices. Ethnic or racial majorities may disfavor persons associated with other groups. Thus majoritarian democracy falls short of full respect for each individual person.

With this in mind, many have argued that the ideal form of democracy is *liberal democracy*, which takes respect for persons a step further by recognizing each person as an autonomous individual with rights that must be recognized by the collective, such as freedoms of belief and expression, legal equality, and rights to privacy and due process (Moshman, 2021). Such rights are often explicitly protected in a constitution, ideally approved by a majority, that limits what even a majority may legally do (*West Virginia v. Barnette*, 1943).

In the past few decades, many have argued further that the ideal form of liberal democracy is deliberative democracy (Bächtiger, Dryzek, Mansbridge, & Warren, 2018). *Deliberative democracy* may be defined as *a form of liberal democracy that takes as its ideal the achievement of consensus through rational processes of argumentation* (Moshman, 2021). Deliberative democracy takes the liberal respect for persons as autonomous individuals a step further in recognizing them as rational agents, with reasons of their own.

Full respect for persons requires respect for reasons, which requires conditions for collaborative reasoning—argumentation aimed at achieving a justifiable consensus. If consensus cannot be reached, there may be no alternative to majority rule, within constitutional limits, but institutions of deliberative democracy enhance the rationality of the process by requiring serious discussion of beliefs and reasons prior to action.

Even if deliberative democracy is a worthy ideal, is it psychologically possible? Psychological research since the 1960s has shown not only that human reasoning is sometimes flawed but that our conclusions are often driven more by automatic and intuitive heuristics and biases than by deliberate and reflective processes (Kahneman, 2011; Moshman, 2015, 2021; Stanovich, 2021). Many fear that human reasoning may not be up to the task of democracy. But despite the evidence for human irrationality, human reasoning shows strong developmental trends toward rationality across childhood and often long beyond, and education can do much to advance the ongoing development of rationality (Moshman, 2011a; 2021).

Deliberative democracy also has a superpower not seen in other forms of democracy. Decades of research has shown that groups of people engaging in argumentation under conditions of mutual respect perform more rationally, on average, than do individuals or less democratic groups (Moshman, 2021; for a detailed review of this extensive literature, see Laughlin, 2011).

Moshman and Geil (1998), for example, compared individual and collaborative reasoning in college students on a notoriously difficult logical task. Each student was presented with a sheet of paper picturing four cards that showed, from left to right, E, K, 4, and 7. Each card, they were informed, had a letter on one side and a number on the other. Below the cards was this hypothesis: "If a card has a vowel on one side then it has an even number on the other side." Students were asked, either individually or in groups of 5 or 6, to select the card or cards they would need to turn to determine conclusively whether the hypothesis was true or false for the set of four cards. The correct response is to select E, the only vowel, because an odd number on the other side would falsify the hypothesis, and 7, the only odd number, because a vowel on the other side would falsify the hypothesis. Neither of the other cards needs to be turned because neither could falsify the hypothesis.

The correct response pattern was selected by only 9% of individuals working alone but was the consensus choice for 75% of the groups. Students in groups routinely engaged in collaborative reasoning: working together to solve the problem through argumentation, they challenged each other to justify their selections and encouraged each other to consider consequences and alternatives. Final selections reflected voluntary agreement based on emerging logical insights rather than passive conformity to views favored by peers. The process was both rational and democratic, rooted in respect for persons, reasons, and truth.

A study by Curșeu, Jansen, & Chappin (2013) compared deliberative democracy to enlightened dictatorship in 176 small groups of college students working on a set of decision-making tasks. Some of the groups, randomly selected for the "collaborative" condition, were instructed to reach consensus on each task. These groups functioned as small deliberative democracies in which decisions were made through discussion under conditions of mutual respect. In the other groups, designated the "consultative" condition, one member of the group was randomly appointed the leader and instructed to make the decisions after getting input from each of the other group members, who were not permitted to discuss the task with each other. These groups functioned as enlightened dictatorships in which the dictator received input from others but then made a final decision.

As predicted based on earlier research, the deliberative democracies achieved, on average, higher levels of rational decision making than the enlightened dictatorships. That is, groups operating on a basis of mutual respect did better, on average, than those set up hierarchically with a single authority receiving input from others. Getting input from multiple sources is good, but not as good as free discussion among all concerned.

Deliberative democracy, then, is not just a political theory of how governments ought to function. At its foundation, deliberative democracy is a psychological reality of small-group human functioning that enables groups to transcend the many foibles of individual people. The challenge is to scale it up to societal levels (Landemore, 2013). And education may be central to achieving that (Leiviskä, 2023; Moshman, 2021).

In the next four sections, I consider the four values and commitments that not only distinguish education from indoctrination, but also relate education for rationality to rational group functioning and deliberative democracy: (1) respect for reasons, (2) respect for persons, (3) respect for truth, and (4) intellectual freedom. I then conclude the chapter with a brief discussion of education for deliberative democracy.

RESPECT FOR REASONS

Research on collaborative reasoning provides clear evidence that, under ideal conditions, people routinely show respect for reasons (Laughlin, 2011; Moshman, 2021, 2024). They provide reasons for their claims and proposals, listen and respond to others' reasons, consider objections to their own reasons, and sometimes change their minds.

Research has also shown serious limitations, however. One is that collaborative reasoning is most beneficial when, as in Moshman and Geil (1998), the group faces a problem of logic that has a necessarily correct answer that can be determined through reflection on the problem itself. In most problems there is a need for additional evidence. Even with such evidence, moreover, there may be no single correct answer, though some potential responses may be clearly incorrect, and some of the remaining responses may be better justified than some others. Reasons remain relevant, even when they consist of empirical evidence and even when they are less than conclusive, but respect for reasons is complicated by epistemological complexities concerning the nature of justification and truth beyond the domain of logic (Greene, Sandoval, & Bråten, 2016; Moshman, 2015, 2021).

Another limitation on the rational functioning of groups is that powerful psychological forces come into play when people have ideological biases favoring or disfavoring particular conclusions or decisions. Strong ideological biases, usually related to deep identity commitments, often direct us toward or away from particular ideas. Respect for reasons is routinely undermined by ideology and identity (Leiviskä, 2023; Moshman, 2021, 2024; Stanovich, 2021).

Education should promote rationality, but education for rationality is not a matter of teaching logic or instilling respect for reasons. Even young children make logical inferences and respect reasons (Moshman, 2021). The challenge for educators is to promote better understanding of the nature and role of reasons, a matter of epistemic cognition and development (Greene et al., 2016; Moshman, 2015, 2021). This requires academic settings in which both teachers and students are expected to provide reasons for their claims, including claims about sensitive and controversial matters, and to consider alternative ideas and reasons. At a societal level, good governance requires institutions that encourage respect for reasons, including opportunities for rational deliberation. That is, good governance requires deliberative democracy (Bächtiger et al., 2018).

RESPECT FOR PERSONS

Research on collaborative reasoning also shows respect for persons. When groups operate under ideal conditions, everyone has ample opportunity to speak, but no one is required to do so. Students listen to each other's ideas and reasons and take them seriously, even when they find the reasons unconvincing. Students disagree without attacking each other personally. They treat each other with mutual respect.

Once we go beyond logical and other noncontroversial tasks, however, respect for persons, like respect for reasons, is readily undermined by identity-related processes of dichotomization and dehumanization (Klein, 2020; Moshman, 2011b, 2024). We conceptualize our social worlds by dividing people into categories, leading in the extreme to perceiving everyone as one of "us" or one of "them" and perceiving "them" as less human than us. Dehumanization involves seeing others as driven by ideology and social pressures rather than by legitimate reasons. Thus lack of respect for persons becomes lack of respect for reasons.

To educate students we must respect them as persons, which is to respect them as developing rational agents. Their reasons are not always good reasons but we cannot simply replace bad ideas with good ones or bad reasons with better ones. We must engage students' rational agency in order to promote the development of rationality (Siegel, 1988).

At a societal level, respect for persons requires each of us to respect people we have never met and will never meet, with the expectation that this abstract sort of respect will be reciprocated. This doesn't mean we have to like or admire everyone. It means we must treat them as persons at least in the sense of construing them as rational agents, operating on the basis of reasons of their own.

RESPECT FOR TRUTH

Returning once again to ideal cases of collaborative reasoning, the psychological literature also shows respect for truth. On matters of logic, group members are not generally pressured to conform to a majority view just to create unanimity. Aiming for logical truth, groups seek to achieve a correct solution, not just an end to the argument. In contrast to debate, where the aim is to win, collaborative reasoning is aimed at the truth.

Outside the realm of logic, of course, truth is a far subtler matter than logical proof. In matters of science or history there may be more than one justifiable interpretation or theory, leading some to conclude that, at least beyond the realm of logic, truth is just a matter of perspective. But even in cases where truth is contested, some ideas may be better justified than others and some may be clearly false. And even where this is not obvious at a glance, there may be a justified consensus among experts. Respect for truth remains meaningful and important even in cases involving something more subtle than logical proof (Moshman, 2015, 2021).

Outside the realm of logic, moreover, ideological biases and identity commitments may generate active denial of truths we find threatening. Respect for truth may be undermined not just by epistemological misunderstandings but by active processes of protecting our core beliefs and identities (Bardon, 2020; Leiviskä, 2023; Moshman, 2011b, 2024).

Respect for truth is arguably the core value, even the defining value, of any academic institution. Institutions may have multiple aims, but having a mission to seek and communicate the truth is what makes an institution academic. This commitment to truth requires respect for reasons, which requires respect for persons. With all this in mind, education should aim to engage students in the pursuit of truth, which promotes their epistemic development, including their understanding of and respect for expertise.

Respect for truth and expertise are also crucial to democracy (Leiviskä, 2023). If consensus cannot be achieved, democracy may rely on the will of the majority, but the fact that a majority choose or believe something does not make it justified or true. The ideal democracy is a deliberative democracy, which, like the ideal academic institution, engages in deliberation to seek the truth.

INTELLECTUAL FREEDOM

Consistent with respect for reasons, persons, and truth, collaborative reasoning on logical tasks typically takes place in contexts of intellectual freedom, a natural condition of rational argumentation. It is simply taken for granted that all persons are free to express all views about the matter at hand. Participants understand that to maximize their chances of identifying the logically correct solution they should limit their speech to the current topic but set no limits on viewpoints regarding the logic of the task or the correct solution. Incorrect views are refuted, not censored. Such views disappear not because those who hold them are silenced or intimidated but because those who held them are convinced to change their views.

Outside the realm of logic, many ideas are deemed intolerant, offensive, hateful, dangerous, or otherwise objectionable. When ideology and identity come into play, calls for censoring expression or restricting access to ideas are common (Moshman, 2011b, 2017; PEN America, 2023; Strossen, 2018). But even when we disagree about the scope and limits of intellectual freedom, we should keep in mind that a basic level of intuitive respect for intellectual freedom is a natural condition of peer argumentation (Moshman, 2021, 2024).

Education is commonly seen as a social context that requires respect for the intellectual freedom of both teachers and students (Moshman, 2009, 2017). This is most clearly true for conceptions of education that highlight the promotion of rationality, given that rationality is the outcome of developmental processes that require active intellectual engagement (Moshman, 2011a, 2021). Teachers must have the academic freedom to teach the truth but they must teach in a manner that respects the academic freedom of their students to reach their own conclusions (Laats & Siegel, 2016; Siegel, 1988).

Indoctrination, then, is not protected by academic freedom. But the fact that someone objects to what a teacher teaches is not enough to justify a charge of indoctrination. To demonstrate indoctrination one must show either that what is being taught is not academically justifiable or that it is being taught in a manner that undermines the intellectual autonomy of students by coercing belief. All people have a right to their beliefs, but in academic contexts both teachers and students may be expected to provide reasons for their claims and may be evaluated on their ability to do so.

Democracy is commonly seen as a form of governance that requires respect for intellectual freedom. This is most clearly true for deliberative democracy, in which democratic deliberation plays a central role. All people have a right to say what they believe, but democratic deliberation involves exchanging reasons, not just claims, and genuine engagement with others. That is, deliberative democracy requires not just freedom of expression but a social context of respect for reasons, persons, and truth.

EDUCATION FOR DELIBERATIVE DEMOCRACY

Education for rationality engages students in rational deliberation under conditions of intellectual freedom to promote developmental progress in the use of reasons and stronger commitment to reasons. Thus in both its means and its outcomes, education for rationality prepares students for democratic deliberation. Unlike indoctrination, education for rationality thus serves deliberative democracy.

Education for deliberative democracy must fully address matters of social justice, including questions of diversity, equity, and inclusion, however "political" or "controversial" these may be deemed. Education for democracy cannot avoid leaning into politics, but educators must respect the intellectual and political freedoms of their students, including their right to determine and express their beliefs. As we have seen, indoctrination is different from education, and inconsistent with deliberative democracy.

Education for deliberative democracy can take many forms (Samuelsson, 2016, 2018; Samuelsson & Bøyum, 2015). It is not a specific technique or a set of exercises. What marks education for deliberative democracy, I suggest, is an academic context of intellectual freedom rooted in respect for reasons, persons, and truth. Even when we find ourselves tempted to join a game of "Facts Don't Matter," we should remind ourselves, and those around us, that they do.

REFERENCES

Andersen, M. L. (2022). *Race in society: The enduring American dilemma, 2nd ed.* Rowman & Littlefield.

Bächtiger, A., Dryzek, J. S., Mansbridge, J., & Warren, M. E. (Eds.). (2018). *The Oxford handbook of deliberative democracy*. Oxford University Press.
Bardon, A. (2020). *The truth about denial: Bias and self-deception in science, politics, and religion*. Oxford University Press.
Brint, S. (2023). The political machine behind the war on academic freedom. *Chronicle of Higher Education*, August 28. https://www.chronicle.com/article/the-political-machine-behind-the-war-on-academic-freedom
Callan, E., & Arena, D. (2009). Indoctrination. In H. Siegel (Ed.), *Oxford handbook of philosophy of education* (pp. 104–121). Oxford University Press.
Curșeu, P. L., Jansen, R. J. G., & Chappin, M. M. H. (2013). Decision rules and group rationality: Cognitive gain or standstill? *PLOS ONE*. https://doi.org/10.1371/journal.pone.0056454
Dator, J. (2017). *Fact don't matter*. https://www.facebook.com/newyorker/photos/a.430906773868/10155334077878869/
Graves, J. L., Jr. (2001). *The emperor's new clothes: Biological theories of race at the millennium*. Rutgers University Press.
Greene, J. A., Sandoval, W. A., & Bråten, I. (Eds.) (2016). *Handbook of epistemic cognition*. Routledge.
Kahneman, D. (2011). *Thinking, fast and slow*. Farrar, Straus, and Giroux.
Klein, E. (2020). *Why we're polarized*. Avid Reader Press.
Laats, A., & Siegel, H. (2016). *Teaching evolution in a creation nation*. University of Chicago Press.
Landemore, H. (2013). *Democratic reason: Politics, collective intelligence, and the rule of the many*. Princeton University Press.
Laughlin, P. R. (2011). *Group problem solving*. Princeton University Press.
Leiviskä, A. (2023). Democratic education and the epistemic quality of democratic deliberation. *Theory and Research in Education, 21*, 113–134. doi.org/10.1177/14778785231187304
Morley v. State of Vermont (2022). https://www.courtlistener.com/docket/61446908/morley-v-state-of-vermont/
Moshman, D. (1989). *Children, education, and the First Amendment: A psycholegal analysis*. University of Nebraska Press.
Moshman, D. (2009). *Liberty and learning: Academic freedom for teachers and students*. Heinemann.
Moshman, D. (2011a). *Adolescent rationality and development: Cognition, morality, and identity, 3rd edition*. Psychology Press.
Moshman, D. (2011b). Identity, genocide, and group violence. In S. J. Schwartz, K. Luyckx, & V. L. Vignoles (Eds.), *Handbook of identity theory and research* (pp. 917–932). Springer.
Moshman, D. (2015). *Epistemic cognition and development: The psychology of justification and truth*. Psychology Press.
Moshman, D. (2017). Academic freedom as the freedom to do academic work. *AAUP Journal of Academic Freedom, 8*. https://www.aaup.org/JAF8/academic-freedom-freedom-do-academic-work#.Wcqm7I6QzuR
Moshman, D. (2021). *Reasoning, argumentation, and deliberative democracy*. Routledge.

Moshman, D. (2024). Democratic character and virtues: Developmental responses to group conflict and oppression. In M. D. Mathews & R. M. Lerner, (Eds.), *Multidisciplinary handbook of character development*. Routledge.

Moshman, D., & Geil, M. (1998). Collaborative reasoning: Evidence for collective rationality. *Thinking & Reasoning, 4*, 231–248.

PEN America (2023). Index of educational gag orders. https://docs.google.com/spreadsheets/d/1Tj5WQVBmB6SQg-zP_M8uZsQQGH09TxmBY73v23zpyr0/edit#gid=107383712

Piaget, J. (1965). *The moral judgment of the child*. Free Press. (Original work published 1932)

Samuelsson, M. (2016). Education for deliberative democracy: A typology of classroom discussions. *Democracy & Education, 24*(1), Article 5. https://democracyeducationjournal.org/home/vol24/iss1/5

Samuelsson, M. (2018). Education for deliberative democracy and the aim of consensus. *Democracy & Education, 26*(1), Article 2. https://democracyeducationjournal.org/home/vol26/iss1/2

Samuelsson, M., & Bøyum, S. (2015). Education for deliberative democracy: Mapping the field. *Utbildning & Demokrati, 24*(1), 75–94.

Siegel, H. (1988). *Educating reason: Rationality, critical thinking, and education*. Routledge.

Stanovich, K. E. (2021). *The bias that divides us: The science and politics of myside thinking*. MIT Press.

Strossen, N. (2018). *Hate: Why we should resist it with free speech, not censorship*. Oxford University Press.

Vivian, B. (2023). *Campus misinformation: The real threat to free speech in American higher education*. Oxford University Press.

West Virginia State Board of Education v. Barnette, 319 U.S. 624 (1943).

Whittington, K. E. (2023). Professorial speech, the First Amendment, and legislative restrictions on classroom discussions. *Wake Forest Law Review, 58*, 463–524.

CHAPTER 16

THE PROXIMATE POWER OF STUDENT-LED NONPARTISAN POLITICAL ENGAGEMENT EFFORTS

Alexander S. Kappus
Michigan State University

ABSTRACT

What can we learn from the lived experiences of college students leading nonpartisan political activity? While previous research has shown that college students vote more often when they are taught about the importance of voting and when they are provided with support for navigating the processes of voting, little is known about how to support student-led nonpartisan political engagement work. Using qualitative data collected from semi-structured interviews and focus groups with Campus Vote Project Democracy Fellows from eight different states and fourteen campuses during the 2020 election, this chapter analyzes the proximate power of student-led political learning. In assessing student experiences, findings demonstrate the need for more institutional support for such efforts. The chapter also provides recommendations for colleges and universities interested in advancing student-led nonpartisan political engagement.

Despite espoused civic values, college and university civic engagement efforts often focus heavily on apolitical service-learning and volunteer activities (Finley, 2011; Saltmarsh & Hartley, 2011). Although meaningful, many service-learning and volunteer activities routinely fall short in educating students about democracy and how to access and engage the political system. In one study, for example, students involved in service-learning became more politically conscious but could not articulate an understanding of or interest in engaging in the political process (Harker, 2016). In another study, almost all respondents participated in civic activities, yet only 36% of the students voted (Hylton, 2018). These statistics underpin concerns among scholars and practitioners that young people are not prepared to engage in democracy.

Voting serves as only one, though very important, metric for gauging student political participation. In addition, Title IV of the 1998 Higher Education Act (20 U.S.C. 1094(a)(23), compels colleges and universities to uphold a "good faith effort" (Sec. 162) to inform students about voter registration. In recent years, voting among those aged 18–29 years have experienced steady increases, yet young people remain the voting block with the lowest turnout rate and data suggests disparities among young voters based on different demographic backgrounds (CIRCLE, 2021). Higher education therefore needs to look to new, promising practices in civic learning and democratic engagement.

Previous studies of nonpartisan political engagement examine interventions and experiences within a formal classroom environment (Bardwell, 2011; Beaumont et al., 2006; Bennion, 2006; Mann et al., 2018; Rank & Tylock, 2018). For example, Rank and Tylock (2018) studied students enrolled in a course that implemented political engagement activities accompanying a get-out-the-vote effort. The study offered many insights, including finding that students held a stronger appreciation for the time and energy invested in political campaigns and politics more broadly. In another study, students observed polling locations on election day and made recommendations to influence the efficiency of the voting process (Mann et al., 2018). As a result of their proximity to the democratic process, students gained greater interest in the political system itself (Mann et al., 2018). Despite the contributions provided by these studies, few scholars focus on civic and political engagement in the co-curricular setting. Yet, by getting involved in meaningful out-of-class activities, students practice democracy, exercise leadership skills, and develop civic perspectives (Strachan & Bennion, 2016; Strachan & Bennion, 2023).

Meanwhile, over the past decade, several nonpartisan organizations have provided training and support for students leading civic engagement, and especially voter education, efforts across higher education (see also Miles et al. and Rank in this volume). Whereas early external entities, such as Rock the Vote, focused on entertainment to draw students in (Jacoby, 2006), more recent efforts have sought to build partnerships with institutions and student leaders. For example, the organization at the center for this study, the Campus Vote Project, was founded by the Fair Elections Center in 2012 and provides robust support, training, and guidance to student leaders. Organizations like Civic Nation, which facilitates the ALL IN Campus Democracy Challenge (see Domagal-Goldman & King in this volume) provides guidance and associated recognition to institutions actively engaged in the work. The American Political Science Association (2023) maintains a list of over 20 nonpartisan organizations leading in nonpartisan political engagement activities in higher education. Rank (this volume) questions the influence of partner organization in Chapter 5, stating, "what is explicitly and implicitly encouraged is the process of casting a ballot with little discussion of where that process fits within the larger political landscape" (p. 66). This is an important consideration, and reinforces the argument made in this chapter that institutions need to take more responsibility for such efforts including by providing support to peer educators leading nonpartisan political engagement work (see also Harrison & Healey in this volume). Indeed, their work includes voter education, but also often includes broader work to build a campus culture of civic and political engagement through a variety of educational activities.

THE WHAT AND WHY OF NONPARTISAN POLITICAL ENGAGEMENT

Because terminology is often used inconsistently (Finley, 2011; Jacoby, 2009), readers need clarity on the relationship between civic and political engagement. Civic engagement is a broader term describing activities with an assumed priority placed on community-based values and the "common good" (Barrett & Pachi, 2019, p. 3). Political engagement is a subset of experiences encompassed within the larger civic engagement domain, explicitly promoting learning about and involvement with the political system itself (Rios, 2014). Political engagement activities include formal actions like serving as an election worker, or more informal activities, such as engaging in a conversation with a roommate about politics (Hildreth, 2003). A previous study, the Political Engagement Project (PEP), examined promising practices designed to engender student's political knowledge, skills, motivation, and participation (Colby et al., 2010). Volunteer, civic, and service-learning activities were excluded from the PEP unless there was a demonstrated tie to the political system (Colby et al., 2010). From leading get-out-the-vote campaigns to organizing debate watch parties, students included in this study participated in a diverse array of over 80 different nonpartisan political engagement activities (Kappus, 2021).

The word nonpartisan refers to the intentional choice to educate in a manner whereby no partisan perspective, candidate, or issue is privileged over another. Nonpartisan does not mean the absence of partisan perspectives. For example, a peer educator may organize a local candidate forum where all candidates for a selected office are invited. The line of nonpartisanship can be difficult to define. As one student in this study said, a question she and her peers frequently asked one another was, "could someone misconstrue this (action or statement) as partisan?" (Kappus, 2021). Unfortunately, promotion of voter education among college students in and of itself has been characterized by some as a partisan issue (Anderson, 2019). Furthermore, some politicians have publicly argued young people only vote for liberal candidates and ideas (Nolan, 2011). Typecasting young voters as mindlessly voting one way ideologically ignores research demonstrating the diversity of perspectives present among college student voters (Binder & Kidder, 2022). More importantly, legal scholars contend registering to vote and casting a ballot should receive full protections under the Constitution's First Amendment right to free expression (Derfner & Herbert, 2016). By taking an explicitly nonpartisan approach to voter engagement efforts, colleges and universities can support student leaders in protecting this fundamental activity to advance democracy.

METHODS

Evidence suggests students' experiences are influenced by their various, intersecting social identities (Strachan, 2019). Understanding how students make meaning of their political engagement experiences is therefore best understood through a qualitative approach. To implement this study, I partnered with Campus Vote Project (CVP), a nonpartisan nonprofit organization, and sought nominations for students participating in their Democracy Fellows program. I selected CVP due to the organization's steadfast commitment to a nonpartisan approach and the credibility offered with their association to the Fair Elections Center. Students who serve as Democracy Fellows receive support from CVP, including training, ongoing professional development, and a small stipend to catalyze their efforts. A purposeful sampling approach to secure a rich data sample for this study yielded 15 participants in eight different states at a variety of institutional types, including 12 public and private four-year institutions, and two community colleges.

After developing interview protocols using a theoretical framework based on Thomas and Brower's (2018) model on campus climate for political learning and engagement in democracy, I facilitated in-depth, semi-structured interviews prior to the 2020 election and then conducted several focus group interviews after Election Day. The individual interviews sought to probe students' motivations for getting involved with the Campus Vote Project and to elicit stories that brought to life their lived experiences in those roles. In the focus groups, I invited students to reflect on their experiences following the election, and to share how serving in the role might influence their future civic engagement, including a discussion of career choice.

Student participants were evenly distributed in terms of academic year standing and not surprisingly, several of the students were political science majors. Students studying political science as a discipline hold implicit motivation and interest, hence the disproportionate representation of students in the study. All but one student was between the ages of 18 and 23. Eleven of the students identified as female-identified while four identified as male. Most of the students described their race as White, while two students identified as Asian, one as Latinx, and one as Black. In addition to filing with the Institutional Review Board (IRB) and adhering to ethical standards in research, I also enacted several trustworthiness strategies, including member-checking, which is the practice of sharing data analysis and interpretations with participants and soliciting on-going feedback throughout the process (Kappus, 2021). Each participant was assigned a pseudonym, and their institution received an alias to protect their privacy. I utilized narrative techniques, attempting to focus on students' lived experience, characterized by storytelling, interpretation of experiences, and an expression of meaning making (Boylorn, 2012). This methodological approach aligned with my constructivist research paradigm, whereby my relationship with participants was co-creative and collaborative in nature (Broido & Manning, 2022). Student quotes and stories are intended to provide evidentiary support for claims. The pseudonyms used in this chapter honor and represent the first names of young people who participated in Freedom Summer, the 1964 effort by over 700 young people to counter voter intimidation and injustice at the polls in Mississippi.

NAVIGATING UNCERTAINTY THROUGH A TENUOUS ELECTION SEASON

The first research question I aimed to address was: What are the lived experiences of politically engaged college students involved in nonpartisan political activity leading up to the 2020 U.S. election? Democracy Fellows' responses to this question demonstrated an election season rife with uncertainty and disruption, whereby students leveraged digital and online tools and worked tirelessly to persuade their peers to be politically aware and engaged. The lived experience of nonpartisan political engagement during the 2020 election season mirrored the country's reaction to the COVID-19 global pandemic. Most students began their roles in January 2020. By March 2020, every student in the study abruptly moved their political engagement efforts online as the country went into lockdown. Students pivoted to social media and other outlets for engagement. Sue said, "every aspect of my life was kinda consumed by Zoom." Summer 2020 brought continued, unexpected social unrest and uncertainty following the murder of George Floyd. Several students viewed speaking out against racial injustice as part of their nonpartisan political engagement efforts. Dona described her reasoning for participating in racial justice demonstrations saying, "when you play this both sides game, it's very harmful to our democracy and to those whose lives are being marginalized." Other students also referenced concerns about racial injustice and the conflation of the issue with partisanship.

In the fall of 2020, the election season continued to unfold in uncertain terms, with campuses responding to the ongoing pandemic in different ways. Whereas some students returned to highly controlled physical campuses, the majority of students coped with the reality of continued online learning throughout the Fall 2020 semester. Even students who returned to a physical campus relied heavily on a socially distanced environment. In addition to navigating their institution's responses to COVID, students also responded to evolving state and local guidance, or lack thereof, regarding voter registration, mail-in voting, and more. The students in the study therefore sought to provide trusted information to peers, turning to digital and online tools for dissemination.

LEVERAGING DIGITAL AND ONLINE TOOLS FOR POLITICAL ENGAGEMENT

Students instituted new strategies in a highly virtual world to engage their peers in the 2020 Election. Describing his student organization's reaction to the pandemic, William said, "We had to get more creative than we did before, and the physical restrictions forced us to think outside of the box." Democracy Fellows realized their peers were increasingly fatigued by virtual events, so they were strategic about which events they moved to a virtual modality. Students tapped into emerging digital platforms like Discord, an interactive streaming service to host events, such as debate watch parties where students could interact with each other at their own campuses and also with other students from campuses across the country. Instead of visiting classrooms in-person to discuss voting, students made presentations via Zoom. Kelly developed what she referred to as a "Faculty Champion

Toolkit," a digital suite on voting that professors could incorporate into their course management platform.

Students described feeling connected but said their interactions lacked the same depth as in-person interactions. In describing this dynamic of being able to connect online but missing interpersonal connection, Richard said, "hitting a like button is way different than having an in-person conversation." Closer to Election Day, students felt like social media became oversaturated with political messaging, so they emphasized more personal digital outreach. For example, students organized text banking efforts referred to as "couch parties," capitalizing on peer-to-peer outreach through personalized text messages via mobile phones.

MOTIVATING PARTICIPATION

The student-led approach exhibited a promising practice for encouraging political participation. Democracy Fellows encountered peers who felt apathetic to, disillusioned by, disconnected from, and intimidated by the political process. Naomi described a view shared by several of her peers saying, "I think young people care a lot, but sometimes they don't know what to do with it." The Fellows helped to demystify the mechanics of politics and of the voting process by sharing access to trusted nonpartisan resources and information, engaging in authentic conversations, and even disclosing their own experiences, such as their initial fear of the voting process.

Campus Vote Project trained Democracy Fellows to be prepared with data to help motivate peers to participate in elections. Joan, for example, said she encountered peers who said the older generations dictate the results of elections, so many peers resisted participation. Equipped with data, she shared how 18–29-year-old voters could influence the outcomes of elections in her state if a higher percentage of students voted. Similarly, Diane reminded peers that young voters would not be ignored if they voted. She and other students also used messaging that tapped into the concept of civic duty, the responsibility members of a community should feel to generations prior and generations to come.

Many students the Democracy Fellows encountered expressed that they were disillusioned by the polarized nature of the election. Kelly, who had been involved in previous elections, said she found herself frequently defending the value of electoral politics this election cycle. Similarly, Diane said students cared deeply about issues but did not feel like they had a voice in politics. She and other Fellows discussed how they shared with their peers the variety of ways, in addition to voting, to express themselves in the political process, especially the importance of doing so at the local level. Joan said peers often expressed dissatisfaction with the two parties, to which she reminded them that they still needed to decide who represented their viewpoints more.

Some students the Fellows encountered expressed concerns that they were not informed enough to vote. Richard described an interaction he had with a student who said they never voted because their vote did not matter. He showed the student how to look up a nonpartisan voter guide where he could learn about the stances candidates took on various issues. The student registered to vote on the spot. He simply helped the student see that he could have an influence in using his voice.

The Fellows also shared about the barriers their peers faced in accessing the ballot. How to physically get to their polling location was a particularly salient theme for many students the Fellows encountered. Catherine described the barrier of not having a polling location on or near campus, particularly for a campus with a high number of students who use wheelchairs. Similarly, Richard discussed the multilayered basic needs challenges students he helped were experiencing on his campus:

> There's this idea that people at community college don't give a shit. But I would push back on that concept. It's not a question of political efficacy. It's a question of eating. It's a question of having a house. It's a question of being able to find a job. I really hate how people malign students for being disinterested. Last time I checked, my boss doesn't give me a day off to vote, and never has. And I've never had a job where I get a paid day off to vote. And I'm a White guy, so I've got the privilege. So that makes me wonder what happens with people who don't have my gender, who don't have my skin color.

NONPARTISANSHIP IN THE FACE OF TURMOIL

Democracy Fellows embraced the nonpartisan approach offered by the Campus Vote Project for several reasons. Not only did nonpartisanship allow them to access spaces, like classrooms, but also, they felt like nonpartisanship helped them make more authentic connections with students. Roger, who also worked as a Resident Assistant in a campus dorm, said students would come to him for insight on the voting process. Several students previously worked in partisan capacities prior to serving as Democracy Fellows for the Campus Vote Project. They described past experiences where peers would shut down once they disclosed that they were working for a candidate or party. In the Democracy Fellow role, however, they built trust more quickly.

Despite their nonpartisan approach, the students still encountered substantial turmoil within their campus environments. For example, when asking a student if they were registered to vote, Naomi said a student aggressively questioned her intentions and whether she would throw away her registration if she indicated a party Naomi did not support. Naomi assured the student she was a nonpartisan actor and taught the student how to confirm that her voter registration had been received. Some students faced hostility from faculty members on their campus. In one example, a faculty member warned their colleagues via a departmental email to not allow Lyn to visit their classes. The faculty member falsely claimed that Lyn had a partisan agenda to brainwash her peers. In another example, a faculty member invited Catherine into the class to present and yet proceeded to tell everyone voting was a waste of their time.

Students of color in the study disproportionately described negative, hostile interactions. Diane, who identified as Latina, shared on several occasions she was the target of aggressive remarks directed at her while engaged in voter education efforts. Lyn recounted how she felt when an off-campus fraternity invited her to present. As the daughter of Indian immigrants, she felt particularly uncomfortable when members forcefully made it known to her that they were voting for Donald Trump, erupting in a chant as she distributed voter registration cards. She also was shown a photo someone took captioned with derogatory language. In another particularly egregious example of hostility, Ella, a Black student, described being coughed on while working at a polling location, completely unprovoked. She assumed it was because she was wearing a mask, but also questioned if the act was a result of her racial identity.

Consistent with the hostility Ella faced, the toxicity also came from outside of the students' campus communities. For example, non-students frequently responded to the Fellows' nonpartisan social media posts through student organization accounts with partisan comments. In a more troubling example, while working the polls on Election Day, Henry recalled a member of the community marching into the polling location and shouting about the state of democracy in America. The person needed to be removed by security for disrupting the polling site. Henry and other students felt these incidents only heightened the importance of people willing to serve their communities as nonpartisan actors. Nancy recruited peers to join her as a poll worker, and she felt a sense of pride in counting absentee ballots.

DEFENDING DEMOCRACY

Students were on the front lines in upholding the democratic process. Democracy Fellows worked to learn the changing election guidance around absentee and mail-in voting as provisions were made during the pandemic. Subsequently, they also fielded concerns about the security and trust of mail-in voting. The preponderance of misinformation and purposeful disinformation arising in their communities caused concern among the

Fellows. They educated students about the presence of misinformation and disinformation by highlighting trusted nonpartisan sources.

This study also found evidence of voter intimidation in local election boards. For example, in one particularly intense interaction, a board of elections official in North Carolina intimidated Henry when they dropped off a box of voter registration cards, claiming he could go to jail for committing election fraud. The official said the students were using an invalid address because it was a residence hall. Henry knew the students had the correct information, and ultimately protected over 70 students in registering to vote. Another time, a board of elections official denied a set of 40 registrations without cause. He contacted the Campus Vote Project for legal support, and ultimately the students' voter registrations were accepted.

In Texas, Judy described the voter suppression tactics as "sneaky." For example, on her campus, the zip code for student's P.O. Boxes were different from the zip code of their residence hall. If students completed their voter registration with the wrong zip code, their registrations were discarded. The day prior to the voter registration deadline, Judy learned that over 1,000 students on her campus had their voter registrations rejected. Later, on the final day of early voting, Judy learned about students being turned away from the campus polling location. She brought her records from her voter registration drives and helped over 50 students on her campus obtain provisional ballots.

Finally, students were particularly concerned about the threats of violence in their communities. For Dona, these fears were born out of the White supremacist march and violence in her hometown, Charlottesville in 2017. Reading concerning language, particularly on social media, caused Dona significant stress. Nancy referred to the foiled kidnapping of her state's governor, Gretchen Whitmer as her awakening to the threat of violence. Even though the students anticipated there would be a delay in election results, the anxiety grew strong. Judy described her concerns about a militia of White nationalists marching downtown, right near campus. The students' concerns were expressed during the focus group interviews in November and December, and foreshadowed the January 6, 2021 insurrection at the U.S. Capitol.

LACK OF INSTITUTIONAL SUPPORT

As the election season ended, the students reflected on the lack of institutional support they received from their campus administration to engage in their roles. Only two students in this study participated in nonpartisan political engagement efforts led through an established college or university department. Instead, most students worked through student organizations with little to no formal institutional support. Sue, for example, had a faculty advisor, but had not communicated at all with them during the election season. For some students, the institutions came to rely upon them as the campus experts on voting. For example, Joan said she was commonly referred to by administrators as "the voting person" on her campus. In fact, she received requests from senior level administrators who redirected questions to her. Nearing graduation, she drew up a plan based on her experience and attempted to gain institutional support. She had trouble getting anyone to take a meeting to discuss the proposal. Eventually, she met with the Vice Chancellor who responded that the institution would not take any ownership. William shared a similar experience, saying the administration was hesitant to support voter engagement efforts. After the lukewarm reception, he went to the faculty senate to propose ideas like a university holiday on Election Day. The faculty were quick to dismiss him and simply came up with reasons why that was not a viable option. Roger also shared resistance he faced, even with something as simple as putting up voter registration information on residence hall bulletin boards. Students felt they were treated like a nuisance instead of valued partners.

A couple of students were able to make progress in institutionalizing voter engagement efforts, the active incorporation of nonpartisan voter engagement into campus cultures and processes (Rank, 2023). Lyn, for example, started to garner administrative support when she presented the Campus Vote Project's Voter Friendly Campus distinction to administrators. She leveraged the potential for the school to be recognized to move ideas forward, such as posting nonpartisan voter information on the webpage and in the student's course management platform. Henry received little support from the administration until he reached out directly to the president of the university. With a positional champion to support his proposal, stakeholders began to mobilize to support voter education efforts. Not every student viewed the lack of institutional support as problematic. Kelly, for example, felt being student-led offered protection from a hostile state legislature in Texas.

LONG TERM INFLUENCE ON STUDENT ASPIRATIONS

My second research question sought to understand how these experiences of nonpartisan political activity influenced student aspiration for future civic engagement. Despite the challenges faced by students in the study, all maintained optimism for the future and expressed aspiration for continued civic engagement. They based their perceptions of remaining engaged in civic life on: their desires to improve the political system; trust that the political system will be responsive to their efforts; and a sense of responsibility to act. Their future aspiration to remain civically engaged was underpinned by two elements: the skills they gained and a vision for incorporating civic engagement into their career choice.

Students described the skills they developed through the nonpartisan political engagement work, which only made them more eager to be involved in the future. Specifically, students recounted stronger understanding of government and politics as well as increased emotional intelligence, and leadership skills. For example, by operating from a nonpartisan approach, students said they gained skills about regulating their emotions and engaging with people they disagree with on issues. By presenting in classes and facilitating activities, students referenced their increased confidence with public speaking and competence with event planning.

Every student shared their emerging career choice and indicated how civic engagement would remain central to their work, in roles ranging from education to government, legal, and nonprofit worlds. Some students went so far as to say that this experience made them want to pursue a career advancing voting rights. Lyn, for example, credited her role as her motivation for a legal career saying, "The biggest impact of Campus Votes and all of the nonpartisan and partisan stuff I've done is that I want to be a voting rights litigator. There are just so many frameworks that we accept in the voting rights space that have deliberately been built up in order to prevent people from voting." Even for students who did not envision working in the voting space, they spoke about how they planned to engage in future civic engagement in their career choice.

IMPLICATIONS

Colleges and universities can take tangible actions to establish, foster, and support student-led nonpartisan political engagement. Faculty and staff at colleges and universities should play a more active role in supporting student leaders involved in nonpartisan political engagement, and not just during presidential election years. As stewards of campus life, student affairs professionals should ensure that if efforts are led by student organization leaders that they have a strong advisor trained in nonpartisan voter education. Student affairs professionals should also partner with tenured faculty members who can offer a level of protection to staff concerned about repercussions for supporting nonpartisan political engagement efforts. Faculty members supporting students engaged in this work similarly should seek out partners in administrative capacities to support student leaders. Ideally, campuses will build coalitions of faculty, staff, students, and community leaders working together to bring people in (see Murray in this volume). Strong partnerships can help to bridge equity gaps that may exist on the campus.

Practitioners should be proactive in addressing the role of identity in supporting peer educators carrying out nonpartisan political engagement efforts. As described by Democracy Fellows in this study, students of color faced greater hostility when performing their duties. Student affairs professionals and faculty should help students understand where they can get support, including how to file reports of bias incidents, discrimination, and violence. White faculty and staff must be more proactive in recognizing their role in addressing the racial climate in relation to civic life. For example, if certain student populations are underrepresented among politically engaged student groups, bridges should be intentionally built to address equity concerns (see Murray in this volume). Additionally, advisors can help students from privileged identities understand their own positionality and subsequent responsibilities when engaging in this work. For instance, a White male-identified student may not understand the barriers faced by peers in navigating government and political arenas, such as the discomfort felt in spaces that have historically excluded certain groups and continue to lack representation. I agree with the students in the study that educating for an inclusive and equitable democracy is in alignment with nonpartisan political engagement efforts.

As demonstrated in this study, third-party organizations like the Campus Vote Project can provide guidance, funding, and support in developing student-led initiatives. As Rank (this volume) explains in Chapter 5, institutions need to make sure efforts need go beyond just voter education and encourage other learning experiences that center democracy, such as designing experiences that foster purposeful dialogue across political differences. At a previous institution, I assisted in the implementation of a campus-wide civic education challenge. Instead of tracking student voter registrations, we encouraged students to pledge to take one civic action that semester and provided examples of activities students could take part in. One student who was not eligible to vote told me they wanted to encourage their peers to get registered to vote as their action. Another student wanted to attend a city council meeting to advocate for an issue impacting students. In short, nonpartisan political engagement encompasses a vast array of learning experiences and should be fostered as such.

The presence of voter suppression and intimidation revealed in discussions with Democracy Fellows in this study also underscores the need for greater legal support for students doing this work. My study did not include a large sample size, and yet, I found evidence of voter intimidation and suppression. Chances are, countless other students have faced similar issues, both as students encouraging their peers to vote, and typical students navigating changing processes or voting for the first time. Colleges and universities should establish open lines of communication and collaboration with local elections board officials, brainstorming proactive strategies and keeping track of any concerns that arise. Nonpartisan organizations can offer expertise as institutions and students navigate state and local issues. For example, the nonpartisan Election Protection Coalition (866ourvote.org), represents over 300 partners across the country in upholding the right to vote. The group is well known for establishing a free hotline, 866-OUR-VOTE, for legal guidance in navigating the voting process. In addition to leading key litigation and advocacy efforts, the Fair Elections Center (fairelectionscenter.org), the parent organization to the Campus Vote Project, provides state guides with updates on election law, vote-by-mail guidelines, and other resources to help people understand their rights.

Finally, the study demonstrated the importance of leadership to guide the work happening at colleges and universities. To encourage political participation that strengthens democracy, policy makers should consider requiring colleges and universities to designate a coordinator for student civic and voter education, tasked with, among other duties, supporting student-led efforts and building a campus coalition (a recommendation also made by Murray in this volume). Relevant to the study reviewed in this chapter, these coordinators could be charged with advising, training, and supporting student peer educators. The concept of designating a campus official to civic and voter engagement was introduced in 2021 through House Resolution 1, the "For the People Act," which failed to pass into law. The state of California, however, codified the Student Civic and Voter Empowerment Act (AB963) requiring California State Universities, California Community Colleges, and requesting the Universities of California to enact a number of provisions, including the appointment of a campus Coordinator for Civic and Voter Empowerment, developing an action plan, and more. This kind of state-level legislation could prove to be influential in institutionalizing voter education and civic engagement efforts at colleges and universities.

CONCLUSION

The creativity of students leading nonpartisan political engagement efforts, coupled with support from invested faculty and staff advisors and mentors, strengthen campus efforts. This study only scratched the surface of insights into student experiences with political engagement efforts. Future studies might account for regional, state, and institutional differences, as well as the unique contexts of each election season. Future studies might also expand upon the role that racial identity plays in how students experience nonpartisan political engagement. Nonpartisan political engagement efforts should include, but go beyond voter education, such as robust discussions on public issues (see Moshman in this volume). When done well, these efforts can help students across the political spectrum to engage meaningfully in democracy.

REFERENCES

American Political Science Association. (2023, October 21). *Civic engagement groups*. https://connect.apsanet.org/raisethevote/civic-engagement-groups/

Anderson, G. (2019). Tug-of-war over students' votes. *Inside Higher Ed*. https://www.insidehighered.com/news/2019/11/12/students-across-country-faced-voting-barriers-election-day

Bardwell, K. (2011). Fact checks, voter guides, and GOTV: Civic learning projects in American politics courses. *Journal of Political Science Education, 7*(1), 1–13. http://doi.org/10.1080/15512169.2011.539899

Barrett, M., & Pachi, D. (2019). *Youth civic and political engagement*. Routledge.

Bennion, E. A., & Nickerson, D. W. (2016). I will register and vote, if you teach me how: a field experiment testing voter registration in college classrooms. *PS: Political Science & Politics, 49*(4), 867–871. http://doi.org/10.1017/s1049096516001360

Beaumont, E., Colby, A., Ehrlich, T., & Torney-Purta, J. (2006). Promoting political competence and engagement in college students: An empirical study. *Journal of Political Science Education, 2*(3), 249–270. http://doi.org/10.1080/15512160600840467

Binder, A. J., & Kidder, J. L. (2022). *The channels of student activism: How the left and right are winning (and losing) in campus politics today*. University of Chicago Press.

Boylorn, R. (2012). Lived experience. In A. Given (Ed.), *The SAGE encyclopedia of qualitative research methods* (pp. 490–491). SAGE. http://dx.doi.org/10.4135/9781412963909

Broido, E. M., & Manning, K. (2002). Philosophical foundations and current theoretical perspectives in qualitative research. *Journal of College Student Development, 43*, 434–445. https://eric.ed.gov/?id=EJ650160

Center for Information & Research on Civic Learning and Engagement (2021). Half of youth voted in 2020, an 11-point increase from 2016. CIRCLE Latest Research. Retrieved from https://circle.tufts.edu/latest-research/half-youth-voted-2020-11-point-increase-2016

Chadjipadelis, T., & Panagiotidou, G. (2021). Students Teaching Democracy to Other Students: The Effects on Political Engagement. *GLOBALLY*, 185.

Clandinin, D. J. (2016). *Engaging in narrative inquiry*. Routledge.

Colby, A., Beaumont, E., Ehrlich, T., & Corngold, J. (2010). *Educating for democracy: Preparing undergraduates for responsible political engagement*. Wiley.

Derfner, A., & Gerald, H. J. (2016). Voting is speech. *Yale Law & Policy Review, 34*(2), 471–491. Retrieved from https://ylpr.yale.edu/voting-speech

Finley, A. (2011). *Civic learning and democratic engagement: A review of the literature on civic engagement in post-secondary education.* Association of American Colleges and Universities. Paper prepared for the U.S. Department of Education.

Harker, D. (2016). Political consciousness but not political engagement: Results from a service-learning study. *Michigan Journal of Community Service Learning, 22*(2), 31–47. https://eric.ed.gov/?id=EJ1137442

Higher Education Act (HEA). (1998). 20 U.S.C. 1094(a)(23)

Hylton, M. E. (2018). The role of civic literacy and social empathy on rates of civic engagement among university students. *Journal of Higher Education Outreach and Engagement, 22*(1), 87–106.

Jacoby, B. (2006). Making politics matter to students: Voting as civic engagement. *About Campus, 11*(4), 30–32. http://doi.org/10.1002/abc.178

Jacoby, B. (2009). *Civic engagement in higher education: Concepts and practices.* Wiley.

Junco, R., Kawashima-Ginsberg, K., Amado, L., Fahlberg, V., & Bliss, L. (2018). *Expanding the electorate: How simple changes in election administration can improve youth participation among low-income youth.* Center for Information & Research on Civic Learning and Engagement. https://circle.tufts.edu/sites/default/files/2020-01/expanding_electorate_oyu_report.pdf

Kappus, A. (2021). *Examining the lived experience of politically engaged college students participating in nonpartisan political activity during the 2020 U.S. election.* Available from ProQuest Dissertations & Theses Global. (2572599252). Retrieved from https://proxying.lib.ncsu.edu/index.php/login?url=https://www.proquest.com/dissertations-theses/examining-lived-experience-politically-engaged/docview/2572599252

Komives, S. R. (2019). Engagement with campus activities matters: Toward a new era of educationally purposeful activities. *The Journal of Campus Activities Practice and Scholarship, 1*(1), 14–25.

Linder, C., Quaye, S. J., Lange, A. C., Evans, M. E., & Stewart, T. J. (2019). *Identity-based student activism: Power and oppression on college campuses.* https://ebookcentral-proquest-com.cmich.idm.oclc.org

Mann, C. B., Alberda, G. A., Birkhead, N. A., Ouyang, Y., Singer, C., Stewart, C., Herron, M. C., Beaulieu, E., Boehmke, F., Boston, J., Cantu, F., Cobb, R., Darmofal, D., Ellington, T. C., Finocchiaro, C. J., Gilbert, M., Haynes, V., Janssen, B., Kimball, D., Kromkowski, C. (2018). Pedagogical value of polling-place observation by students. *PS: Political Science & Politics, 51*(4), 831–837. http://doi.org/10.1017/S1049096518000550

Nolan, J. (2011). House speaker O'Brien addresses Rochester 9–12ers; Many changes planned by republican new wave. *Fosters.* https://www.fosters.com/article/20110113/GJNEWS04/701139913

Pritzhiker, S., Springer, M., & McBride, A. M. (2015). Learning to vote: Informing political participation among college students. *Journal of Community Engagement and Scholarship, 8*(1), 69–79. https://digitalcommons.northgeorgia.edu/jces/vol8/iss1/8

Rank, A. D., & Tylock, A. R. (2018). Vote Oswego: Developing and assessing the campaign-as-course model. *Journal of Political Science Education, 14*(3), 376–389. http://doi.org/10.1080/15512169.2017.1413653

Rios, A. R. M. (2013). Teaching civic engagement: Debates, definitions, benefits, and challenges. In A. R. M. McCartney, E. A. Bennion, & D. Simpson (Eds.), *Teaching civic engagement: From student to active citizen* (pp. 9–20). American Political Science Association.

Saltmarsh, J., & Hartley, M. (Eds.). (2011). *"To serve a larger purpose": Engagement for democracy and the transformation of higher education.* Temple University Press.

Strachan, J. C. (2019). Giving all college students what they need to become active citizens: Tailoring civic learning to students' lived experiences. *Political Science Now.* https://politicalsciencenow.com/giving-all-college-students-what-they-need-to-become-active-citizens-tailoring-civic-learning-to-students-lived-experiences/

Strachan, J. C., & Bennion, E. A. (2016). New resources for civic engagement: The National Survey of Student Leaders and the Consortium for Inter-Campus SoTL Research. *eJournal of Public Affairs, 5*(2), 41–91. ISSN 2162-9161

Stolzenberg, E. B., Eagan, K., Aragon, M., Cesar-Davis, N. M., Jacobo, S., Couch, V., Rios-Aguilar, C. (2017). *The American freshman: National norms Fall 2017.* UCLA Higher Education Research Institute. https://heri.ucla.edu/publications-tfs/

Thomas, N., & Brower, M. (2018). Conceptualizing and assessing campus climates for political learning and engagement in democracy. *Journal of College and Character, 19*(4), 247–263. http://doi.org/10.1080/2194587x.2018.1517651

Wawrzynski, M. R., LoConte, C. L., & Straker, E. J. (2011). Learning outcomes for peer educators: The National Survey on Peer Education. In L. B. Williams (Ed.), *New Directions for Student Services: No. 133. Emerging issues and practices in peer education* (pp. 17–27). Wiley.

CHAPTER 17

SPACE, PLACE, AND COMMUNITY

Engaging With College Students Where They Are

Brian F. Harrison
University of Minnesota–Twin Cities

Robert Healy
Carleton College

ABSTRACT

College campuses can be spaces where students, often passionate about political topics, can be encouraged to engage with democracy, politics, and civic organizing. At Carleton College in Northfield, Minnesota, efforts to do just this were co-coordinated by a faculty member and an undergraduate student to activate and to motivate students in a complex registration and voting process. In the six months prior to the 2022 midterm election, we engaged in nonpartisan efforts focused on three tactics: (1) the formation, development, and/or continuation of student-led campus nonpartisan organizations; (2) novel communication channels and locations to capture student interest; and

(3) finding common ground with existing institutions within the college. At a liberal arts college with students from all over the country and the world, our tactics supported political learning and augmented existing campus culture, pushing boundaries of existing nonpartisan voter engagement efforts. Our chapter highlights the challenges and the benefits to creating a grassroots student community committed to political engagement, including the process of identifying student leaders and working within (and outside of) the confines of institutional structures to accomplish engagement goals. We end with a discussion of how our experience adds to efforts to build responsible democratic participants among college students on campuses across the country.

Political science scholarship has long shown that education and age are reliable predictors of political engagement and participation (Verba and Nie 1972; Wolfinger and Rosenstone 1980; Verba, Schlozman and Brady 1995; Plutzer 2002; Leighley and Nagler 2013). Generally speaking, younger voters tend to turnout less often than older voters (Kam and Palmer 2008), with additional years of formal education increasing the propensity to vote (Hanson & Tyner 2021). Establishing voting habits earlier in life has been shown to increase the likelihood of future voting (Plutzer 2002; Gerber, Green and Shachar 2003; Coppock and Green 2016; Meredith et al. 2009). These trends suggest that engaging students in college may be fruitful in increasing propensity to vote and increasing overall interest in the political process. There are, however, unique challenges to engage younger voters such as the high mobility among younger people (Ansolabehere, Hersh and Shepsle 2012) and difficulty measuring student engagement because of high non-contact rates in surveys (Abraham, Maitland and Bianchi 2006). Further, when scholars research student voting, they often seek the most effective interventions to increase registration and turnout by looking at how students think and feel about voting (Nickerson 2006; Eustice et. al, 2021; Dalton & Crosby, 2008; Green & Gerber, 2015). Knowing that college students and young voters have different needs and wants when it comes to political engagement, we tailored our approach at Carleton College to answer a simple question: How can we connect students to think and feel about themselves and their campus community in ways that increase political engagement and voting?

Central to this question, and our approach, is the creation of democratically-engaged citizens. Voting is often the gateway to being a citizen in a democratic country but should not be where engagement efforts end. With this in mind, we pushed to create an organization that encourages students not just to vote but to think of themselves as voters. By tapping into the community of the college and students' own networks, the voting process transformed from something transactional, that an individual does, to something empowering, that a community does. Our goal was not just to encourage students to vote but to create a community of voters.

This chapter focuses on ways to create and implement civic engagement plans on college campuses to activate and motivate students to turn out to vote. We focus on three broad concepts: (1) the formation, development, and/or continuation of student-led campus nonpartisan organizations; (2) novel communication channels and locations to capture student interest, from satirical campus publications and in-class presentations to QR codes in the bathroom stalls in the physics hall; and (3) finding common ground with existing institutions within the college, while maintaining autonomy to focus on our stated goals.

We focus on each concept in turn detailing our work at Carleton College leading up to the 2022 midterm election, with a focus on how to turn academic literature into practice rapidly and efficiently. We hope our approach will provide a practical framework for other students, faculty, or institutions to create their own nonpartisan, student-led, voter engagement initiatives that can contribute to creating good citizens that will help to fulfill the public mission of higher education.

STUDENT CLUBS: ORGANIZING STUDENTS TO DO THE WORK

On many college campuses, as in broader society, there is significant variance of interest in politics, with a core group of politically active students far more interested in the median student (Simmons & Lilly 2010). In building a nonpartisan voter education and engagement initiative, our first step was to identify and to organize a subset of students which would lead wider, campus-wide efforts. While there was somewhat of a voter education infrastructure at Carleton College, our goal was to develop a focused and enduring student organization that would be dedicated year-round and year-after-year to further such efforts. Setting up the structures to have a successful voter turnout operation was time-intensive but necessary to maintain engagement by core leadership for future election cycles.

In the early stages, this effort was largely faculty-led: Brian Harrison, a member of the political science faculty at the time, gauged interest in organizing and engagement work in several of his classes during the 2022 Spring term prior to the election. The assumption was that students engaged in American political science might already be more interested in the political process (Fernandez 2021). To cast a wider net, an email was also sent to the political science listserv, including all majors and prospective majors at Carleton. During this timeframe, there was a fair amount of student interest but no formal structure was established. Work during the summer proved challenging as well: while Harrison set up video meetings to create an action plan for the upcoming term, moving the effort forward proved almost impossible until students were back on campus at the outset of the Fall semester. It may have been challenging to organize because the goals that students were asked to consider were both abstract and far off in the future.

Upon recognition of this problem, Harrison contacted LeadMN, a Minnesota-based organization focused on college student political engagement, to lead an initial session to help develop a structure for a new student group. LeadMN has extensive experience with workshops and trainings to teach students interpersonal leadership skills essential to political and social organizing (LeadMN.com). This partnership proved to be instrumental to our success. LeadMN offers myriad resources to bring structure to developing a campus action plan, helping students see easily digestible ways that the nascent organization would function and creating achievable small tasks that would contribute to increasing voter turnout. These plans were made at the beginning of the term and were created to be evaluated on a week-by-week basis.

Student leaders started to take initiative and to do some of the work on their own outside of class. Targeted groups looking at messaging, branding, organizing, developed multiple forms of communication (e.g., Slack, text message, email, Google Drive) so that students could collaborate on their work with the group. Perhaps most importantly, a general planning document was created in Google Docs that took all the goals from the campus action plan and distilled specific steps students could take to get started on these tasks. Each task was assigned its own Google document where students could collaborate on the project. While mainly organizational in nature, these efforts were crucial to the success of overall efforts. Undergrad Robert Healy emerged as a leader of these efforts and was chosen as the first president of the new organization called CarlsVote.

Harrison maintained a working relationship with LeadMN, which has a robust fellowship program that provides funds for campus fellows to lead efforts on voter turnout on college campuses. We were able to secure funding from LeadMN in the amount of $3000 for three paid fellowships which were advertised to students who had expressed interest in the project. The selection process for these positions targeted students who had already shown commitment to the work as well as to students who were already embedded in formal structures of the college campus, including the Carleton student government known as the *College Student Association*. One recipient of the fellowship highlighted how instrumental the paid position was: the money pushed him to spend more time focused on voter engagement than he would have been able to contribute for a purely volunteer position (Q. Buhman, personal communication, February 23, 2023).

Our next task was to get everyone in a room and start to develop a viable structure to run the newly developed student organization. With the promise of sugar and carbs in the form of department-provided snacks, we developed a decentralized structure focusing on engagement and communication. Students chose one of the two broad categories based on their interests and skill sets. The engagement side of the organization was to help develop organizing workshops, dorm storms, candidate fora, and more broadly engage with campus offices and other student groups. The communication branch was dedicated more explicitly to written and artistic forms of communication around campus. Each branch chose a leader who was responsible for developing a cohesive strategy and a communication plan for keeping students on track. This leadership differentiation proved key, particularly as schoolwork became more intense over the course of the term and students became busier and unable to devote as much time as they could earlier in the semester.

CAMPUS COMMUNICATION STRATEGIES

We employed several communication strategies to encourage involvement and engagement among as many students as possible. First, we tried appealing to an in-group identity as a Carleton student. Material highlighted at club meetings and in on-campus literature outlined that one of our broad goals was to try to beat St. Olaf College, one of Carleton's rival schools in the same town of Northfield, Minnesota, in voter turnout numbers in the midterm election. The reason behind this approach was to explore how a friendly college rivalry might increase motivation and performance among constituents regarding electoral engagement for the 2022 midterm elections (Cikara and Fiske 2011). St. Olaf College also happened to have one of the highest voter turnout rates in the country in 2020 (IDHE 2021).

Second, we encouraged student organization members to leverage social relationships and to talk to their friends and peers to get them involved more informally, allowing club members to continue to be engaged with the mission of the club even if they were not working on a specific project at the time. We provided ideas for students to spark conversations, whether over lunch or in a residence hall lounge, to build a broader network of students engaged in student turnout efforts. This second tier of students played a role in making voting an important social activity on campus. At small colleges, relying on social networks can be an inexpensive and impactful way to begin to craft a culture of engagement.

Next, we led brainstorming sessions with the club to think about key locations, messages, and strategies that would help us reach beyond traditional channels. With guidance from LeadMN, we designed a short, 4-minute presentation that provided concrete logistical information about registration requirements, voting times, information about voting-by-mail and early voting, and locations where students could vote. Members of the communication subgroup of the club then contacted their professors asking if they could speak to their classmates for a few minutes at the beginning or the end of classes as Minnesota voter registration deadlines, early voting deadlines, and Election Day itself approached. We did not emphasize at this point that Minnesota has same-day voting registration since our focus was getting students to register immediately. Our strategy shifted as the election approached to remind students they could still vote even if they hadn't yet registered. Professors were mostly agreeable to allowing these nonpartisan, informational presentations in a wide variety of majors and we again leveraged the power of hearing this information from a peer rather than from a faculty member or a different institutional source.

CarlsVote developed a series of posters to be displayed in key residence halls and academic buildings, focusing on the science complex. Though these were not typical posters that you see posted on college bulletin boards in the hundreds: they were silly posters employing "potty humor" designed to go in bathroom stalls (one such poster read "Don't be a [poop emoji], Vote"). They also included a QR code linking to the Minnesota Secretary of State website and instructions for voter registration. With posters going up 5 days before the Minnesota registration deadline, 102 unique students on campus scanned the QR code, representing more than 5% of the student body on campus during the Fall of 2022. If employed earlier in registration season with full coverage of the campus community, we might expect to see an even greater percentage of the student body registering with this method in 2024.

Unsurprisingly, food was also key to bringing students together prior to the election to talk about voting and how to get friends to go to the polls with them. The week before Election Day, we hosted an event with food from a local taco restaurant for sixty students, with financial assistance from LeadMN. We advertised the event through the @CarlsVote Instagram page and through a campus announcement sent via email from the head of communication. The event brought in more than the sixty people we had planned. Utilizing the space that a campus provides to host events, that brings students together through food or for the love of voting is one of the key advantages a college has to organizing voter turnout efforts.

In addition to in-person events, we targeted campus news outlets in ways that would be engaging to students, focused on a relatively new app called Yik Yak. Yik Yak is a location-based social media platform designed to let community members anonymously post X (formerly Twitter)-length messages to people within a five-mile radius. In the runup to the election, CarlsVote members would frequently post reminders to register to vote and where polling locations in both serious formats as well as meme formats, imitating other top posts at the time. Frequently these posts would make it into the top two or three posts in the radius which included both Carleton College and St. Olaf College.

We also replicated social media phenomena from past campaigns for activism, a trend we called an "Instagram Blitz." This is the process through which a single central account posts an infographic about a topic of activism and then several community members repost on their stories which leads to more community members reposting. The result is that members of the community are inundated with the same message. Our commutations team devised a few slides about the importance of voting to post on our Student Organization Instagram page, @CarlsVote, and we encouraged our members to repost it on their story and tell their friends to do the same.

One final way we met students where they are online was using Google calendar invites. Students at Carleton rely on Google calendar so much that if an event is not on their official Google calendar, most people forget to go to it. While this may be a Carleton-specific quirk, it's likely that other campuses use Google calendar or another similar application as the primary way to schedule one's day. Knowing this, members invited friends or acquaintances to go vote during common times (periods of time on campus when classes aren't in session) that many students are free. Club members led small groups to the polls together during those times and we encouraged students to do the same. We wanted to create a sense of community of people who are voters and to add mild social pressure to voting which is an effective way to get people to the polls (Gerber, Green, & Larimer 2008). Even if students do not go and vote with a group, we sent them a notification about going to vote when they get the invite as well as the time set for the invite on Election Day, bringing the election to the center of their minds and providing an important reminder using technology they already use every day.

NAVIGATING INSTITUTIONS

A key part of student organizing is finding ways to collaborate with campus resources and offices while retaining autonomy and some control over the student group. We did, of course, welcome institutional support for our efforts. However, due to the rigidity of higher education bureaucratic systems and the territorial nature of office politics, this was a slow and oftentimes frustrating process. Even still, much was accomplished in just a few months and work continues to be done to institutionalize these voter engagement efforts.

There were several key on-campus entities that were beneficial to our efforts. Our first and primary point of contact was the Carleton College's Center for Community and Civic Engagement (CCCE). This office was an obvious place to start given the nature of the related work that they engage in on a day-to-day basis. However, Harrison and other club members reached out to a variety of offices and departments that could be helpful, including the provost and president, residential life, student affairs, the library, the chaplain's office, dining services, the gender and sexuality center, media relations, office of student fellowships, student activities, and the on-campus Humanities Center at Carleton College. With each conversation, we determined a concrete ask for the particular department or office. For example, the Chaplain's office put language in their campuswide newsletter that extolled the virtues of being engaged in the political process. The Gender and Sexuality Center offered to mention our efforts during their many programs and clubs. The Humanities Center had an ongoing exhibit on civic engagement and art in politics. We wanted multiple campus actors to contribute something unique to the overall effort and to publicize the work the club was doing.

In election cycles prior to the 2022 midterm elections, Carleton refused to release data to the National Study of Learning, Voting, and Engagement (NSLVE) because of privacy concerns. NSLVE examines college voting rates based on race, sex, and major, which allows stakeholders to access data pertinent to voter mobilization efforts. NSLVE is the first and only study to objectively examine student and institution-level data on student voting and to share these data with participating campuses. Participation is free, easy, and protective of student privacy. As such, we dedicated much of the beginning of the term to encouraging the school to join NSLVE, requesting meetings with both the provost's office as well as the president's office. Our arguments focused on both the club's ability to assess how successful our efforts were in the 2022 cycle but also as a forward-looking mechanism: we wanted to see how effective our 2022 plan was to optimize the action plan leading up to the 2024 election cycle. Harrison and several students met with administration officials underscoring the importance of NSLVE data for both future efforts on campus as well as the opportunities for academic research on the subject. Likewise, the CCCE had discussions with the provost on its importance as well. Ultimately our efforts proved successful and the college enrolled to receive data about the 2022 midterm from the NSLVE.

On the topic of "success," we conceived of success in a few different ways. First, we wanted to usher in a sense of agency for students on campus when it came to the efforts geared toward student political engagement. The campus had their efforts that they felt were adequate; what was missing was a "bottom-up" approach. Students were not included in the administration of voter engagement efforts outside of a small group of fellows hired by the CCCE. Expanding the degree to which interested students could contribute their insight, time, and energy was a primary goal of the effort and we hope it will continue into the future.

Next, we conceived success as encouraging students to tap into their social networks to encourage participation. These organic efforts, in tandem with more traditional efforts by the CCCE, fostered the idea that talking about politics and policy is a normal, regular part of everyday life, even when you're a college student. On the path to deeper democratic engagement, we wanted students to feel comfortable incorporating the normative importance of voting and voter turnout on campus. These tactics fostered civic skills in two ways: the most straightforward way was, obviously, registering voters and encouraging them to turn out when they would not have done so without prodding from CarlsVote. In addition to raw turnout numbers which were very encouraging post-election, conversations with students suggested they felt far more comfortable and confident engaging in political conversations and efforts than they were previously. Building civic skills is such an important precursor to deeper political engagement and to life-long habits related to voting.

Secondly, students who were engaged in the leadership and execution of CarlsVote efforts improved their own civic skills by being part of organizing efforts, messaging strategy, and interacting with elected officials that visited campus and local election leaders. Many of these student leaders mentioned they had never been engaged in "real politics" before the CarlsVote effort drew them in.

Lastly, measurement was an important metric of success. NSLVE is a widely-used tool to gauge turnout in a given election year but most important from year-to-year. At first, Carleton was patently unwilling to join the NSLVE movement to the degree that we were told in no uncertain terms to not even approach the administration on the topic. However, in ways big and small, our efforts showed key members of the administration how important it was to join peer institutions to measure student voting turnout securely and safely.

As we mention above, voting is only one part of democratic engagement; efforts moving forward will focus on ways to deepen and broaden engagement into activism and conversations across differences. Next steps on campus include becoming the newest chapter of Havel's Place, a project named after Václav Havel, to promote dialogue, discussion, and freedom of speech. After the first installation at Georgetown University in Washington D.C., it has been instituted on campuses across the world. Havel's Place brings people of different views, ideologies, identities, and beliefs to a conversation that adheres to the best practices associated with democratic dialogue. Tomáš Halík, a close friend of Havel, paraphrased Havel when he said, "Even as people of different opinions, different political beliefs and different religions, it is still immensely important to sit down at a table and talk to one another in search for the truth" (Czech Radio, 2013). We viewed a student-centered voter turnout effort as a gateway into these next-level engagement efforts, reliant upon key democratic values like free expression and genuine attempts to empathize with others of different viewpoints and backgrounds.

Despite our successes, we encountered several institutional barriers along the way. For example, our goals and the CCCE's were not always in alignment and there was often a sense of territoriality when it came to working with the office or with other offices on campus. One such instance occurred when the club tried to connect with residential life to have Resident Assistants (RAs)— students charged with maintaining floor life— send messages to their floor about voting information. The Residential Life offices responded that such requests needed to go through the CCCE. When we got in communication with the CCCE, we were told they could not accept such material as it was not made in consultation with the office, nor did it have the CCCE logo on it.

However, the club proceeded without institutional support. A friend of a club member was an RA, who agreed to compile a list of most other RAs and their contact information. Club members took to individually emailing everyone on the list, asking them to share the voting information to their residents. We cannot be certain of how many did but this example highlights that working within institutional channels can make things easier. However, if it is not possible to work within institutional channels, or if they do not exist in the first place, it should not deter from engaging in the work of organizing and pushing ahead anyway.

Another source of tension we encountered was when trying to post flyers around the library. According to the librarians, the library acted as a "neutral place" and they would not allow any posters that were political in nature. Unfortunately, they deemed nonpartisan registration information to be too political as well. Similar to the setback with the residential life office, we hung posters throughout the library anyway.

Small acts of political defiance like this may have forced us to have an uncomfortable conversation with library staff after the fact but in our calculations such discomfort was still worth increasing awareness on campus. So long as such small acts of defiance did not impinge a potential future working relationship with offices and institutional bodies on campus, we had no issues with pushing the limits. While we still asked for permission, we also found ourselves occasionally asking for forgiveness as well. This method of institutional engagement afforded us the ability to find areas where we could work with the administration and then figure out a path forward on their own if they were not helpful. Post-election engagement with a variety of offices on campus has only increased, however, lending credence to the idea that our boundary-pushing didn't harm our image within the administration.

After the midterm election (December 2022), club attendance started to drop off quite quickly. For many students, the election is a motivating factor to be involved in civic engagement and turnout efforts. A strategic evaluation of our actions in the 2022 midterms highlighted that additional integration into the more formal institutions of the college may allow the club to have greater reach in the campus community moving forward. As we have continued to engage with campus institutions like the CCCE, other less formally organized groups dedicated to civic engagement, discourse, and voter turnout have reached out to us. They have a desire to expand programming to create a whole ecosystem of interconnected organizations on campus. Likewise, alumni groups have engaged with our efforts to expand civil discourse norms. Each of these connections constitute an opportunity to build momentum for civic engagement programming and we plan to take advantage of it.

We learned several lessons in the process of developing CarlsVote. Organizations on other college campuses will likely face similar challenges and struggles to develop a program that has sufficient stakeholder support to accomplish all desired goals. CarlsVote, however, provides a strong case study of how to maximize visibility utilizing limited resources. One of the most eye-opening discoveries that other campuses should consider: while there is an assumption that college students are knowledgeable and politically engaged, our experience (and significant data) shows that they still need significant and targeted activities to encourage them to register and to turn out. Existing on-campus institutions may believe they engage in the correct activities but as we found, past efforts fell short of best practices and there was little to no measurement of efforts to acknowledge successes and to reflect on future changes to best meet the needs of students. We hope this chapter encourages campuses to take a closer, more empirical look at their engagement activities to ensure they are consistent with the latest research on how to turn out younger college students, whether these efforts are new or have been existing for some time.

Other organizations looking to replicate some of the successes at Carleton should look to find several committed students to create the backbone of a nonpartisan voter engagement organization. With a group of five or so students, a large portion of the media-focused engagement activities can be accomplished. These students are also best positioned to determine which platforms to target on their respective campuses. In focusing on non-traditional social media platforms, CarlsVote found that it was easier to capture a wider array of the campus community.

CONCLUSION

Our efforts on Carleton's campus were multifaceted, with support from off-campus organizations as well as students, faculty, and on-campus personnel. While these strategies and tactics were only an initial attempt to create processes and longevity of engagement on campus, attempts to reach students through emerging social media platforms and localized social networks proved fruitful. Further, leveraging the physical space of a college campus through poster campaigns allowed students to be reached when their attention was not focused elsewhere, perhaps increasing the salience of the message. In combination, these results show that organizers need to conceive of college campus both as a physical community as well as an online community and to tap into spaces where students are most likely to be willing to engage with voting materials.

After the election, it became clear that it was not feasible to continue as a separate entity from the CCCE and CarlsVote needed to be more ingrained in existing institutions. While institutionalization has its drawbacks, it is done with an eye toward expanding the role of the organization. Our long-term goal is to move past simple voter turnout efforts and more towards a holistic view of what it means to be democratic citizens. We want to emphasize that democracy is something that you engage in all the time— it is, in its fundamental form, a means of conflict resolution as well as the way you engage with your community every day. Volunteer work and community engagement are actions that you buy into and therefore express yourself politically through your actions. And while voter turnout efforts will continue to be a core component of our programming, figuring out how to incorporate those broader ideals into that same program could more easily be done with the help of staff members and students within the offices of the college.

To this end, CarlsVote formally became part of the CCCE during the 2023–2024 academic year.

Having access to institutional support lends a sense of credibility to the organization to both students looking to get involved as well as to other offices we hope to engage with. It will also expand the role of institutional knowledge within the organization and allow for more efficient navigation of college structures and bureaucracy. It provides CarlsVote access to resources that can sustain long-term year-round efforts to build responsible citizens. In the past term alone, several events focused on broader political engagement were sponsored by CarlsVote that had more than twenty attendees. Moreover, CarlsVote student leadership was tasked with creating campus voter engagement reviews and plans that the College president's cabinet has adopted. This proves our primary thesis——a dedicated group of students and faculty can organize rapidly to engrain itself into the campus community and promote real democratic engagement by augmenting known strategies with a little innovation.

Further developing the CarlsVote initiative will be met with opportunities and challenges but in total, the inaugural CarlsVote efforts at Carleton College expanded student-led efforts and clubs, pushed communication boundaries, and started important conversations about how engagement efforts can be a better collaboration between existing institutions and students moving forward. Fresh and creative ways of tapping into informal social networks increased civic skills on campus and signaled to students that it was socially appropriate and acceptable to engage in non-partisan voting turnout efforts. In the short term, we wanted to create voting consumers; in the long term, we wanted to start down the road of developing a sustainable organization dedicated to building responsible democratic participants who will embrace the ongoing need to engage in our democratic process at every turn possible.

REFERENCES

Abraham, K., Maitland, A., & Bianchi, S. (2006). *Non-response in the American time use survey: who is missing from the data and how much does it matter?* National Bureau of Economic Research. http://dx.doi.org/10.3386/t0328

Ansolabehere, S., Hersh, E., & Shepsle, K. (2012). Movers, stayers, and registration: Why age is correlated with registration in the U.S. *Quarterly Journal of Political Science, 7*(4), 333–363. https://doi.org/10.1561/100.00011112

Cikara, M., Botvinick, M. M., & Fiske, S. T. (2011). Us versus them. *Psychological Science, 22*(3), 306–313. https://doi.org/10.1177/0956797610397667

Coppock, A., & Green, D. P. (2015). Is voting habit forming? New evidence from experiments and regression discontinuities. *American Journal of Political Science, 60*(4), 1044–1062. https://doi.org/10.1111/ajps.12210

Czech Radio. (2013). "Halík: Je dobře, že je to lavička, a ne bronzová socha..." https://www.rozhlas.cz/halik-je-dobre-ze-je-lavicka-a-ne-bronzova-socha-8004492

Dalton, J., & Crosby, P. (2008). From volunteering to voting: Higher education's role in preparing college students for political engagement. *Journal of College and Character, 9*(4). https://doi.org/10.2202/1940-1639.1138.

Eustice, K., Cook-Davis, A., Springer, B., & Brown, K. (2021). "There are issues that I care about": What drives civically engaged student voters. Pre- and post-election analysis of Arizona State University student voting behavior and attitudes. *Morrison Institute for Public Policy.* Accessed from https://eric.ed.gov/?id=ED615095.

Fernandez, F. (2021). Turnout for what? Do colleges prepare informed voters? *Educational Researcher, 50*(9), 677–678. https://doi.org/10.3102/0013189X211045982

Gerber, A. S., Green, D. P., & Shachar, R. (2003). Voting may be habit-forming: Evidence from a randomized field experiment. *American Journal of Political Science, 47*(3), 540–550. https://doi.org/10.1111/1540-5907.00038

Green, D. P., & Gerber, A. S. (2019). *Get out the vote: How to increase voter turnout.* Brookings Institution Press.

Gerber, A, Green D., & Larimer C. (2008). Social pressure and voter turnout: Evidence from a large-scale field experiment. *American Political Science Review, 102*(1), 33–48. https://doi.org/10.1017/S000305540808009X

Hansen, E.R., Tyner, A. (2021). Educational attainment and social norms of voting. *Political Behavior, 43,* 711–735. https://doi.org/10.1007/s11109-019-09571-8

Institute for Democracy & Higher Education: National Study of Learning, Voting, and Engagement. (2021). *Student voting rates for St Olaf.* https://drive.google.com/file/d/17iBO46cDcw43XNL-eERKamA8zT8yh2wM/view

Kam, C. D., & Palmer, C. L. (2008). Reconsidering the effects of education on political participation. *The Journal of Politics, 70*(3), 612–631. https://doi.org/10.1017/s0022381608080651

Kilduff, G. J. (2014). Driven to win. *Social Psychological and Personality Science, 5*(8), 944–952. https://doi.org/10.1177/1948550614539770

LeadMN. (2023). *What we do.* LeadMN. Retrieved April 27, 2023, from https://www.leadmn.org/what-we-do

Leighley, J. E., & Nagler, J. (2013). *Who votes now?: Demographics, issues, inequality, and turnout in the united states.* Princeton University Press.

Meredith, M. (2009). Persistence in political participation. *Quarterly Journal of Political Science, 4*(3), 187–209. https://doi.org/10.1561/100.00009015

Nickerson, D. W. (2006). Hunting the elusive young voter. *Journal of Political Marketing, 5*(3), 47–69. https://doi.org/10.1300/j199v05n03_03

Plutzer, E. (2002). Becoming a habitual voter: Inertia, resources, and growth in young adulthood. *American Political Science Review, 96*(1), 41–56. https://doi.org/10.1017/s0003055402004227

Simmons, J., & Lilly, B. (2010). The university and student political engagement. *PS: Political Science & Politics, 43*(2), 347–349. https://doi.org/10.1017/S1049096510000260

Verba, S., & Nie, N. H. (1987). *Participation in America: Political democracy and social equality.* University of Chicago Press.

Verba, S., Schlozman, K. L., & Brady, H. E. (1995). *Voice and equality: Civic voluntarism in American politics.* Harvard University Press.

Verba, S. and N. H. Nie. (1972). *Participation in America.* Harper and Row.

Wolfinger, R. E., & Rosenstone, S. J. (1980). *Who votes?* Yale University Press.

SECTION IV

CHARTING COURSES: CREATING CLASSROOMS THAT PREPARE STUDENTS FOR DEMOCRACY

CHAPTER 18

TEACHING AND MODELING DEMOCRACY IN THE CLASSROOM DURING POLITICAL POLARIZATION

The Amalgamation Pedagogy Project

Mark K. McBeth
Idaho State University

Donna L. Lybecker
Idaho State University

ABSTRACT

These are difficult times. Challenges such as climate change, a global pandemic and declining life expectancy confront us. Perhaps more importantly, democracy itself is under strain globally. Yet, there are also encouraging developments including reductions in poverty, increases in literacy and expansion in health care. Today's college students need tools to navigate this complex world, including an understanding of the benefits of political engagement and democracy, and a degree of optimism about the possibilities to address or solve existing problems. While there is literature on how teaching impacts civic engagement and political efficacy (see Rice and Moffett in this volume), there is a dearth of work on how pedagogy itself impacts a student's view of the world. Thus, in this chapter we examine this topic from a theoretical perspective, first suggesting that pedagogy should promote civil discourse while also exploring opposing views. Second, we contend that faculty should focus on balancing optimism and pessimism, helping students recognize today's problems, and believe in the possibility of solutions.

For those who watch the news, our world can appear bleak; we are facing many issues that challenge our capacities. Today the world faces problems but also generates possibilities at an intensity unseen for generations. On one hand, democracy itself is under strain, negative partisanship and polarization are on the rise (Abramowitz & Webster, 2018), and compromise appears limited as authoritarian populism and nationalism increase both in the United States and around the world (Repucci & Slipowitz, 2021). In addition, the devastating, extreme weather effects of climate change are regularly witnessed (IPCC, 2021), and a global pandemic brought an unprecedented healthcare crisis (Woolf et al., 2021). On the other hand, there are global increases in literacy, and expansion of healthcare (Pinker, 2018). Additionally, there is evidence that much of the Millennial and Gen Z generations support initiatives to address global issues such as climate change and reject the status-quo politics that uphold racism and inequality (Dalton, 2021).

Despite encouraging developments, problems, and their perceived immensity, are clearly a concern for college students today. Thus, as faculty we must inspire students to obtain the tools to navigate the complex world, gain the knowledge to support individual engagement through democracy, and find the desire to make a difference in the world. This is no easy task.

To address this task, we offer pedagogical techniques and strategies that promote civil discourse (McCoy & Scully, 2002) and advocate exploring opposing views with the goal of helping students develop a more nuanced understanding of society, produce stronger support for democracy and inspire students to see possibilities rather than problems. In doing so, we place ourselves within the literature on democracy in the classroom (Brookfield & Preskill, 2012; Davidson & Katopodis, 2022; Longo & Shaffer, 2019).

BACKGROUND

Democracy in the classroom literature is extensive, thus we provide only elements of this literature and how the literature influences our work. A democratic classroom encourages dialogue and listening (Longo & Shaffer,

2019) or silence (Drury, 2019), and teaches students how to engage in deliberative democracy (Barker, 2019) and collaborative action to solve public problems (Longo & Shaffer, 2019). These deliberations occur within a set of ground rules which helps students learn the substance of their discipline and how to engage in democratic practices (Davidson & Katopodis, 2022; Thomas, 2019). Utilizing these ideas allows for the development of pedagogical practices that both teach and model democracy. In an attempt to collect and sharpen this type of pedagogy practice, we created an Amalgamation Pedagogy Project (APP) that emphasizes the need to recognize combined strengths while still maintaining individual perspectives (amalgamating). In particular, the APP draws upon ideas from scholars such as Freire (2021) and bell hooks (1994) and seeks to encourage active participation, critical thinking and problem-solving to confront power structures, yet also promotes listening and a willingness to engage with individuals who hold different perspectives (Longo & Shaffer, 2019). Additionally, the APP provides students with techniques to move from pessimism toward politics and the political future, to greater optimism (McBeth, et al., 2023), where students value divergence and varying perspectives as a means to achieve an amalgamation—visibly different parts coming together to create a whole. Overall, the APP's goals include describing pedagogical techniques that promote civil discourse and advocate exploring opposing views to help students understand the complexities of society and to inspire students to see possibilities rather than problems by presenting examples where divergent ideological backgrounds worked together to find solutions. Our goal for this chapter is to determine if APP pedagogy techniques and methods help students engage in the classroom and develop a realistic optimism. We hope the APP will produce stronger support for democracy (understanding compromise can produce advantageous outcomes) by showing students that politics do not have to be dominated by the win-lose narratives and outcomes that dominate contemporary politics.

CHAPTER OVERVIEW: THE APP AND BUILDING SUPPORT FOR DEMOCRACY

As teachers of political science, we are directly confronted with the topic of democracy, and find connection to scholarship that discusses the role of education for democracy and civic participation (Freire, 2021; Longo & Schaffer, 2019; Scapp 2003). As such, and aligning with the goals of the APP, we suggest it is critical to promote civic engagement and civil discourse while also exploring opposing views (Thomas, 2019; see also Moshman in this volume), and to examine increasing political efficacy (e.g., Goldberg, et al., 2022; Moffett & Rice in this volume) and political participation (e.g., Moffett & Rice, 2015). Our interest is on specific pedagogical classroom techniques that teach and model public engagement and build support for democracy.

This chapter proceeds with an overview of the conceptual: what we have found to be effective pedagogical approaches for students. We then provide a pedagogical discussion of the developed APP techniques, showing the intersection of politics and pedagogy, and how we believe it can impact democracy—strengthening society through greater understanding of opposing views and by offering solutions to problems instead of only discussing them. Finally, we present data from two courses where these pedagogical approaches were applied. These data reveal what worked and did not work, and challenges that arose.

CONCEPTUAL: PEDAGOGICAL APPROACHES AND CHALLENGES

Reflecting on teaching practices, noting what has and has not worked during one author's more than 30 years of teaching public administration and U.S. politics, and the second author's more than 20 years of teaching international relations, comparative politics and environmental politics, we constructed three overarching pedagogical approaches. These create the foundation of the APP; clearly identified approaches that, although not uncommon, are not always acknowledged.

1. Pedagogical Approach 1: Focus on the optimistic (realistic, evidenced based and contextual solutions) along with the pessimistic (existence of problems)— don't go overboard in either direction.
2. Pedagogical Approach 2: Promote civil discourse WHILE also exploring opposing views.
3. Pedagogical Approach 3: Recognize classroom sociality (Eyler, 2018), students learn best when provided opportunities to engage and bring their own unique experiences and perspectives into the classroom.

Along with showing the three overarching pedagogical approaches, it is necessary to identify possible challenges. First, every class is composed of unique individuals who react differently to teaching approaches. Faculty need to be flexible, not solely bending to students but working with them to facilitate critical thinking and learning. Second, with generational changes in students comes changes in experiences, understanding and learning styles (Dalton, 2021). Showing students strengths and weaknesses of multiple generations can be challenging. Finally, students learn differently depending on their optimism or pessimism (Stankovska et. al., 2020) yet many variables impact optimism and pessimism (Hecht, 2013). It takes concerted effort to find a balance.

Keeping both the overarching approaches and challenges in mind, we utilized self-reflection of teaching methods and data from courses to develop the APP suggestions for pedagogical strategies and methods for teaching in these times.

PEDAGOGICAL STRATEGIES FOR TEACHING IN THESE TIMES

We identified five pedagogical strategies to help implement Pedagogical Approach one.

1. Have Students Consider the Principle Behind an Idea As Well As How the Idea Is Applied

Too often students make general statements showing cynicism about issues such as trust of democratic institutions. Faculty need to help students understand the principles behind an idea or institution and how implementation often introduces the flaws. Faculty should help students weigh the benefits of an idea against its costs, and think through possible reforms. For example, students may claim, "The U.S. jury system is rigged and should be eliminated." Although racial bias continues to be a problem in jury selection, as faculty, we need to address why there is a jury system, what the ideal would be, what a legal system would look like without a jury system and ways to reform the jury system. This progression upholds the importance of democratic principles while also recognizing problems and needed reform.

2. Provide Students With an Understanding of What Has Improved in the World and What Still Needs to Be Fixed

Using examples to push students to discuss what works and what needs to be changed opens the door for young minds to tackle today's issues. The goal is not to make students complacent, but rather to help them see that through political action and involvement problems can be addressed. For example, discussing climate change exposes students to the political and environmental complexity of such an issue. To understand the issue of climate change, students should recognize the threats due to lack of action, but also the significant environmental improvements, often achieved through policy changes, in the world over the past 50 years. Other issues like racism, sexism and homophobia could likewise be addressed showing ongoing problems but also significant advances made by politics in democratic settings throughout the world. As explained in recent articles (e.g., Baron et al., 2019), helping students develop a realistic or skeptical optimism about the world inspires a sense of empowerment.

3. Offer and Discuss Solutions, Allowing Students to Push the Envelope But Also Recognize the Reality of Limitations

Students thrive when guided to recognize change is possible (Glaeser et al., 2007), encouraging creativity but also giving structure. Helping students recognize that problems and challenges are opportunities for new directions, rather than an impasse, is important for empowerment. Students gain insights working through assignments that invite them to think innovatively about solutions while recognizing there are political, social and economic limitations that stem, in part, from pluralistic democratic systems which attempt to meet the needs of many, not just the few. For example, providing access to shelter is a clear solution to homelessness. However, communities do not have resources to build all the needed structures. Asking students to think creatively about solutions for this problem leads to suggestions such as providing 3D printed homes rather than single-family dwellings or addressing structural causes and sustainable solutions (creating a world that does not need homeless shelters). Students recognize there are solutions even within limitations.

4. Focus Both on the Positive and Negative Contributions of Politics

Too often students view politics as negative and manipulative (Webster, 2020) rather than a method for creating change. They are exposed to media sources that question the strength of U.S. democracy, rather than viewing democratic politics as a means to change the world for the better. Providing students with examples of how individuals used the democratic system to change views of gender, the environment or war can capture students' imagination and help students see the positive aspects of politics. Likewise, having students research Harvey Milk, Cesar Chavez or Greta Thunberg can challenge students to see politics changing the world for the better (while also helping them understand that these individuals have/had distractors).

5. Focus on Generational Politics and Have Positive Assumptions

Personal experiences shape individuals' views of issues, politics and democracy. Recognizing the experiences and reactions of individual generations can help identify past transitions and possible future transformations. Having students connect with their grandparents about a political issue discussed in class can highlight generational differences and help them understand past progress. Furthermore, making positive assumptions that the current generation will also make progress can help alleviate despair of current challenges. As Dalton (2021) shows, young people are increasingly engaged citizens with high expectations for government performance, including in collective action challenges. If these positive attributes are highlighted it can help students see their generation as capable of solving problems, increase political efficacy and strengthen support for democracy.

PEDAGOGICAL METHODS FOR TEACHING IN THESE TIMES

Using our combined 54 years of college teaching experience and assessing our own experiences in the classroom, in addition to consulting literature, we determined nine pedagogical methods to help implement Pedagogical Approaches two and three; to help with teaching about democracy in polarizing times. You can think of these as teaching strategies used to effectively implement the five approaches just discussed.

1. Engage in Intellectual Humility

As teachers, we need to both accept and admit that we do not have all the answers. Acknowledging this in discussions can push students to engage and suggest solutions to challenges. The political polarization throughout the world is partially caused by a lack of such humility (Bowes, et al., 2020), and democracy itself requires the ability to admit when one is wrong. Modeling this to students is important.

2. Set Up Parameters and Use Theory for Guided Discussions

As is discussed in difficult conversations literature (e.g., Connor et al, 2012) it is important to structure discussions of sensitive topics. Students come into classes with pre-existing knowledge about political issues, much of which comes from media sources, families, religious institutions, and social groups and may or may not be factual. Of course, one of democracy's shortcomings is the freedom to spread misinformation (or disinformation). Faculty can be put in the difficult situation of telling students that some information is incorrect, which can shut down learning or move a student to think that the faculty member is biased. When discussing controversial issues in class, it is necessary to have a carefully planned and executed presentation, to use political science concepts and theories, such as democracy, to guide the exploration and to be responsive when conflict arises (Barker, 2019, Drury, 2019). For students to see the world differently, structuring and guiding discussions that address multiple sides to an issue and thus pushes students to question their preconceived attitudes and beliefs, favorite news channel or social media meme, is key. As faculty, it is our role to help students think critically by providing them with theoretical and philosophical frameworks to move them beyond their prior knowledge.

3. Teach Skepticism, Not Cynicism

A skeptic questions as a means to understand evidence and find the truth, they are open to changing their mind. A cynic questions not to hear evidence but to show disagreement; cynics are disbelievers and are not likely to change their mind. Teaching students to question as a means to identify fallacy, but also to gain understanding and possibly adopt a new perspective both allows for a greater vision of possible solutions and supports democratic norms. This can be achieved by asking students to research an issue, such as the U.S. death penalty, which often divides people, and argue for the side they would not normally support. This exercise allows students to question, but also to see that legitimate points can be argued on both sides of the issue—supporting skepticism rather than cynicism. Teaching the distinction between the two is key for democracy.

4. Substantively Focus on Collaboration As Well As Competition

Political science often suggests that humans are by nature competitive. Whether it is Hobbes' (1651/1968) definition of life in a state of nature as being "solitary, nasty, brutish, and short," the prisoner's dilemma, or the fictional example of the *Lord of the Flies*, competition is central to politics. Yet, as seen with scholars of theories such as Liberalism, for example, John Locke, Hernado de Soto and Martha Craven Nussbaum, collaboration is also central to politics. Combining these, Bregman (2020) argues that we need a more realistic view of human nature, one that focuses on both competition and collaboration. One contemporary example that can be used involves the COVID-19 pandemic within the United States: it led to political conflict, however, it also led to a remarkable amount of collaboration in science, wearing masks and getting vaccinated. Once we are attuned to the idea that humans both compete and collaborate, it is easier for students to find examples of democratic collaboration as well as competition.

5. Help Students Have a High Error Tolerance and Learn From Failure

Students will fail; however, we learn from failure (Eyler, 2018; Bain, 2021). Having a high error climate, where students feel comfortable discussing, writing and thinking even if it is "wrong," along with a method for "productive failure" (Bain 2021, p. 23), where students are led to identify the strengths and weaknesses within their problem solving is key for teaching. Encouraging students to learn from failure facilitates humility and opens the door for additional learning. It also necessitates faculty investing time to understand students' perspectives and explain correct answers. For example, a student might suggest that Japanese-Americans, during World War Two, were sent to internment camps for their own protection. While this is factually untrue, there are many narratives that take this stance. Helping students understand the fallacy of this narrative and why individuals circulate such narratives helps them to trace why they believed the narrative and to critically think about other narratives. Seeing "failure" as a means to grow and learning to question narratives prepares students to recognize that beliefs (even their own) can be factually incorrect, and feel empowered to correct them—a fundamental attribute of a democratic society.

6. Engage in Sociality

Sociality is a means to connect the science behind how students learn (through interactions with others) to pedagogical methods (Eyler, 2018). It emphasizes a social classroom with all students engaging as a means to build a sense of belonging and promote collaboration and peer learning. Utilizing sociality functions as a way to model democracy, and thus reinforces the teaching of democracy. It encourages students to engage with each other and allows for greater understanding among those with divergent views, the possibility of bridging ideological spectrums. Sociality can occur through class discussion, think-pair-share and other pedagogical techniques (Davidson & Katopodis, 2023).

7. Use Narratives to Build Emotional Connections

Academia focuses on cognition, often seeing emotion as negative. Yet, increasingly, we know that emotion and cognition are linked and cannot be separated in decision making (Immordino-Yang, 2016). Too much emotion (either hate or love) can limit learning, but increasingly we understand that some emotion in the classroom is appropriate and that the use of narrative is one way to productively use emotion (Eyler, 2018). Many fields, including political science, focus on things that we care about (e.g., freedom, equality and justice), which are value laden and invoke emotion. Acknowledging this emotion within controlled interactions in the classroom can help students make lasting connections to concepts and understand why others react. This can be used to teach how concepts such as political tolerance are key for democracy. For example, starting with a narrative that shows both tolerance and intolerance, such as the story of the Black Power salute at the 1968 Olympics in Mexico City, can elicit emotional responses. The difference between post-Olympic treatment of the U.S. athletes and their competitor from Australia, often draws emotion from students. It helps connect students to the complexity of political tolerance in democratic settings.

8. Purposely Include, Acknowledge and Encourage Divergent Voices, and Create the Environment for Them to Be Heard

Pluralist democracy is based on divergent voices: differences in political ideologies, race and ethnicity, gender, sexuality, religion, geographic location and socio-economic class, among others. In order to model democracy, faculty must maintain an open yet controlled discussion (see also Moshman in this volume). Although people fear greater instability, in the classroom or in a government, with more diverging voices, diverse perspectives can provide new ideas and creative solutions for current problems. Both modeling this in the classroom and teaching the value of diversity to students are key. This can be achieved through the use of examples, such as the development of the COVID-19 vaccine—where scientists from around the world worked together to address global issues. Allowing diverse perspectives can stimulate creativity, reduce the us-versus-them mindset, and help model democracy.

9. Teach Students to Practice Empathy

The ability to put oneself in the shoes of others is an important part of democracy, and one that is often forgotten in today's politically polarized world.

Teaching and modeling empathy can be done through investigating an issue such as vaccine hesitancy in rural communities. Students see data which show rural vaccination rates are often lower than in urban centers, and the often-mocking attitudes of celebrities and others toward such vaccine hesitancy or denial. Coupling this with an explanation (e.g., Delizza 2021) focusing on rural communities' income, lack of trust of pharmaceutical companies, in part due to the opioid epidemic that ravaged rural areas, and lack of insurance and access to health care, provides a counterargument. The takeaway for students is that in a democracy we should strive to understand varied beliefs rather than ridiculing them (Thomas, 2019; Barker, 2019). We want students to be empathetic with not only their own groups but also with those they might consider outgroups (Yabar & Hess, 2007).

METHODS

To test the APP approaches, we utilized these teaching techniques and methods within two lower-division political science classes in the fall 2022: Introduction to Politics and Critical Thinking and Introduction to International Relations. We realize that more testing is needed and that there are questions of causality unaddressed but we are providing a baseline of data for future APP studies. Throughout the semester we noted when approaches engaged students and when they did not. This technique allowed us to sharpen or add to the ideas as the semester progressed, to bring us to the more completely developed techniques and methods listed above. As teachers know, this is a normal process—working to improve teaching practices as you learn more about your students.

In addition, we collected data via pre- and post-tests, measuring student-identified optimism and/or pessimism. (The survey is available upon request.) Thirty-one students participated in the Introduction to Politics pre-test and 25 of those students participated in the post-test. Twenty-two students participated in the Introduction to International Relations pre-test and 21 of those students participated in the post-test. Our research protocol was ruled exempt by the university's Human Subjects Committee.

Overall, our goal was to determine if APP pedagogy techniques and methods helped students engage in the classroom and develop a realistic optimism, which we hope will ultimately push students to engage in their community.

SURVEY DATA

The following provides an overview of data from the surveys, which largely focused on students' perceptions of optimism and/or pessimism concerning politics, their generation and the future. In response to a general question concerning politics, the post-test shows more students, in both courses, saw politics as positive by semester's end (see Table 18.1).

The number of students in the post-test who said politics was positive, increased by 16 percentage points for those in Introduction to Politics, and 25 percentage points in Introduction to International Relations. Furthermore, both courses concluded with the majority of students viewing politics as positive.

In looking at students' optimism toward specific issues, the results vary between the two courses. For Introduction to Politics, the percentage of students who were optimistic about the issues increased in all cases; this was not the case for Introduction to International Relations (see Table 18.2).

TABLE 18.1 Positive Politics

	Introduction to Politics Students		Introduction to International Relations Students	
	Pre-test	Post-test	Pre-test	Post-test
Students responding politics are positive	16/31 (52%)	17/25 (68%)	7/21 (33%)	11/19 (58%)

Note: For all tables, the data were collected using a five-point Likert scale but collapsed for presentation purposes. For Table 18.1, the number of students saying that politics is positive is first, followed by the number of students answering the question. The percentage is the percent of students saying that politics is positive. The survey question was: "Some people view politics as something negative (it is corrupt and manipulative) whereas others view politics as something more positive (it is how the world changes for the better)."

TABLE 18.2 Student Optimism

	Introduction to Politics Students		Introduction to International Relations Students	
	Pre-test	Post-test	Pre-test	Post-test
Racial equality	20/32 (63%)	17/25 (68%)	18/22 (82%)	14/21 (67%)
Gender equality	22/32 (69%)	21/25 (84%)	19/22 (86%)	16/21 (76%)
Economic equality	12/32 (38%)	10/25 (40%)	9/22 (41%)	2/21 (10%)
Sexuality equality	18/32 (56%)	16/25 (64%)	12/22 (55%)	8/21 (38%)
Climate change	4/32 (13%)	6/25 (24%)	8/20 (40%)	4/21 (19%)
Democracy	10/31 (32%)	13/25 (52%)	7/22 (32%)	9/21 (43%)
Access to health care	11/32 (34%)	9/25 (36%)	4/22 (18%)	3/21 (14%)
Affordable public higher ed	10/32 (31%)	12/25 (48%)	3/22 (14%)	5/21 (24%)
Economic prosperity	11/32 (34%)	11/24 (46%)	2/22 (9%)	2/21 (10%)

Note: The survey question read: "Generally, when you look to the future, how pessimistic or optimistic are you about the following issues:"

Table 18.2 shows shifts in the percentage of students, in both courses, reporting optimism toward specific issues. A majority of students in both courses started the semester with a positive opinion of issues of social equality (versus economic equality) while a much lower percentage had a positive outlook on climate change, democracy and economic issues. However, post-test results show the percentage of students in Introduction to Politics reporting optimism toward these issues increased in all cases. On the other hand, the percentage of students in Introduction to International Relations reporting optimism for these issues dropped in all cases except democracy, affordable public higher education, and economic prosperity.

We also explored the larger question of optimism. Table 18.3 shows the percentage of students who expected/experienced optimism from their course and toward their generation.

In Table 18.3, in Introduction to Politics, the course (compared to what the students expected) made the students slightly more optimistic, and delivered the expected level of what is right (advances in literacy, health care access, social equity...) and wrong (racism, poverty, climate destruction....) with the world. There was a larger jump between the expectation the course would make students more hopeful and the final percentage who believed the course made them more hopeful. Finally, the students were optimistic about their generation and their ability to solve the world's problems. In Introduction to International Relations, fewer students at semester's end reported the course made them more optimistic compared to what they expected. There was a slight increase in the percent of the students at the course's end who

TABLE 18.3   Outcomes of the Course

Question	Introduction to Politics Students Pre-test	Introduction to Politics Students Post-test	Introduction to International Relations Students Pre-test	Introduction to International Relations Students Post-test
The course will/did make you more optimistic	26/32 (81%)	21/25 (84%)	17/22 (77%)	10/21 (48%)
Course expectations/ What the course delivered (what is "right" and "wrong" with the world)	30/32 (94%)	24/25 (96%)	21/22 (95%)	20/21 (95%)
Impact of Course, Hopeful	10/21 (48%)	16/25 (64%)	8/22 (36%)	11/21 (52%)
Optimism about your generation	17/32 (53%)	19/25 (76%)	10/22 (45%)	10/20 (50%)

Note: The first number is the number of students answering the question in the way the choice is presented. The second number is the total number of students answering the question. The percentage is the percentage of students answering the question presented as the choice is presented.

said the course delivered "what is wrong and wrong with the world." There was a substantial increase in the belief the course made them more hopeful (compared to expectations at the beginning of the class).

Overall, the survey findings indicate students became more optimistic over the semester, yet their optimism was qualified as they wanted to understand what is working in the world and what needs to be improved. It was also clear there was substantial variation in students' levels of optimism. Today's students need to find a realistic optimism to see opportunities and feel empowered to take action (Baron et al, 2019), but also recognize that challenges exist, and that what some see as an opportunity, others may see as a challenge. Taking account of divergent perspectives such as opportunities versus challenges, acknowledging divergent voices, is key to both strengthening the tenets of democracy and finding solutions. This is amalgamation teaching.

From the results of our class analyses, we believe the APP pedagogical techniques promoted civil discourse and facilitated students' exploration of opposing views, developing a more nuanced understanding of society and inspired students to see possibilities rather than problems. Thus, we believe APP pedagogy techniques and methods encourage student engagement in the classroom and the development of a realistic optimism. We realize that pedagogical challenges differ depending on the class topic, issues addressed and student composition, and that there are benefits and drawbacks to all choices. Yet recognizing the array of strategies and methods available will improve pedagogical practices and, hopefully, student advancement in learning and life.

CONCLUSION

Through identifying shared pedagogical practices, and our views of education, we found key strategies and methods to teaching and modeling democracy. Utilizing these APP techniques has allowed for productive relationships with and among students who are ideologically, economically, socially and generationally diverse. Our APP research contends that faculty should focus on balancing optimism and pessimism to help students develop a more nuanced understanding of society, produce stronger support for democracy (understanding compromise can produce advantageous outcomes) and inspire students to see possibilities rather than problems, and that pedagogy should promote civil discourse and sociality while exploring opposing views. Our study challenges faculty to consciously choose how they teach, consider why they teach, and be purposeful about the outcomes they hope to achieve. Higher education has a role to play in rebuilding democracy and part of that role involves pedagogy. We hope these techniques and methods add to a larger conversation.

REFERENCES

Abramowitz, A. I., & Webster, S. W. (2018). Negative partisanship: Why Americans dislike parties but behave like rabid partisans. *Political Psychology, 39,* 119–135.

Bain, K. (2021). *Super courses: The future of teaching and learning.* Princeton University Press.

Baron, H., Blair, R. A., & Grossman, S. (2019) Teaching Trump: Why comparative politics makes students more optimistic about US democracy. *Political Science & Politics, 52*(2), 347–352.

Barker, D. W. M. (2019). Deliberative civic engagement: Toward a public politics in higher education. In N. V. Longo & J. Shaffer (Eds.) *Creating space for democracy: a primer on dialogue and deliberation in higher education* (pp. 57–68). Stylus Publishing.

Bowes, S. M., Blanchard, M. C., Costello, T. H., Abramowitz, A. I., & Lilienfeld, S. O. (2020). Intellectual humility and between-party animus: Implications for affective polarization in two community samples. *Journal of Research in Personality, 88,* 103992.

Bregman, R. (2020). *Humankind: A hopeful history.* Bloomsbury Publishing.

Brookfield, S. D., & Preskill, S. (2012). *Discussion as a way of teaching: Tools and techniques for democratic classrooms.* John Wiley & Sons.

Connor, J. M., & Killian, D. (2012). *Connecting across differences: Finding common ground with anyone, anywhere, anytime* (2nd ed.). PuddleDance Press.

Dalton, R. J. (2021). *The good citizen: How a younger generation is reshaping American politics.* CQ Press.

Davidson, C. N., & Katopodis, C. (2022). *The new college classroom.* Harvard University Press.

Delizza, T. (2021, July 9). What the media gets wrong about red state vaccine hesitancy. *Salon.* https://www.salon.com/2021/07/09/what-the-media-gets-wrong-about-red-state-vaccine-hesitancy_partner/

Drury, S. A. M. (2019). Cultivating dialogue and deliberation through speech, silence, and synthesis. In N. V. Longo & J. Shaffer (Eds.), *Creating space for democracy: A primer on dialogue and deliberation in higher education* (pp. 69–82). Stylus Publishing.

Eyler, J. (2018). *How humans learn: The science and stories behind effective college teaching.* West Virginia University Press.

Freire, P. (2021). *Pedagogy of hope: Reliving pedagogy of the oppressed.* Bloomsbury Publishing.

Gans, J. (2023, March 31). Majority of Americans don't think college degree is worth the cost: Poll. *The Hill.* https://thehill.com/blogs/blog-briefing-room/3928015-majority-of-americans-dont-think-college-degree-is-worth-cost-poll/

Glaeser, E. L., Ponzetto, G. A. M., & Shleifer, A. (2007). Why does democracy need education? *Journal of Economic Growth, 12,* 77–99. https://doi.org/10.1007/s10887-007-9015-1

Goldberg, A., Pastor, D. A., & Whaley, C. O. (2022). Let's get political: Co-creating and assessing civic learning and engagement. *PS: Political Science & Politics, 55*(2), 398–400. https://doi.org/10.1093/oxfordhb/9780199604456.013.0029.

Hecht, D. (2013). The neural basis of optimism and pessimism. *Experimental Neurobiology, 22*(3),173–199. https://doi.org/ 10.5607/en.2013.22.3.173

Hobbes, T. (1651/1968). *Leviathan.* Penguin Books.

hooks, b. (1994). *Teaching to transgress.* Routledge.

Immordino-Yang, M. H. (2016). *Emotions, learning, and the brain: exploring the educational implications of affective neuroscience.* Norton.

IPCC. (2021). *Climate change 2021: The physical science basis. Contribution of working group I to the sixth assessment report of the intergovernmental panel on climate change* [Masson-Delmotte, V., P. Zhai, A. Pirani, S. L. Connors, C. Péan, S. Berger, N. Caud, Y. Chen, L. Goldfarb, M. I. Gomis, M. Huang, K. Leitzell, E. Lonnoy, J. Matthews, B.R., Maycock, T.K., Waterfield, T., Yelekçi, O., Yu R., & Zhou, B. (Eds.). Cambridge University Press.

Longo, N. V., & Shaffer, J. (2019). Discussing democracy: learning to talk together. In N. V. Longo & J. Shaffer (Eds.), *Creating space for democracy: A primer on dialogue and deliberation in higher education* (pp. 13–40). Stylus Publishing.

McBeth, M. K., Blakeman, J. W. L., Tyler, A. C., Kearsley, L. K., & Villanueva, E. E. (2023). Teaching generation z students about politics: optimism or pessimism? *International Journal for the Scholarship of Teaching and Learning, 17*(1), 1–9. https://doi.org/10.20429/ijsotl.2023.17105

McCoy, M. L., & Scully, P. L. (2002). Deliberative dialogue to expand civic engagement: What kind of talk does democracy need? *National Civic Review, 91*(2), 117–135.

Moffett, K. W., & Rice, L. L. (2015). Taking college-level political science courses and civic activity. In S. M. Chod, W. J. Muck, & S. M. Caliendo (Eds.), *Technology and civic engagement in the college classroom* (pp. 13–47). Palgrave Macmillan. https://doi.org/10.1007/978-1-137-50451-7_2

Pinker, S. (2018). *Enlightenment now: The case for reason, science, humanism, and progress.* Penguin.

Repucci, S., & Slipowitz, A. (2021). Democracy under siege. *Freedom house.* Retrieved August 15, 2021, from https://freedomhouse.org/sites/default/files/2021-02/FIW2021_World_02252021_FINAL-web-upload.pdf

Scapp, R. (2003). *Teaching values.* Routledge.

Stankovska, G., Braha, R., & Pandiloska Grncharovsa, S. (2020). Relationship between optimism–pessimism, learning and teaching style among medical students. *Educational Reforms Worldview,* Bulgarian Comparative Education Society, Conference Books, 18. (Online June 2020). https://eric.ed.gov/?id=ED608401

Thomas, N. (2019). Readiness for discussing democracy in supercharged political times. In N. V. Longo & J. Shaffer (Eds.), *Creating space for democracy: a primer on dialogue and deliberation in higher education* (pp. 41–56). Stylus Publishing.

Webster, S. (2020). *American rage.* Cambridge University Press.

Woolf, S. H., Masters, R. K., & Aron, L. Y. (2021). Effect of the covid-19 pandemic in 2020 on life expectancy across populations in the USA and other high income countries: simulations of provisional mortality data. *BMJ (Clinical research ed.), 373,* n1343. https://doi.org/10.1136/bmj.n1343

Yabar, Y., & Hess, U. (2007). Display of empathy and perception of out-group members. *New Zealand Journal of Psychology, 36*(1), 42–49.

CHAPTER 19

MOVING FAST WITHOUT BREAKING DEMOCRACY

Computer Science Education for a Just Future

Julie M. Smith
University of North Texas

ABSTRACT

Mark Zuckerburg famously said that one of Facebook's core values was moving fast, which necessitated breaking things. But what if one of the broken things is democracy? (See Runciman, 2018). Facebook has been implicated in anti-democratic activities, but the problems of democracy-breaking algorithms extend far beyond Facebook to virtually every corner of modern technology, from facial recognition software used to suppress political dissent to Google searches that sexualize young women from minoritized groups. As an ever-increasing number of students learn computer science concepts, it is important to explore what they are—and are not—learning about responsible computing. This paper considers the status quo of undergraduate computer science education in relation to democratic norms; it also explores alternative approaches to teaching future computer scientists about their professional responsibilities. Finally, it suggests a framework of best practices for the development of responsible computing.

In recent years, public discourse has frequently focused on many moral and ethical issues related to technology: should police be required to wear body cameras? Is excessive social media use harmful to adolescent girls? Should TikTok be banned for reasons of national security? Ironically, the one venue where such issues are unlikely to be discussed is in the classrooms where students are taught to design these technologies: many college-level computer science courses are not equipping students to consider the social and political issues related to emerging technologies.

This chapter will sketch some of the ways in which emerging technologies challenge visions of a just world. Then, it will explore the current state of instruction in computer science courses as well as emerging and alternative approaches to such instruction. It will conclude with a framework for best practices for preparing future computer scientists to work toward a just future. It is hoped that these suggestions would be applicable in other domains as well.

The term *responsible computing* will be used herein to include concepts such as ethics, a concern for social justice, civic engagement, accessibility, environmental impact and so on. Similarly, those who use the artifacts that computer scientists produce will be referred to as *consumers* (not the more common appellation *users*) to emphasize that they should occupy the same social position as consumers of other products, such as food or medicine.

THE STATUS QUO: TROUBLED TECH

This section explores five instances where emerging computing technologies have led to disastrous outcomes, emphasizing the contribution of the culture and priorities of computing to each situation.

First, the chair of the U.N. Independent International Fact-Finding Mission on Myanmar concluded that Facebook had the "determining role" in the Rohingya genocide (Miles, 2018), via its spread of Islamophobic sentiment and other disinformation. Facebook—like most online platforms—prioritizes consumer engagement over other metrics, and extremism that arouses intense emotions of disgust, hatred and fear is quite engaging (Berger & Milkman, 2012).

Second, the data consulting firm Cambridge Analytica, which has been accused of enabling Russian election interference in the US, has also been implicated in inappropriate involvement in elections in Kenya, India, Australia, Mexico and the Philippines. The firm gathered extensive data on Facebook's consumers and their friends in a manner that was permitted by

Facebook at the time (Granville, 2018). While Facebook has since banned the firm's approach to data gathering, the incident serves as an example of the problems implicit with novel platforms that permit the gathering of vast quantities of personal data and also permit that data to be used in unexpected ways. It may even be the case that political parties and factions are morphing into groups manufactured by technology instead of groups developed based on shared interests (Zack, 2016). Computer science does not have a tradition of thinking deeply about potential uses of its platforms and products; rather, the atomized nature of modern programming (Rentsch, 1982)—where developers often work in large teams but are largely concerned with one small portion of functionality, with little knowledge of or concern about what others are doing or what properties and possibilities might emerge from their team's combined effort.

Third, in the United States, about two-thirds of the population receives—or is denied access to—health care on the basis of decisions made by commercial risk assessment software. A study of one of these tools found that it systematically discriminated against Black patients to the extent that shifting to an unbiased algorithm would result in a change in the rate of additional care offered to Black patients from under 20% to over 45% (Obermeyer et al., 2019). The disparity stems from the fact that the software uses future health care costs as a proxy for future health care needs. Of course, given the unequal access to healthcare in the US as well as historical biases against Black patients, projected future costs of their health care are not in fact a good proxy for their future need for health care (LaVeist et al., 2023). This situation suggests two problems in the practice of computing: the uncritical use of data sets that include historical biases and the use of not-entirely-accurate variables to make decisions.

Fourth, Amazon developed an automated tool that would assess resumes, but it showed a systematic preference for male job applicants (Dastin, 2018). Why? Because it deduced the characteristics of successful applicants based on Amazon's previous hiring data. The problem was caused by reliance on machine learning techniques, where the software 'learns' to make decisions by creating a system that weighs various factors—a system that is inaccessible to humans. The recent boom in machine learning applications suggests a willingness on the part of computer scientists to embrace decision-making approaches that are not reviewable by human auditors.

Fifth, the introduction in 2022 of publicly accessible tools capable of generating realistic text has galvanized a race for control of the AI industry. While these chatbots are capable of plausibly answering almost any question, some of their responses are wildly inaccurate. For example, they have created citations to academic research that does not exist in response to prompts for references. Even though they knew that the chatbots were sometimes inaccurate, Google, Microsoft, and OpenAI released them anyway, and within months over 100 million people were using them. The willingness to rush out a product with known flaws stems from a common attitude in computing circles, encapsulated by a comment in an email from a Microsoft executive regarding its chatbot that it is an "absolutely fatal error in this moment to worry about things that can be fixed later" (Grant & Weise, 2023). This approach would be anathema in other industries planning the launch of consumer products, but it is common in computing, where the idea of releasing a 'minimum viable product' and then improving it based on consumer feedback is a core tenet of modern approaches to software design. In a matter of months, these chatbots have been accused of encouraging suicide (Sellman, 2023) and spreading conspiracy theories (Hsu & Thompson, 2023).

The incidents described in this section show how attitudes and beliefs common among computer scientists seed the ground for vexing social and political problems. They indicate the ways in which the training of computer scientists has neglected inculcating a concern for a just world or preparing students for the unique requirements of civic engagement that their profession will demand. Specifically, social media tools that are designed to maximize engagement can also lead to social discord, health care decisions based on historical data extend the biases in that data and an attitude privileging being first to market is willing to accept faulty tools with the potential for large real-world impacts.

THE STATE OF COMPUTER SCIENCE EDUCATION

There is wide variety in whether and how the social dimensions of computing are taught to computer science students, but the overall picture is one where a variety of barriers conspire to limit the attention paid to any non-technical topics, such as ethics, in computer science classrooms. Smith et al. (2023) identified many barriers to incorporating instruction in ethics based on a survey of instructors, including a sense of inadequacy to discuss the topics, a higher priority placed on other topics, a sense that the course content is unrelated to ethics, a lack of control over curriculum, a lack of time and motivation and a concern that ethics would detract from a course's technical content. Thus, it is not surprising that there is limited discussion about social concerns related to computing in higher education (Lin, 2022). The current political situation, where some states are limiting tenure protections (Brown, 2023) and underfunding higher education (Hartocollis, 2023), also contributes to some instructors' unwillingness to introduce topics with social and ethical dimensions (see also Lassabe Shepherd and Kraemer-Holland in this volume).

Several other challenges distinct to computer science as a discipline augment the factors identified above: there is a need to scale instruction given rapidly rising enrollment (Shapiro et al., 2021), but at the same time, it is difficult to attract instructors given the disparity between academic and industry salaries for those with advanced computing skills. One strategy to manage burgeoning enrollment is to automate grading, but this likely cannot be done for assignments related to the social implications of computing. Further, course content and tools change more rapidly in computing than most other disciplines, necessitating more attention to course (re) development. Failure rates in computer science are already relatively high, pressuring instructors to focus their attention on improving instruction on core content. And students, who are often career-focused and drawn by the promise of high salaries at high tech companies, can be resistant to devoting time to what they perceive to be extraneous concerns.

The result of these barriers and challenges is that the social responsibilities of computer scientists are not widely taught: an analysis of syllabi from university-level technology ethics courses found that the most common topic was law and regulation, that just over half of syllabi mention issues of justice and inequality, and that civic responsibility is included in fewer than one-third of courses (Fiesler et al., 2020). The focus on law and regulation is concerning: ethical requirements and legal requirements are not the same; for example, the 2008 banking crisis was rooted in predatory loans that, while usually legal, were not ethical—and ultimately led to widespread economic devastation. But courses may skew toward legal issues because they appear to be more objective, less controversial, and easier to assess (Baumer et al., 2022). And while some critics may argue that students should be receiving instruction in ethics from their general education classes, there are issues that are specific to computing technology and/or have technical aspects, thus making them more appropriate to computing courses. Further, the elimination of ethical considerations from computing courses advances a hidden curriculum that ethics are not relevant to computing courses.

Empirical evidence suggests that the lack of attention to the social and political implications of technology has a strong impact on computer science students: one research team has found that, while students in most majors are more committed to global citizenship as their college career progresses, computer science majors were *less* committed, and to a degree greater than that of students in any other major (Núñez et al., 2021). While extant research does not explain *why* this is the case, it may be that instruction focused on technical topics leaves students with the impression that those technical topics are all that matter. In the context of the power that computer science majors are likely to wield professionally as designers of the next generation of technology products, this lack of concern for responsible computing is especially worrisome.

ALTERNATIVE APPROACHES TO JUSTICE IN COMPUTER SCIENCE EDUCATION

And yet despite the pervasive lacunae outlined above, there is a growing movement to improve the teaching and learning of social responsibility in computer science. In fact, interest in the topic appears to be increasing dramatically: the newly proposed version of computer science curriculum guidelines by the Association for Computing Machinery devote nearly twice the amount of time to ethics as the previous iteration. Fiesler et al. (2020) found that almost a fourth of the references to 'ethics' in the publications of the Special Interest Group on Computer Science Education of the Association for Computing Machinery (SIGCSE), which is the main association for computer science education research, were published in just the last few years. For example, one research article (Shapiro et al., 2021) described an intervention where students were asked to engage in a role play as various stakeholders—such as a disability advocate, city planner, and union leader—in addition to the more typical technical roles such as a cybersecurity expert or a computer vision expert. Another intervention relied on a repository of lesson modules that use narratives, including recent news articles, podcast episodes, and popular movies, as springboards to ethical discussions (Bullock et al., 2021).

There is growing interest in the idea of embedded ethics, or interweaving themes of social responsibility into the traditional computer science courses, as opposed to requiring students to take a stand-alone course in ethics or professional responsibility. This approach has the advantage of making clear to students that social concerns are intimately related to technical concerns; it avoids the 'hidden curriculum' which tacitly implies that ethics is separate from their technical work that can be assumed when ethical concepts are taught separately from technical concepts. In other words, if their training doesn't integrate ethics into technical work, then it is likely that, when they are practitioners, students won't integrate ethics into technical work either; the hidden curriculum must be aligned with the goal of a tech workforce trained in responsible computing. A focal point for this work is Stanford University, where an embedded ethics program seeks to help instructors incorporate ethics into the core undergraduate computer science curriculum. Its learning goals are to enable students to identify ethical issues, reason through these issues, communicate about them and design responsible technologies; curricular modules that combine technical topics with their social implications are publicly available (see embeddedethics.stanford.edu). For example, in an assignment for an artificial intelligence, the student is asked to implement a sentiment classifier that could be used for online reviews; in the ethical portion, students grapple with the fact that the techniques used in classification can be biased against minoritized groups (*Sentiment classification and maximum group loss*, n.d.). The program is quite new, but preliminary evidence suggests that it holds promise for mitigating some of the concerns (e.g., lack of expertise) that inhibit ethics instruction (Grosz et al., 2019).

Another emerging trend is the use of interdisciplinary approaches (Lin, 2022) to responsible computing. For example, a philosopher holding a post-doctorate role might introduce an ethics framework to a computer science course, and the students would then complete an assignment where their software design would be informed by the framework. Or, a standing requirement for one ethics course and one computing course could be changed to require one six-hour course, co-taught by one instructor from the humanities and one from computing; this approach would address the problem that computer science instructors often feel unprepared to teach social issues while at the same time allowing integrated instruction in technical and social issues.

FRAMEWORK FOR BEST PRACTICES

I conclude with five suggestions for framing the implementation of responsible computing (see Table 19.1).

First, instructors should explicitly and implicitly convey that every technology encodes a value system. Note that this position runs counter to the common sentiment that a technology is neutral until its consumer makes decisions about its use. But all technology involves design decisions, all design decisions require choices, and all choices reflect values. Those values might be unexamined or they might be carefully considered, but they always underpin choices. Thus, there is no such thing as value-free technology. As discussed previously, many social media platforms use algorithms that provide their consumers with content designed to maximize engagement. This might initially appear to be—and is often considered to be—value-free

TABLE 19.1 Best Practices for Teaching Responsible Computing

1. Teach that there is no value-free or value-neutral technology.
2. Critically examine habits of mind such as encapsulation.
3. Teach that there is no bright line between social and technical issues.
4. Focus on the concept of responsible computing.
5. Leverage computing concepts such as edge cases.

design in that the algorithm is not, for example, designed to promote liberal or conservative perspectives on a hot-button political issue. But engagement-maximizing algorithms, such as those used by YouTube, often provide increasingly radical content (Reviglio & Agosti, 2020). Thus, what seemed to be a value-neutral decision in fact reflected the value that radicalizing consumers is acceptable, despite the consequences to society.

Computer science curricula can help students understand that every technology has a value system. Not only is this an important first step to the analysis and evaluation of those value systems, but it also provides a gentle on-ramp to instructors who may, for a variety of reasons, be hesitant to incorporate responsible computing in their classrooms: they can begin with simply identifying values encoded in systems. Similarly, courses can be redesigned to more explicitly consider the values of the technology that are explored. For example, computer science majors generally take a course on the design and analysis of algorithms, where they learn how to design algorithms that work quickly and require reasonable amounts of memory. These courses normally do not engage in any sort of non-technical analysis of algorithms, such as whether the algorithm reifies extant patterns of discrimination against women or against people of color. In other words, they can unintentionally, implicitly convey the value that the only kind of analysis of algorithms that counts is their speed and memory usage, not their differential impact on human beings.

Second, several habits of mind common to computer scientists need to be critically examined. The problem isn't just that responsible computing is ignored in many computer science courses; the problem is that some of the thinking patterns common to the discipline are applied in ways that actively encourage irresponsible computing, as the instances of troubled technologies presented at the beginning of this paper illustrated. These habits of mind are often discussed under the umbrella of computational thinking, which is a set of approaches to a problem that are commonly used by computer scientists. For example, encapsulation allows a computer program to output the date by using a command to retrieve the current date. The programmer likely does not know—and does not need to know—how precisely the command actually determines what the current date is. Encapsulation is an important building block in computing since without it, a programmer would be buried under an avalanche of complex details. But encapsulation also inculcates the habit of mind that the programmer need not be concerned with *any* aspects of a program's functionality other than their own narrow task, a problem discussed above in the context of Facebook's interaction with Cambridge Analytica. In contrast, responsible computing requires computer scientists to think carefully about the social implications of not just their own small portion of a project but also of the impact of the project as a whole (Smith, 2021). Similarly, abstraction allows computer scientists to enhance program usability by abstracting away certain details, such as in an inventory management program that has the ability to store data about any kind of soda, regardless of its manufacturer. But the decision to bracket information from a program is inherently value-laden since someone must decide what data is or is not relevant to the task at hand (Malazita & Resetar, 2019). Consider software designed to recommend sentencing guidelines for those convicted of crimes: should exculpatory information about, for example, childhood trauma be considered or be abstracted away? Should incriminating information about the history of disciplinary action in middle school be included?

Third, curriculum should be rooted in the idea that there is, ultimately, no division between social and technical issues in the sense that both fall under the umbrella of responsible computing. By analogy, architects and engineers do not consider building safety to be a tangential, non-technical concern; rather, they see it as a completely integrated component essential to their design work. Similarly, software developers should view the safety—both physical and social—of their products not as a separate issue from its technical merit but rather as a component of responsible design on at least equal footing with other concerns. Computer science should be fundamentally understood not as a technical field but rather as a field tasked with the responsible development of new technologies—with responsibility defined to include not only the traditional factors such as speed, reliability and functionality but also of factors such as the consumer's safety.

Problematic habits of mind can also be evidenced on pedagogical and systemic levels. For example, advanced math is normally a prerequisite for computer science majors, but a sociology course is not. The implication of this design choice is that computer scientists need advanced math to be successful practitioners, but they do not need to understand sociology. This is a difficult position to justify when they are likely to design products with rapid and massive impacts on society. Similar arguments could be made about understanding history (especially of minoritized persons), government, psychology and other disciplines.

In short, computer science has traditionally been viewed as a discipline located on technical ground with students who might take occasional trips into non-technical fields to better understand topics such as ethics. But instead of planning more field trips, we could think of computer science as situated on ground neither technical nor social but responsible.

Fourth, the frame of 'responsible computing' should be leveraged in several ways. One is to de-emphasize high salaries as a motivation for students to study computer science—a view that can lead implicitly to the attitude that the goal of computing is making money for the individual or for big tech companies (Lin, 2022). In contrast, Vogel et al. (2017) articulate six other motivations for encouraging the study of computing: advancing justice, gaining competence, enabling active citizenship, encouraging innovation, improving schools and personal fulfillment. Another way to leverage the concept is to view it as far more than a synonym for ethics; it might include (as outlined previously) application of concepts from sociology and a concern with accessibility. It also suggests that students of computing need to develop skills such as the ability to explain their work in a non-technical way to general audiences.

Fifth and finally, discussing responsible computing using terminology and concepts already common to computing will smooth the path for both instructors and students. For example, computer scientists are used to considering edge cases—unusual or atypical situations that might cause a program to malfunction, such as input that causes a program to attempt to divide a number by zero. The concept of edge cases lends itself to include social issues of marginalized or minoritized persons, such as individuals with names containing characters not common in the United States, who often struggle to complete online forms without generating error messages. Similarly, so-called bug bounties are sometimes offered in industry or in classrooms, rewarding those who identify an error in a program. Instructors might offer their students bug bounties for identifying errors related to program performance and the practice of responsible computing, such as identifying software that does not function well with the screen readers commonly used by people with low vision. Or, test cases—scenarios designed to assess a program's functionality—could be intentionally expanded to include cases of individuals from diverse backgrounds to avoid problems such as the inequitable decisions about patient care mentioned previously. Computer science students are used to the language of design requirements and of optimizing a program within given constraints; adopting this language while expanding it to include social concerns creates a bridge from the status quo to responsible computing.

CONCLUSION

Baumer et al. describe the "default position of indifference [to ethics] prevalent in the tech community" (2022). There is an urgent imperative to change this dynamic in a world where the reach of computation—from driverless cars to chatbot therapists—is ever expanding. That change can begin by changing the culture, pedagogy, and content of computer science courses to ensure that future practitioners understand that they have a responsibility to use their skills to create a more just world.

REFERENCES

Baumer, B. S., Garcia, R. L., Kim, A. Y., Kinnaird, K. M., & Ott, M. Q. (2022). Integrating data science ethics into an undergraduate major: A case study. *Journal of Statistics and Data Science Education, 30*(1), 15–28.

Berger, J., & Milkman, K. L. (2012). What makes online content viral? *Journal of Marketing Research, 49*(2), 192–205.

Brown, D. J. (2023, March 29). *FL university system imposes 5-year tenure review; profs, other advocates criticize the change.* Florida Phoenix. https://floridaphoenix.com/2023/03/29/fl-university-system-imposes-5-year-tenure-review-profs-other-advocates-criticize-the-change/

Bullock, B. B., Nascimento, F. L., & Doore, S. A. (2021, March). Computing ethics narratives: Teaching computing ethics and the impact of predictive algorithms. In *Proceedings of the 52nd ACM Technical Symposium on Computer Science Education* (pp. 1020–1026).

Dastin, J. (2018, October 10). Amazon scraps secret AI recruiting tool that showed bias against women. *Reuters.* https://www.reuters.com/article/us-amazon-com-jobs-automation-insight/amazon-scraps-secret-ai-recruiting-tool-that-showed-bias-against-women-idUSKCN1MK08G

Fiesler, C., Garrett, N., & Beard, N. (2020, February). What do we teach when we teach tech ethics? A syllabi analysis. In *Proceedings of the 51st ACM technical symposium on computer science education* (pp. 289–295).

Grant, N., & Weise, K. (2023, April 10). In A.I. race, Microsoft and Google choose speed over caution. *The New York Times.* https://www.nytimes.com/2023/04/07/technology/ai-chatbots-google-microsoft.html

Granville, K. (2018, May 14). Facebook and Cambridge Analytica: What you need to know as fallout widens. *The New York Times.* https://www.nytimes.com/2018/03/19/technology/facebook-cambridge-analytica-explained.html

Grosz, B. J., Grant, D. G., Vredenburgh, K., Behrends, J., Hu, L., Simmons, A., & Waldo, J. (2019). Embedded EthiCS: Integrating ethics across CS education. *Communications of the ACM, 62*(8), 54–61.

Hartocollis, A. (2023, August 18). *Slashing its budget, West Virginia University asks, what is essential?* The New York Times. https://www.nytimes.com/2023/08/18/us/west-virginia-university-budget-cuts-deficit.html

Hsu, T., & Thompson, S. A. (2023, February 13). Disinformation researchers raise alarms about A.I. chatbots. *The New York Times.* https://www.nytimes.com/2023/02/08/technology/ai-chatbots-disinformation.html

LaVeist, T. A., Pérez-Stable, E. J., Richard, P., Anderson, A., Isaac, L. A., Santiago, R., ... & Gaskin, D. J. (2023). The economic burden of racial, ethnic, and educational health inequities in the US. *JAMA, 329*(19), 1682–1692.

Lin, K. (2022, February). CS education for the socially-just worlds we need: The case for justice-centered approaches to CS in higher education. In *Proceedings of the 53rd ACM Technical Symposium on Computer Science Education V. 1* (pp. 265–271).

Malazita, J. W., & Resetar, K. (2019). Infrastructures of abstraction: how computer science education produces anti-political subjects. *Digital Creativity, 30*(4), 300–312.

Miles, T. (2018, March 12). U.N. investigators cite Facebook role in Myanmar crisis. *U.S.* https://www.reuters.com/article/us-myanmar-rohingya-facebook-id UKKCN1GO2PN

Núñez, A., Mayhew, M., Shaheen, M., & Dahl, L. (2021, March 15). Let's teach computer science majors to be good citizens. The whole world depends on it. *EdSurge.* https://www.edsurge.com/news/2021-03-15-let-s-teach-computer-science-majors-to-be-good-citizens-the-whole-world-depends-on-it

Obermeyer, Z., Powers, B., Vogeli, C., & Mullainathan, S. (2019). Dissecting racial bias in an algorithm used to manage the health of populations. *Science, 366*(6464), 447–453.

Rentsch, T. (1982). Object oriented programming. *ACM Sigplan Notices, 17*(9), 51–57.

Reviglio, U., & Agosti, C. (2020). Thinking outside the black-box: The case for "algorithmic sovereignty" in social media. *Social Media+ Society, 6*(2), 2056 305120915613.

Runciman, D. (2018). *How democracy ends.* Profile Books.

Sellman, M. (2023, March 31). AI chatbot blamed for Belgian man's suicide. *The Times.* https://www.thetimes.co.uk/article/ai-chatbot-blamed-for-belgian-mans-suicide-zcjzlztcc

Shapiro, B. R., Lovegall, E., Meng, A., Borenstein, J., & Zegura, E. (2021, March). Using role-play to scale the integration of ethics across the computer science curriculum. In *Proceedings of the 52nd ACM Technical Symposium on Computer Science Education* (pp. 1034–1040).

Sentiment classification and maximum group loss. (n.d.). Stanford Embedded Ethics. https://embeddedethics.stanford.edu/assignment/sentiment-classification

Smith, J. M. (2021). Is computational thinking critical thinking?. In *Expanding Global Horizons Through Technology Enhanced Language Learning* (pp. 191–201). Springer Singapore.

Smith, J. J., Payne, B. H., Klassen, S., Doyle, D. T., & Fiesler, C. (2023, March). Incorporating ethics in computing courses: Barriers, support, and perspectives from educators. In *Proceedings of the 54th ACM Technical Symposium on Computer Science Education V. 1* (pp. 367–373).

Vogel, S., Santo, R., & Ching, D. (2017, March). Visions of computer science education: Unpacking arguments for and projected impacts of CS4All initiatives. In *Proceedings of the 2017 ACM SIGCSE Technical Symposium on Computer Science Education* (pp. 609–614).

Zack, N. (2018). *Reviving the Social Compact: Inclusive Citizenship in an Age of Extreme Politics* (Vol. 2). Rowman & Littlefield.

CHAPTER 20

FORCED MIGRATION, CIVIC ENGAGEMENT, AND EDUCATIONAL EXCHANGE IN THE TIME OF COVID-19

Prakash Adhikari
Central Michigan University

ABSTRACT

How can institutional infrastructures of campuses be leveraged to promote civic engagement among students, even during disruptive natural calamities? While COVID-19 adversely affected thousands of activities around the world and created opportunities for political leaders to restrict individual rights, the pandemic also created unique opportunities for higher education institutions to promote civic engagement by virtually connecting students with populations living in remote and hostile areas, such as refugee camps and fragile democracies. As classes shifted online in 2020, we launched a virtual education program called Global Classroom that allows refugee students in Malawi to enroll in classes at Central Michigan University and share their lived experiences with U.S. students, creating an international student community. So far, a total of 330 students, including 94 refugees, have successfully participated, suggesting that innovative programs can help promote global civic engagement and democracy even during a pandemic. This chapter describes the efficacy of the Global Classroom program.[1]

While scholars generally agree that civic literacy contributes to a vibrant democracy (Milner, 2002), students' engagement with civic education has declined as democracies around the world have come under attack (Diamond, 2021; Freedom House, 2022). The COVID-19 pandemic contributed to the deterioration in the "health of democracy" when "schools were closed and thus the right for education limited" (Kneuer & Wurster, 2023, 616). Such measures raised questions as "to what extent democracy would also be quarantined" (*ibid*). In its 2022 annual report, Freedom House warned: "global freedom faces a dire threat" and "[i]n countries with long-established democracies, internal forces have exploited the shortcoming in their systems, distorting national politics to promote hatred, violence, and unbridled power" (Freedom House, 2022, 1). This warning sums up sixteen "consecutive years of decline in global freedom" since this negative pattern began in 2006 (Diamond, 2021; *ibid*), with the pandemic intensifying already existing democratic deficits (Kneuer & Wurster, 2023). Given the decline in democratic freedoms, it cannot be a coincidence that a record 108.4 million people worldwide were forced from their homes by the end of 2022 due to "persecution, conflict, violence, human rights violations and events seriously disturbing public order" (UNHCR, 2023a). Existing research on forced migration has established that autocracies that do not respect human rights, and regime change, armed conflicts, and violence in general are the primary causes of forced migration (Adhikari, 2013; 2012; Davenport et al., 2003; Melander & Öberg, 2006; Moore & Shellman, 2004). While authoritarian regimes in places such as China, Iran and Saudi Arabia discourage development of education policies that promote democracy (Freedom House, 2022; Kneuer & Wurster, 2023), countries such as Afghanistan, Myanmar and the Democratic Republic of Congo (DRC) that are mired in decades of civil war simply lack the educational infrastructure to promote formal education and civic engagement.

With such high and ever-increasing displacement, the need for initiatives to educate displaced youths could not be greater (UNHCR, 2021). According to the United Nations High Commissioner for Refugees (UNHCR), over 40% of forced migrants are children, with only 7% of college-age refugees having access to higher education by the end of 2022 (UNHCR, 2023b). Over 75% of the displaced persons globally are living in "low and middle-income countries" such as Pakistan, Bangladesh, Uganda, Colombia and Malawi where educational opportunities for their own citizens are limited, let alone for displaced persons (Ferris & Kerwin, 2023; UNHCR,

2023a), and the COVID-19 pandemic further dampened educational opportunities for refugee youth globally.

Because the conditions in their country of origin are too dangerous for them to return home, many college-age refugees in places like Dzaleka in Malawi are left with no option but to languish in refugee camps. The Global Classroom (GC) is organized to fill this gap (ROC, n.d.) by providing an innovative way for students experiencing forced displacement to receive a college degree from a university in the United States without leaving the refugee camp. Similarly, the GC gives college students in the United States the opportunity to interact with individuals from the other side of the world without having to leave the country. Such interactions are extremely valuable for promoting global understanding of democratic freedoms and civic engagement for young people from both sides. The GC serves as a model of innovative and alternative educational pathways that can be used when resettlement is not an immediate option. Additionally, sharing virtual classroom space with people who have been forcibly displaced raises awareness and increases civic engagement among students in the United States. By pairing U.S. students with refugees living in Dzaleka, the GC provides them with a rare opportunity to teach and learn from each other and enhances civic engagement (Chadjipadelis & Panagiotidou, 2021). This chapter highlights some of the strategies adopted to engage students in the United States in conversations on challenging topics related to forced migration with the individuals who are experiencing it.

PROTRACTED REFUGEE SITUATIONS AND THE NEED FOR VIRTUAL EDUCATION

While incidents of protracted refugee situations have substantially increased since the end of the Cold War, there is now a general lack of enthusiasm from developed countries to resettle refugees (Gibney, 2004; Selm, 2014). As a result, more people are living in refugee camps and experiencing terrible conditions such as lack of food, shelter and access to education (Milner, 2014). Meanwhile, many host countries introduced stringent measures on refugee integration in the midst of the COVID-19 pandemic, with some reversing their previous integration policies. For example, in 2021, the Malawian government rescinded its previous decision to integrate refugees, ordering those who had married locals and started businesses to return to the camp (Kunchezera, 2021); and Pakistan started deporting Afghan refugees in 2023 (Shah, 2023). Failure of the UNHCR and individual states to address protracted refugee situations has left places such as Dzaleka with little to no hope.

The shift to online education through the GC provides an opportunity for campuses to address this problem by leveraging their institutional infrastructures. For faculty members, it is an opportunity to engage their students in conversations with peers and with individuals experiencing forced migration to better understand a global issue currently plaguing the international community. GC serves as a bridge between U.S. students and Dzaleka residents as well as a link between citizens living in a developed democracy and those fleeing homes due to a fear of persecution from authoritarian governments. By completing course work on topics such as international relations, U.S. foreign policy, and liberal democracy, as well as American politics, Dzaleka students are exposed to civic education in the United States and U.S. students gain firsthand experience working with forced migrants, most of whom lack basic individual rights, like the right to an education.

Dzaleka provides a classic example of a protracted refugee situation and an ideal case for implementing the GC. The facility, which previously served as a political prison to around 9,000 inmates, was converted into a UNHCR Refugee camp in 1994. Originally, the camp was established to house up to 12,000 individuals displaced due to the civil war in the DRC. They were later joined by individuals fleeing deteriorating political situations in Mozambique, Somalia, Ethiopia and other countries (Kariya, 2023). Today, the population in the camp has increased to approximately 50,000 (Human Rights Watch, 2023).

With support from the UNHCR and the Malawian government, school-age children in Dzaleka are offered a K–12-level education. But opportunities for high school graduates to get tertiary education without leaving the camp are limited. For example, when a 20-year-old resident in the camp was asked what they wanted to do upon graduation from secondary school, they stated that they wished to be a doctor. But when the same individual was asked the same question after graduating from high school, they stated "Here in Dzaleka it cannot happen. When you live in camp you change your behaviors, your expectations. It can't happen because I am a refugee" (Healy, 2012, 2). The rising population of the camp and the lack of higher education opportunities made Dzaleka a good starting point for the GC program.

GLOBAL CLASSROOM AND CIVIC ENGAGEMENT

Initiated in the midst of a global pandemic, the GC is a collaboration between a student-led non-governmental organization known as the Refugee Outreach Collective (ROC) and Central Michigan University (CMU). The program offers a unique two-way learning and teaching experience, providing access to higher education for displaced individuals, while focusing on cross-cultural exchanges and civic engagement between CMU students and

Dzaleka residents. Each year, the ROC selects up to 20 qualified individuals from Dzaleka for admission into the program. Once admitted, they are enrolled in undergraduate-level online classes and provided an opportunity to complete coursework alongside CMU students. The GC aims to allow refugee students to obtain a college degree so that they can leave the camp to start a career.

LANGUAGE EXCHANGE PROGRAM[2]

As a first step to launching the GC, we ran a pen pal program from 2016–2018, pairing students from ROC chapters at various universities in the Midwest region of the United States with Dzaleka residents, allowing the pen pals to conduct informal conversations via WhatsApp. The unstructured format of the program allowed a free flow of ideas and worked remarkably well in raising cross-cultural and political awareness among the students. Once students became comfortable interacting with each other, we reshaped the pen pal program into a Language Exchange Program (LEP) that ran until 2020 where CMU students were tasked with teaching an English language curriculum to their Dzaleka partners in exchange for a similar Swahili language curriculum taught to them. In addition to providing an opportunity to gain first-hand experience of teaching a foreign language and establishing deeper connections between U.S. students and refugees in Dzaleka, the LEP created a foundation for the GC program by encouraging participants to engage in discussions of the policies and politics of their respective countries. For example, the LEP overlapped with Donald Trump's presidency when immigration policy was marked by controversial measures such as emphasizing a border wall, family separation and travel bans to stop the inflow of people from seven Muslim majority countries, including Somalia and Sudan where some of the Dzaleka students originate. Thus, it was natural for Dzaleka students to ask questions about U.S. immigration policy, curious to know how a country that had historically been known for its generous resettlement program could suddenly become hostile towards refugees. To facilitate dialogue on such sensitive topics, students in the LEP were simultaneously enrolled in a course on refugees and forced migration in which they were tasked with the responsibility of conducting weekly group discussions that included their LEP partners. Despite the sensitive nature of the topic, these group discussions played a crucial role in fostering a sense of community among the students on both sides, with some expressing profound impacts on their political knowledge. One CMU student wrote:

> In most classes, you read and write and watch videos, but you rarely get the chance to have first-hand contact with someone who has experienced what

you're learning about. Talking to a refugee in a camp allowed me to see that this problem is a huge one that so many people around the world face every day. Interacting with someone that has a life, family, and friends just like me helped to put into perspective that refugees are people, and they deserve every ounce of protection that the international community has to offer.

Another CMU student said:

Throughout this course we learned about the core principles, and concepts that [are critical to understanding] international relations and have reflected our knowledge of these core principles and concepts in our global classroom, discussing the course materials with our Dzaleka partners. I feel that the global classroom program was a great addition to this course. I have not only been able to participate in real international relations but have also been able to apply the concepts learned in this course in understanding a real-world problem.

As a community of learners, students in the course discussed political processes in the United States where the president issues executive orders without approval from the legislature and they compared and contrasted the United States with parliamentary democracies in Sub Saharan Africa, such as South Africa and Botswana, and countries with presidential forms of government like Malawi. Many Dzaleka students reported gaining deeper knowledge from their group discussions in terms of their skill development, expressing ideas and engaging in sensitive topics. These exercises also helped students in the course to compare advanced democracies such as the United States with fragile democracies such as Malawi and Rwanda and understand the impact of government policies on individual's lives. One CMU student reflected:

This program helped me to be able to take the knowledge I was learning in class and think about it in the context of someone who is actually a refugee instead of only understanding the refugee experience in a theoretical manner.

The above experience of teaching each other provided students with opportunities to share experiences of living in dramatically different circumstances. By creating a partnership between two sides in which one is living a more comfortable life than the other, the LEP eliminated some of the feelings of superiority or the so called "White savior" complex that tends to exist in many humanitarian exchange programs (Biddle, 2021). By opening channels of communication for learning each other's culture, political situations and government policies that affect ordinary citizens' lives, such exchanges breed opportunities for students to develop civic knowledge (Krishnan, et. al., 2021), and to learn about college life in the United

States and that of a refugee. Such educational exchanges promote civic engagement among students by prompting students to learn about issues and political conditions in their respective countries. A majority of CMU students come from rural Michigan and have never left the state. The LEP opened their eyes to other people and countries in a way that taking regular classes has not. One CMU student reflected:

> Working with my language partner definitely provided me with a new perspective specifically in my view of refugees. I did not know how much of a person's life can be established in a refugee camp. I was so in awe at all of the things my language partner was involved in and all the roles he played in the camp. It shifted my previous perception and assumptions about refugee's lives and the struggles they can face and overcome.

While a majority of the Dzaleka students simply expressed their gratefulness for the opportunity, many reported learning a "great deal about American people" from their study partners. The LEP contributed to building trusting relationships and a respectful virtual environment for civic engagement between CMU students and Dzaleka residents and a solid foundation for launching the GC.

NEGOTIATING A GLOBAL CLASSROOM

The idea for the global classroom was rooted in students' interest in tackling a real-world problem. In fall 2016, CMU students started an organization to work with refugees around the world and in 2018, it became a chapter of a 501(c) non-profit organization called the ROC. When COVID-19 forced classes to be shifted online, I used this as an opportunity to open my classes to Dzaleka residents whom we already had connections to through the LEP and I invited U.S. students to do the groundwork in Dzaleka. ROC members from eight different colleges in the Midwest region of the United States, along with counterparts in Dzaleka, collaborated to register a ROC chapter in Malawi, a process which is still ongoing (as of December 2023). Students also started negotiations with the CMU administration and after two years in December 2022, CMU and ROC concluded an agreement to allow Dzaleka residents to enroll at CMU as non-degree seeking students.

The processes of creating the ROC and negotiating an agreement with a public university bureaucracy proved to be an eye opener for U.S. and Dzaleka students alike. U.S. students had to write a constitution for a brand-new organization, engage in fund-raising for the organization, hold campus events to raise awareness of the problem of forced migration and navigate the process of registering the NGO. In general, students, especially undergrads around the globe have very little knowledge about university and government bureaucracies. For example, in trying to register the ROC chapter in Malawi, students have had to revise their constitution more than three times, have hired numerous lawyers in Malawi to help them with the process and refugee students have made many trips to the capital of Lilongwe to meet with government officials. Despite being time consuming and often frustrating, this process has been highly educational for students in building a community of learners and for laying a foundation for changing the lives of forced migrants around the world. While the CMU experience taught students that democratic processes are slow and that they demand perseverance, the Dzaleka experience is teaching them that new democracies, such as Malawi, are even more bureaucratic. These experiences are expected to have lasting impacts on the lives of the GC students in terms of their civic knowledge and their understanding of democratic processes around the world.

INFRASTRUCTURE, STUDENT RECRUITMENT, AND FUNDING FOR A GLOBAL CLASSROOM

Making physical arrangements for launching a GC in the middle of a global pandemic inside a refugee camp provided additional civic engagement opportunities for the students. Starting the GC involved careful planning, where U.S. students were required to work remotely with Dzaleka partners not only to find a classroom but also to understand UNHCR and Malawian government policies. When the program was launched in fall 2020, arrangements were made to meet students inside a tin-roofed community center at the camp, but the noise made learning impossible, so ROC had to rent a room in a building across the street with a concrete roof where students can attend classes in a peaceful environment. While this room now serves as an Education Center for the GC, paying for utilities presents the students with another challenge and an opportunity to develop fundraising skills, which can be an important exercise for citizens in democracies. Internet service is very expensive in Malawi, but because the GC is conducted virtually, it requires uninterrupted internet service that ROC is responsible for paying. A local program Site-Coordinator, who is also a refugee, performs logistical tasks including preparing the classroom and paying bills in return for a small stipend from ROC. In 2022, a UK-based charity called Turing Trust donated 13 fully functional desktops for the Center, and ROC purchased four laptops. To combat frequent nation-wide power outages in Malawi that interrupt virtual classes, the Education Center is run on a gas-powered generator, which also has to be maintained and fueled by the ROC. U.S. students accomplished all these tasks working with their Dzaleka partners remotely despite the challenges of unreliable internet service and an irregular power supply, not to mention a 6–7-hour time difference.

In consultation with CMU, ROC developed a standard procedure to recruit Dzaleka students into the GC program. To meet CMU admission criterion, Dzaleka individuals must meet some baseline qualifications, such as English proficiency, evidence of completion of high school and experience in an educational setting. While not all forced migrants in Dzaleka are fluent in English, CMU courses are taught in English so those who are not fluent in English are disqualified. ROC screens the applications and invites qualified applicants for an in-person interview. To mitigate potential chances of interference with the selection process, the program Site-Coordinator consults with ROC before announcing the final list of program participants. Selected candidates are referred to CMU for admission. While the recruitment process provides U.S. students with an opportunity to screen various applications and make decisions based on strict merit-based criteria, Dzaleka applicants gain the opportunity to compete for their spots while also promoting the program in the camp. By participating in the recruitment and selection processes, students develop skills such as evaluating applications, conducting interviews and administering competitive tests that are likely to play critical roles in producing civically engaged citizens needed for a healthy democracy.

To pay for the operating cost of the Education Center, U.S. students regularly organize campus fundraising activities that range from selling doughnuts and cider to organizing campus-wide dinner events, silent auctions and similar activities that require students to work as a community and negotiate with business organizations as well as university officials. These activities contribute to building a sense of community among the students that is likely to have a lasting impact on the health of democracy in the United States. While Dzaleka students do not directly participate in fundraising activities in the United States, they get the opportunity to witness their counterparts' work and appreciate the process. Fundraising activities can contribute to developing interpersonal skills, commitment to a cause, determination and perseverance, all of which are important for promoting democracy (Chhabra, 2018; Sandmann et al., 2009).

In sum, the various service-learning activities described above foster leadership skills in GC students and give them the tools to promote civic engagement and democracy. GC students learn about the causes and consequences of forced migration and how it can be prevented. Students may choose to join international organizations such as the UNHCR to work with refugees or Amnesty International to work in human rights. By being actively involved in negotiating the agreement with CMU, preparing a space for the GC in Dzaleka, and screening students for enrollment into different courses, students learn about collective problem solving. To inculcate a civic engagement habit among students, faculty members need to provide students with opportunities to discuss problems and challenges and give them the opportunity to explore potential solutions to address the problems (CIRCLE, 2003). The GC affords students with a voice in providing educational access to college-age refugees.

GLOBAL CLASSROOM "STUDY BUDDIES"

The GC provides students with an opportunity to engage in conversations that connect course content to ongoing political situations around the world. Research shows that "[W]hen young people have opportunities to discuss current issues in a classroom setting, they tend to have greater interest in politics, improved critical thinking and communications skills, more civic knowledge, and more interest in discussing public affairs out of school" (CIRCLE 2003, 6). While the exact nature of class work in the GC program will vary by course and instructor, some of the activities include attending online lectures, written assignments, group projects, virtual joint study sessions, group presentations, participation in discussion boards and taking quizzes and exams. For example, faculty members teaching GC courses at CMU frequently include group projects designed to better promote an exchange of ideas between CMU and Dzaleka students.

To foster civic engagement, CMU students are provided with an orientation on engaging in discussions on sensitive topics such as refugees and survivors of political violence. These include topics such as being respectful and mindful of individuals with refugee backgrounds, being sensitive to current political conditions in their country of origins and the importance of avoiding conversation on circumstances that forced them to flee. CMU students are then paired with Dzaleka students and asked to complete course work. Building on the group activities discussed above, students in the GC are split into 'study buddies' and tasked with the responsibility to conduct study sessions, exchange notes, do virtual group presentations and share their experience in the form of a reflection paper at the end of the semester. These activities allow students to share diverse perspectives pertaining to course materials, as well as lived experiences.

During the spring 2023 semester, for example, students in the GC were asked to learn and present their findings on women in politics in their respective countries. As a community of learners, students in the course learned about the cross-country differences in political freedoms accorded to women and the impact that something basic like regime types can have on young people's choices of career paths. This exercise allowed the students to compare the freedoms of citizens in a developed democracy versus less developed countries such as the DRC and Malawi. In their final reflection, most Dzaleka students mentioned that they were surprised to find out "how much freedom women have in America." One female student from Dzaleka said, "here in Africa women don't have rights." This was an eye opener for CMU students. One CMU student wrote:

> It's quite amazing that we are able to have students in our class that are on the other side of the world. Hearing their point of view provided an important perspective. For example, during the final week, one of the [Dzaleka] students was talking about how important it is to have women in power. Africa does not have a lot of women in positions of power. I'll be honest, I didn't know much about refugees' situations prior to taking this class. I knew they existed, but I hadn't ever considered what refugees would be doing in these camps.

The testimonies of GC participants are perhaps the best way to illustrate the impact that GC activities have had. Reflecting on the contribution of the GC, a Dzaleka student wrote: "with the classes I have taken from this program, I am able to relate political affairs that interfere with my daily life and the political circumstances that are affecting our communities." A CMU student reflected that the GC gave him the chance to explain democracy to his study buddy in Dzaleka:

> For Americans, most information is easily available because of technology. For a student in Dzaleka, internet connection is scarce. Because of this, it is easier to understand why they ask questions as simple as "what is democracy?" When this question was first asked, my study group was almost stunned and lost for words in terms of an actual definition as it is so common and almost unspoken in our culture. A difference in the way the global classroom student interpreted the information is that most Americans hope to use the information learned in this class in their future career. The Dzaleka student seemed to hope to use this information in hopes of bringing democracy and freedom to their country by studying what other countries have done. While this is a very different interpretation, we were able to see each other's perspectives and adapt the information to fit the others' experiences.

Many CMU students also reflected that the program helped them realize their privileges and opportunities, as well as responsibilities associated with being a citizen of an advanced democracy.

> I think this program is invaluable. Playing a small role in providing education to refugees has been an extraordinary privilege and a highlight of my academic career so far. I believe this program is worth keeping and expanding as much as possible. I would love to have the opportunity to do this again.

A Dzaleka student dreams to return to his country of origin, run for political office—if and when conditions in his country of origin are suitable—and introduce democracy so that people don't have to flee. He reported getting this idea after taking an introduction to international relations course and interacting with his CMU study buddies. In his final reflection, the student wrote: "This program is very important; it is the type of program that can develop good leaders."

Another Dzaleka student reflected that he had stopped dreaming after becoming a refugee, but the GC helped him start dreaming again and made him a better person:

> I am in Dzaleka Refugee [camp], due to constant wars in my country [of origin]. I had become desperate, lacking the joy of life and some of the dreams I had have died and disappeared after I became a refugee. I didn't expect that one day I could have the opportunity to get a higher education with my refugee status. Two years ago, unexpectedly, I had the opportunity to join ROC and become one of the students of the Global Classroom. Through this education, I have become a better person in the refugee community and brought great changes to my fellow refugees. ROC here in Malawi is changing the lives of many refugees through Education.

Another Dzaleka student wrote, "With the knowledge I have acquired from this class, I have been helping my community deal with some problems and bring solutions with a better understanding. Which is total happiness to me, my family, and the whole community."

Another Dzaleka student in the program mentioned that the GC revived his hopes:

> I arrived in Malawi after passing through many African countries in search of peace and education. I lost everything except my life. I have seen many hostilities and hatreds towards refugees and had become hopeless. My hopes started coming back after joining the Global Classroom. ROC is rebuilding hopelessness into hope through Education. Now I believe I can promote peace in the world through Education.

The GC is contributing not only to promoting education to forced migrants in Dzaleka, but also preparing young people for changing their communities and producing young leaders that are committed to promoting global citizenship and democracy. This is best captured by a Dzaleka student who wrote:

> The Refugee Outreach Collective is preparing me to be a change agent in my community. The Global Classroom has given me the opportunity to pursue my dreams. I am confident that after completing this program, I will be able to properly care for others. This program has helped me understand both

myself and the world we live in. I am becoming a global citizen as a result of the Global Classroom.

CONCLUSION

In this chapter, we have described one way in which institutional infrastructures of campuses can be leveraged to support civic engagement, even during a disruptive global pandemic. The GC program is partially a product of the pandemic. Social scientist Andrew Shacknove (1985) argued, "[F]or even an ideally just state cannot save us from earthquakes, hurricanes, or eventual death.... but [t]he devastation of a flood or a supposedly natural famine can be minimized or exacerbated by social policies and institutions" (p. 279). Institutions of higher education offer infrastructure for faculty and students to be innovative in tackling some of the most challenging problems in the world. The GC provides opportunities where "students can take agency in their studies" (Sato & Horne, 2020, 70). With their active participation and engagement in one of the most challenging topics facing the world today, over 300 young people have developed a relationship with someone across the world. While our students may not be able to prevent disruptive calamities from reoccurring, the GC has introduced conceptual tools for addressing real world problems. Students who participated in the GC have harnessed civic knowledge that has equipped them to become agents of change for promoting peace and democracy in the world. This chapter shows that students can also contribute to the goal of making post-secondary education accessible to some of the forcibly displaced youths around the world. The 2022 annual report of the Freedom House recommended:

> Fostering a strong public understanding of democratic principles, especially among young people, empowers citizens to defend freedom domestically and support foreign policies that protect democratic rights and values abroad. As democracies struggle, and authoritarian rulers promote the narrative that democracy is unable to deliver on its promises, it is essential that those living in free countries understand and are able to articulate how effective democratic governance protects rights and freedoms. (Freedom House, 2022, p. 33)

The GC promotes valuable interactions among college students and a global understanding of democratic freedoms and contributes to civic engagement by building a community of learners and agents of change. Students want to be heard (Levin-Goldberg, 2009). The GC affords young people across eight colleges in the Midwest region of the United States a rare opportunity to voice their opinions with university administration in addressing one of the most pressing issues of their time. For refugee students, this is an opportunity to negotiate access to higher education in their place of displacement. Recalibrating the goals of encouraging civic engagement and promoting democracy at a time when they are under attack from populism, the GC is preparing the next generation of civically engaged students who can work across the world. GC students cultivate virtual learning environments where all students in the program can build on their classroom knowledge and experiences for helping college-age refugees progress on their journey towards brighter futures. Students in the program cultivate civic engagement and academic skills that are important for promoting democracy. Through their participation in the GC, U.S. students not only make a difference in the lives of Dzaleka students, but also acquire valuable skills that prepare them to become the next generation of civically engaged leaders. Similarly, for college-age refugees who possess untapped potential, the GC helps to tap it by engaging them in conversation with U.S. students. The GC creates productive and involved citizens who are expected to contribute to promoting democracy around the world.

The GC program is not without challenges. First, funding is an ongoing issue; the ROC has had to continuously engage in fundraising just to keep the electricity and internet functioning in the camp. Second, language and cultural differences may pose some challenges during the initial phase of the program. An informal program such as the LEP can be a useful starting point to initiate interactions between college students and refugees. Finally, anyone interested in replicating the GC faces the challenge of convincing university administrators to allow forcibly displaced students to enroll in courses; the GC program does not generate revenue to CMU. While no one can say that providing college students in the United States with an opportunity to take classes alongside college-age refugees, while also providing refugees with a chance to access higher education, is a bad idea, administrators may need to be convinced that the educational benefits outweigh any foregone tuition revenue from the refugee students. In the case of CMU, students who are members of ROC did the convincing. Faculty interested in initiating similar programs on their campus should encourage their students to take the lead. Such a strategy will contribute to building leadership skills among the students, who after all are in the best position to convince administrators that the program will have a profound impact on their education and futures and the lives of the refugees.

So far, 330 students have participated in 9 different courses taught at CMU, with more courses being planned. An increasing number of universities have expressed interest in introducing the program on their campuses in the near future. Since 2019, the UNHCR and its partner organizations have been working on a goal to provide educational access to 15% of the forcibly displaced students by 2030 (UNHCR, 2023b). Interested institutions of higher education around the world can join this campaign.

ACKNOWLEDGMENT

I thank Dr. Richard Rothaus, Dean of the College of Liberal Arts and Social Science at CMU and Kathy Rise for their continued support, Max Ranger for his contribution to the LEP, Emily Worline for her untiring leadership, ROC members for their commitment to the welfare of forced migrants, and Dr. Wendy L. Hansen at the University of New Mexico for her selfless support of my work on forced migration.

NOTES

1. The Global Classroom program was launched in partnership between a student-led non-governmental organization called Refugee Outreach Collective (ROC) and Central Michigan University (CMU). As described in the following pages, a number of individuals, including students participating in the program, played a critical role in making the program possible. The inclusive term 'we' is used throughout the chapter to reflect the collective contribution from all the parties involved in making the program a success.
2. Students submit final papers reflecting on their experiences with the GC. I use students' reflections to evaluate the impact of the program. Quotes are taken from student papers with their written permission and with approval from CMU institutional review board (CMU IRB # 2023-751).

REFERENCES

Adhikari, P. (2012). The plight of the forgotten ones: Civil war and forced migration. *International Studies Quarterly, 56*(3), 590–606.

Adhikari, P. (2013). Conflict-induced displacement, understanding the causes of flight. *American Journal of Political Science, 57*(1), 82–89.

Biddle, P. (2021). *Ours to explore: Privilege, power, and the paradox of voluntourism.* Potomac Books.

Carnegie Corporation of New York, CIRCLE. (2003). *The civic mission of schools* (Carnegie Corporation of New York and CIRCLE, 2003).

Chadjipadelis, T., & Panagiotidou, G. (2021). Students teaching democracy to other students: The effects on political engagement. In E. C. Matto, A. R. M. McCartney, E. A. Bennion, A. Blair, T. Sun, & D. M. Whitehead (Eds). *Teaching civic engagement globally: Spreading the word* (pp. 185–203). American Political Science Association.

Chhabra, S. (2018). *Handbook of research on civic engagement and social change in contemporary society.* IGI Global. https://doi.org/10.4018/978-1-5225-4197-4

Crea, T. M., & McFarland, M. (2015). Higher education for refugees: Lessons from a 4-year pilot project. *International Review of Education, 61*(2), 235–245.

Davenport, C. A., Moore, W. H., & Poe, S. C. (2003). Sometimes you just have to leave: Domestic threats and forced migration, 1964–1989. *International Interaction, 29*(1), 27–55.

Diamond, L. (2021). Democratic regression in comparative perspective: Scope, methods, and causes. *Democratization, 28*(1), 22–42. https://doi.org/10.1080/13510347.2020.1807517

Ferris, E., & Kerwin, D. (2023). Durable displacement and the protracted search for solutions: Promising programs and strategies. *Journal on Migration and Human Security, 11*(1), 3–22.

Freedom House. (2022). *Freedom in the world 2022: The global expansion of authoritarian rule.* https://freedomhouse.org/sites/default/files/2022-02/FIW_2022_PDF_Booklet_Digital_Final_Web.pdf

Gibney, M. J. (2004). *The ethics and politics of asylum: Liberal democracy and the response to refugees.* Cambridge University Press.

Healy, L. (2012). Unable to see the future: Refugee youth in Malawi speak out. *Forced Migration Review, 40*, 5–6.

Human Right Watch. (June 5, 2023). *Malawi: Refugees, including children, forcibly relocated.* https://www.hrw.org/news/2023/06/05/malawi-refugees-including-children-forcibly-relocated

Karasik, T. (February 2, 2022). Africa's 'coup belt' facing further upheaval. *Arab News.* https://arab.news/ypd45.

Kariya, J. (June 29, 2023). Malawi's refugee problem. *Africa Arguments.* https://africanarguments.org/2023/06/malawis-refugee-problem/

Kneuer, M., & Wurster, S. (2022). Democratic health in the corona pandemic. The corona pandemic as a trigger or amplifier of democratic erosion or autocratization? *Zeitschrift Für Vergleichende Politikwissenschaft, 16*(4), 615–634.

Krishnan, L. A., Sreekumar, S., Sundaram, S., Subrahmanian, M., & Davis, P. (2021). Virtual "study abroad": Promoting intercultural competence amidst the pandemic. *The Hearing Journal, 74*(4), 38–40.

Kunchezera, B. (2021, November 25). Return to the refugee camp: Malawi orders thousands back to 'congested' Dzaleka. *The Guardian.* https://www.theguardian.com/global-development/2021/nov/25/return-to-the-refugee-camp-malawi-orders-thousands-back-to-congested-dzaleka.

Melander, E., & Öberg, M. (2006). Time to go? Duration dependence in forced migration. *International Interactions, 32*(2), 129–152.

Milner, H. (2002). *Civic literacy: How informed citizens make democracy work.* University Press of New England [for] Tufts University.

Milner, J. (2014). Protracted refugee situations. In E. Fiddian-Qasmiyeh, G. Loescher, K. Long, & N. Sigona (Eds.) *The Oxford handbook of refugee and forced migration studies* (pp. 151–162). Oxford University Press.

Moore, W. H., & Shellman, S. M. (2004). Fear of persecution: Forced migration, 1952–1995. *Journal of Conflict Resolution, 48*(5), 723–745.

Moore, W. H., & Shellman, S. M. (2007). Whither will they go? A global study of refugees' destinations, 1965–1995. *International Studies Quarterly, 51*(4), 811–834.

Refugee Outreach Collective, ROC. (n.d.). Refugee Outreach Collective. https://www.rocyourworld.org/

Sandmann, L. R., Thornton, C. H., Jaeger, A. J., & Jaeger, A. J. (2009). Institutionalizing community engagement in higher education: The first wave of carnegie classified institutions. In *Institutionalizing community engagement in higher education* (Vol. 96). John Wiley & Sons, Incorporated.

Sato, K., & Horne, B. (2020). Cultivating students' communication skills for the global workplace: A cross-cultural online exchange project with non-native speakers. *International Journal of Teaching & Education, 8*(1), 64–83.

Selm, J. V. (2014). Refugee resettlement. In E. Fiddian-Qasmiyeh, G. Loescher, K. Long, & N. Sigona (Eds.) *The Oxford handbook of refugee and forced migration studies* (pp. 512–524). Oxford University Press.

Shacknove, A. (1985). Who is a refugee? *Ethics, 95*(2), 274–284.

Shah, S. (2023). Pakistan begins deporting Afghans who fled Taliban. *The Wall Street Journal.* https://www.wsj.com/world/asia/pakistan-begins-deporting-afghans-who-fled-taliban-085b5842

UNHCR. (2021). *Model UN refugee challenge background guide—Improving access to education for refugees.* https://www.unhcr.org/5df9f1767.pdf

UNHCR. (2023a). *Global trends: Forced displacement in 2022.* United Nations High Commissioner for Refugees. https://www.unhcr.org/global-trends-report-2022

UNHCR. (2023b). *Refugee higher education global newsletter 2023—Volume 2.* https://www.unhcr.org/media/refugee-higher-education-global-newsletter-2023-volume-2

CHAPTER 21

POETRY AT THE END OF DEMOCRACY

Envisioning Democracy Through Poetry

Angelo Letizia
Notre Dame of Maryland University

ABSTRACT

Democracies do not last forever. This might be a terrifying statement. But it is a prospect that citizens in a democracy must confront. The purpose of this chapter is to show how professors and students can use poetry to strengthen their current democracies and imagine new political and social arrangements when those democracies end. In this chapter, I examine some relevant theories of democracy and citizenship, as well arts-based research and poetic inquiry. I ground the analysis in John Dewey's notion of creative democracy. Most importantly, this chapter contains actual professor and student-created poetry which illustrates how democracy and more generally, a robust social life, can be reimagined.

Democracies are always under construction. By utilizing the tenets of arts-based research and poetic inquiry, professors and students can use poetry to strengthen and when appropriate, reimagine democracy. Arts-based research is a type of research activity which utilizes the arts (e.g., painting, fiction, poetry, drama, music, etc.) in the research process (Barone & Eisner, 2011; Leavy, 2019b). Arts-based researchers do not strive for objectivity, but rather, create works which are participatory, emotionally resonant and which are invested with multiple meanings (Barone & Eisner, 2011; Leavy, 2019a; McNiff, 2019). Poetic inquiry is a subset of arts-based research which specifically utilizes poetry in the research process in various ways, draws on multiple disciplines and focuses on poetry as product and method, as well as having autobiographical elements (James, 2017; Faulkner, 2019a; Prendergast, 2009). While traditional scientific research is important, it is not the only way to understand and change the world (Barone & Eisner, 2011; McNiff, 2019).

Following Faulkner (2019a, xi), who advocates the use of poetic inquiry for political and social justice causes, this chapter seeks to use poetic inquiry to "engage a political voice." Faulkner explains that through poetry we can "create and tell stories that advocate for social justice and change." Moreover, Leggo notes, "poetry invents worlds and teaches us how to live in them" (2017, 28). This is precisely what I want to accomplish—the creation of a new world through poetry, for myself and my students, especially in this volatile time. Democracy is not only the responsibility of political scientists. *Everyone* has to take part and has the responsibility to imagine better ways of living together. This chapter details how this task can be achieved, at least in small part, in a college course.

I utilize aspects of arts-based research and poetic inquiry in two ways. For one, I am a poet *and* an academic. My poetry draws heavily on scholarly literature. However, scholarly literature is constrained in many ways. Poetry allows me to play with ideas from the literature. I can reformulate the literature, as well as my own more personal experiences, ideas and inclinations into a creative piece.

Second, I utilize aspects of arts-based research and poetic inquiry with students in the classroom through poetry assignments. The use of poetry should not only be a theoretical or abstract exercise with little attention paid to the living body. The brain itself is activated in various ways by the arts (Leavy, 2019a). Wiebe and Sameshima (2017) proclaim that more than just abstract and empty talk is needed to change political arrangements; people have to seek pleasure, make love, talk, and laugh and take action. Poetry is visceral. Poetry, with its imagery, emotive aspects, rhyming and alliteration can be a way to call attention to and to cultivate our bodies along with our minds (Leavy, 2019b; Prendergast, 2009; Shusterman, 2008). Poetry and literature show us life on the ground, in all its sweat, grief and sadness (Greene, 2007; Wiebe & Sameshima, 2017). Similarly, democracy is not only grandiose proclamations. I want to show how professors and students can imagine better forms of living with poetry and how this process is not only theoretical, but a truly lived phenomena. We are not only abstract citizens, but real human beings and poetry can capture some of this lived experience.

My method somewhat follows Maxine Greene (2007). In her work, *The Public School and Private Vision*, Greene juxtaposed works of literature, such as those written by Nathanial Hawthorne, Herman Melville and Walt Whitman, against the ideas of educational philosophers such as Thomas Jefferson, Horace Mann and John Dewey. Greene (2007) argued that philosophers did not capture the truly lived and felt experiences of most people. The philosophers tended toward lofty rhetoric, but Greene (2007) argues that the literature truly captures living in all its terror and mundanity. The artists, she notes, "press against the human creatures listening, feeling their pulse, their warmth, their chill" (Greene, 2007, p. 4). Literature, in this fashion, is used as a "foil" (Greene, 2007, p. 4). I want to do something similar, and juxtapose my own poetry against ideas from the scholarly literature to capture something more visceral. When I read scholarly literature, sometimes it inspires me to write a poem or sometimes I will pair a poem that I have already written to certain points in it. In this way, I "speak" to the scholarly literature, but not as an academic, and not just as an abstract citizen, but rather, as a real person with hopes and dreams and fears. I also facilitate this process with students.

The following section briefly examines the notions of democracy and citizenship. In this section, I make poetry "talk" to the scholarly literature by bringing out new insights through interspacing my own poems in the scholarship. From this conversation, new insights can emerge. For example, I will take a point, such as citizenship or democracy, and use my own poems to refine, recast and/or reimagine it. I also urge the reader to join the conversation. I introduce each poem with some relevant information and questions and use the poem to raise questions and invite discussion. As such, mine is not the last word. *What questions do my poems pose for you? What disagreements do you have with me?*

I then show how I facilitate this process with my students in my courses. For this chapter, I included the assignment I use in my Educational Philosophy Course. The assignment is meant to make students speak to the scholarly literature and things they learned in the course, not just as a student, but as a real person with life experiences, fears and dreams. From this assignment, I present four student poems and some responses to these poems which were on discussion boards (some responses were written, others were in audio form so I transcribed and paraphrased them). These poems and responses constitute the data sources for this chapter. Again, I ask the reader to reflect on my students' poems and think about what questions and comments they can contribute. Finally, I offer some concluding thoughts.

DEMOCRACIES AND CITIZENSHIP

What is a democracy? Miller (2018) notes how many politicians and countries try to brand themselves as democratic, such as the laughable examples of Russia and North Korea. Even if we factor those examples out, democracies across the world and across history have differing aims and procedures (Christiano & Sameer, 2022; Miller, 2018). One specific area that Miller (2018) discusses is the spectrum of participation; some democratic configurations allow more participation, while some allow less. Moreover, democracies do not necessarily guarantee freedom. Miller (2018) surveys a number of historical episodes (e.g., the Reign of Terror in France) where democratic action led to dictatorship and bloodshed. Some have argued that democracies and liberalism are being separated—liberalism, while a multifaceted term, usually denotes some commitment to individualism, freedom of speech, press and religion and the rule of law to name a few—and turning to oppressive configurations or "illiberal democracies" (Miller, 2018; Plattner, 2019). Hungary, under the leader Viktor Orban, is an example of an illiberal democracy (Miller, 2018; Plattner, 2019). Miller (2018) also surveys democratic arrangements which privilege the rule of elites such as Woodrow Wilson and Franklin D. Roosevelt, who expanded the administrative and executive functions in the United States in the early 20th century. While there are commonalities and combinations of democratic configurations, the important point here is that democracies are variable and take on a multitude of forms (Christiano & Sameer, 2022; Miller, 2018).

Perhaps the most important point for any democracy is that it constantly evolves, and citizens must take an active part in this creative process (Dewey, 1939/2008; Parker, 1996). In *Democracy and Education*, Dewey (1916/1985, 93) wrote: "A democracy is more than a form of government; it is primarily a mode of associated living..." where stimuli and variation of members is key. For Dewey, democracy depends on experience; its members must constantly be moving, acting, reflecting and building new ideas and forms to govern their lives (Johnson & Reed, 2012). Moreover, Dewey (1916/1985) believed that education was integral to democracy, members of a democracy had to be educated, resourceful and versatile so they would not "be overwhelmed by the changes" and volatility (pp. 93–94). Dewey (1938/1963) pointed to the role of experience in educational practices and democracy, teachers had to work to facilitate good experiences for their students (Johnson & Reed, 2012). And for Dewey (1916), the arts, far from being only a leisure activity, had a crucial role to play in education as well. Dewey reminds us: "an education which does not succeed in making poetry a resource in the business of life as well as in its leisure, has something the matter with it- or else the poetry is artificial" (1916/1985, p. 250).

Poetry at the End of Democracy ▪ **343**

Democracies, while variable, have some commonalities and perhaps the most important feature is that they are not static, they evolve and change. The individual and the intersubjective creation of new ideas through the use of poetry may open up new ways of seeing and practicing citizenship. Citizens must create democracy anew through their experience, and poetry may help people to refine and reflect on their experience and imagine new ways of living.

Democracies are based on decision making of various parties. But even beyond politics, decision-making at an individual and existential level can be terrifying (Flynn, 2006). How do we as citizens, and really, individuals, decide anything? The poem below tackles this issue. Making certain decisions is lonely and terrifying, because we must face our awesome freedom. Maybe we seek refuge in things we know, perhaps things that might be oppressive (e.g., oppressive archetypes, forms in the garden and messiahs in the poem) because they at least provide some comfort.

> I populate the vacuum
> To drain the stars
> Into hammers and pistons
> To crush the geography of decision
> It is lonely here
> There are only the forms in the garden
> Awaiting to inflict their tyranny
> Oppressive archetypes, ghosts of modern life
> But I am here
> I am the metal messiah
> I will pulverize the forms
> And scatter their ashes
> in the sea

What if the evolution of democracy, and existence itself, is just too terrifying for people because they truly cannot decide? Or what if they only know how to choose oppression and convenience but think they are freely choosing (Fromm, 1969)? Maybe these are the ghosts of modern life, as suggested above. How can a democracy survive if people cannot choose? *What do you, reader, take from this poem? What can you add to the conversation?*

> the secret becomes something else
> the secret becomes a sun
> so it can burn
> all the things we love
> the secret planted itself in the ocean
> to show us
> how stupid our norms and expectations are

> the secret wrapped itself in gold
> and told itself
> so it could die (and not be a secret anymore)
> so it could teach us
> how foolish we are,
> and now we are nomads
> who wander from star to star
> in search of a new secret to ignore
> we are the joke the universe tells itself
> when it is afraid

What is the secret to democracy and its evolution? Is the secret a realization that it has to end at some point? When it ends, do we become homeless or just continue to think our democracy is fine? Are we the punchline?

> The moon is not the moon
> But a mouth
> And each star
> Turned out to be
> A battery
> Streets become pears
> Windows turned to grass
> The sanctuary is not safe
> As the ground melts to oil
> And jelly
> I am awash in the jelly
> That used to be my home
> Swimming in closets and other hidden places
> I finally learn the secrets

Is any democracy or political arrangement safe? As indicated above, there might not be any sanctuary. How do democracies evolve? *What do you think?* In America, the passage of the 13th, 14th, 15th, and 19th amendments; the verdict in the *Brown v. Board of Education* Supreme Court Case; and the passage of the Civil Rights Act of 1964 and the Voting Rights Act of 1965, were all crucial (but incomplete) advancements in American democracy (Parker, 1996). Despite these monumental achievements, American democracy still has much work to do and there is no guarantee that it will survive. While these advancements were all positive, there is no guaranteed end in sight, no utopia waiting for us. A more perfect union might not be in the cards.

Just as we cannot speak of some eternal or monolithic democracy, it is also important to note that the notion of citizenship means different things to different groups. The question of citizenship and what it means to be a good citizen are foundational to any discussion of politics and democracy, however, there is little agreement on this question (Westheimer & Kahne, 2004; Vickery, 2014).

Westheimer and Kahne (2004) posit three different types of citizenship (some of which can be contradictory). These forms are the personally responsible citizen, the participatory citizen and the justice-oriented citizen. The concept of the personally responsible citizen is largely rooted in obedience and character. Responsible citizens follow the laws, are patriotic and have good character. Participatory citizens participate in the democracy in various ways while justice-oriented citizens are concerned with fairness and justice and they will fight peacefully against unjust laws and norms.

However, as Vickery (2014) notes, different groups of people experience citizenship differently. She gives the example of African Americans who view citizenship more in communal terms. Misco and colleagues (2020) go so far as to note that some groups in America, such as many indigenous peoples, never wanted citizenship in the first place and citizenship was actually used as a tool of colonial assimilation to eradicate their culture. Therefore, we must be wary of prescribing any immutable forms of citizenship or democracy. The answer to the question of what constitutes good citizenship highly depends on who you ask. We need to always be open to new information to answer this question. What might good citizenship look like for a democracy in transition or in decline?

As the introduction to this book makes clear, American democracy is backsliding in many respects (Repucci, 2021). I think this notion of a backsliding democracy, while forcing people to take some action to defend it, might also make citizens ask a much more existential question: When is faith lost in a democracy? The poem below begins to suggest this prospect. Do we as citizens begin to lose faith in all of our institutions? Do some continue to hold on to them out of blind faith while some just give up (see the last three lines)?

> I no longer believe in Thursday
> Fahrenheit or food labels
> I no longer believe in shower handles
> or gardening tools
> October is a myth
> and so is the formula for area
> I no longer believe in MS medications
> or diagnoses
> or Epstein-Barr disease
> put them in a church
> for others to worship and
> just let me wander the desert

We must come face-to-face with the prospect that American democracy is in flux, under strain and could possibly end and give way to...something else. Right now, democracies the world over are under strain and citizens must face the prospect that their democracies might end or change drastically (Gotokhovkain et al., 2023; Levitsky & Ziblatt, 2018; Runciman, 2018). *What do you take from the poem above? What can you add to the conversation?*

Dewey (1939/2008) talked of creative democracy, but does democracy eventually transition to something completely different? While it is tempting to see the election of Donald Trump as the cause of all of this discord, these strains have been present for decades. There is not enough space in this short chapter to detail all these changes, but rising wealth inequality; racial disparities; dark money in politics; social media; distrust in journalism and public institutions and expertise; the dehumanization of political rivals; and extreme partisan polarization are some of the culprits (Levitsky & Ziblatt, 2018; Runciman, 2018; Repucci, 2021).

Do we have to give back the name? Do we have to give back democracy because we have finally outgrown it? When does this happen? The poem below grapples with these questions.

> The end is not as sad as you would think
> There is peace here
> And a somber realization
> That all your regrets do not matter
> There is some pain, sure
> But it is momentary and fleeting
> And finally, you give back your name
> Because you have outgrown it

In regard to democracy, Runciman states that "clinging on too long could do as much harm as giving up too early. It could be even worse" (2018, p. 165). Sometimes, because of the success of democracy, it seems as if there are no other options, but there are alternatives and some are more terrifying than others (Runciman, 2018).

If democracies are evolving and changing, the highest form of citizenship might be one rooted in imagination. We as thinking and feeling human beings, no matter what democracy or governing structures we live in, must imagine new and better political arrangements. Students must be taught to imagine a better political arrangement. But this cannot be some abstraction. Like Greene (2007) and Weibe and Sashemia (2017), we as citizens must come face-to-face with life, that is democracy. Democracy is not a stale notion in a textbook or political science dissertation or something we do in a voting booth every four years- democracy is a palpable, lived thing in our bones. Democracy, or social living more generally, is despair and anxiety, arbitrariness as well as justice. And all of this must constantly be reimagined. Sometimes we have to reject what we know to see more clearly as the poem below posits.

The New Prophecy[1]
I reject subjectivity
I reject objectivity
I have burnt all right angles
Because I hate symmetry
I have burnt the firehouse
And the 5-paragraph form
I reject the hypothesis and the null
I threw away my heart medication
I reject my wife's ex-lovers
And the insurance payment
I know the world is an idea
In my brain
An image in my retina but
I reject matter and the idea and
All the corners
Which parse the undifferentiated whole
I reject logic, significance and prestige
I have cracked every septic tank in America
And want to break every toilet with a 10-inch rough in size
The fire does not burn me because I don't believe it
Your metaphysics are profitable
But mine are pitiless

Cohen and colleagues (2010) argue that citizens in a democracy need to possess certain skills and dispositions to effectively function in the democracy. Some examples of skills are listening and effective communication. Some examples of dispositions are responsibility and an appreciation of social justice (Cohen et al., 2010). Imagination is a skill that is necessary for citizenship now. Citizens must imagine something different and then actually work toward making this a reality. There is no eternal singular form of democracy. The use of poetry may allow citizens to insert themselves in this elasticity and create ever new forms of democracy and perhaps forms that go beyond. The poem below tackles this idea of creation in a very strange way and posits the idea that we must be radical creators even if our creations eventually leave us behind.

Superman
I built a universe
With ammonia,

> Chocolate and electrons
> This primal jelly oozed on the
> Linoleum
> Little microbes
> Began to flutter
> And I saw life for the first time
> In its raw form
> And I instantly loved it
> More than anything
> I had ever known
> I saw its strange laws
> And equations begin to form
> Against the designs in my kitchen floor
> I saw little elemental batteries yawn and struggle
> Getting ready
> To power millions of years of life
> And I waited for this new universe to devour me
> But it took longer than I thought
> So, I prepared a microwavable meal of salted chicken and
> Sat down to eat alone

In addition, the individuals that populate these states are not abstract homogenous entities. As noted above there are different conceptions of citizenship. But even more than the academic or political science definitions, citizens are real people, with flesh and blood, people who laugh and fuck and smoke weed and who contract MS. Indeed, many people are not even political. While we are solitary individuals, we must also forge some type of intersubjective unity. But is it even possible to truly understand what goes on in someone else's head? If not, how can a democracy with shared interests be built? Can you not see my dreams, as the poem below suggests? *What do you think?*

> There is meaning in everything
> But I cannot explain it to you
> There is solace
> In darkness
> There is a room in the stars
> Where all the names of things are stored
> And the names are holy
> Because no one is there to speak them
> I dream the world before I walk in it
> But you cannot follow
> You must dream your own

POETRY IN THE CLASSROOM

I require a poetry assignment in almost all of my courses because I want all my students to think deeply about democratic decline, rejuvenation and new creations all together. I focus specifically on asynchronous courses in this chapter because that is where I utilize these assignments. Students will post their poems on discussion boards and comment on their classmate's poems. I generally require students to do this in written and audio form. In my experience, the use of audio in asynchronous courses usually gives the class a more communal and personal feel. I also believe that asynchronous courses offer unique possibilities for students, mainly because students have time to reflect on their classmate's work.

As Daniels (2021, p. 1) argues, American universities have really only been "bit players in the project of educating the citizenry." Universities, for a variety of reasons, have not taken civics education seriously, although, some colleges as of late have begun to take up the challenge by implementing some civics-themed general education classes (Daniels, 2021). In addition, this discussion has taken on new significance amidst the volatile debates over CRT and diversity initiatives across the US. Integrating poetry assignments in individual classrooms may be another way to integrate civics education.

Poetry usually starts as an individual effort but then can be brought into the intersubjective realm when students begin to share and critique each other's work. This can happen in a face-to-face setting, or increasingly, in virtual settings. Will creating a poem and then commenting on other poems change the world or create a new world? Probably not, but it can be a start to at least get students thinking creatively, to generate discourse (Baldacchino, 2018).

The poem leaves the reader with more questions. And that is the crux of arts-based research and poetic inquiry—these methods are not meant to describe the world but invite people in to debate and possibly enact change. The use of discussion boards and other technologies in asynchronous courses helps to make poetry a truly social endeavor in an increasingly technological world and in a small way shows how we all can fight democratic decline.

The poems below, which were written by my students, help to start a conversation. The poems help us feel and see. The poems below also incorporate many of the ideas that we read during the semester. It is in these discussions, where the abstract theories of citizenship and democracy can become real. Again, it is important to note that I am not arguing that students automatically make connections or that writing poems instantly make students better citizens, rather, all I am asserting is that student poetry can facilitate good conversations around important topics and get students talking and thinking in new ways.

Below are the directions to the poetry assignment that I use in my courses. I also give my students a poetry cheat sheet and video tutorial, where I give them a refresher on poetic terms. The assignment is meant to make students "speak" to the literature and things they learned in the course, not just as a student, but as a real person with life experiences, fears and dreams. Since this is a small assignment, assessment is more informal. I simply pose some questions when I read my students poems—How did the poem integrate the theories and ideas we read during the semester, and more importantly, what does the poem challenge, and/or how might the poem advance new ideas for social living in a way that goes beyond traditional scholarship (Faulkner, 2019b; Leavy, 2019a)?

The week I assigned this, we had read philosophers who wrote about women's education and issues. Many of the poems were about women's issues, but some also dealt with other ideas as well. I have provided some student comments on some of the poems. Through the writing of the initial poems and commentary, students engaged in a conversation with the literature and each other about an important issue of any democracy: women's rights and education. In addition, I urge the reader to engage with the poems. *What insights do the poems open for you? What can you add to the conversation?* After each poem I have included some student responses to show how rich conversations about citizenship may begin to emerge. Some student responses were in audio form so I transcribed and paraphrased them. In the next section, I will bring this discussion together.

> Directions: Utilize the readings assigned this week and any other readings or ideas learned in the course.
>
> 1. List relevant concepts and vocabulary for this topic
> 2. What do these terms mean to you, and how might they be interpreted or even creatively misinterpreted by others?
> 3. Write your poem! Your poem does not have to rhyme. Put the concepts together in new ways. Leave the readers with questions to think about.
> 4. Comment on two classmates' poems on the discussion board. Remember, do not just say, "I like the poem." Reading a poem is a creative endeavor, you have to be an active participant in the piece. Maybe link it to something else we discussed or even add some more lines to the poem.

STUDENT EXAMPLES

Example 1
Mother, they may now...
After, Plato saw my soul!
After, Aristotle wanted my happiness too!
After, Rousseau saw the value in my freedom!

Poetry at the End of Democracy ▪ **351**

> After, Macaulay believed in my rights, just like Jefferson, Dewey, and Alder!
> And, after Martin felt my pain!
> After, Noddings cared about me & wiped my tears...
> Even Greene fought for me, and Young stepped on the stage too!
> Mother wait! Don't leave yet...
> They may know now...
> Now, Mother, after this long time of hardship and injustice...
> They may hear now, my voice of beauty,
> They may see now, my white & black wings, widespread from East to West,
> They may close their eyes now, to envision my journey in the free space heading
> to your home Mother... far and high, deep in the sky...
> They may learn now the way to your home with no need to return...

In a response, a student subtly challenged the last line in the poem. The student noted that he would like to return and bring others with him to the new home. What a powerful idea and illustration of how poems can engender ongoing conversations.

> *Example #2*
> I am that daisy
> Trampled beneath boots all too willing
> To go to war
> But not to come home
> To be a soldier
> But not a partner
>
> I am that goldfinch
> Clipped wings
> Illegally caged
> By fingers on triggers
> And red buttons
> But not on my pulse
>
> I am that scapegoat
> Blamed for a shared sin
> No more responsible than you
> You are punished with nudity
> I with breaking bones
> Companionship only with the moon
> A cold tent as you sleep well

I am that flood
Towanda: rushing water
Reclaiming desiccated land
Leaving behind fertile soil
I am not for you
To deposit seeds

I am that pained glass
Beneath tired feet
As you go to hold yourself
In the midnight blindness
Brighter than your closed daytime eyes

I am that pillar
Holding the roof over your head
Over the heads of our children
Over the heads of the children of our neighbors
The center of community
The epicenter of awakening

I responded to this poem. The line about being a pillar made me think of the silent people who hold up and support society. We look at the top, but it is really the people at the bottom that perform thankless jobs. I am not sure if that was what was intended, but readers oftentimes find meanings that were not intended by the creators- that is what makes this an active process and conversation.

Example #3
Apologies, Maxine
I dreamed of a heaven
where there was nothing—
no clouds, no gates, or music—
just answers.
To me, it was perfect.

Upon awakening I was saddened
to realize I had fallen in love
with an answer
and not the question.

So maybe heaven is just answers
and where humanity—
intent on asking questions—
ends.

The title of the poem is in reference the philosopher Maxine Greene, who we read in the course. On the discussion board, a student noted how the poem might show that society is more content with knowledge and answers than the questions and the process of discovery. For me, this encapsulates this entire chapter. Maybe we as a society are more content with answers because there is comfort there, but we need to keep pressing forward, questioning old forms to imagine new ones, that is (or should be) the essence of democracy. I also think this poem is a beautiful engagement with Maxine Greene's works.

Example #4
The Metamorphosis

Breaking free of her confines, she stretches, yawns,
Opening her eyes to the world around her.
She explores, but moves slowly, purposefully,
Seeing the limits of her range.

She wanders, traversing her space, taking in all that is new.
Gorging herself on the fruits around her.
But... she sees that predators abound;
She knows how far she is permitted to go.

Suddenly full and tired, she curls back up,
Enveloping herself in the safety of her silk robe.
She digests all she has absorbed;
Reimagining, reinventing, waiting to burst forth.

When she awakens this time, she is not only free,
She is wise, confident, as she unwraps her wings to soar.
Her influence is no longer limited by what she can see,
But only by what she can dream.

One student responded to this poem by noting that women in the present have to carry out the vision of these pioneers who came before them. Another student noted something similar and talked about the obstacles women face but also about hope for the future. This is democracy in action. The respondents placed the future in front of them, the poem helped them visualize a movement and the goal.

CONCLUSION

The purpose of this chapter is to call attention to the terrifying notion of democratic decline, both in the United States and abroad. If democracy is in decline, we have to imagine new ways to do democracy or even think about what might come after. But this is not just the work of political scientists, rather, the responsibility for imagining new forms of democracy falls to teachers, students, janitors, academics, CEOs and everyone in between—really, this responsibility falls to all citizens. And this chapter is a small but tangible result of this process.

As noted earlier, I am not claiming that students automatically become better citizens by simply writing a poem or responding to a classmate. Rather, rich conversations emerge, students and professors begin to discuss important issues related to citizenship in new ways. The poems and responses above are evidence of this in some ways. In the response to the first poem, a student thought deeply about the last line of the poem and subtly challenged it, or at least began to take it in a new direction. The second poem made me think of all of the people in a society that do thankless jobs but that are necessary for the functioning of a society. The responses to the third poem call attention to the endless questioning that drives (or should drive) democracies. The responses to the fourth poem talk about obstacles and goals, which are integral for creative democracy. But again, I am not the last word. *What do you, reader, think about the poems my students wrote?*

My own students (both men and women) wrote poems about the education of women and other issues. But my students did not just write about women's issues from a scholarly view; they wrote about these issues from a scholarly *and* personal view. And that is the point—we are not just debating abstract theories of democracies or stale definitions in stale textbooks. Democracy is a flesh and blood thing; it is something we must feel and live, it is something we all must continually reimagine and poetry can help us accomplish this task.

> The democracy of terror
> and love
> citizens who cry and
> dance together
> build their houses on a cliff
> and watch the sea carry away their garbage
> but at least now
> they have a language
> to name their dreams

NOTE

1. The title and form of this poem was inspired by Donald Hall's poem *Prophecy*.

ACKNOWLEDGMENTS

I would like to thank my students, David Quinton-Schein, Zeina Al-Zaiim, Jessica Cavanaugh and Kara Minchin for allowing me to use their poetry.

REFERENCES

Baldacchino, J. (2018). *Art as unlearning: Towards a mannerist pedagogy*. Routledge.
Barone, T., & Eisner, E. (2011). *Arts based research*. Sage.
Christiano, T., & Sameer B. (2022). Democracy. In E. Zalta (Ed.), *The Stanford encyclopedia of ohilosophy*. Stanford University. https://plato.stanford.edu/archives/spr2022/entries/democracy/
Cohen, J., Pickerel, T., & Levine, P. (2010). The foundation for democracy: Promoting social, emotional, ethical, cognitive skills and dispositions in K–12 schools. *Interamerican Journal of Education for Democracy, 3*(1), 74–94. https://scholarworks.iu.edu/journals/index.php/ried/article/view/618/714
Daniels, R. J. (October, 3, 2021). Universities are shunning their responsibility to democracy. *The Atlantic*. https://www.theatlantic.com/ideas/archive/2021/10/universities-cant-dodge-civics/620261/
Dewey, J. (1938). *Experience and education*. Macmillan Publishers.
Dewey, J. (2008). Creative democracy—The task before us. In Jo Ann Boydston (Ed.), *John Dewey, The later works, 1925–1953. Vol. 14: 1939–1941* (pp. 224–230). Southern Illinois University Press. (Original work published 1939)
Dewey, J. (1985). *Democracy and education*. Southern Illinois Press. (Original work published 1916)
Faulkner, S. (2019a). *Poetic inquiry as social justice and political response*. Vernon Press.
Faulkner, S. (2019b). Poetic inquiry: Poetry as/in/for social research. In P. Leavy (Ed.). *Handbook of arts based research*. (pp. 208–230). Gulliford.
Flynn, T. R. (2006). *Existentialism: A very short introduction*. Oxford.
Fromm, E. (1969). *Escape from freedom*. Avon.
Gotokhovkain, Shahbaz & Slipowitz (2023). Freedom in the world in 2023. *Freedom House*. https://freedomhouse.org/report/freedom-world/2023/marking-50-years#key-finding
Greene, M. (2007). *The public school and the private vision*. The New Press.
James (2017). In P. Sameshima, K. James, C. Leggo & A. Fidyk (Eds). *Poetic inquiry: Enchantment of place* (pp. 23–27). Vernon Press.
Johnson, T., & Reed, R. (2012). Introduction. In *Philosophical documents in education* (4th ed., pp. 1–16). Pearson.
Leavy, P. (2019a). Criteria for evaluating ABR. In P. Leavy (Ed). *Handbook of arts based research*. (pp. 575–586). Gulliford.
Leavy, P. (2019b). Introduction to arts based-research. In P. Leavy (Ed.). *Handbook of arts based research*. (pp. 3–21). Gulliford.
Leggo, C. (2017). Incantation. In P. Sameshima, K. James, C. Leggo & A. Fidyk (Eds). *Poetic inquiry: Enchantment of place* (pp. 28–31). Vernon Press.
Levitsky, S., & Ziblatt, D. (2018). *How democracies die*. Viking Press.

Miller, J. (2018). *Can democracy work? A short history of a radical idea from ancient Athens to our world.* Farrar, Strauss & Giroux.

Misco, T., Molina, E., & Schultz, B. (2021). Citizenship not wanted but received. *The Social Studies, 112*(1), 46–56. https://doi.org/10.1080/00377996.2020.1794772

McNiff, S. (2019). Philosophical and practical foundation of artistic inquiry: Creating paradigms, methods and presentations based in art. In P. Leavy (Ed.). *Handbook of arts based research.* (pp. 22–36). Gulliford.

Parker, W. (1996). Curriculum and democracy. In R. Soder (Ed.), *Democracy education, and the schools* (pp. 182–210). Jossey-Bass.

Plattner, M. F. (2018). Illiberal democracy and the struggle on the right. *Journal of Democracy. 30*(1), 5–19. https://www.journalofdemocracy.org/articles/illiberal-democracy-and-the-struggle-on-the-right/

Prendergast, M. (2009). Introduction: The phenomena of poetry in researc: "Poem is what?" Poetic inquiry in qualitative social science research. In M. Prendergast, C. Leggo & P. Sameshima (Eds.). *Poetic inquiry: Vibrant voices in the social sciences.* (pp. xix–xlii). Sense Publishers.

Repucci, M. (2021). From crisis to reform: A call to strengthen America's battered democracy. *Freedom House.* https://freedomhouse.org/report/special-report/2021/crisis-reform-call-strengthen-americas-battered-democracy

Runciman, D. (2018). *How democracy ends.* Hachette Book Group.

Sameshima, P., (2017). Poetic inquiry: Past, present and possibilities. In P. Sameshima, K. James, C. Leggo & A. Fidyk (Eds). *Poetic inquiry: Enchantment of place* (pp. 16–22). Vernon Press.

Shusterman, R. (2008). *Body consciousness: A philosophy of mindfulness and somoaesthetics.* Cambridge University Press.

Vickery, A. (2015). It was never meant for us: Towards a Black feminist construct of citizenship in social studies. *The Journal of Social Studies Research, 39,* 163–172. https://doi.org/10.1016/j.jssr.2014.12.002

Weibe, S., & Sameshima, P. (2019). *Reframing and reflaming social justice through poetry.* In S. Faulkner. (Ed.), *Poetic inquiry as social justice and political response* (pp. 223–237). Vernon Press.

Westheimer, J., & Kahne, J. (2004). What kind of citizen? The politics of educating for democracy. *American Education Research Journal, 41*(2), 237–269.

CHAPTER 22

READING BANNED BOOKS

Preparing Elementary Teachers to Navigate the Politics of Teaching and Learning

Aaron R. Gierhart
Columbus State University

ABSTRACT

Legislation banning or censoring books and art not only greatly impacts teaching candidates' future work by restricting discourse and knowledge about a range of issues, but it is also antithetical to the democratic ideals upon which the United States was founded. This chapter presents a single-case study in a multicultural children's literature course for pre-service elementary teaching candidates in which they considered how state laws might impact teaching and learning in public schools. It describes a Novel Study Assignment for which participants read a banned young adult novel and engaged in pedagogical dialoguing. This study offers a theoretical framework and an assignment that can be adapted by other educators to help future teachers find creative ways to strive towards democratic ideals as they navigate the politics and legislation that impact their work.

In the past two years, amidst ongoing "culture wars" amplified by opposing political philosophies, debates have raged about how to learn and discuss diversity in public education settings. To date, several states have passed bans in K–12 public schools and higher education institutions and implemented protocols for reviewing and potentially removing books from classrooms and libraries. Dominant discourse about diversity in public school settings is often bereft of the voices of classroom teachers, particularly non-White practitioners (Farag, 2023); instead, these decisions are handed down from policymakers (Penuel & O'Connor, 2018).

In April 2022, Governor Brian Kemp signed two bills into law impacting teaching and learning in Georgia's public schools. House Bill 1084 restricts conversations and teaching about "divisive concepts" in schools, mainly regarding race and diversity. Senate Bill 226 establishes protocols for how school boards and administrators review complaints about books to potentially ban them from district libraries and classrooms. At the time he signed House Bill 1084, Kemp noted that this legislation would place "our children ahead of partisan agenda" (Burnside & Cole, 2022, para. 2). These Georgia bills were among similar legislation passed in other states in recent years, such as Florida and Texas, in a conservative political movement to combat 'woke culture' (Schrader, 2022).

I teach a multicultural children's literature course for pre-service elementary teaching candidates at a mid-sized state university in Georgia. This legislation greatly impacts my candidates' future work as elementary public school teachers, restricting discourse they foster with and books they may curate for students. Given the broad nature of Senate Bill 226, books may be challenged and banned about a variety of topics and populations beyond race and culture, such as the LGBTQIA+ community. As an example, in the wake of recent state legislation requiring reviews of all books on public school and library shelves in Florida, titles like *The Best Man* by Richard Peck have been labeled "pornographic" due solely to representation of same-sex couples (Legum, 2023).

I designed and implemented the Novel Study Assignment in Spring 2023. Candidates read and analyzed a young adult novel that had previously appeared on a banned book list. The assignment did not stipulate or presuppose candidates' personal or political beliefs, nor require them to critique the recent legislation. Rather, I asked them to consider how banning a book may amplify or silence the voices of specific populations of students and individuals and impact their future teaching practices.

I report on findings from this single-case study regarding candidates' interpretations of this recent state legislation and how they are preparing to curate and teach with multicultural children's literature amidst the current political climate. The research question of this case study was as follows:

How do elementary pre-service teaching candidates develop insights about book bans and censorship and their impacts on future teaching practices?

First, I present a brief review of literature and introduce Freire's (1970/2000) conception of praxis as the framework of this study. After describing the Novel Study Assignment and methodology, I present findings, including relevant portions of the participants' essays, public-facing components, and discussion from a group interview to portray and contextualize their work on the assignment. I conclude by discussing implications of the student for preparing pre-service teaching candidates.

FRAMEWORK AND REVIEW OF LITERATURE

Public education in the United States has been subject to cycles of political influence, including state and national standards for teaching and learning from the work of the Committee of Ten in the late 19th century (National Education Association, 1894; Kliebard, 2004) to the Common Core State Standards (National Governors Association, 2010) less than two decades ago. Movements and legislation geared towards neoliberal goals of global competitiveness from "A Nation at Risk" and more recently, the "You Belong in STEM" initiative of the Biden-Harris administration seek to position public schools as venues for bolstering economic superiority and filling 21st century jobs (Hoeg & Bencze, 2017) with varying emphases on student agency or empowerment (Mayes, 2020; Yanez et al., 2019). As public education has shifted towards more neoliberal goals of preparing a globally competitive workforce and improving standardized test scores, pedagogy is often reframed with less emphasis on empowering students and drawing upon their passions and lived experiences (Giroux, 2010; Hoeg & Bencze, 2017).

Teachers and administrators struggle to navigate the current waves of new legislation regulating or limiting how matters of diversity can be integrated into teaching and learning, including books that are read to students or are curated on classroom and school library shelves. For example, Florida public schools have struggled in the wake of House Bill 1467 to meet seemingly ambiguous criteria regarding race and gender to evaluate if books are appropriate; Florida teachers have worked to tread carefully in their practices amidst this new legislation, lest they be charged with third-degree felonies for using books that do not meet new state requirements (Goñi-Lessan, 2023).

Freire (1970/2000) defined praxis as "reflection and action upon the world in order to transform it" (p. 51). In the case of the Novel Study Assignment, candidates were not tasked with the goal of speaking with politicians at the state capitol in Atlanta or making impacts on state or county policy.

Rather, the goal of the assignment was for pre-service and future classroom teachers to engage in an inner pedagogical dialogue with consideration for the restrictions of the state laws (i.e., House Bill 1084, Senate Bill 226) with which they must abide (Gierhart, 2023b; Gierhart & Seglem, 2021).

Public school teachers work within a space that is politically-influenced. Legislation, such as House Bill 1084 and Senate Bill 226 in Georgia, emphasize partisan politics, directing teachers to filter their pedagogies through a specific conservative lens (Britzman, 2003; Krebs, 2022). In this study, candidates considered and reflected on their intended practices for curating and integrating literature, transforming their lenses for their future classroom teaching practices. By reading a banned novel, candidates evaluated whose voices were being emboldened and whose were stifled or silenced by the bans, highlighting inequitable power dynamics of classroom teaching and society at large (Pearce & Wood, 2019). If teacher education programs blindly reinforce partisan decisions, the dominant norms of the day will only become further entrenched in public schools, sustaining inequities and muting diverse voices (Oser & Hooghe, 2018).

THE ASSIGNMENT

Teaching candidates completed the Novel Study Assignment as part of a multicultural children's literature course. After spending one course meeting examining Georgia House Bill 1084, and, more pertinent to the focus of the course, Senate Bill 226, I introduced the Novel Study Assignment and asked the candidates to choose a novel from a series of provided lists of books that had been widely banned by states or school districts in recent years. Candidates selected a banned young adult novel that included diverse perspectives, voices, and experiences that they perceived as relevant to their own lives or future teaching in some way.

In their written essay, the candidates were required to introduce the book and author and provide their rationale and interest in reviewing the book for this assignment. Then, they a) analyzed possible reasons the book had been banned, b) discussed whose voices were challenged and whose were reinforced, and c) considered how book bans impact their current and future teaching as well as their students' learning within and outside of public school settings. Additionally, the candidates designed and submitted a public-facing component, synthesizing major takeaways from their essays. For the public-facing component, most students chose to create social media posts on platforms such as Instagram and X (formerly Twitter). The suggested outline format, page count, and assessment criteria are provided in Table 22.1.

TABLE 22.1 Novel Study Essay Format, Suggested Page Count, and Assessment Criteria

Essay Section	Suggested Page Count	Assessment Criteria
Introduction	1 page	Introduction that includes background of teaching candidate, current program of study, etc.; introduces novel, including title and author, and rationale for selecting it for the assignment.
Overview	1 page	Summarizes the novel, highlighting characters and key events, including the ending of the story
Discussion	2–3 pages	Discuss possible reasons the book has been challenged or banned in past or contemporary times; describes whose perspectives, voices, and experiences are challenged and whose are reinforced as a result of the book being banned
Conclusion	1–2 pages	Draws conclusions, based on the discussion in the essay, about how book bans may impact their current and future teaching as well as their current and future students' learning and experiences in and out of formal school settings
Public-Facing Component	1 page	Synthesizes the major claims from the essay, focusing specifically on impacts of the book being banned

METHODS

A single-case study was conducted with two students from the Spring 2023 section of my multicultural children's literature course, Angel and Ellen (pseudonyms). I solicited the entire class for the study, but only Angel and Ellen consented to participate.

Data sources included the participants' written essays and public-facing components that they submitted for the Novel Study Assignment as well as a focus group interview, which was conducted with a video conferencing tool, audio recorded, and transcribed. The participants' essays and the focus group interview transcript were selectively coded, identifying instances of praxis (Freire, 1970/2000) in which the participants engaged in forms of personal and professional reflection oriented towards transforming how they interpreted state legislation and its impacts on their current and future teaching practices (Flick, 2022). The public-facing components were used to elicit additional discussion during the focus group interview (Walls & Holquist, 2019).

FINDINGS

Angel

"When I [was] first assigned this project," Angel noted in their essay's introduction, "I was appalled. Most of these titles I grew up reading and loving." Angel chose to read George Orwell's *1984* for the Novel Study, because they had not had the opportunity to read it during their high school years. As the war in Ukraine continues, *1984* has become a bestseller in Russia, where the novel was initially banned up until the year 1988, exemplifying how this dystopian classic continues to resonate in contemporary global society (Sharma, 2022). In late-2022, U.S. District Judge Mark Waller cited verbiage from *1984* in a ruling against part of Florida Governor Ron DeSantis's "Stop WOKE Act" that restricted how university professors in the state discussed matters of race. "The State has chosen to eliminate one side of the debate" (Schrader, 2022, para. 8) Waller noted in his ruling against the legislation.

In their essay, Angel proceeded to examine possible reasons this novel has been widely banned, pointing out the irony of government and school officials banning a book that focuses on authoritarian government control:

> [Banning *1984*] challenges the viewpoints of those who believe it's important to discuss tough concepts, regardless of how controversial or difficult they may be [as well as] people who have traditionally been excluded and oppressed by authoritarian governments. Groups who have gone through political repression and censorship may feel as though their experiences and voices are being erased and silenced by the book's ban. Some believe that censorship is essential for upholding their own beliefs in order to prevent [literature] from undermining [their agenda].

Angel concluded that books like *1984* should not be banned from schools and public libraries. "Without novels like [*1984*]," Angel rhetorically inquired in the "Conclusion" section of their essay, "how are our students supposed to learn the perils of living under a totalitarian government? This is an important cautionary tale about the dangers of unchecked political power." Angel perceived the banning of Orwell's *1984* as counterproductive to helping young readers understand what authoritarian government control is like, including what they perceived as overreach by the state and federal government today. They also considered the issue through the lens of their non-binary gender identity, discussing how book bans and other recent legislation seek to prohibit authentic teaching and learning and constrain acceptance in today's public schools.

Ellen

Ellen selected *The Killing of Mr. Griffin* by Lois Duncan for the Novel Study. In her interpretation about why *Mr. Griffin* had been banned or challenged, such as the warning label that was affixed to this book in Collier County, Florida, in 2022 (Riley, 2022), Ellen found some of story's content questionable for younger readers:

> I think the book is banned because it talks about murderers and really self-destructing teens. I think parents will want this book to be banned so their child won't read something that could come across as vulgar. To a certain point, I get it. I wouldn't want an elementary student to read this.

While acknowledging the mature content of this novel, Ellen also decried the idea of outright banning it from adolescents and teenagers. She felt books intended for mature audiences could still contain worthwhile lessons and takeaways:

> Why should a young adult novel [like *Mr. Griffin*] that touches on topics such as growing up living with your mom and grandma, feeling like you have to fit in, not feeling confident in yourself, and not being able to handle your emotions be banned? A lot of these [issues are ones that] kids, especially teens, go through. A majority of teens definitely do not try to kill their teacher, but they do deal with some of the emotional despair and anguish that is [represented] in this book. If a teen wants to read it, then I feel like they should be allowed to. Banning the book doesn't help solve anything. Teens are still going to have those uncertainties of emotions. So even if we try to act like [these issues do not] exist, it will not go away. We should talk about having a feeling of doubt and insecurities. We should use this book as a tool.

In the focus group, Ellen went on to question not only banning contemporary literature like *Mr. Griffin*, but also banning classic literature staples, such as Aldous Huxley's *Brave New World*:

> I had to read *Brave New World* as a freshman in high school. I guess my question revolves around, well...why so? We study this literature because [past generations] think they have some type of, I guess, value to our life. So then, why are you taking [these classics] out? And what qualifies you to just get rid of it? Because these books are important.

Ellen expressed disagreement with banning books like *The Killing of Mr. Griffin*, despite its graphic content, as the character archetypes could be perceived as entertaining or even relatable by young readers. She perceived book banning as counterproductive to teachers leveraging literature as a means for making connections and building relationships with students.

FUTURE PRACTICE

In a written essay, candidates were required to consider how book bans and censorship could impact their future practices as classroom teachers as well as their future students' learning both in and out of public school settings. Prior to completing the Novel Study, Ellen admitted that she had not thought much about the issue of book banning and censorship, but she concluded, "I see why banning books is such a big deal and it's not the solution." Ellen also expressed concern for the long term impact of book bans on arts and entertainment and that banning books would work against what she perceived as the larger purpose of teaching—making genuine connections with students:

> You get to make a stronger connection with your teacher, and that's very important for students. You want to have that good standing—'Oh, I can relate to them on this and that, because they can understand this [book] character.'

In addition to their discussion about the banning of a dystopian novel like *1984*, as someone who identifies as non-binary, Angel expressed concerns about how book bans would continue to suppress matters of authenticity and acceptance in public schools and society:

> I always accepted that parents wouldn't want [me] to quote-unquote "push my gay agenda" on their kids. I, still to this day, have to present as female to all of [my students]. Like, earlier today, I had a job interview to be an assistant teacher. They were fine with using my preferred [non-binary] name, because it was easier for them to say than my actual Hispanic name. [However], they would still address me by "Miss," which I'm not very okay with. Not a lot of people are going to really ever accept it. But, it's just like, I want to be able to show my future students it's okay to be who you want to be, and you shouldn't be silenced. But I kind of feel like a hypocrite if I'm being silenced all the time [and act as if] I'm okay with it. Once people get stifled of their creativity and individuality, there's really nothing left in the world…

Neither participant explicitly described their intended practices for curating and integrating books that had been challenged or banned into their future teaching; however, they both openly challenged the focal legislation and expressed concerns with the outcomes of book banning and censorship. Ellen interpreted the legislation as counterproductive to ensuring that students could engage with literature that authentically represented them and their lived experiences. She also felt that teachers would be less able to leverage literature as a means of forging meaningful connections with students. Angel viewed book bans as a component of a wider effort to extinguish acceptance of individuals like them who do not align with dominant norms. To Angel, book banning was a form of institutionalized silencing and control.

CONCLUSIONS AND IMPLICATIONS

Georgia's Senate Bill 226, which establishes protocols for reviewing and banning books on a county-by-county basis, is not as draconian as what has been implemented in other states. During the summer of 2022 in Forsyth (Georgia) County Schools, a second review of books that had initially been banned was conducted and involved input from "teachers, media specialists, students and parents" (Kerns, 2022, para. 3). Seven of the eight books that were re-reviewed were allowed to be returned to high school library shelves, pending the approval of administration and library specialists in each individual school building. Meanwhile, officials in Llano County, Texas, are going so far as to consider shuttering their entire public library system to prevent patrons from accessing certain books it had removed from shelves that a federal judge ordered them to return (Rose, 2023). Book publication companies, such as Scholastic, have begun to take recent state legislation into account when suggesting revisions to authors to avoid controversy and to make their publications more marketable in the present sociopolitical climate (Bowman, 2023). Publishers of educational textbooks and instructional materials have also begun revising their products to maintain relationships with states and school districts. For example, *Studies Weekly* removed the mention of race as a reason Rosa Parks was asked to switch seats on a Montgomery, Alabama bus in late-1955 in an article used by K–6 teachers in Florida (Gamble, 2023).

As a society, we must be incredibly cautious about forming operating principles and norms that restrict open discourse and exclude diverse voices and experiences, especially given the democratic ideals upon which the United States was founded. How our country defines equality and determines who has which rights has been debated for centuries and continues today as politicians and authoritative forces seek to strip rights and protections from those whose identities do not align with dominant norms and ideologies.

Every teacher engages in a metaphorical (and sometimes literal) pedagogical dialoguing with *internal* beliefs, ideals, and lived experiences and *external* stakeholders, forces, and the politics of society that have always impacted education (Britzman, 2003). Book banning instantiates the dominant political discourse at the state and national levels. By reading banned books, considering how state legislation materializes in classroom settings and engaging in pedagogical dialoguing, teaching candidates can orient their work towards fostering educational equity and democratic principles (Gierhart, 2023a). Assignments such as the Novel Study can provide opportunities for teaching candidates to engage in a form of dialogue rehearsal, a praxis oriented towards internal action and potential external action and pedagogical transformation.

As teaching candidates proceed from coursework and field experiences to their first positions in U.S. public schools, they will very likely navigate the ongoing and evolving issue of book banning and censorship. Teacher educators, beholden to state standards commissions and boards of education, are responsible for informing pre-service candidates about new state laws that may restrict how they curate and integrate literature in their instruction and the conversations they have in their classrooms regarding diverse identities, including race and gender. Teaching candidates will benefit from exercising a critical lens during their pre-service coursework experiences on the politics and legislation that impact their work. Assignments like the Novel Study can provide opportunities for candidates to examine the current educational landscape and project towards future classroom practices (Clandinin & Connelly, 1988). If they are to forge greater educational and social equity, the teachers of tomorrow must find creative ways to strive towards democratic ideals in their professional efforts, especially if current political systems fail those outside of the dominant majority (Oser & Hooghe, 2018).

REFERENCES

Bowman, E. (2023, April 15). Scholastic wanted to license her children's book—if she cut a part about 'racism.' *NPR*. https://www.npr.org/2023/04/15/1169848627/scholastic-childrens-book-racism

Britzman, D. P. (2003). *Practice makes practice: A critical study of learning to teach*. State University of New York Press.

Burnside, T., & Cole, D. (2022, April 28). Georgia Gov. Kemp signs bill into law that limits discussions about race in classrooms. *CNN*. https://www.cnn.com/2022/04/28/politics/georgia-bill-limits-race-discussions-classrooms

Clandinin, D. J., & Connelly, F. M. (1988). *Teachers as curriculum planners: Narratives of experience*. Teachers College Press.

DeCesare, T. (2020). Centered democratic education: Public schools as civic centers. *Philosophical Studies in Education, 51*, 33–43.

Farag, A. (2023). The CRT culture war of the suburbs. *Phi Delta Kappan, 104*(5), 18–23. http://dx.doi.org/10.1177/00317217231156225

Flick, U. (2022). *An introduction to qualitative research* (7th ed.). SAGE.

Freire, P. (2000). *Pedagogy of the oppressed* (M. B. Ramos, Trans.). Continuum National Publishing Group Inc. (Original work published 1970)

Gamble, J. (2023, March 22). Race left out of Rosa Parks story in revised weekly lesson text for Florida schools highlights confusion with Florida law. *CNN*. https://www.cnn.com/2023/03/22/us/florida-textbook-race-rosa-parks-reaj/index.html

Gierhart, A. R. (2023a). Digital pedagogy in dialogue: Student teaching during COVID-19. *Journal of Pedagogical Research, 7*(1), 243–259. https://doi.org/10.33902/JPR.202319642

Gierhart, A. R. (2023b). Fostering science discourse in teacher education: Elementary teaching candidates publish narrative podcasts. In S. L. Finley, P. Correll, C. Pearman, & S. P. Huffman (Eds.), *Empowering and engaging students through academic discourse* (pp. 154–179). IGI Global.

Gierhart, A. R., & Seglem, R. (2021). Narrativizing digital pedagogy. *International Journal of Qualitative Research in Education*. https://doi.org/10.1080/09518398.2021.2003888

Giroux, H. A. (2010). Rethinking education as the practice of freedom: Paulo Freire and the promise of critical pedagogy. *Policy Futures in Education, 8*(6), 715–721. http://dx.doi.org/10.2304/pfie.2010.8.6.715

Goñi-Lessan, A. (2023, March 2). Which books are allowed? Varied interpretations of Florida law lead to confusion at schools. *Tallahassee Democrat*. https://www.tallahassee.com/story/news/education/2023/03/02/florida-book-bans-interpretations-confusion-vary-across-the-state/69888646007/

Hoeg, D., & Bencze, L. (2017). Rising against a gathering storm: A biopolitical analysis of citizenship in STEM policy. *Cultural Studies of Science Education, 12*(4), 843–861. https://doi.org/10.1007/s11422-017-9838-9

Kerns, S. (2022, August 19). Seven of the eight banned books approved to return to Forsyth school libraries. *Forsyth County News*. https://www.forsythnews.com/news/education/seven-eight-banned-library-books-approved-return-forsyth-school-libraries/

Krebs, M. L. (2022). Can't really teach: CRT bans impose upon teachers' First Amendment rights. *Vanderbilt Law Review, 75*, 1925–1955.

Lahman, M. K. E. (2022). *Writing and representing qualitative research*. SAGE.

Legum, J. (2023, February 8). This book is considered pornography in Ron DeSantis' Florida. *Popular Information*. https://popular.info/p/this-book-is-considered-pornography

Mayes, E. (2020). Student voice in school reform? Desiring simultaneous critique and affirmation. *Discourse: Studies in the Cultural Politics of Education, 41*(3), 454–470. https://doi.org/10.1080/01596306.2018.1492517

Neumann, R. (2017). American democracy in distress: The failure of social education. *Journal of Social Science Education, 16*(1), 5–16. https://doi.org/10.2390/jsse-v16-i1-1630

Oser, J., & Hooghe, M. (2018). Democratic ideals and levels of political participation: The role of political and social conceptualisations of democracy. *The British Journal of Politics and International Relations, 20*(3), 711–730. https://doi.org/10.1177/1369148118768140

Pearce, T. C., & Wood, B. E. (2019). Education for transformation: An evaluative framework to guide student voice work in schools. *Critical Studies in Education, 60*(1), 113–130. https://doi.org/10.1080/17508487.2016.1219959

Penuel, W. R., & O'Connor, K. (2018). From designing to organizing new social futures: Multiliteracies pedagogies for today. *Theory Into Practice, 57*(1), 64–71. https://doi.org/10.1080/00405841.2017.1411715

Riley, J. (2022, August 15). A Florida county finds these 115 books questionable. *Metro Weekly.* https://www.metroweekly.com/2022/08/a-florida-county-finds-these-115-books-objectionable/

Rose, A. (2023, April 12). A Texas county that was ordered to return banned books to its shelves is set to consider shutting down its library system. *CNN.* https://www.cnn.com/2023/04/12/us/texas-llano-county-library-banned-books/index.html

Schrader, A. (2022, November 17). Judge heavily references '1984' in striking down parts of DeSantis' 'Stop WOKE Act.' *United Press International.* https://www.upi.com/Top_News/US/2022/11/17/federal-judge-references-1984-strikes-down-parts-desantis-stop-woke-act/7811668732583/

Sharma, S. (2022, December 16). The once-banned dystopian novel that has become Russia's bestseller. *Independent.* https://www.independent.co.uk/news/world/europe/george-orwell-1984-novel-bestseller-russia-b2246388.html

Walls, J., & Holquist, S. E. (2019). Through their eyes, in their words: Using photo-elicitation to amplify student voice in policy and school improvement research. In K. K. Strunk & L. A. Locke (Eds.), *Research methods for social justice and equity in education* (pp. 151–161). Palgrave Macmillan.

Yanez, G. A., Thumlert, K., de Castell, S., & Jenson, J. (2019). Pathways to sustainable futures: A "production pedagogy" model for STEM education. *Futures, 108*, 27–36. https://doi.org/10.1016/j.futures.2019.02.021